THE WORLD'S

THE MALCO
AND OTHER

JOHN MARSTON (1575–1634) was educated at Oxford and the Middle Temple but eschewed a legal career (his father's) for that of writer. His early satirical work earned him displeasure in high circles and so he turned to the stage where a series of brilliant plays, written roughly between 1599 and 1608, proved highly influential in the development of contemporary play-writing. Once more incurring official displeasure, he left the stage, took holy orders, and eventually was accorded the living of Christchurch, Hampshire, where he remained parish priest for fifteen years. He then retired, returned to London, and lived out his last three years in relative obscurity. He was married, but his only child died in infancy. He wrote nine unaided plays, one collaboratively and one unfinished, as well as a number of satirical poems.

KEITH STURGESS was Professor of Theatre Studies at Lancaster University and Director of the Nuffield Theatre, and he is author of a dozen plays that have been performed. He now lives in Greece and is a full-time writer.

MICHAEL CORDNER is Reader in the Department of English and Related Literature at the University of York. He has edited George Farquhar's *The Beaux's Stratagem*, the *Complete Plays* of Sir George Etherege, *Four Comedies* of Sir John Vanbrugh, and, for the World's Classics series, *Four Restoration Marriage Comedies*. He has also co-edited *English Comedy* (Cambridge University Press, 1994) and is completing a book on *The Comedy of Marriage 1660–1737*.

PETER HOLLAND is Judith E. Wilson University Reader in Drama in the Faculty of English at the University of Cambridge.

MARTIN WIGGINS is a Fellow of the Shakespeare Institute and Lecturer in English at the University of Birmingham.

DRAMA IN WORLD'S CLASSICS

J. M. Barrie
Peter Pan and Other Plays

Aphra Behn
The Rover and Other Plays

George Farquhar
*The Recruiting Officer and
Other Plays*

John Ford
*'Tis Pity She's a Whore and
Other Plays*

Ben Jonson
The Alchemist and Other Plays

Christopher Marlowe
Doctor Faustus and Other Plays

John Marston
The Malcontent and Other Plays

Thomas Middleton
*A Mad World, My Masters and
Other Plays*

Arthur Wing Pinero
*Trelawny of the 'Wells' and
Other Plays*

J. M. Synge
*The Playboy of the Western World and
Other Plays*

ed. George Taylor
Trilby and Other Plays
Four Plays for Victorian Star Actors

John Webster
*The Duchess of Malfi and
Other Plays*

Oscar Wilde
*The Importance of Being Earnest and
Other Plays*

William Wycherley
The Country Wife and Other Plays

Campion, Carew, Chapman, Daniel,
Davenant, Jonson, Townshend
Court Masques

Chapman, Kyd, Middleton,
Tourneur
Four Revenge Tragedies

Coyne, Fitzball, Jones, Lewes, Sims
*The Lights o' London and
Other Plays*

Dryden, Lee, Otway, Southerne
Four Restoration Marriage Comedies

THE WORLD'S CLASSICS

━━

JOHN MARSTON

Antonio and Mellida
Antonio's Revenge
The Malcontent
The Dutch Courtesan
Sophonisba

━━

Edited with an Introduction by
KEITH STURGESS

General Editor
MICHAEL CORDNER
Associate General Editors
PETER HOLLAND   MARTIN WIGGINS

Oxford   New York
OXFORD UNIVERSITY PRESS
1997

Oxford University Press, Great Clarendon Street, Oxford OX2 6DP

Oxford New York

Athens Auckland Bangkok Bogota Bombay Buenos Aires
Calcutta Cape Town Dar es Salaam Delhi Florence Hong Kong
Istanbul Karachi Kuala Lumpur Madras Madrid Melbourne
Mexico City Nairobi Paris Singapore Taipei Tokyo Toronto

and associated companies in
Berlin Ibadan

Oxford is a trade mark of Oxford University Press

Editorial material © Keith Sturgess 1997

First published as a World's Classics paperback 1997

British Library Cataloguing in Publication Data
Data available

Library of Congress Cataloging in Publication Data
Marston, John, 1575?–1643.
The Malcontent and other plays / John Marston; edited by Keith Sturgess.
I. Sturgess, Keith. II. Title. III. Series.
PR2692.S78 1997   822'.3—dc21   96–48198
ISBN 0–19–282250–0 (pbk.)

1 3 5 7 9 10 8 6 4 2

Typeset by Pure Tech India Ltd, Pondicherry, India
Printed in Great Britain by
Biddles Ltd.
Guildford and King's Lynn

CONTENTS

Acknowledgements   vi

Introduction   vii

Note on the Texts   xxvi

Select Bibliography   xxx

A Chronology of John Marston   xxxiii

ANTONIO AND MELLIDA   1

ANTONIO'S REVENGE
Or the Second Part of the History of Antonio and Mellida   57

THE MALCONTENT   117

THE DUTCH COURTESAN   177

SOPHONISBA
Or The Wonder of Women   241

Appendix: Felice's Ballad in *Antonio and Mellida*, 3.2   295

Explanatory Notes   298

Glossary   387

ACKNOWLEDGEMENTS

I SHOULD like to thank my two editors, Michael Cordner and Martin Wiggins, for their invaluable help with this book, especially the latter, whose erudition and eagle eye have saved me from countless errors of commission, omission, and transmission, and many of whose suggestions have been accepted silently.

Also, my profound thanks to Sergio Mazzarelli, who provided a great deal of information about the Italian passages and references in the texts; to James Mardock for his collation of the texts; and to Karen Clarke, who sorted out early versions of the typescript. Finally, my thanks to Margaret Eddershaw, who helped greatly in the later stages.

To the latter, I should also like to dedicate this.

KEITH STURGESS

Nafplion
1996

INTRODUCTION

JOHN MARSTON was born in Oxfordshire in 1576. His father was a successful lawyer, with property and civic influence in Coventry, and his mother was a second-generation Italian immigrant, whose physician father had settled in London. Having graduated from Brasenose College, Oxford, Marston entered the Middle Temple, one of the Inns of Court in London, to finish his education. Marston senior, himself a reader of the Middle Temple, hoped that his son would become a lawyer, but Marston junior, as father acidly noted in his will, took 'delight in plays, vain studies and fooleries'. Primed by a cultivation, characteristic of the Inns, of radical ideas in philosophy, politics, and the arts, Marston junior headed instead for a career in letters.

His first extant work was the erotic poem *The Metamorphosis of Pigmalion's Image*, but he published with it, in an evidently more congenial strain, the vituperative *Certain Satires* (1598). This latter exploited the new, literary fashion for Juvenalian satire, and Marston was able to develop here an aggressive and irreverent *persona* in 'Don Kinsayder', an early exercise for the writer in role-play. A second volume in this strain, *The Scourge of Villainy*, followed in the same year, but by order of the Bishop of London and the Archbishop of Canterbury this, together with Marston's other work and any other contemporary writings deemed to be obscene and/or scurrilous, was publicly burned and banned (1599). Within, it seems, months of this, Marston had announced himself as a serious playwright by refashioning *Histriomastix*, probably first written by Marston himself and others for the Inns of Court, for performance by the Paul's Boys.

Ten years later, when Marston left his last play, *The Insatiate Countess*, unfinished in order to begin a new career, he had written eight more, unaided plays and one collaborative piece. *The Insatiate Countess* was finished by others, evidently the little-known William Barksted and Lewis Machin, and published in 1613; and the collaborative play (composed with Chapman and Jonson) was the comic masterpiece *Eastward Ho!*, which got its authors into trouble with the king. But from 1609, Marston would no longer court the kinds of problem that his provocative writing drew him into. In that year he was ordained deacon and then priest; and from 1616 to his retirement in 1631 he held the living of Christchurch in Hampshire.

During these years, he sought and received little publicity, and hence we know little of his activities. He had married in 1605 (his father-in-law was also a cleric), and he seems to have settled down, with loving wife, to the obscure and uneventful life of a country vicar. When a publisher produced an octavo edition of six of his plays in 1633, Marston insisted that all signs of his authorship should be removed from the text. At his death in the next year, his tombstone was inscribed, on his own order, with the words '*Oblivioni Sacrum*', sacred to oblivion. The journey may seem to have come full circle, but we do not know enough of him confidently to explain or understand it.

Marston's dramatic work has engaged a good deal of critical attention during the last three decades, including the publication of at least seven, full-length books; but it remains enigmatic and difficult to place for the modern reader or theatre practitioner. There is little consensus about the source, or sources, of the distinctive dramatic voice we hear, or about the meaning and significance of the texts themselves. And it follows that there is little consensus about what might constitute a competent 'reading' of them. There have been relatively few, modern-day stage revivals, whereas contemporaries such as Webster, Middleton, and Ford have often been performed. And yet the aesthetics of the modern stage ought properly to have prepared the ground for a major and positive reassessment of this most elusive of Jacobean playwrights. We have long, in the theatre, been wooed away from coherent, narrative structures and 'realistic', psychologically plausible characters; and we read with some confidence the performance text which comprises set pieces, which sets ambushes for us, and the discourse of which is truly multi-media. We have learned to identify and order the multiple voices of quotation and allusion, to recognize and enjoy the teasing prismatics of intertextuality and to collude in strategies of deconstruction and metatheatre. At the very least, Marston's restless experimentation and innovativeness with form and his reckless mixing of genres should find an echo in the modern, theatre-going bosom.

Marston's contemporaries and near successors paid him the signal compliment of sitting at his shoulder, sometimes literally, to learn from his dramaturgical expertise and courage. Middleton, Webster, Fletcher, and Ford, a roll-call of the best 'Jacobean' writers, all show special kinds of indebtedness to the series of plays with which

Marston, remixing the established genres of tragedy of blood, romantic comedy, city comedy, comical satire, and classical tragedy, rewrote the dramatic model-book in the first decade of the seventeenth century. One problem with him stems from the fact that we cannot with total confidence discern in the *œuvre* a regular line of artistic development. Nor can we reconstruct from biography and/or work an integrated personality by which we can explain, or at least explain away, his artistic career and its abrupt abandonment. As artist, if not as man, Marston seems to swarm all over us; and yet he remains indistinct and aloof. Fifty years after he wrote it, we must still acknowledge T. S. Eliot's magisterial judgement: 'His merits are still a matter for controversy.'

As a practising dramatist, Marston was ever nervous about the business of seeing his plays in print. First, he feared, or claimed to fear, the characteristic propensity for error of the cavalier processes of the printing-house itself, inevitable without an assiduous surveillance of the printing which he felt he was not always able to provide. (His plays seem to have suffered an average level of damage of this kind.) More especially, he fretted over the artistic loss involved in the transfer of the plays from stage to page, from the theatrical to the literary experience. Of *The Malcontent*, he was concerned 'that some scenes invented merely [= 'wholly'] to be spoken should be enforcively published to be read'. And in 'The Address to the Reader' of *The Fawn*, he wrote: '[the] life of comedy rests much in the actor's voice'; then amplifying that idea into the authoritative: 'Comedies are writ to be spoken, not read; remember, the life of these things consists in action [= 'their performance']'.

With regard to the publication of *Sophonisba*, the playwright had fewer qualms. In that play he had set himself to write the kind of tragic text, careful, literary, less dependent on the players' animating skills and presence, that might in fact be effectively read in the study. In this endeavour, he certainly had one eye on Jonson, whom he alternately admired and despised, and he styled the play, uniquely for him, 'a poem'. He had prepared the way for its publication in 1606 in the quarto edition of *The Fawn*, published in the same year. There he advertised *Sophonisba* as 'a tragedy ... which shall boldly abide the most curious perusal'. But even in this text (or especially in this text) he feeds and directs the readers' visual imagination about the physical realization of the play, not its literary and narrative features, by the inclusion of full and colourful stage-directions of an amplitude that he himself acknowledges is unusual in the publication of plays of the period: 'Let me entreat my reader not to tax me for the fashion of the entrances and music of this tragedy, for know it is printed only as it was presented by youths and after the fashion of the private stage.'

For a consideration of Marston's art that pays due respect to the fact that the texts were written as scripts for performance, we might begin with that phrase, 'presented by youths'. All of Marston's theatre work was written for performance by the children's companies, troupes of juvenile players who flourished during the first decade of the seventeenth century, after some years in the doldrums. These were the 'little eyases' who, Rosencrantz tells Hamlet in a meta-theatrical passage that would have caught Marston's eye, were all in fashion (*Hamlet*, 2.2.339–44). The two main companies, both nominally chorister groups but professionalized and commercialized (and perhaps even employing a separate personnel from that dedicated to the singing activity), were the Paul's Boys and the Children of the Chapel (later, and more obviously registering their specialized function, the Children of the Queen's Revels). Marston's work was shared equally between the two, the first five plays played by the Paul's Boys, the last four by the Chapel Children. In fact, Marston's own writing may have prompted the success from 1599 of the Paul's Boys by equipping them with a repertory of exciting new plays at the point when they were striving to re-establish their reputation. Later, in about 1603, the playwright himself became a partner in the Chapel Children's operation when he evidently bought a sixth share in the company, a financial connection he relinquished in 1608 when he left the theatre to prepare for ordination.

It is often claimed that the boys' companies' stock-in-trade, and the secret of their successful competition with the adult players on the London theatre scene in the period, was their performing talents in the related areas of music, satire, and parody. Because, the argument runs, the boys were unable to compete with the adults in terms of the realistic portrayal of weighty and passionate (adult) characters and the telling of grave and affecting stories, so they deployed their innate or learned skills in comic mimicry, aping the adult world (children appearing as grown-ups) and parodying the conventions and practices of adult play-making. But we need to be wary. The boy players in performance would not at all anticipate a twentieth-century kind of children's theatre that we meet in school and village hall. Most, if not all, of the players were highly trained, carefully rehearsed, and skilful. Jacobean audiences were accustomed to watching boy actors play mature and passionately engaged female roles in the adult theatre. And as the decade developed (by the time of the playing of the later Marston plays) the Chapel Children, at least, had matured into a significantly older troupe than the Paul's Boys, 10 to 14 years old, who had played the *Antonio* plays. In any case, and from the outset, Marston's own dramatic *œuvre* shows that it was entirely possible onstage to show age-differences through casting, and even a variety of physical appearances. When *The Malcontent* somehow became detached from the repertoire of the Chapel Children and so available for performance elsewhere, the King's Men, pre-eminent adult company of the time, not only deigned to perform this play formerly 'presented by youths' but added an Induction to show their enthusiasm for the venture. In that Induction, no doubt with a degree of archness, they present a character who has seen the boys act the play and as a consequence is keen to coach the adult actors in how to perform the main play. (See 'The Induction' to *The Malcontent*, Addition A, ll. 13–14.)

The boy players were certainly accomplished in singing and in instrumental music: it was a part of their education and their official *raison d'être* as choristers. But we should not assume that they were incapable of playing 'straight', with all due regard for character and situation, if the piece required it. *Sophonisba*, painfully vulnerable to parody and ridicule because of its solemn presentation of idealistically virtuous and heroic characters in tortuously involved, moral dilemmas, is clear proof that the boys could attempt this, or at least that a major playwright might expect them to. Those special kinds of irony, and the characteristic intermixture of comic and tragic typical of Marston and the other mannerist writers of his period, are more probably a product of a newly formed audience sensibility (though originating in the private theatres) than a concession to the limitations of range of the child performers. If parody is a frequent intention of the plays, it lies (and should be seen to lie) in the writing and, therefore, more or less in Marston's conscious control, rather than in the given circumstances of the playing. When the actor of Antonio in the Induction to *Antonio and Mellida* (l. 70) claims that he does not possess the voice to play his character when disguised as an Amazon, this is because he considers himself too physically mature to cope. That is, his voice has broken or is in the process of breaking. (The joke lies in his new consciousness of that fact.)

On the other hand, Marston everywhere availed himself of the musicality of his actors and of the musical tradition and fine acoustics of the private (indoor and intimate) theatre, and he was constantly concerned to incorporate music and musical effects into the special strategies of his drama. It was evidently customary at Paul's, and at the Blackfriars where the Chapel Children played, to preface the performance with an hour-long concert played by the resident band, and also to mark the act-intervals, during which the candles would be trimmed and reset, with musical interludes. (Candles comprised most, perhaps all, of the artificial lighting in the indoor playhouses.) But if not uniquely, then more consistently than in any other dramatic *œuvre* of the period, Marston's plays incorporate music into their basic design and meaning. A character may, metatheatrically, call for music at the end of an act. (Mulligrub orders up therapy music for himself and the audience at the ends of Acts 2 and 3 of *The Dutch Courtesan*, and Cocledemoy stage-managerially cues the band at the end of Act 4 of the same play, and see likewise the end of Act 1 of *Antonio's Revenge*.) Often, a dance or masque introduced semi-realistically into the narrative quickly generates symbolic meanings, usually ironic in that the celebratory function typical of such an event is actually being subverted. See for three different versions of this effect the last scene of *Antonio's Revenge*, 4.1 of *The Dutch Courtesan*, and 1.2 of *Sophonisba*.

Songs, low in impact, colour, and energy for the play reader, figured, and figure, vitally in the Marston play-in-performance. In the first seven of the unaided plays there are, on average, six songs per play, not all carefully motivated or integrated narratively but contributing, individually and cumulatively, a significant structural and atmospheric element in the plays' overall effect. *The Fawn* uncharacteristically includes only one song, and the sung elements of *Sophonisba* are much reduced because of its special status as a tragic poem. But it is this last play which most notably, because of its austere design, gives best evidence of Marston's ambitious demands on music, in this case instrumental music, to articulate thematic and psychological motifs of the play. The stage-directions, for the inclusion of which the author disarmingly apologizes in the published text (see above), nominate five different, musical instruments, played singly and in combination and intended to produce a wide range of acoustical and emotional effects. The first scene of Act 4, in which Erichtho, demon enchantress, is summoned, deploys instrumentalists in different areas offstage, above and below, to create a rich orchestration which enacts the magical properties and superhuman forces of the episode. The term 'melodrama' in its strict sense of 'music theatre' is not inappropriate here. (See Notes to 4.1 for a detailed discussion.) In *The Malcontent*, theatrical music provides a literal underscoring of the play's redemptive movement from discord (first scene: 'The vilest out-of-tune music being heard') to resolution and harmony (last scene: a dance reunites the couples in a new accord).

Music, however, is only one aspect (though the most difficult to recapture) of Marston's continuous commitment to creating eloquent stage effects. Elsewhere, he might call for a single striking entrance: *'Enter Antonio, his arms bloody'*; *'Enter Franceschina with her hair loose, chafing'*; *'Enter Masinissa all in black'*. Or it might be a more complexly composed image, such as this spectacular event in *Antonio and Mellida*, 3.3, after l. 116:

> *Enter Balurdo, backward; Dildo following him, with a looking-glass in one hand and a candle in the other hand, Flavia following him backward, with a looking-glass in one hand and a candle in the other; Rosaline following her. Balurdo and Rosaline stand, setting of faces. And so the scene begins*

Felice, already onstage, acts as mediator for the audience and notates this half-a-minute or so of stage time, flat in the reading but potentially richly comic and resonant in performance, as 'a rare scene of folly, if the plot could bear it'. In these words we hear Marston as dramatist/director approving a piece of (in the best sense) pure theatre.

The elaborate and formal dumbshows that appear early and late in the playwright's work (three in *Antonio's Revenge*, one in *The Malcontent*, two in *Sophonisba*) also show the director's confidence in the visual language of theatre. Jacobean staging conventions, we are fond of assuming, were relatively simple. The playing area was a thrust stage backed by a tiring-house wall, the latter, probably in the case of both Paul's playhouse and the Blackfriars, offering door entrances left and right (i.e. upstage). Between them, centre-stage, was a third, larger, curtained opening offering access to a small playing area, the so-called 'discovery-space'. Above was an upper level, with a 'practical' window centre-stage for actors and balcony space either side which could be occupied by musicians or audience or both. The main stage could be furnished with free-standing, scenic units and furniture as appropriate to the narrative, and it had a trap. At Paul's, the playing area was sufficiently small that stage-sitters (audience onstage) were not allowed, but at the Blackfriars they were a regular feature and formed part of the stage scene. At the Blackfriars, the roofed and candle-lit auditorium accommodated about a thousand, closely packed spectators, sitting at three levels, but at Paul's, the audience was much smaller.

The apparent simplicity of such facilities (no scenery in the modern sense of a completely realized, narrative setting, only basic stage machinery for flying and concealment, no manipulable lighting for effects) is in fact deceptive, and Marston exploits the staging possibilities available to full effect. For example, he utilizes offstage areas to surprise and startle (the Ghost concealed 'betwixt the music houses', 1.2, and the body hung up in the window, 5.3, in *Antonio's Revenge*; Erichtho's sinking through the floor in *Sophonisba*, 4.1, and the same scene's offstage sound effects referred to above; or the beds, often in the 'discovery space', that in several plays reveal or conceal their occupants from characters and/or audience). We cannot recover all the exact detail, but enough is obvious to allow us to see Marston's theatrical mind constantly at work.

As in the pantomime of Balurdo and Rosaline quoted above, the playwright's concern is seldom with realism but more usually with a theatricality that edges always towards or into metatheatre. The boy players inevitably would accentuate the audience's double consciousness, inherent in all theatre, of actor and role, real world and fictional world. But in true mannerist fashion, Marston sought to sharpen that consciousness further by a periodical intervention into the imaginative world of the play in which he breaks the frame of the fiction, thus inviting a sophisticated interaction between drama and audience. The strategy appears baldly in the Induction to *Antonio and Mellida* where the actors enter before the play proper, their scripts in hand, cloaks over costumes, to discuss their various problems in playing the play. Alarmingly (or disarmingly), the production seems in fact to be hardly rehearsed. In *Antonio's Revenge*, Balurdo enters in 2.1 'with a beard half off, half on' and explains that the tireman, working backstage, has not had sufficient time during the performance to glue it properly in place. Before our eyes, actor and role switch positions with absurdist effect. It is Balurdo's idea to don the beard, but it is the theatre's failure to make it stick. So whom/what are we observing? What universe are we/they inhabiting? Even in *Sophonisba*, the play by Marston most fictionally insulated from the real world of the theatre performance (because intended, self-consciously, as tragic poem as well as performance text), the frame breaks there too when Sophonisba (at 4.1.25–7) marks her disciplined

self-control by declaring that in her tragic circumstances she might
be expected to

> Cleave my stretched cheeks with sound, speak from all sense,
> But loud, and full of players' eloquence.—
> No, no! What shall we eat?

For a moment, the fiction splits open and through the gap the
'hypocritical' world of theatrical role-play becomes visible, but,
ironically, in order to provide a standard of sincerity and modesty.
Sophonisba, in her iron maturity, will not indulge in histrionic role-
play, even though the boy actor of the role in a sense must.

Indeed, role-play itself is a major concern in Marston's art. It is a
mechanism generally of the art of theatre (and of satiric poetry) and
it functions here, as metaphor, as an element of the playwright's
world-view (or views). It is arguable, in fact, that Marston's interest
in metatheatre as philosophic statement tends to overload *Antonio
and Mellida*, the first of the major plays, almost to destruction.
When the eponymous young lovers are reunited on the seashore in
4.1, they engage in a lyrical exchange in Italian verse, a stretched
Petrarchan sonnet. It is as though their love is insulated from a 'real'
world depicted elsewhere in the play and Marston is signalling to us
the failure of realistic dialogue to render the truth of the moment.
The obvious echo is of Romeo and Juliet at the ball (*Romeo and
Juliet*, 2.1.92–109), but the experience is abstracted yet further from
the contingent world by the use of Italian. And the playwright then
deflates the episode with a knowing wink when the page, onstage for
the purpose, wryly observes to the audience: 'I think confusion of
Babel is fallen upon these lovers.' There follow references to Marston's own Italian origins as further in-jokes are embedded in the
ironies.

Antonio and Mellida is arguably the least effective of the plays in
this edition (its justification here being, in part at least, to 'explain'
Antonio's Revenge, a much stronger piece). And yet it is full of
brilliant and bold effects. The playwright begins with a revenge story
(of Andrugio and Antonio, father and son, exiled from their dukedom by the usurping and violent Piero), bolts onto this, quite successfully, the motif of frustrated love (Antonio loves Piero's
daughter) and then goes looking for a happy ending. Nothing much
actually happens as Andrugio bides his time in his pastoral retreat
and Antonio, disguised as an Amazon, remains inactive in Piero's
court. Father and son suffer and make speeches, but they fail to take

purposeful action; and Antonio feeds a self-indulgent habit of casting himself on the ground when particularly frustrated (he does this four times). Finally, in separate and unco-ordinated actions, father and son blackmail their tormentor into an unlikely repentance by throwing themselves publicly onto his mercy.

Marston is evidently concerned in the play to probe the pathology of grief and suffering. Andrugio and Antonio play foils to each other in their, respectively, stoic and anti-stoic reponses to the catastrophes that befall them. Father is all stoic fortitude, embodying the principle of sovereignty over self as a consolation for the loss of his dukedom. Son embraces grief and despises the idea of consolation. And to fill out the thematic treatment, Felice, Antonio's friend, exemplifies, as his name tells us, the stoic's disciplined resistance to the seductive, human propensity to envy the good fortune of others. Nevertheless, unable to resist a good joke and suspicious of Felice's stoicism as merely a kind of role-play, Marston composes, without warning, Felice's fit of spiteful jealousy of the successful amatory pursuits of others (3.2.68 ff.).

The play, anticipating the construction of Fletcherian tragi-comedy, lacks deaths though it brings some close to death. At the last, and risking more than a little the charge of implausibility, a tongue-in-cheek, happy ending is contrived. But another comic impulse also tugs the play away from the tragic world of pain and death that it partly inhabits and towards the satirist's world of court vanity and folly. If there is a fine line drawn between the serious and mock-serious in the main action of the play, no ambiguities complicate the simply comic impulse of the secondary action, that concerning the host of minor courtiers, namely Alberto, Castilio Balthazar, Rosaline, Flavia, and Balurdo. And presenter of this parade of folly, a kind of genial Don Kinsayder, is Felice. Rosaline, witty and self-parodying, and borrowed from Shakespearian romantic comedy, is queen of this world, and around her is created a merry-go-round of fatuous foolery entirely at odds with the violence and evil that orbit Piero.

In writing a kind of sequel, *Antonio's Revenge*, Marston in effect admitted to the strains of the earlier play. Neither the happy end nor the parade of court vanity was really to the point, and the second play follows through, with iron resolve, the implications contained in the first play of the destructive malice of Piero's personality. The playwright certainly did not set out to write a two-part play but saw in the unresolvable elements of the first *Antonio* play the impulse towards a different kind of comi-tragic mix. The result in the second is a ferocious, sometimes ferociously comic, revenge tragedy that achieves as brutal and sadistic a climax as any on the Elizabethan/Jacobean stage. Sources include Seneca at his bloodiest in *Thyestes* and Shakespeare at his bloodiest in *Titus Andronicus*, together with a parodic subplot drawn from the melodrama of Kyd's *The Spanish Tragedy*. And melded into this volatile mix, for purposes we cannot entirely fathom, is a stock of extra-narrative events and references drawn from the story of Hamlet, itself concurrently being dramatized in its most enduring form by Shakespeare at the Globe.

In *Antonio's Revenge*, Marston continues his experiments in dramaturgy and tone of the first *Antonio* play but distils the parade of folly there into the single figure of the egregious Balurdo. (Other comic characters survive in name only.) And Balurdo's folly connects now not with the vanities of court behaviour but with an altogether blacker and fallen world of ignorance/innocence and (corrupting) knowledge. In part, Balurdo's pathetic lack of grasp maps out a world incapable of rational explanation (and so for the modern audience the episode of the half-glued beard properly mobilizes ideas of an 'absurd' universe). But equally, Marston employs Balurdo as a comic foil (not comic relief, which is quite other and, here at least, quite wrong) to the inflatedly rhetorical and morbidly savage content of the rest of the play. He is a comic subplot in himself, invariably present at the most solemn or scarifying moments, always generating the effect of burlesque that allows the main plot to stay on the right side of seriousness. Critics almost invariably regret his presence, especially at the death of Piero at the climax of the play. But to miss the fineness of Marston's handling of this character is to miss what is essentially Marstonian. Through Balurdo, we are allowed a glimpse, comic that it is, of a lost world of innocence that provides rich commentary on the fallen world of Italianate vice that surrounds him. He is a kind of touchstone in his exile, and Piero (of course) understands his meaning: 'He that speaks he knows not what shall never speak sin against his own conscience' (2.1.37–8).

We might say that innocence makes Balurdo incapable of role-play, and it is the operation of role-play and its narrative extension into intrigue and conspiracy that provide the play's main structural elements. Stoic identities are again explored. Pandulfo, whose son Felice is dead at the play's opening, becomes a substitute father for Antonio, thus repeating with variations the role of Andrugio, also dead. And he plays the stoic to the life, ostentatiously laughing at his own son's death, arguing the consolatory notion that early death merely saved the young man from life's pain, and triumphing over exile at Piero's hands by claiming as his birthright the stoic's personal kingdom of the unpassionate mind. Antonio is again the anti-stoic. He parades and mocks at Seneca's *De Providentia*, a handbook of Renaissance stoicism (see 2.2 and notes) and he despises stoicism's inadequacy to provide an authentic moral programme for the suffering human being. And so, perhaps inevitably, he embraces the role of bloody revenger, slaughtering Piero's child in a brutal scene (3.1) and then, with others, torturing and killing Piero in the sadistic finale. In effect, Antonio is forced by the logic of his anti-stoicism to take on the degrading role of murderer that is properly that of his antagonist, and he is joined in this project by Pandulfo who abandons his own stoicism. In a curious role-reversal, Antonio displays a hardening to evil at the moment when Piero, in a graphic stage-direction, 'seems to condole his son' (5.3 after l. 82) and thus exhibits a new or unsuspected humanity.

The ending is not a crude moral compromise on Marston's part. Rather, in the kind of poised withdrawal of clear-cut judgement that many plays of the period favour, the playwright signals a world of moral relativism and philosophic skepticism. *Antonio's Revenge* is the darkest of Marston's plays, partly because of its savage humour. In it, the playwright adumbrates a world in which the moral adept may survive only at the expense of a deep and lasting compromise. The effect is not unlike that of *King Lear*.

Role-play and its external manifestation in disguising feature strikingly in what is the masterpiece of Marston's group of Italianate plays, *The Malcontent*. This was his first play for the Chapel Children (1603) and was written after a two-year layoff in which he had had time to mull over criticisms made of his dramatic style, particularly by Jonson. The latter had guyed Marston onstage in the person of Crispinus in *The Poetaster* (1601), and Marston replied in a manner by dedicating the printed version of *The Malcontent* to him as 'his frank and heartfelt friend' (see Explanatory Notes, p. 325).

The play has the almost unique distinction of having been performed not only by the boys but then by an adult company, indeed, *the* adult company, the King's Men. The unusual printing history of the play in part, though not at all clearly, marks this odd career. There are three, virtually separate editions of the text, all dated 1604 (the year after the probable first performance) and all emanating from the same printing-house. The first and second editions, referred to as

QA and QB, are nearly identical, apart from customary transmission changes and the inclusion in QB of a little extra text. But the third, QC, which alone registers that the play was 'played by the King's Majesty's servants', has substantial additions. These take the form of a lengthy Induction scene and about 450 extra lines of dialogue in the main body of the play. These extra lines in the main play comprise eleven passages, scattered throughout but with nine of them in Acts 1 and 5. The title-page of QC and its first page of text (i.e. the first page of the Induction) contradictorily suggest (1) that Webster wrote all the new material; and (2) that the play was 'augmented' by Marston while Webster supplied 'additions'. Modern scholarship has generally agreed that most probably Webster composed the Induction and five of the eleven, main-text passages and that Marston supplied the other six.

The Induction, written for the revival by the King's Men, talks wittily about how the adult company acquired, perhaps stole, the play to compensate for a parallel takeover by the boys (or rather their managers) of another (unnamed) piece. It goes on to suggest why additions were thought necessary for the Globe presentation: 'as salad to your great feast [i.e., presumably, the Induction] and to abridge the not-received custom of music in the theatre'. In other words, the play needed extending to compensate for the lack at the Globe of the musical embellishment normal in the private theatre.

How both Marston and Webster were involved in this whole process of augmentation is not obvious, and it is entirely possible that the extra Marston passages had in fact belonged to the original play text but had been cut for performance by the Chapel Children. (Quartos A and B had then, it would follow, been set from the cut version.) The extra Marston material is all dramatically relevant and theatrically effective and the play (as in QA and QB) seems the poorer without it. The same, however, cannot be said for Webster's main-text additions. Four of the five passages (printed here as Additions B, C, D, and E in the Explanatory Notes, pp. 349–57) contain a new character, Passarello, a professional fool assigned to Bilioso, and almost certainly intended, in addition to lengthening the play, to provide a role for the King's Men's popular comic actor, Robert Armin. But the material itself is feeble, merely jest-book routines, and it is barely at all integrated into the play proper. The fifth passage (printed here as Addition F, p. 357), which does not contain Passarello, alone requires a cancelling of a main-text passage for its inclusion, as it in part repeats material crucial to the plot. It is the Marston play without the Webster additions that we might consider the authentic, original text, even though, paradoxically, it might never have been played by the Chapel Children (and certainly not by the King's Men) exactly in that form. (For this edition's handling of the problem of this layering of texts, see Note on the Texts.)

The title of the play is a tease because properly there is no malcontent in it. That is merely a disguise, a role-play for the deposed duke, Altofronto, so that he might at once be not seen and be conspicuously present. Antonio's disguise as an idiot in *Antonio's Revenge*, 4.1, had served as a rehearsal and Marston explored there how a 'licensed' figure of that kind could provide a critical commentary on the life on which it battens and yet remain both detached from it and invulnerable. And so, ironically, it is with Altofronto's *alter ego*, the Malcontent, that Altofronto's adversary in the play, the usurping Pietro, closely identifies: 'I like him, faith; he gives good intelligence to my spirit, makes me understand those weaknesses which others' flattery palliates' (1.1.34–6). Like Shakespeare's dukes-in-hiding, Vincentio and Prospero, Altofronto will plan and execute a complicated strategy of reformation and renewal (here for all but one of his errant opponents in the play) and then reassume his regency.

Both Altofronto's apparent reliance on providence to bring his plans to fruition and his unholy alliance with Malevole have exercised the play's commentators. But in fact his belief in the interventionist operation of providence does not commit him to a programme of merely passive waiting. Instead, he readies himself for the opportunity to reassert himself, preparing as the beneficent avenger to initiate action, confident, as the wise ruler, that God will be on his side. His energy and commitment to positive action are finely caught by the graphic word 'scuffle': 'When the ranks are burst, then scuffle Altofront (1.1.237); and so is his willingness to scheme and deceive. In a world where the feebly opportunistic Pietro makes it possible for the truly evil Mendoza to prosper, Altofronto must adopt the enemy's practice to be assured of defeating him. In other words, the high principles of the neo-stoic must necessarily be tempered with the *realpolitik* of the moral Machiavell. As a legitimate ruler, that is, one not intent on personal ends, Altofronto may 'temporise' (he uses the word crucially at 1.1.226), but without destructively swapping roles with his enemy, as does Antonio in *Antonio's Revenge*.

However, Altofronto must also somehow keep himself insulated from the spoiling, prurient, corruption-loving Malevole; he must play Malevole but not be or become the role. Of course, the problem is rather one of life than dramatic art where the ability to assume a role 'to the life' and yet remain separate from it is both a convention of the dramaturgy of the Jacobean stage and an actual requirement of theatrical presentation itself. In a way, Altofronto is no more likely to be taken over by the role of Malevole than is the boy player of Altofronto to be taken over by the role of the Duke of Genoa. And Marston tactfully rehearses the gap between Altofronto and his role when he allows him to tire of the playing of it (5.1.98–101). At the end of the play, the removal of the disguise is done with aplomb. Altofronto as masquer reveals the figure which Mendoza identifies as Malevole, Malevole then reveals Altofronto, and those assembled finally re-identify Altofronto as duke (5.2.148–51). The metamorphoses do not at all belong to the world (or art) of realism, but they are fine, and finely judged, in a piece of poetic theatre.

Much of the force of the play depends on the liveliness and rude vigour of the Malevole role-play. Marston's writing here is at its best, and Malevole's rumbustious prose is one of the great achievements of what we loosely term 'Jacobean theatre'. (The play was probably on stage before the death of Elizabeth.) It is energetic and supremely gestural, inviting its live delivery, an actor's delight. And it is radically irreverent in content, though urging on its audience inside and outside the play a value system of ordering rationality and moderation that is the opposite of its outward and formal operation. Take, for example, Malevole's exposition to Pietro of Mendoza's plans to have him, Pietro, assassinated, 3.2.48–58. Note its approximations to the rhythms and shapes of the real, speaking voice, and also its pithy economy of expression. The epithets at the end of the third sentence, 'loathsome', 'gracious', and 'loose' have a great, but shorthand force. There is a quick, salacious wit in the 'egress'/'regress' formula and a rude physicality in 'toused thy sheets'. And the final, rhetorical question is designed to draw Pietro into a world of robust candour that is at once true and ironic. Altogether, this is an inventive but classically composed species of high comedy, at once deeply serious and richly funny. The role provided great acting material for the Chapel youth who originated the part and no doubt too for Burbage, the greatest performer of his time, who adopted it.

In *The Dutch Courtesan* Marston moves on. The Italianate world of
court depravity is replaced by a semi-realistic account of London life
in what is a very early version of a new Jacobean dramatic genre,
satirical London comedy. The writer attached a *Fabulae argumentum*
to the reading text (see Explanatory Notes, p. 358) to encourage us to
see the piece as a kind of morality play built on the ethical opposition
of the classic antagonists, love and lust, represented here, respectively, by Freevill in his love for Beatrice and Malheureux in his lust
for Franceschina (not Beatrice and Franceschina themselves, as some
commentators have mistakenly assumed). However, the simple-
minded, moral programme that such a scheme entails is wonderfully
compromised by the presiding but invisible genius of the play, Montaigne, who is much quoted (unacknowledged) by the characters (see
the notes) and whose festive, onstage representative is the quicksilver
Cocledemoy. Montaigne's skepticism and moral realism inform the
play at every stage and encourage Marston to explode any simple,
moral structures of right/wrong, black/white by engaging with the
genuine complexity of human experience, armed with a kind of
humane relativism. And so the play is more interested in Malheureux's psychological problems than his moral ones (though the two
are consistently and properly connected), and role-play here lies not
only in the obvious disguising of Freevill but more engagingly in the
hypocritical mask of the man (Malheureux) who is unwilling to
acknowledge and deal with his own baser instincts.

In this radical mix of morality and realism, the play can be seen to
mark a new maturity of outlook in its author, still fascinated by greed
and sexual depravity but generous now to accept and allow the
imperfectibility of human nature, suspicious, moreover, of those with
idealist or absolutist claims. As Freevill, the successful *homme
moyen sensuel* of the play, puts it: 'consider man furnished with
omnipotency and you overthrow him' (3.1.235–6). It is a line that
might have come from what is in many ways a companion piece,
Measure for Measure.

At the heart of the play is neither Freevill (right way) nor Malheureux (wrong way) but Cocledemoy. Nowhere is Marston's con-
viction that the life of comic plays 'consists in the action' better
illustrated than here. The character has no impact on the main plot,
he is unmotivated in terms of realistic characterization, and his language of demotic swagger laced with scraps of classical learning, tag
lines, non-lexical cries and the like, comes quite stutteringly off the
page. But both in his intrigues and in his discourse, Cocledemoy as

stage-presence is vibrantly alive, a comic anarchist. And like Mal-evole, he is a moral agent by implication, punishing the fake-puritan pretentiousness of Mulligrub while at the same time, by embodying anti-puritan attitudes, helping to define Malheureux's depraved pru-dery. Cocledemoy's is a supremely actable role, as shape-changer run riot and a comic vice; and his comfortable access to Franceschina's world and culture of flesh-mongering invites us to question any instinct we may have to too-easy censoriousness.

Freevill's career in the play has been more compromised by the passage of time than has Cocledemoy's. He can slide (Marston lets him) from the cynical liaison with Franceschina to blessed wedlock with Beatrice without apparent strain or stain. It is true that the playwright ensures that Franceschina does not attract audience sym-pathy, but this leaves Beatrice with the problem typical of the romantic heroine (as with Hero in *Much Ado About Nothing*) caught up in a semi-realistic and grainy, city play. (The aggressive Crispi-nella, her sister, counterpart to *Much Ado*'s Beatrice, might have demanded greater restitution for the philandering.) But as notions of sexual propriety are quizzically interrogated by all the main characters (even by Mrs Mulligrub), so a sense of compromise, perhaps tolerance, is generated which the comic failures of the law in Act 5 (again the borrowing is from *Much Ado*) serve to under-write *The Dutch Courtesan* is a luminously intelligent play about sex and self-discipline, and in reading it we must bear in mind that the youthful cast of its Chapel Children players would have bestowed on the play, through good humour and high spirits, a certain geni-ality in the original performance that Marston could count on. Later productions would and will find the whole thing darker and cruel-ler. But Tysefew says it all: 'you must live by the quick, when all is done' (5.2.78–9).

In *Sophonisba*, we are back in a world of moral absolutes, heroic virtue and total depravity. Marston finally locates his obsession with stoicism in its natural home, the ancient, part-literary, world that first developed it. However, little else in Marston's *œuvre*, or in Elizabethan/Jacobean drama generally, prepares us for this strange play. The nervous energy that informs the playwright's best work (in parts of *Antonio's Revenge* and *The Dutch Courtesan* and pre-eminently in *The Malcontent*) is muted here, the ferocious humour mostly, not entirely, banished, and the strategies used elsewhere to keep an audience off-balance a good deal less blatant.

Marston, we must suppose, had, fittingly, himself signed a pledge of stoic austerity and self-restraint, and the result is a play which is both unified in intent and uncomfortable in outcome. The characters, nobly virtuous like Masinissa, Sophonisba, and Gelosso, or viciously depraved like Syphax, Hasdrubal, and Carthalon, cannot surprise us. The spirit of compromise and accommodation that Altofronto learns and Freevill (and Cocledemoy) live by is available now only to the wicked, in whose mouths it becomes the hypocritical cover of, or special pleading for, egotism. (With this regard, 2.3, in which the political strategists fall to acrimony and, in Hasdrubal's case, hysterical incoherence at the failure of their plans, is finely done and very Marstonian.) At the finale, the moral protagonists are brought to their tragic end by their own high-mindedness. They have won the argument, and seemingly, the worldly contest; but when the defeated Syphax hastily improvises his final trap (by making Sophonisba appear to be a danger to Scipio), Masinissa and Sophonisba spring that trap themselves by insisting that only Sophonisba's death can unlock the paradox of two conflicting vows.

So the play, ultimately, is about martyrdom, and its recourse to spectacular stagecraft (despite, or because of, the pledge of austerity) is deployed in the final scene to furnish Sophonisba with the baroque exequies appropriate to martyrdom itself. There is a histrionic solemnity about it all that evidently caught Ford's eye, for the later tragedian, himself a more consistently baroque artist, reproduced much of the style, sentiment, and actual stagecraft of this episode in the finale of his *The Broken Heart*, the play of the period most like *Sophonisba*.

The austerity in the writing of *Sophonisba* takes the form of an often ineloquent laconicism and severe compression that would scarcely favour the live delivery of the romantic actor. Except in the Erichtho scenes, there is little of the energy and colour that marks Marston's most distinctive dialogue. Notably absent is the close approximation to the impromptu verbalisms, non-lexical items, of live speech that Marston is so expert at imitating. These are not allowed to 'localize' in speech acts Marston's experiment in tragic ('classic') poetry, intended for reader as much as, even in preference to, auditor.

The play, in fact, was performed 'sundry times' by the Chapel Children, or so we are informed by its title-page. But it is difficult to imagine that it was ever liked, rather than admired. T. S. Eliot claimed to find in the play 'an underlying serenity', but he had little sympathy for Marston's other dramatic work. Those who respond to the nervous mannerism of *The Malcontent* may want to substitute 'frigidity' here for 'serenity'.

Sophonisba, not surprisingly, has never been performed professionally in the modern period (indeed, probably not since its Blackfriars days), though all the other plays of this edition have been, in some form or other, *The Dutch Courtesan* several times. Marston's *œuvre* is larger and more various than that of the other Jacobean playwrights with whom he is commonly associated, Webster, Middleton, and Ford. In an era of outstanding talent, he was the most innovative and experimental of the theatre writers. While leading others towards their best work, he wrote a number of masterpieces which, a pleasure to read, will still handsomely respond to the supreme test for a dramatic text, namely theatrical production.

NOTE ON THE TEXTS

FOUR of the five plays printed here were first published in a single quarto within a year or two of their first production and then (unauthoritatively) in a collected, octavo edition in 1633. These quartos provide the copytext for the present edition. The odd one out is *The Malcontent*. This appeared in three separate, quarto editions in 1604, all produced by the same publisher and printer. These editions are generally known (and are so referred to in the Explanatory Notes here) as QA, QB, and QC. QB is a carefully edited and slightly enlarged version of QA, while QC is a greatly extended version of QB, with a good deal of new text, apparently supplied both by Marston himself and by fellow dramatist John Webster. (See the Introduction, pp. xviii–xx, for a longer discussion of this.) QB of *The Malcontent*, together with the six Marston additions in QC, provides the copytext for the present edition. The Webster additions in QC are relegated here to the Explanatory Notes, pp. 343–57. The Marston additions (or restorations) included in the main text are: (a) 1.1.134–75 ('—think it.'); (b) 1.1.182–98; (c) 1.1.241 S.D.–'*Exit Bilioso*' after 1.284; (d) 2.2.54–68; (e) 5.1.120 S.D. '*Enter Bilioso*'– 150; (f) 5.2.172–93.

Marston prepared all the plays, however lightly, for their first printing, and the copy for the press was evidently his own manuscript or, in the case of QB, his own editing of QA. (The octavo of 1633, on the other hand, was worked up only from printed material and without the writer's blessing.) Marston supplied a 'Persons in the Play' for three of the texts (not for the *Antonio* plays), an Epistle to the Reader for two, and an end-note for one. (All this extra-playhouse material is relegated here to the Explanatory Notes, as it did not form part of the play proper, i.e. of the performance. Included in this is a so-called 'Prologue' for *The Malcontent*, which, it is assumed here, was also provided only for the printed text.) All the texts were divided into acts, and all but *Antonio and Mellida* into scenes. The scene divisions in the other four play texts operate according to two different principles. In *The Dutch Courtesan* and *Sophonisba*, scene divisions follow the staging (Elizabethan-style) in that an empty stage marks the end of a scene. In

Antonio's Revenge and *The Malcontent*, the 'classical' principle is followed, a new 'scene' being indicated at each new, important entrance. Two of the texts were furnished with a Latin motto and *The Malcontent* with two, one for QA, a different one for QB and QC (and all are also printed here in the Explanatory Notes).

Evidence that printing-house copytext derived from a production version exists forcefully in only one case, *Antonio and Mellida*, where at 4.1.28 S.D. (present edition) the names of two Paul's Boys actors of the period, required on stage at this point, appear in the entry-direction. Elsewhere, what evidence there is would suggest that copy was non-theatrical in provenance. Nevertheless, the quartos are generally well supplied with stage-directions, often of a graphic, sometimes of a literary nature. This may suggest either Marston's original concern to direct to the company the precise staging activity of the play or his later concern to improve the play's accessibility for the reader. The end-note to *Sophonisba* tells us that at least in the case of that play it was the former.

The full title of *Sophonisba* as it appears on the title-page of the quarto (1606) is *The Wonder of Women / Or / The Tragedy of Sophonisba*. However, the running title (which heads each page of text) is *The Tragedy of Sophonisba*. We have no notion by what title the play was known to its first audiences and it is the unadorned *Sophonisba* that has been universally adopted in later editions and critical discussions. To 'restore' *The Wonder of Women* in this edition would seem unwarrantably pedantic.

No new editions of the play texts appeared between 1633 and 1856. In that latter year, J. O. Halliwell brought out a three-volume, complete edition, but based largely on the (non-authoritative) octavo edition. This was followed by two other complete editions, A. H. Bullen's edition of 1887 and J. H. Wood's old-spelling version of 1934–5 (both also in three volumes). Each of the latter has proved valuable in the preparation of this edition. All five plays here reprinted also appear in *The Selected Plays of John Marston*, ed. MacD. P. Jackson and M. Neill (Cambridge, 1986). This has been a source of constant reference for the present editor for its innumerable insights into text, interpretation, and criticism. In particular, its original device of not including in the main text the Webster additions of QC has been adopted here.

Single editions of the five texts, all of which have been consulted for this edition, are:

Antonio and Mellida: ed. G. K. Hunter, Regents, 1965; ed. R. Gair, Revels, 1991

Antonio's Revenge: ed. G. K. Hunter, Regents, 1965; ed. R. Gair, Revels, 1978

The Malcontent: ed. M. L. Wine, Regents, 1965; ed. B. Harris, New Mermaid, 1967; ed. G. K. Hunter, Revels, 1975

The Dutch Courtesan: ed. M. L. Wine, Regents, 1965; ed. P. Davison, Fountainwell, 1968

Sophonisba: ed. W. Kemp, Garland, 1979 (old-spelling edition).

Single plays also appear in a number of anthologies, several of which have been consulted here.

The texts in this edition have been modernized in punctuation and spelling, and character-names in speech prefixes and stage-directions have been regularized. Abbreviations, ampersands, and numerals have been expanded, obvious misprints corrected, and evidently 'correct' emendations from previous editors adopted, all silently. Latin stage-directions have been mostly (silently) translated and where stage-directions have been amplified or supplied, the new material is printed in square brackets. 'And' meaning 'if' or 'if it' has been silently changed to 'an' or 'an't'. The act division of the original texts has been retained, but the scene division has been supplied or regularized on the Elizabethan principle (see above).

The quarto texts are variable in their accuracy, and a problem in editing them relates to Marston's especial interest in registering in his dialogue some of the untidiness typical of real speech. Characters exclaim or falter, they lose their thread or they become incoherent with emotion; often they are interrupted in full flow. Sudden hiatuses are marked here with a dash or with three stops, the former indicating a sudden break-off, the latter a gentle trailing-off. However, the distinction is not always clear. In a general way, this tendency towards 'realism' in the writing has somewhat inhibited editors in their identifying and attempting to reform textual problems. Often, what is probably a printing-house lapse is identified as a character's solecism and consequently retained. In this edition, more frequent emendation is attempted (never silently), often working from an attempt to identify the force and meaning of the particular theatrical situation, as well as the bibliographical one.

Marston's evident fluency of composition, amounting at times to carelessness, probably contributed to a frequent blurring of the transition between verse and prose. No textual emendation in the present edition has been proposed specifically to regularize the metre, and the typographical distinction between verse and prose, often a mystery to Marston's first printers (if a greater problem to eye than to ear) has been attempted here, often with no great confidence. However, the convention has been followed of marking stressed syllables in the past participle and preterite as 'èd' but not recording unstressed syllables as '-'d' except where this retains a significant, quarto spelling.

SELECT BIBLIOGRAPHY

THE fullest account of critical writing about Marston is contained in T. P. Logan and D. B. Smith (eds.), *The New Intellectuals* (Lincoln, Nebr., 1977), 171–247, by C. M. McCulley. Chapter 1 of G. L. Geckle's *John Marston's Drama: Themes, Images, Sources* (Rutherford, Madison, Teaneck, 1980) outlines major trends, and R. W. Ingram's *John Marston* (Boston, 1978) has a short bibliography.

Two scholarly, book-length studies from the 1960s provide the best introduction to Marston's writing career: A. Caputi's *John Marston, Satirist* (Ithaca, NY, 1961) and P. J. Finkelpearl's *John Marston of the Middle Temple* (Cambridge, Mass., 1969). The former locates Marston's work within the context of literary satire and identifies as a key to the integrity of the artist a consistently 'serio-comic view of the Renaissance world'. Emphasis is placed here on Marston's neo-stoicism which, for Caputi, informs the satire with a consistent moral philosophy. Finkelpearl's equally persuasive account locates Marston's literary development within the intellectual, artistic and moral context of the Inns of Court (and provides a thorough introduction to that institution's practice, culture, and influence). The satirical impulse in Marston's work is examined in a number of wide-ranging books. These include: O. J. Campbell's *Comicall Satyre and Shakespeare's 'Troilus and Cressida'* (San Marino, Calif., 1938); A. J. Kernan's *The Cankered Muse* (New Haven, 1959); and B. Gibbons's *Jacobean City Comedy* (London, 1968).

Marston has had something of a mixed press. The introduction to A. H. Bullen's excellent edition of the plays (1887) reserved its best praise, with no apparent sense of irony, for *Eastward Ho!*, in the composition of which Marston had only a share. Elsewhere, Bullen deplored both the playwright's harsh bitterness and his 'noisy verbiage', charges that have found frequent echoes in later critics who have discerned in Marston a morbidity and a tendency to neuroticism that stems, it is argued, from mental instability. An authoritative essay in this vein is S. Schoenbaum's 'The Precarious Balance of John Marston' (*Publications of the Modern Language Association*, 67 (1952), 1069–78). For some, what was 'read' as Marston's nihilism, prurience, sensationalism, and plagiarism became synonymous with the early manifestations of what was fashionably regarded as Jacobean decadence.

In fact, most of the negative criticism, if not too much of all Marston criticism, concerns itself with the (self-evidently experimental) *Antonio* plays, and much ink has been spilt over the vexed question of how far a major impulse there is parody. An important proponent of the idea that the plays are primarily parodic (and therefore ironic in their deliberate excesses of style) is R. A. Foakes in his essays, 'John Marston's Fantastical Plays' and 'Tragedies at the Children's Theatre after 1600' (*Philological Quarterly*, 41 (1962), 229–39; and *The Elizabethan Theatre*, ii, ed. D. Galloway (London, 1970), 35–59). The counter-argument, that the plays are not ironic but simply excessive in their style and therefore bad, is well put in R. Levin's 'The New *New Inn* and the Proliferation of Good Bad Drama' (*Essays in Criticism*, 22 (1972), 41–7). In the same volume, there is a reply by Foakes and a further rejoinder by Levin. There are two effective essays on the same theme by T. F. Wharton: '*The Malcontent* and "Dreams, Visions, Fantasies"' and 'Old Marston or New Marston: The *Antonio* Plays' (*Essays in Criticism*, 24 (1974), 261–74; and 25 (1975), 357–69).

The question of parody relates in part to the qualitative impact of the initial playing of Marston's plays by boy actors, for whom Marston intended them. Any approach to the plays *via* theatrical criticism is welcome, but the assumption that the boys' acting lent itself only to mimicry and satire has been strongly overstated. J. S. Colley, in *John Marston's Theatrical Drama* (Salzburg, 1974), rightly stresses the self-conscious theatricality of Marston's writing and his manipulation of stage technique, and he claims that more than most these plays reveal their true meaning only in performance. Colley and others, such as M. Scott in *John Marston's Plays: Theme, Structure and Performance* (London, 1978), explore the modernity of Marston's drama by comparing it with the work of such twentieth-century theatre innovators as Pirandello, Artaud, Brecht, and Genet.

Individual features of the theatrical shape and flavour of Marston's plays are illuminated in other studies. His use of dumbshows and mime sequences is usefully analysed in D. Mehl's *The Elizabethan Dumb Show* (London, 1965); and the important place of music in the plays is discussed by C. Kiefer in 'Music and Marston's *The Malcontent*' (*Studies in Philology*, 51 (1954), 163–71) and by R. W. Ingram in 'The Use of Music in the Plays of Marston'

(*Music and Letters*, 37 (1956), 154–64) and by D. G. O'Neill in 'The Influence of Music in the Works of John Marston (*Music and Letters*, 53 (1972), 122–33, 293–308, and 400–10). Two complementary books discuss the operation of the boys' companies of the early seventeenth century and Marston's own place in that operation: M. Shapiro's *Children of the Revels* (New York, 1977), and R. Gair's *The Children of Paul's: The Story of a Theatre Company, 1553–1608* (Cambridge, 1982).

Individual plays have been critically well served by later editors. The work of G. K. Hunter, with his insights into the mannerist strain in Marston's plays and their strategic discontinuities, has been especially valuable. See the introductions to his editions of *Antonio and Mellida* and *Antonio's Revenge* (Regents, 1965 and 1966), and *The Malcontent* (Revels, 1975). Other illuminating commentaries are: for *The Malcontent*, M. L. Wine (Regents, 1965) and B. Harris (New Mermaid, 1967); for *The Dutch Courtesan*, P. Davison (Fountainwell, 1968); and for *Sophonisba*, W. Kemp (Garland, 1979). Other notable essays, not connected with editions, are: G. K. Hunter's 'English Folly and Italian Vice' (*Jacobean Theatre*, ed. J. R. Brown and B. Harris (London, 1960), 84–111); G. D. Aggeler, 'Stoicism and Revenge in Marston' (*English Studies*, 51 (1970), 507–17); P. Ure's 'John Marston's *Sophonisba*: A Reconsideration' (in his own *Elizabethan and Jacobean Drama* (Liverpool, 1974)); W. Babula's 'The Avenger and the Satirist: John Marston's Malevole' (*The Elizabethan Theatre*, ed. G. R. Hibbard (London, vi, 1978), 48–58); and J. Dollimore's 'Marston's *Antonio* Plays and Shakespeare's *Troilus and Cressida*: The Birth of a Radical Drama' (in his own *Radical Tragedy* (Brighton, 1984), ch. 2). Finally, there is a persuasive account of the originality, structure, and influence of *The Malcontent* in M. Wiggins's *Journeymen in Murder* (Oxford, 1991).

Much work remains to be done. The theatrical shapes fashioned by Marston's supple dramaturgies have yet to be convincingly expounded analytically (or, perhaps, explored theatrically). Several of the plays, especially *The Dutch Courtesan, Sophonisba*, and (reluctantly absent from the present volume) *The Fawn*, remain scandalously neglected. A whole new assessment of the Senecal strain in Marston's writing (and its related neo-stoicism) is still to follow on from G. Braden's *Renaissance Tragedy and the Senecan Tradition* (New Haven, 1985). And a comprehensive, post-structuralist account of Marston is strangely overdue.

A CHRONOLOGY OF JOHN MARSTON

1575   Parents John Marston and Marie Guarsi married at Wardington, Oxfordshire.

1576   Born at Wardington. Christened, 7 October.

1591   Takes up residence at Brasenose College, Oxford.

1592   Matriculates at Brasenose College, Oxford, 4 February.
             Entered as a member of the Middle Temple, 2 August.

1594   Graduates Bachelor of Arts, 23 March.

1595   Takes up residence in the Middle Temple.

1597   Shares father's chambers at the Middle Temple.

1598   Poems published: *The Metamorphosis of Pigmalion's Image, and Certain Satires*; *The Scourge of Villainy*.

1599   Order of Conflagration bans Marston's (and others') Satires, 1 June.
             Philip Henslowe, theatre impresario, records loan of two pounds on behalf of the Admiral's Men to 'Mr. Marston, the new poet', 28 September.
             Father dies; will proved, 29 November.

?1599   *Histriomastix* performed by Paul's Boys (printed 1610).

1599/1600   *Antonio and Mellida* performed by Paul's Boys (printed 1602).

1600   *Jack Drum's Entertainment* performed by Paul's Boys (printed 1601).

1600/1   *Antonio's Revenge* performed by Paul's Boys (printed 1602).

1601   *What You Will* performed, probably by Paul's Boys (printed 1607).
             Contributes verses (with Shakespeare, Chapman, and Jonson) to Robert Chester's *Love's Martyr*.
             Portrayed on stage as Crispinus in Jonson's *The Poetaster*.

1603   *The Malcontent* performed by the Children of the Chapel Royal (printed 1604).

1604   Buys sixth share in the Children of the Queen's Revels Company.
             The Fawn performed by the Children of the Queen's Revels (printed 1606).
             Revised version of *The Malcontent* performed by the King's Men at the Globe.

1605   *The Dutch Courtesan* performed by the Children of the Queen's Revels (printed same year).
             Contributes prefatory verses to Jonson's *Sejanus' Fall*.

Collaborates with Jonson and Chapman on *Eastward Ho!* Forced to flee London to escape imprisonment because of offence given by the play to the king and authorities.

Listed as major British poet by William Camden.

?1605   Marries Mary Wilkes, daughter of Dr William Wilkes, Rector of Barford St Martin's, Wiltshire; lives at Barford for eleven years.

Sells share in Children of the Queen's Revels Company at marriage or in 1608 (conjectural).

1606   *Sophonisba* performed by the Children of the Queen's Revels (printed same year).

Writes city pageant to welcome Christian IV of Denmark to London.

1607   Masque, *The Entertainment of the Dowager Countess of Derby* performed at Ashby.

1608   Committed to Newgate Prison, 8 June, for short period (offence unknown).

The Insatiate Countess left incomplete (printed 1613).

1608/9   *The Insatiate Countess*, completed by William Barksted and Lewis Machin, probably performed by the Children of the King's Revels.

1609   Ordained deacon in parish church of Stanton Harcourt, Oxfordshire, 24 September.

Ordained priest, 29 December.

1616   Presented to the Curacy of Christchurch, Hampshire, 10 October.

1621   Mother dies.

1624   Only son, John, dies in infancy.

1631   Resigns living at Christchurch, 13 September, and returns to London.

1633   Octavo edition of six of the plays printed without author's approval.

1634   Dies at his house in Aldermanbury, London, 25 June.

1657   Widow dies; is buried next to him, 4 July.

ANTONIO AND MELLIDA

THE PERSONS OF THE PLAY

Piero Sforza°	Duke of Venice
Andrugio	former Duke of Genoa
Antonio	son of Andrugio, disguised as Florizell the Amazon
Felice°	Venetian gentleman
Galeazzo	son of the Duke of Florence
Mazzagente°	son of the Duke of Milan
Jeffrey Balurdo°	wealthy heir of Venice
Alberto	Venetian gentleman
Castilio Balthazar°	Venetian gentleman
Forobosco°	the parasite
Cazzo°	page to Castilio
Dildo°	page to Balurdo
Lucio	counsellor to Andrugio
A Painter	
Mellida	daughter to Piero Sforza
Rosaline	cousin to Mellida
Flavia	gentlewoman to Mellida
Pages	
A Boy	
Attendants	

2

Antonio and Mellida

INDUCTION

Enter [the actors of] Galeazzo, Piero, Alberto, Antonio,
Forobosco, Balurdo, Mazzagente, and Felice, with parts° in
their hands, having cloaks cast over their apparel

'GALEAZZO'° Come sirs, come! The music will sound straight for
entrance. Are ye ready? Are ye perfect?°

'PIERO' Faith, we can say our parts. But we are ignorant in what
mould we must cast our actors.°

'ALBERTO' Whom do you personate?   5

'PIERO' Piero, Duke of Venice.

'ALBERTO' O, ho! Then thus frame your exterior shape
To haughty form of elate majesty,
As if you held the palsy-shaking head
Of reeling chance under your fortune's belt   10
In strictest vassalage. Grow big in thought,
As swoll'n with glory of successful arms.

'PIERO' If that be all, fear not, I'll suit it right.
Who cannot be proud, stroke up the hair, and strut?°

'ALBERTO' Truth! Such rank custom is grown popular;   15
And now the vulgar fashion strides as wide
And stalks as proud upon the weakest stilts
Of the slight'st fortunes, as if Hercules
Or burly Atlas shouldered up their state.°

'PIERO' Good. But whom act you?   20

'ALBERTO' The necessity of the play forceth me to act two parts:°
Andrugio, the distressed Duke of Genoa, and Alberto, a Venetian
gentleman enamoured on the Lady Rosaline, whose fortunes being
too weak to sustain the port of her, he proved always disastrous in
love, his worth being much underpoised by the uneven scale that   25
currents all things by the outward stamp of opinion.

'GALEAZZO' Well, and what dost thou play?

'BALURDO' The part of all the world.

'ALBERTO' The part of all the world? What's that?

'BALURDO' The fool. Ay, in good deed la now, I play Balurdo, a   30
wealthy, mountebanking,° *Bergamasco*'s° heir of Venice.

3

'ALBERTO' Ha, ha! One whose foppish nature might seem create only for wise men's recreation, and, like a juiceless bark, to preserve the sap of more strenuous° spirits; a servile hound that loves the scent of forerunning° fashion; like an empty hollow vault still giving an echo to wit; greedily champing what any other well-valued judgment had beforehand chewed.   35

'FOROBOSCO' Ha, ha, ha! Tolerably good, good faith, sweet wag.

'ALBERTO' Umh! Why 'tolerably good, good faith, sweet wag'? Go, go, you flatter me.   40

'FOROBOSCO' Right, I but dispose my speech to the habit of my part.

'ALBERTO' (to ['Felice']) Why, what plays he?

'FELICE' The wolf° that eats into the breast of princes, that breeds the lethargy and falling sickness° in honour, makes justice look asquint, and blinks the eye of merited reward from viewing desert-   45
ful virtue.

'ALBERTO' What's all this periphrasis, ha?

'FELICE' The substance of a supple-chapped flatterer.

'ALBERTO' O, doth he play Forobosco, the parasite? Good, i'faith!—[To 'Forobosco'] Sirrah, you must seem now as glib and   50
straight in outward semblance as a lady's busk, though inwardly as cross as a pair of tailor's legs;° having a tongue as nimble as his needle, with servile patches of glavering flattery to stitch up the bracks of the° unworthily honoured.

'FOROBOSCO' I warrant you! I warrant you! You shall see me prove   55
the very periwig to cover the bald pate of brainless gentility. Ho! I will so tickle the sense of *bella graziosa madonna*° with the titilla-tion of hyperbolical praise that I'll strike it in the nick,° in the very nick, chuck.

'FELICE' Thou promisest more than, I hope, any spectator gives faith   60
of performance.—(To ['Antonio']) But why look you so dusky, ha?

'ANTONIO' I was never worse fitted since the nativity of my actor-ship. I shall be hissed at, on my life now.

'FELICE' Why, what must you play?

'ANTONIO' Faith, I know not what—an hermaphrodite, two parts   65
in one; my true person being Antonio, son to the Duke of Genoa, though for the love of Mellida, Piero's daughter, I take this feigned presence of an Amazon,° calling myself Florizell and I know not what. I a voice to play a lady! I shall ne'er do it.°

'ALBERTO' O, an Amazon should have such a voice, virago-like. Not   70
play two parts in one? Away, away; 'tis common fashion. Nay, if you cannot bear two subtle fronts under one hood,° idiot, go by, go by;° off this world's stage! O time's impurity!

'ANTONIO' Ay, but when use hath taught me action to hit the right
point° of a lady's part, I shall grow ignorant, when I must turn   75
young prince again, how but to truss my hose.°
'FELICE' Tush, never put them off, for women wear the breeches still.
'MAZZAGENTE' By the bright honour of a Milanese,
And the resplendent fulgor of this steel,°
I will defend the feminine to death,   80
And ding his spirit to the verge of hell
That dares divulge a lady's prejudice.
    [Exeunt ['Mazzagente'], ['Forobosco'], and ['Balurdo']
'FELICE' Rampum scrampum! Mount tufty Tamburlaine! What rat-
tling thunderclap breaks from his lips?
'ALBERTO' O, 'tis native to his part. For acting a modern   85
Bragadoch° under the person of Mazzagente, the Duke of Milan's
son, it may seem to suit with good fashion of coherence.
'PIERO' But methinks he speaks with a spruce Attic accent of adul-
terate Spanish.°
'ALBERTO' So 'tis resolved. For Milan being half Spanish, half   90
High Dutch and half Italian,° the blood of chiefest houses is
corrupt and mongrelled. So that you shall see a fellow vainglorious
for a Spaniard, gluttonous for a Dutchman, proud for an Italian,°
and a fantastic idiot for all. Such a one conceit this Mazzagente.
'FELICE' But I have a part allotted me which I have neither able   95
apprehension to conceit, nor what I conceit gracious ability to
utter.
'GALEAZZO' Whoop! In the old cut? Good, show us a draught of thy
spirit.
'FELICE' 'Tis steady, and must seem so impregnably fortressed with   100
his own content that no envious thought could ever invade his
spirit; never surveying any man so unmeasuredly happy whom I
thought not justly hateful for some true impoverishment; never
beholding any favour of Madam Felicity° gracing another, which
his well-bounded content persuaded not to hang in the front of his   105
own fortune;° and therefore as far from envying any man as he
valued all men infinitely distant from accomplished beatitude.
These native adjuncts appropriate to me the name of Felice.—
[To ['Galeazzo'] But last, good, thy humour.
    Exit ['Alberto']
'ANTONIO' 'Tis to be described by signs and tokens. For unless I   110
were possessed with a legion of spirits, 'tis impossible to be made
perspicuous by any utterance.° For sometimes he must take austere state, as for the person of Galeazzo, the son of the Duke of

Florence, and possess his exterior presence with a formal majesty, keep popularity in distance; and on the sudden fling his honour so prodigally into a common arm,° that he may seem to give up his indiscretion to the mercy of vulgar censure. Now as solemn as a traveller and as grave as a puritan's ruff; with the same breath, as slight and scattered in his fashion as ... as ... as ... a ... a ... anything. Now as sweet and neat as a barber's casting-bottle; straight, as slovenly as the yeasty breast of an ale-knight.° Now lamenting, then chafing, straight laughing, then ...

'FELICE' What then?

'ANTONIO' Faith, I know not what. 'T'ad been a right part for Proteus° or Gew. Ho! blind Gew° would ha' done 't rarely, rarely!

'FELICE' I fear it is not possible to limn so many persons in so small a tablet as the compass of our plays afford.

'ANTONIO' Right. Therefore I have heard that those persons, as he and you, Felice, that are but slightly drawn in this comedy, should receive more exact accomplishment in a second part,° which, if this obtain gracious acceptance, means to try his fortune.

'FELICE' Peace, here comes the Prologue. Clear the stage.

    Exeunt

PROLOGUE

[Enter] the Prologue

PROLOGUE The wreath of pleasure and delicious sweets
    Begirt the gentle front of this fair troop!°
    Select and most respected auditors,
    For wit's sake do not dream of miracles.
    Alas, we shall but falter if you lay   5
    The least sad weight of an unusèd hope°
    Upon our weakness. Only we give up
    The worthless present of slight idleness°
    To your authentic censure. O that our muse
    Had those abstruse and sinewy faculties°   10
    That with a strain of fresh invention
    She might press out the rarity of art,
    The pur'st elixèd juice of rich conceit,
    In your attentive ears; that with the lip
    Of gracious elocution, we might drink   15
    A sound carouse unto your health of wit.
    But O, the heathy dryness of her brain,
    Foil to your fertile spirits, is ashamed
    To breathe her blushing numbers to such ears.
    Yet, most ingenious, deign to veil our wants;°   20
    With sleek acceptance polish these rude scenes;°
    And if our slightness your large hope beguiles,
    Check not with bended brow, but dimpled smiles.
        Exit [the] Prologue

1.1

The cornets sound a battle within. Enter Antonio, disguised like
an Amazon

ANTONIO   Heart, wilt not break? And thou abhorrèd life,
Wilt thou still breathe in my enragèd blood?
Veins, sinews, arteries, why crack ye not,
Burst and divulsed with anguish of my grief?
Can man by no means creep out of himself   5
And leave the slough of viperous grief behind?
Antonio, hast thou seen a fight at sea,
As horrid as the hideous day of doom,
Betwixt thy father, Duke of Genoa,
And proud Piero, the Venetian prince,   10
In which the sea hath swoll'n with Genoa's blood,
And made spring tides with the warm reeking gore
That gushed from out our galleys' scupper-holes,
In which thy father, poor Andrugio,
Lies sunk or, leaped into the arms of chance,   15
Choked with the labouring ocean's brackish foam;
Who, even despite Piero's cankered hate,
Would with an armèd hand have seized thy love
And linked thee to the beauteous Mellida?
Have I outlived the death of all these hopes?   20
Have I felt anguish poured into my heart,
Burning like balsamum in tender wounds,
And yet dost live? Could not the fretting sea
Have rolled me up in wrinkles of his brow?
Is death grown coy, or grim confusion nice,   25
That it will not accompany a wretch,
But I must needs be cast on Venice' shore
And try new fortunes with this strange disguise
To purchase my adorèd Mellida?
          The cornets sound a flourish [within]; cease
Hark how Piero's triumphs beat the air.°   30
O ruggèd mischief, how thou grat'st my heart!
Take spirit, blood; disguise, be confident;
Make a firm stand; here rests the hope of all:
Lower than hell, there is no depth to fall.

The cornets sound a sennet° [*within*]. *Enter Felice and Alberto,*
Castilio and Forobosco, a Page carrying a shield, Piero in
armour, Cazzo and Dildo, and Balurdo. All these (saving
Piero) armed with petronels.° *Being entered, they make a stand*
in divided files.° [*Antonio steps aside*]

PIERO Victorious Fortune, with triumphant hand,   35
Hurleth my glory 'bout this ball of earth,
Whilst the Venetian duke is heavèd up
On wings of fair success, to overlook
The low-cast ruins of his enemies,
To see myself adored and Genoa quake: 40
My fate is firmer than mischance can shake.

FELICE Stand! The ground trembleth.

PIERO Ha, an earthquake!

BALURDO O, I smell a sound.

FELICE Piero, stay, for I descry a fume   45
Creeping from out the bosom of the deep,
The breath of darkness, fatal when 'tis whist
In greatness' stomach. This same smoke, called pride,°
Take heed, she'll lift thee to improvidence
And break thy neck from steep security;   50
She'll make thee grudge to let Jehovah share
In thy successful battles. O, she's ominous;
Enticeth princes to devour heaven,
Swallow omnipotence, outstare dread fate,
Subdue eternity in giant thought;   55
Heaves up their heart with swelling, puffed conceit
Till their souls burst with venomed arrogance.
Beware, Piero, Rome itself hath tried;°
Confusion's train blows up this Babel pride.°

PIERO Pish! *Dimitto superos, summa votorum attigi.*—°   60
Alberto, hast thou yielded up our fixed decree
Unto the Genoan ambassador?
Are they content, if that their duke return,
To send his and his son Antonio's head,
As pledges steeped in blood, to gain their peace?   65

ALBERTO With most obsequious, sleek-browed entertain,
They all embrace it as most gracious.

PIERO Are proclamations sent through Italy,
That whosoever brings Andrugio's head,
Or young Antonio's, shall be guerdonèd   70

9

With twenty thousand double pistolets,°
And be endearèd to Piero's love?

FOROBOSCO They are sent every way. Sound policy,
Sweet lord.

FELICE (*aside*) Confusion to these limber sycophants!   75
No sooner mischief's born in regenty
But flattery christens it with 'policy'.

PIERO Why then, *O me caelitum excelsissimum!*°
The intestine malice and inveterate hate
I always bore to that Andrugio   80
Glories in triumph o'er his misery.
Nor shall that carpet-boy, Antonio,°
Match with my daughter, sweet-cheeked Mellida.
No, the public power makes my faction strong.

FELICE Ill, when public power strength'neth private wrong.   85

PIERO 'Tis horse-like not for man to know his force.

FELICE 'Tis god-like for a man to feel remorse.

PIERO Pish! I prosecute my family's revenge,
Which I'll pursue with such a burning chase
Till I have dried up all Andrugio's blood.   90
Weak rage, that with slight pity is withstood.
          The cornets sound a flourish [within]
What means that fresh triumphal flourish sound?

ALBERTO The Prince of Milan and young Florence' heir°
Approach to gratulate your victory.

PIERO We'll girt them with an ample waist of love.°   95
Conduct them to our presence royally.
Let volleys of the great artillery
From off our galleys' banks play prodigal
And sound loud welcome from their bellowing mouths.
          *Exit only Piero. The cornets sound a sennet [within]. Enter
          above, Mellida, Rosaline, and Flavia. Enter below,° Galeazzo
          with Attendants. Piero [enters,] meeteth him, embraceth [him];
          at which the cornets sound a flourish. Piero and Galeazzo
          exeunt. The rest stand still*

MELLIDA What prince was that passed through my father's
guard?   100

FLAVIA 'Twas Galeazzo, the young Florentine.

ROSALINE Troth, one that will besiege thy maidenhead,
Enter the walls, i'faith, sweet Mellida,
If that thy flankers be not cannon-proof.°

MELLIDA O, Mary Ambree! Good thy judgment, wench,°   105
    Thy bright elections clear; what will he prove?°
ROSALINE H'ath a short finger and a naked chin,
    A skipping eye; dare lay my judgement, faith,
    His love is glibbery; there's no hold on't, wench.°
    Give me a husband whose aspect is firm,   110
    A full-cheeked gallant with a bouncing thigh;
    O, he is the *paradiso delle madonne contente*.°
MELLIDA Even such a one was my Antonio.
    The cornets sound a sennet [within]
ROSALINE By my nine-and-thirtieth servant, sweet,
    Thou art in love. But stand on tiptoes, fair;   115
    Here comes Saint Tristram Tirlery Whiff, i'faith.°
    Enter Mazzagente; Piero [enters,] meets him, embraceth [him],
    at which the cornets sound a flourish. They two stand, using
    seeming compliments, whilst the scene passeth above
MELLIDA Saint Mark, Saint Mark! What kind of thing appears?
ROSALINE For fancy's passion, spit upon him. Fie!°
    His face is varnished. In the name of love,°
    What country bred that creature?   120
MELLIDA What is he, Flavia?
FLAVIA The heir of Milan, Signior Mazzagent.
ROSALINE Mazzagent? Now by my pleasure's hope,
    He is made like a tilting-staff, and looks
    For all the world like an o'er-roasted pig.   125
    A great tobacco-taker too, that's flat,
    For his eyes look as if they had been hung
    In the smoke of his nose.
MELLIDA What husband will he prove, sweet Rosaline?
ROSALINE Avoid him, for he hath a dwindled leg,   130
    A low forehead, and a thin, coal-black beard;
    And will be jealous too, believe it, sweet,
    For his chin sweats, and h'ath a gander neck,
    A thin lip, and a little, monkey'sh eye.°
    Precious! What a slender waist he hath!   135
    He looks like a maypole, or a notchèd stick;
    He'll snap in two at every little strain.
    Give me a husband that will fill mine arms,
    Of steady judgment, quick and nimble sense;
    Fools relish not a lady's excellence.   140

Exeunt all [except the disguised Antonio] on the lower stage;
at which the cornets sound a flourish, and a peal of shot is
given

MELLIDA The triumph's ended.
[*Notices Antonio on the lower stage*]
                              But look, Rosaline,
What gloomy soul in strange accoutrements
Walks on the pavement.

ROSALINE Good sweet, let's to her, prithee, Mellida.

MELLIDA How covetous thou art of novelties!   145

ROSALINE Pish, 'tis our nature to desire things
That are thought strangers to the common cut.

MELLIDA I am exceeding willing, but...

ROSALINE But what? Prithee, go down; let's see her face.
God send that neither wit nor beauty wants,   150
Those tempting sweets, affection's adamants.°
        Exeunt [Mellida, Rosaline, and Flavia from the upper
        stage]

ANTONIO Come down! She comes like—O, no simile
Is precious, choice or elegant enough
To illustrate her descent. Leap heart! She comes,°
She comes. Smile, heaven, and softest southern wind   155
Kiss her cheek gently with perfumèd breath.
She comes; creation's purity, admired,
Adored, amazing rarity, she comes.
O now, Antonio, press thy spirit forth
In following passion, knit thy senses close,   160
Heap up thy powers, double all thy man.°
        Enter Mellida, Rosaline, and Flavia [on the lower stage]
She comes.
O how her eyes dart wonder on my heart!
Mount, blood; soul, to my lips, taste Hebe's cup;°
Stand firm on deck when beauty's close-fight's up.°   165

MELLIDA Lady, your strange habit doth beget
Our pregnant thoughts, even great of much desire
To be acquaint with your condition.

ROSALINE Good sweet lady, without more ceremonies,
What country claims your birth, and, sweet, your name?   170

ANTONIO In hope your bounty will extend itself
In selfsame nature of fair courtesy,
I'll shun all niceness: my name's Florizell,

My country Scythia; I am Amazon,
Cast on this shore by fury of the sea.   175
ROSALINE Nay faith, sweet creature, we'll not veil our names.
It pleased the font to dip me Rosaline;
That lady bears the name of Mellida,
The Duke of Venice' daughter.
ANTONIO [to Mellida, kissing her hand] Madam, I am obliged to kiss
    your hand   180
By imposition of a now-dead man.°
ROSALINE Now, by my troth, I long beyond all thought
To know the man. Sweet beauty, deign his name.
ANTONIO Lady, the circumstance is tedious.
ROSALINE Troth, not a whit, good fair, let's have it all.   185
I love not, I, to have a jot left out
If the tale come from a loved orator.
ANTONIO Vouchsafe me then your hushed observances.
Vehement in pursuit of strange novelties,
After long travel through the Asian main,   190
I shipped my hopeful thoughts for Brittainy,
Longing to view great nature's miracle,
The glory of our sex, whose fame doth strike°
Remotest ears with adoration.
Sailing some two months with inconstant winds,   195
We viewed the glistering Venetian forts,
To which we made; when lo, some three leagues off,
We might descry a horrid spectacle:
The issue of black fury strewed the sea
With tattered carcasses of splitted ships,   200
Half-sinking, burning, floating topsy-turvy.
Not far from these sad ruins of fell rage,
We might behold a creature press the waves;
Senseless he sprawled, all notched with gaping wounds.
To him we made, and, short, we took him up.   205
The first word that he spake was 'Mellida',
And then he swooned.
MELLIDA   Ay me!
ANTONIO   Why sigh you, fair?
ROSALINE Nothing but little humours. Good sweet, on.°
ANTONIO His wounds being dressed and life recoverèd,
We 'gan discourse; when lo, the sea grew mad,   210
His bowels rumbling with windy passion.

Straight swarthy darkness popped out Phoebus' eye
And blurred the jocund face of bright-cheeked day,
Whilst curdled fogs masked even darkness' brow.
Heaven bade's goodnight, and the rocks groaned   215
At the intestine uproar of the main.
Now gusty flaws struck up the very heels
Of our mainmast, whilst the keen lightning shot°
Through the black bowels of the quaking air.
Straight chops a wave, and in his sliftered paunch   220
Down falls our ship, and there he breaks his neck,
Which, in an instant, up was belched again.°
When thus this martyred soul began to sigh;
'Give me your hand', quoth he; 'Now do you grasp
Th'unequalled mirror of ragg'd misery.°   225
Is't not a horrid storm? O well-shaped sweet,
Could your quick eye strike through these gashèd wounds,
You should behold a heart, a heart, fair creature,
Raging more wild than is this frantic sea.
Wilt do me a favour if thou chance survive?   230
But visit Venice, kiss the precious white
Of my most . . . nay, all, all epithets are base
To attribute to gracious Mellida.
Tell her the spirit of Antonio
Wisheth his last gasp breathed upon her breast'.   235
ROSALINE Why weeps soft-hearted Florizell?
ANTONIO Alas, the flinty rocks groaned at his plaints.
'Tell her', quoth he, 'that her obdurate sire
Hath cracked his bosom.' Therewithal he wept
And thus sighed on: 'The sea is merciful;   240
Look how it gapes to bury all my grief.
Well, thou shalt have it, thou shalt be his tomb.
My faith in my love live; in thee, die woe,
Die unmatched anguish, die Antonio.'
With that he tottered from the reeling deck,   245
And down he sunk.
ROSALINE Pleasure's body, what makes my lady weep?
MELLIDA Nothing, sweet Rosaline, but the air's sharp.—
   [*To Antonio*] My father's palace, madam, will be proud
   To entertain your presence, if you'll deign   250
   To make repose within.—Ay me!
ANTONIO Lady, our fashion is not curious.°

14

ROSALINE Faith, all the nobler; 'tis more generous.
MELLIDA Shall I then know how fortune fell at last,
  What succour came, or what strange fate ensued?   255
ANTONIO Most willingly. But this same court is vast
  And public to the staring multitude.
ROSALINE Sweet lady, nay, good sweet; now by my troth,
  We'll be bedfellows. Dirt on compliment froth!°
    Exeunt, Rosaline giving Antonio the way

2.1

[The Duke's state is set out.] Enter Cazzo with a capon, eating;
Dildo following him

DILDO Ha, Cazzo, your master wants a clean trencher. Do you hear?
Balurdo calls for your diminutive attendance.

CAZZO The belly hath no ears,° Dildo.

DILDO Good pug,° give me some capon.

CAZZO No capon, no, not a bit, ye smooth bully. Capon's no meat 5
for Dildo. Milk, milk, ye glibbery urchin, is food for infants.

DILDO Upon mine honour—

CAZZO Your honour with a pah! 'Slid, now every jackanapes loads
his back with the golden coat of honour; every ass puts on the
lion's skin and roars his honour. Upon your honour! By my lady's 10
pantable, I fear I shall live to hear a vintner's boy cry, ' 'Tis rich
neat canary, upon my honour'.

DILDO My stomach's° up.

CAZZO I think thou art hungry.

DILDO The match of fury is lighted, fastened to the linstock of rage, 15
and will presently set fire to the touch-hole of intemperance,
discharging the double culverin of my incensement in the face of
thy opprobrious speech.

CAZZO I'll stop the barrel thus. [*Gives him the capon*] Good Dildo,
set not fire to the touch-hole. 20

DILDO My rage is stopped, and I will eat to the health of the fool thy
master Castilio.

CAZZO And I will suck the juice of the capon, to the health of the
idiot thy master Balurdo.

DILDO Faith, our masters are like a case of rapiers sheathed in one 25
scabbard of folly.

CAZZO Right Dutch° blades. But was't not rare sport at the sea-
battle, whilst rounce-robble-hobble° roared from the ship sides, to
view our masters pluck their plumes and drop their feathers for
fear of being men of mark.° 30

DILDO ' 'Slud!' cried Signor Balurdo, 'O for Don Besicleer's armour
in the *Mirror of Knighthood*!° What coil's here? O for an armour,
cannon-proof! O, more cable,° more featherbeds, more featherbeds, more cable!'—till he had as much as my cable hatband° to
fence him. 35

Enter Flavia in haste, with a rebato

CAZZO Buxom Flavia, can you sing? Song, song!

FLAVIA My sweet Dildo, I am not for you at this time. Madam
Rosaline stays for a fresh ruff to appear in the presence. Sweet,
away!

DILDO 'Twill not be so put off, delicate, delicious, spark-eyed, sleek-   40
skinned, slender-waisted, clean-legged, rarely shaped—

FLAVIA Whoa!° I'll be at all your service another season. Nay, faith,
there's reason in all things.

DILDO Would I were reason, then, that I might be in all things.

CAZZO The brief and the semiquaver° is, we must have the descant°   45
you made upon our names, ere you depart.

FLAVIA Faith, the song will seem to come off hardly.

CAZZO Troth, not a whit, if you seem to come off quickly.

FLAVIA Pert Cazzo! knock it lustily then.

> *They sing. Enter Forobosco, [carrying] two torches, Castilio*
> *singing fantastically, Rosaline running a coranto pace,° and*
> *Balurdo [dressed in crimson]; Felice following, wondering at*
> *them all*

FOROBOSCO Make place, gentlemen.—[*To Cazzo and Dildo*] Pages,   50
hold torches. The prince approacheth the presence.

DILDO What squeaking cartwheel have we here? Ha? 'Make place,
gentlemen.—Pages, hold torches. The prince approacheth the
presence.'

ROSALINE Faugh! What a strong scent's here! Somebody useth to   55
wear socks.

BALURDO By this fair candlelight, 'tis not my feet. I never wore
socks since I sucked pap.

ROSALINE Savourly° put off.

CASTILIO Ha! Her wit stings, blisters, galls off the skin with the tart   60
acrimony of her sharp quickness. By sweetness, she is the very
Pallas that flew out of Jupiter's brainpan!°—Delicious creature,
vouchsafe me your service;° by the purity of bounty, I shall be
proud of such bondage.

ROSALINE I vouchsafe it; be my slave.—Signor Balurdo, wilt thou   65
be my servant too?

BALURDO O God! Forsooth, in very good earnest la, you would
make me as a man should say...as a man should say...

FELICE 'Slud, sweet beauty, will you deign him your service?

ROSALINE O, your fool is your only servant. But good Felice, why   70
art thou so sad? A penny for thy thought, man.

17

FELICE I sell not my thought so cheap; I value my meditation at a
higher rate.

BALURDO In good sober sadness, sweet mistress, you should have
had my thought for a penny; by this crimson satin that cost eleven   75
shillings, three pence halfpenny a yard, that you should, la.

ROSALINE What was thy thought, good servant?

BALURDO Marry, forsooth, how many strike of peas would feed a
hog fat against Christ-tide?

ROSALINE Paugh! [*She spits.*°—*To Castilio*] Servant, rub out my   80
rheum; it soils the presence.

CASTILIO By my wealthiest thought, you grace my shoe with an
unmeasured honour. I will preserve the sole of it as a most sacred
relic, for this service.

ROSALINE I'll spit in thy mouth, an thou wilt, to grace thee.   85

FELICE O that the stomach of this queasy age
Digests or brooks such raw unseasoned gobs
And vomits not them forth! O slavish sots!
'Servant', quoth you? Faugh! If a dog should crave
And beg her service, he should have it straight.   90
She'd give him favours, too, to lick her feet,
Or fetch her fan, or some such drudgery;
A good dog's office, which these amorists
Triumph of. 'Tis rare. Well, give her more ass,
More sot, as long as dropping of her nose   95
Is sworn rich pearl by such low slaves as those.

ROSALINE Flavia, attend me to attire me.

Exeunt Rosaline and Flavia

BALURDO [*to Forobosco*] In sad good earnest, sir, you have touched
the very bare of naked truth; my silk stocking hath a good gloss,
and, I thank my planets, my leg is not altogether unpropitiously   100
shaped. There's a word: 'unpropitiously'! I think I shall speak
'unpropitiously' as well as any courtier in Italy.

FOROBOSCO So help me your sweet bounty, you have the most
graceful presence, applausive elocuty,° amazing volubility,
polished adornation, delicious affability—   105

FELICE [*aside*] Whoop! Fut, how he tickles yon trout under the gills!
You shall see him take him by and by, with groping flattery.°

FOROBOSCO —that ever ravished the ear of wonder. By your sweet
self, than whom I know not a more exquisite, illustrate, accomplished, pure, respected, adored, observed, precious, real,°   110
magnanimous, bounteous—if you have an idle, rich, cast jerkin

or so, it shall not be a castaway if—Ha! here's a forehead, an eye, a
head, a hair that would make a—or if you have any spare pair of
silver spurs, I'll do you as much right in all kind offices—

FELICE [*aside*] —of a kind parasite.   115

FOROBOSCO —as any of my mean fortunes shall be able to.

BALURDO As I am true Christian now, thou hast won the spurs.°

FELICE [*aside*] —for flattery.

   O how I hate that same Egyptian louse,°
   A rotten maggot, that lives by stinking filth   120
   Of tainted spirits. Vengeance to such dogs
   That sprout by gnawing senseless carrion!
     Enter Alberto

ALBERTO Gallants, saw you my mistress, the Lady Rosaline?

FOROBOSCO My mistress, the Lady Rosaline, left the presence even
now.   125

CASTILIO My mistress, the Lady Rosaline, withdrew her gracious
aspect even now.

BALURDO My mistress, the Lady Rosaline, withdrew her gracious
aspect even now.

FELICE [*aside*] Well said, echo.   130

ALBERTO My mistress, and his mistress, and your mistress, and the
dog's mistress!—[*Aside*] Precious dear heaven, that Alberto lives to
have such rivals!—
[*To them*] 'Slid! I have been searching every private room,
   Corner, and secret angle of the court;   135
   And yet, and yet, and yet she lives concealed.
   Good sweet Felice, tell me how to find
   My bright-faced mistress out.

FELICE Why man, cry out for lantern and candlelight.° For 'tis your
only way to find your bright-flaming wench, with your light-   140
burning torch; for most commonly, these light creatures live in
darkness.

ALBERTO Away, you heretic. You'll be burnt for—

FELICE Go, you amorous hound; follow the scent of your mistress'
shoe. Away!   145
   [*Exit Alberto*]

FOROBOSCO Make a fair presence; boys, advance your lights. The
princess makes approach,

BALURDO An please the gods, now in very good deed la, you shall
see me tickle the measures,° for the heavens! Do my hangers
show?   150

Enter Piero, Antonio [disguised as Florizell], Mellida, Rosaline,
Galeazzo, Mazzagente, Alberto, and Flavia. As they enter,
Felice and Castilio make a rank for the Duke to pass through.
Forobosco ushers the Duke to his state. Then whilst Piero
speaketh his first speech, Mellida is taken by Galeazzo and
Mazzagente to dance, they supporting her; Rosaline in like
manner by Alberto and Balurdo; Flavia by Felice and
Castilio

PIERO [*to Antonio*] Beauteous Amazon, sit, and seat your thoughts
  In the reposure of most soft content.—
  Sound music there!—Nay, daughter, clear your eyes
  From these dull fogs of misty discontent.
  Look sprightly, girl. What? Though Antonio's drowned,   155
  That peevish dotard on thy excellence,
  That hated issue of Andrugio,
  Yet may'st thou triumph in my victories;
  Since, lo, the highborn bloods of Italy
  Sue for thy seat of love.—Let music sound!   160
  Beauty and youth run descant on love's ground.°
    [*Music sounds for dancing*]
MAZZAGENTE [*to Mellida*] Lady, erect your gracious symmetry;°
  Shine in the sphere of sweet affection
  Your eye, as heavy as the heart of night.°
MELLIDA My thoughts are as black as your beard, my fortunes as ill-   165
  proportioned as your legs, and all the powers of my mind as leaden
  as your wit and as dusty as your face is swarthy.
GALEAZZO Faith, sweet, I'll lay thee on the lips° for that jest.
MELLIDA I prithee, intrude not on a dead man's right.
GALEAZZO No, but the living's just possession: 170
  Thy lips and love are mine
MELLIDA You ne'er took seisin on them yet. Forbear!
  There's not a vacant corner of my heart,
  But all is filled with dead Antonio's loss.
  Then urge no more; O, leave to love at all;   175
  'Tis less disgraceful not to mount than fall.
MAZZAGENTE Bright and refulgent lady, deign your ear.
  You see this blade; had it a courtly lip,
  It would divulge my valour, plead my love,
  Jostle that skipping feeble amorist°   180
  Out of your love's seat. I am Mazzagent.
GALEAZZO Hark thee, I pray thee taint not thy sweet ear

With that sot's gabble. By thy beauteous cheek,
He is the flagging'st bulrush that e'er drooped
With each slight mist of rain. But with pleased eye,   185
Smile on my courtship.

MELLIDA What said you, sir? Alas, my thought was fixed
Upon another object. Good, forbear;
I shall but weep. Ay me, what boots a tear?
Come, come, let's dance.—O music, thou distill'st   190
More sweetness in us than this jarring world;
Both time and measure from thy strains do breathe,
Whilst from the channel of this dirt doth flow°
Nothing but timeless grief, unmeasured woe.°

ANTONIO [aside] O how impatience cramps my crackèd veins,   195
And curdles thick my blood with boiling rage!
O eyes, why leap you not like thunderbolts
Or cannon-bullets in my rival's face?
Ohimè infelice misero, o lamentevol fato!°
    [*He falls to the ground*]

ALBERTO What means the lady fall upon the ground?°   200
ROSALINE Belike the falling sickness.
ANTONIO [aside] I cannot brook this sight; my thoughts grow wild.
Here lies a wretch on whom heaven never smiled.
ROSALINE [to Alberto] What, servant, ne'er a word and I here, man?
I would shoot some speech forth to strike the time   205
With pleasing touch of amorous compliment.
Say, sweet, what keeps thy mind? What think'st thou on?
ALBERTO Nothing.
ROSALINE   What's that nothing?
ALBERTO   A woman's constancy.
ROSALINE Good, why, wouldst thou have us sluts,
And never shift the vesture of our thoughts?   210
Away, for shame!
ALBERTO O no, th'art too constant to afflict my heart,°
Too too firm fixèd in unmovèd scorn.
ROSALINE Pish, pish! I fixèd in unmovèd scorn?
Why, I'll love thee tonight.
ALBERTO   But whom tomorrow?   215
ROSALINE Faith, as the toy puts me in the head.°
BALURDO An't pleased the marble heavens, now would I might
be the toy, to put you in the head, kindly to conceit
my...my...my...— Pray you, give m' an epithet for love.

FELICE 'Roaring', 'roaring'.   220
BALURDO O love, thou hast murdered me, made me a shadow, and
    you hear not Balurdo but Balurdo's ghost.
ROSALINE Can a ghost speak?
BALURDO Scurvily, as I do.
ROSALINE And walk?   225
BALURDO After their fashion.
ROSALINE And eat apples?
BALURDO In a sort, in their garb.
FELICE Prithee Flavia, be my mistress.
FLAVIA Your reason, good Felice?   230
FELICE Faith, I have nineteen mistresses already, and I not much
    disdain that thou shouldst make up the full score.
FLAVIA O, I hear you make commonplaces° of your mistresses, to
    perform the office of memory by. Pray you, in ancient times were
    not those satin hose? In good faith, now they are new dyed, pinked   235
    and scoured, they show as well as if they were new.
ROSALINE What, mute, Balurdo?°
FELICE Ay, in faith; an 'twere not for printing and painting, my
    breech and your face would be out of reparation.
BALURDO Ay, in faith, an 'twere not for printing and painting, my   240
    breech and your face would be out of reparation.
FELICE Good again, echo.
FLAVIA Thou art, by nature, too foul to be affected.
FELICE And thou, by art,° too fair to be beloved.
BALURDO By wit's life, most spark spirits, but hard change.°   245
PIERO Gallants, the night grows old, and downy sleep
    Courts us to entertain his company.
    Our tirèd limbs, bruised in the morning fight,
    Entreat soft rest and gentle hushed repose.
    Fill out Greek wines, prepare fresh cresset-light;   250
    We'll have a banquet, princes, then goodnight.
            The cornets sound a sennet, and the Duke goes out in state.
            As they are going out, Antonio stays Mellida. The rest
            exeunt
MELLIDA What means these scattered looks? Why tremble you?
    Why quake your thoughts in your distracted eyes?
    Collect your spirits, madam. What do you see?°
ANTONIO Dost not behold a ghost?   255
    Look, look where he stalks, wrapped up in clouds of grief,
    Darting his soul upon thy wond'ring eyes.

Look, he comes towards thee. See, he stretcheth out
His wretched arms to girt thy loved waist
With a most wished embrace. See'st him not yet?   260
Nor yet? Ha, Mellida, thou well may'st err;
For look, he walks not like Antonio,
Like that Antonio that this morning shone
In glistering habiliments of arms
To seize his love, spite of her father's spite;   265
But like himself, wretched and miserable,
Banished, forlorn, despairing, struck quite through
With sinking grief, rolled up in seven-fold doubles°
Of plagues unvanquishable. Hark, he speaks to thee.
MELLIDA Alas, I cannot hear nor see him.   270
ANTONIO Why? All this night about the room he stalked
And groaned, and howled with raging passion
To view his love, lifeblood of all his hopes,
Crown of his fortunes, clipped by strangers' arms.
Look but behind thee.   275
MELLIDA O, Antonio, my lord, my love, my—
ANTONIO Leave passion, sweet; for time, place, air and earth
Are all our foes. Fear, and be jealous. Fair,
Let's fly.
MELLIDA   Dear heart, ha, whither?
ANTONIO O, 'tis no matter whither, but let's fly.   280
Ha! now I think on't, I have ne'er a home;
No father, friend, no country to embrace
These wretched limbs. The world, the all that is,
Is all my foe; a prince not worth a doit!
Only my head is hoisèd to high rate,   285
Worth twenty thousand double pistolets
To him that can but strike it from these shoulders.
But come, sweet creature, thou shalt be my home,
My father, country, riches and my friend;
My all, my soul. And thou and I will live ...   290
Let's think like what. And thou and I will live
Like unmatched mirrors of calamity.
The jealous ear of night eavesdrops our talk.
Hold thee, there's a jewel; and look thee, there's a note
That will direct thee when, where, how to fly.   295
Bid me adieu.
MELLIDA   Farewell, bleak misery.

ANTONIO Stay, sweet; let's kiss before you go.
    [They kiss]°
MELLIDA Farewell, dear soul.
ANTONIO   Farewell, my life, my heart.
    [Exeunt in different directions]

3.1

Enter Andrugio in armour, Lucio with a shepherd gown in his hand, and a Page

ANDRUGIO Is not yon gleam the shuddering morn, that flakes
  With silver tincture the east verge of heaven?

LUCIO I think it is, so please your excellence.

ANDRUGIO Away! I have no excellence to please.
  Prithee observe the custom of the world,   5
  That only flatters greatness, states exalts.
  'An't please my excellence!' O Lucio,
  Thou hast been ever held respected, dear,
  Even precious to Andrugio's inmost love;
  Good, flatter not. Nay, if thou giv'st not faith   10
  That I am wretched, O read that, read that!
  [Gives him a proclamation]

LUCIO [*reads*] 'Piero Sforza, to the Italian princes, fortune:
  Excellent, the just overthrow Andrugio took in the Venetian Gulf
  hath so assured the Genoese of the injustice of his cause and the
  hatefulness of his person, that they have banished him and all his   15
  family; and for confirmation of their peace with us have vowed
  that if he or his son can be attached, to send us both their heads.
  We therefore by force of our united league forbid you to harbour
  him or his blood; but if you apprehend his person, we entreat you
  to send him or his head to us. For we vow by the honour of our   20
  blood to recompense any man that bringeth his head with twenty
  thousand double pistolets, and the endearing to our choicest
  love.   From Venice: Piero Sforza.'

ANDRUGIO My thoughts are fixed in contemplation
  Why this huge earth, this monstrous animal   25
  That eats her children, should not have eyes and ears.
  Philosophy maintains that nature's wise,
  And forms no useless or unperfect thing.
  Did nature make the earth or the earth nature?
  For earthly dirt makes all things, makes the man,   30
  Moulds me up honour; and like a cunning Dutchman°
  Paints me a puppet even with seeming breath,
  And gives a sot appearance of a soul.°
  Go to, go to; thou liest, philosophy!

Nature forms things unperfect, useless, vain.   35
Why made she not the earth with eyes and ears,
That she might see desert and hear men's plaints?
That when a soul is splitted, sunk with grief,
He might fall thus upon the breast of earth,
[*Throwing himself to the ground*]
And in her ear halloo his misery,   40
Exclaiming thus: 'O thou all-bearing earth,
Which men do gape for till thou cramm'st their mouths
And chok'st their throats with dust, O chawn thy breast
And let me sink into thee,
[*Beats on the ground*]
                  Look who knocks;
Andrugio calls.' But O, she's deaf and blind;   45
A wretch but lean relief on earth can find.
LUCIO Sweet lord, abandon passion, and disarm.
Since by the fortune of the tumbling sea
We are rolled up upon the Venice marsh,
Let's clip all fortune lest more louring fate—   50
ANDRUGIO 'More louring fate!' O Lucio, choke that breath.
Now I defy chance. Fortune's brow hath frowned
Even to the utmost wrinkle it can bend;
Her venom's spit. Alas, what country rests,°
What son, what comfort that she can deprive?   55
Triumphs not Venice in my overthrow?
Gapes not my native country for my blood?
Lies not my son tombed in the swelling main?
And yet 'more louring fate'? There's nothing left
Unto Andrugio but Andrugio;   60
And that nor mischief, force, distress, nor hell can take.
Fortune my fortunes, not my mind shall shake.
LUCIO Spoke like yourself; but give me leave, my lord,
To wish your safety. If you are but seen,
Your arms display you. Therefore put them off   65
And take—°
ANDRUGIO Wouldst thou have me go unarmed among my foes,
Being besieged by passion, ent'ring lists
To combat with despair and mighty grief,
My soul beleaguered with the crushing strength   70
Of sharp impatience? Ha, Lucio, go unarmed?
Come soul, resume the valour of thy birth;

26

Myself myself, will dare all opposites.
I'll muster forces, an unvanquished power;
Cornets of horse shall press th' ungrateful earth;   75
This hollow-wombèd mass shall inly groan
And murmur to sustain the weight of arms;
Ghastly amazement with upstarted hair
Shall hurry on before and usher us,
Whilst trumpets clamour with a sound of death.   80
LUCIO Peace, good my lord; your speech is all too light.
Alas, survey your fortunes, look what's left
Of all your forces and your utmost hopes:
A weak old man, a page, and your poor self.°
ANDRUGIO Andrugio lives, and a fair cause of arms;   85
Why, that's an army all invincible.
He who hath that hath a battalion royal,
Armour of proof, huge troops of barbèd steeds,
Main squares of pikes, millions of harquebus.
O, a fair cause stands firm and will abide;   90
Legions of angels fight upon her side.
LUCIO Then, noble spirit, slide in strange disguise
Unto some gracious prince and sojourn there,
Till time and fortune give revenge firm means.
ANDRUGIO No, I'll not trust the honour of a man.   95
Gold is grown great and makes perfidiousness
A common waiter in most princes' courts;
He's in the chequer-roll. I'll not trust my blood.°
I know none breathing but will cog a die
For twenty thousand double pistolets.   100
How goes the time?
LUCIO   I saw no sun today.
ANDRUGIO No sun will shine where poor Andrugio breathes.
My soul grows heavy.—[*To the Page*] Boy, let's have a song;
We'll sing yet, faith, even despite of fate.
        They sing°
ANDRUGIO 'Tis a good boy; and by my troth, well sung.   105
O, an thou felt'st my grief, I warrant thee
Thou wouldst have struck division to the height,°
And made the life of music breathe.
        [*The Page weeps*]
                                Hold, boy; why so?
For God's sake call me not Andrugio,

That I may soon forget what I have been.   110
For heaven's sake name not Antonio,
That I may not remember he was mine.
Well, ere yon sun set, I'll show myself myself,
Worthy my blood. I was a duke; that's all.
No matter whither but from whence we fall.°   115

>   *Exeunt*

3.2

>   *Enter Felice walking unbraced°*

FELICE Castilio! Alberto! Balurdo! None up?
Forobosco! Flattery, nor thou up yet?
Then there's no courtier stirring; that's firm truth.
I cannot sleep; Felice seldom rests
In these court lodgings. I have walked all night   5
To see if the nocturnal court delights
Could force me envy their felicity;
And by plain truth—I will confess plain truth—
I envy nothing but the traverse light.°
O, had it eyes and ears and tongues, it might   10
See sport, hear speech of most strange surquedries!
O, if that candlelight were made a poet,
He would prove a rare firking satirist
And draw the core forth of impostumed sin.
Well, I thank heaven yet that my content   15
Can envy nothing but poor candlelight.
As for the other glistering copper spangs
That glisten in the tire of the court,
Praise God, I either hate or pity them.
Well, here I'll sleep till that the scene of up   20
Is past at court.
>   [*Lies down on the ground*]
>   O, calm, hushed, rich content,
Is there a being blessedness without thee?°
How soft thou down'st the couch where thou dost rest;
Nectar to life, thou sweet ambrosian feast.°
>   [*He sleeps.*] *Enter Castilio and his Page, [Cazzo]; Castilio with
>   a casting-bottle of sweet water in his hand, sprinkling himself*

CASTILIO Am not I a most sweet youth now?   25
CAZZO Yes, when your throat's perfumed your very words
  Do smell of ambergris. O stay, sir, stay;°
  Sprinkle some sweet water to your shoes' heels,
  That your mistress may swear you have a sweet foot.
CASTILIO Good, very good! Very passing passing good!   30
FELICE [starting up] Fut! What treble minikin° squeaks there, ha?
  'Good! very good; very, very good!'
CASTILIO I will warble to the delicious concave of my mistress' ear,
  and strike her thoughts with the pleasing touch of my voice.
    [Castilio and Cazzo] sing
CASTILIO Felice, health, fortune, mirth and wine—   35
FELICE To thee my love divine.
CASTILIO I drink to thee, sweeting.
FELICE Plague on thee for an ass!
CASTILIO Now thou hast seen the court, by the perfection of it dost
  not envy it?   40
FELICE I wonder it doth not envy me.
  Why man, I have been borne upon the spirit's wings,
  The soul's swift Pegasus, the fantasy,°
  And from the height of contemplation
  Have viewed the feeble joints men totter on.   45
  I envy none, but hate or pity all;
  For when I view with an intentive thought
  That creature fair, but proud; him rich, but sot;
  Th'other witty, but unmeasured arrogant;
  Him great, yet boundless in ambition;   50
  Him high-born, but of base life; th'other feared,
  Yet feared fears, and fears most to be most loved;°
  Him wise, but made a fool for public use;
  Th'other learned, but self-opinionate:
  When I discourse all these, and see myself   55
  Nor fair, nor rich, nor witty, great, nor feared,
  Yet amply suited with all full content,
  Lord, how I clap my hands and smooth my brow,
  Rubbing my quiet bosom, tossing up
  A grateful spirit to omnipotence!   60
CASTILIO Ha, ha! But if thou knew'st my happiness,
  Thou wouldst even grate away thy soul to dust
  In envy of my sweet beatitude.
  I cannot sleep for kisses; I cannot rest

For ladies' letters that importune me   65
With such unusèd vehemence of love
Straight to solicit them, that—
FELICE Confusion seize me, but I think thou liest.
Why should I not be sought to then as well?
Fut! Methinks I am as like a man.   70
Troth, I have a good head of hair, a cheek
Not as yet waned, a leg, faith, in the full.
I ha' not a red beard, take not tobacco much,°
And 'slid! for other parts of manliness—
CASTILIO Pooh! Whoa! You ne'er accourted them in pomp,   75
Put your good parts in presence graciously.
Ha! an you had, why, they would ha' come off,
Sprung to your arms, and sued and prayed and vowed
And opened all their sweetness to your love.
FELICE There are a number of such things as thou   80
Have often urged me to such loose belief.
But 'slid! you all do lie, you all do lie.
I have put on good clothes and smugged my face,
Struck a fair wench with a smart-speaking eye,
Courted in all sorts, blunt and passionate,   85
Had opportunity, put them to the 'Ah!';
And by this light, I find them wondrous chaste,
Impregnable; perchance a kiss or so,
But for the rest, O most inexorable.
CASTILIO Nay then, i'faith, prithee look here.   90
          Shows him the superscription of a seeming letter
FELICE [*reads*] 'To her most esteemed, loved, and generous
servant, Signor Castilio Balthazar.'—Prithee, from whom
comes this? Faith, I must see.—[*Reads*] 'From her that is devoted
to thee, in most private sweets of love, Rosaline.'—Nay God's
my comfort, I must see the rest. I must *sans* ceremony, faith, I   95
must!
          Felice takes away the letter by force
CASTILIO O, you spoil my ruff, unset my hair! Good, away!
FELICE [*reads*] 'Item, for straight° canvas, thirteen pence halfpenny.
Item, for an ell° and a half of taffeta to cover your old canvas
doublet, fourteen shillings and threepence.'—'Slight, this is a   100
tailor's bill.
CASTILIO In sooth, it is the outside of her letter, on which I took the
copy of a tailor's bill.

30

CAZZO [*aside*] But 'tis not crossed,° I am sure of that. Lord have
mercy on him, his credit hath given up the last gasp. Faith, I'll 105
leave him; for he looks as melancholy as a wench the first night
she...°
>*Exit [Cazzo]*

FELICE Honest musk-cod, 'twill not be so stitched together. Take
that and that, [*strikes him*] and belie no lady's love. Swear no more
'By Jesu, this madam, that lady—'. Hence, go. Forswear the pre- 110
sence, travel three years to bury this bastinado. Avoid, puff-paste,
avoid!

CASTILIO And tell not my lady mother. Well, as I am true gentleman, if she had not willed me on her blessing not to spoil my face,
if I could not find in my heart to fight, would I might ne'er eat a 115
potato pie° more.
>*Exit [Castilio]. Enter Balurdo, backward; Dildo following him,*
>*with a looking-glass in one hand and a candle in the other hand,*
>*Flavia following him backward, with a looking-glass in one*
>*hand and a candle in the other; Rosaline following her. Balurdo*
>*and Rosaline stand, setting of faces.° And so the scene begins*

FELICE [*aside*] More fools, more rare fools! O for time and place long
enough and large enough to act these fools! Here might be made a
rare scene of folly, if the plot could bear it.

BALURDO By the sugar-candy sky, hold up the glass higher, that I 120
may see to swear in fashion. O, one look° more would ha' made
them shine. God's nigs! they would have shone like my mistress'
brow. Even so the duke frowns, for all this curson world. O, that
girn kills, it kills! By my golden...What's the richest thing about
me? 125

DILDO Your teeth.

BALURDO By my golden teeth, hold up, that I may put in. Hold up,
I say, that I may see to put on my gloves.

DILDO O delicious sweet-cheeked master, if you discharge but one
glance from the level of that set face, O, you will strike a wench; 130
you'll make any wench love you.

BALURDO By Jesu, I think I am as elegant a courtier as...How lik'st
thou my suit?

DILDO All, beyond all, no paregal; you are wondered at—[*aside*] for
an ass! 135

BALURDO Well, Dildo, no Christian creature shall know hereafter
what I will do for the heretofore.

ROSALINE Here wants a little white, Flavia.

DILDO Ay, but master, you have one little fault: you sleep open-
mouthed.   140

BALURDO Pooh! Thou jest'st. In good sadness, I'll have a looking-
glass nailed to the tester of the bed, that I may see when I sleep
whether 'tis so or not. Take heed you lie not; go to, take heed you
lie not.

FLAVIA [*to Rosaline*] By my troth, you look as like the princess now,   145
ay, but her lip is—

ROSALINE Lip?

FLAVIA —is a little ... redder, a very little redder.

ROSALINE But by the help of art or nature, ere I change my periwig,
mine shall be as red.°   150

FLAVIA O, ay, that face, that eye, that smile, that writhing of your
body, that wanton dandling of your fan becomes prethily, so
sweethly. [*Rosaline gives her money*] 'Tis even the goodest lady
that breathes, the most amiable—faith, the fringe of your satin
petticoat is ripped. Good faith, madam, they say you are the most   155
bounteous lady to your women that ever—[*Rosaline gives more
money*] O most delicious beauty!° Good madam, let me kith° it.

    Enter Piero

FELICE Rare sport, rare sport! A female fool and a female flatterer.

ROSALINE Body o' me, the duke! Away the glass.

PIERO [*seeing Antonio's note*] Take up your paper°, Rosaline.   160

ROSALINE Not mine, my lord.

PIERO Not yours, my lady? I'll see what 'tis.

BALURDO And how does my sweet mistress? O lady dear, even as
'tis an old say, ' 'Tis an old horse can neither whinny° nor wag his
tail', even so—[*aside to Dildo*] do I hold my set face still?—even so,   165
'tis a bad courtier that can neither discourse nor blow his nose.

PIERO [*reads*] 'Meet me at Abraham's, the Jew's, where I bought my
Amazon's disguise. A ship lies in the port, ready bound for Eng-
land. Make haste; come private. Antonio.' [*Calling*] Forobosco,
Alberto, Felice, Castilio, Balurdo!   170

    Enter Castilio, Forobosco

Run, keep the palace, post to the ports, go to my daughter's
chamber. Whither now? Scud to the Jew's. Stay, run to the gates;
stop the gondolets;° let none pass the marsh. Do all at once.
Antonio! His head, his head! [*To Felice*] Keep you the court.—
The rest stand still, or run, or go, or shout, or search, or scud, or   175
call, or hang, or d - d - do s - s - s - something. I know not wh -
wh - wh - what I d - d - do, nor wh - wh - wh - where I am.

O trista traditrice, rea, ribalda fortuna,
Negandomi vendetta mi causa fera morte.°
    [*Exeunt all save Felice*]

FELICE Ha, ha, ha! I could break my spleen at his impatience.   180
    [*Enter Antonio below and Mellida above*]

ANTONIO *Alma e graziosa fortuna siate favorevole,*
    E fortunati siano i voti della mia dolce Mellida, Mellida.°

MELLIDA Alas, Antonio, I have lost thy note.
    A number mount my stairs. I'll straight return.°
    [*Exit Mellida. Antonio throws himself on the ground*]

FELICE Antonio,   185
    Be not affright, sweet prince; appease thy fear,
    Buckle thy spirits up, put all thy wits
    In wimble action, or thou art surprised.

ANTONIO I care not.

FELICE Art mad or desperate? or—   190

ANTONIO Both, both, all, all. I prithee, let me lie;
    Spite of you all, I can and I will die.

FELICE You are distraught; O, this is madness' breath.

ANTONIO Each man takes hence life, but no man death;
    He's a good fellow and keeps open house;   195
    A thousand thousand ways lead to his gate,
    To his wide-mouthèd porch; when niggard life
    Hath but one little, little wicket through.
    We wring ourselves into this wretched world
    To pule and weep, exclaim, to curse and rail,   200
    To fret and ban the fates, to strike the earth
    As I do now. Antonio, curse thy birth,
    And die.

FELICE Nay, heaven's my comfort, now you are perverse;
    You know I always loved you; prithee live.   205
    Wilt thou strike dead thy friends, draw mourning tears?

ANTONIO Alas, Felice, I ha' ne'er a friend;
    No country, father, brother, kinsman left
    To weep my fate or sigh my funeral.
    I roll but up and down, and fill a seat   210
    In the dark cave of dusky misery.

FELICE 'Fore heaven, the duke comes! Hold you; take my key,
    Slink to my chamber. Look you, that is it.
    There shall you find a suit I wore at sea;
    Take it and slip away. Nay, precious,   215

If you'll be peevish, by this light I'll swear
Thou rail'dst upon thy love before thou died'st
And called her strumpet.
ANTONIO   She'll not credit thee.
FELICE Tut, that's all one. I'll defame thy love
  And make thy dead trunk held in vile regard.   220
ANTONIO Wilt needs have it so? Why then, Antonio,
  Viva speranza in dispetto del fato.°
          [*Exit Antonio.*] *Enter Piero, Galeazzo, Mazzagente,*
          Forobosco, Balurdo, and Castilio, with weapons
PIERO O my sweet princes, was't not bravely found?
  Even there I found the note, even there it lay.
  I kiss the place for joy that there it lay.   225
  This way he went; here let us make a stand.
  I'll keep this gate myself. O gallant youth!
  I'll drink carouse unto your country's health,
  Even in Antonio's skull.
          Enter Antonio [*disguised as a mariner*]
BALURDO Lord bless us! His breath is more fearful than a sergeant's   230
  voice when he cries 'I arrest'.
ANTONIO Stop Antonio! Keep, keep Antonio!
PIERO Where, where, man? Where?
ANTONIO Here, here. Let me pursue him down the marsh.
PIERO Hold, there's my signet; take a gondolet.   235
  Bring me his head, his head, and by mine honour,
  I'll make thee the wealthiest mariner that breathes.
ANTONIO I'll sweat my blood out till I have him safe.
PIERO Spoke heartily, i'faith, good mariner.
          [*Exit Antonio*]
  O, we will mount in triumph. Soon, at night,   240
  I'll set his head up. Let's think where.
BALURDO Upon his shoulders, that's the fittest place for it. If it be
  not as fit as if it were made for them, say, 'Balurdo, thou art a sot,
  an ass'.
          Enter Mellida in page's attire,° *dancing*
PIERO Sprightly, i'faith. In truth, he's somewhat like   245
  My daughter Mellida. But alas, poor soul,
  Her honour's heels, God knows, are half so light.
MELLIDA [*aside*] Escaped I am, spite of my father's spite.
          [*Exit Mellida*]
PIERO Ho, this will warm my bosom ere I sleep.

Enter Flavia, running

FLAVIA O my lord, your daughter!   250

PIERO Ay, ay, my daughter's safe enough, I warrant thee.
This vengeance on the boy will lengthen out
My days unmeasuredly.
It shall be chroniclèd, time to come,
Piero Sforza slew Andrugio's son.   255

FLAVIA Ay, but my lord, your daughter—

PIERO Ay, ay, my good wench, she is safe enough.

FLAVIA O then, my lord, you know she's run away.

PIERO Run away? away? how run away?

FLAVIA She's vanished in an instant, none knows whither.   260

PIERO Pursue, pursue, fly, run, post, scud away!

FELICE [*singing*] *And was not good King Solomon* [etc.]°

PIERO Fly, call, run, row, ride, cry, shout, hurry, haste!
Haste, hurry, shout, cry, ride, row, run, call, fly!
Backward and forward, every way about!°   265
Maledetta fortuna che con dura sorte...
Che farò, che dirò, per fugir tanto mal?°
[*Exeunt all but Felice and Castilio*]

CASTILIO 'Twas you that struck me even now, was it not?

FELICE It was I that struck you even now.

CASTILIO You bastinadoed me, I take it.   270

FELICE I bastinadoed you, and you took it.

CASTILIO Faith, sir, I have the richest tobacco in the court for you.
I would be glad to make you satisfaction if I have wronged you. I
would not the sun should set upon your anger;° give me your
hand.   275

FELICE Content, faith, so thou'lt breed no more such lies.
I hate not man, but man's lewd qualities.
[*Exeunt*]

4.1

Enter Antonio in his sea gown,° running

ANTONIO [*calling aloud*] Stop, stop Antonio! Stay Antonio!—
[*To himself*] Vain breath, vain breath; Antonio is lost.
He cannot find himself, not seize himself.
Alas, this that you see is not Antonio;
His spirit hovers in Piero's court,   5
Hurling about his agile faculties
To apprehend the sight of Mellida.
But poor, poor soul, wanting apt instruments
To speak or see, stands dumb and blind; sad spirit,
Rolled up in gloomy clouds as black as air,   10
Through which the rusty coach of night is drawn.
'Tis so, I'll give you instance that 'tis so.
Conceit you me, as, having clasped a rose
Within my palm, the rose being ta'en away,
My hand retains a little breath of sweet;   15
So may man's trunk, his spirit slipped away,
Hold still a faint perfume of his sweet guest.
'Tis so; for when discursive powers fly out
And roam in progress through the bounds of heaven,
The soul itself gallops along with them,   20
As chieftain of this wingèd troop of thought,
Whilst the dull lodge of spirit standeth waste,
Until the soul return from . . . What was't I said?
O, this is nought but speckling Melancholy
That morphews the tender-skinned; I have been   25
Cousin-german. Bear with me, good Mellida.°
[*Falling to the ground*] Clod upon clod thus fall;
Hell is beneath, yet heaven is over all.

Enter Andrugio, Lucio [and the Page]

ANDRUGIO Come, Lucio, let's go eat. What hast thou got?
Roots, roots? Alas, they are seeded, new cut up.°   30
O, thou hast wrongèd nature, Lucio;
But boots not much; thou but pursu'st the world°
That cuts off virtue 'fore it comes to growth
Lest it should seed and so o'errun her son,
Dull purblind error.—Give me water, boy;   35

There is no poison in't I hope. They say
That lurks in massy plate; and yet the earth°
Is so infected with a general plague
That he's most wise that thinks there's no man fool,
Right prudent that esteems no creature just;   40
Great policy the least things to mistrust.
Give me assay.
   [*Lucio tastes the roots and water*]
       How we mock greatness now!
LUCIO A strong conceit is rich, so most men deem;
 If not to be, 'tis comfort yet to seem.
ANDRUGIO Why man, I never was a prince till now.   45
 'Tis not the barèd pate, the bended knees,
 Gilt tipstaves, Tyrian purple, chairs of state,°
 Troops of pied butterflies that flutter still
 In greatness' summer, that confirm a prince;
 'Tis not the unsavoury breath of multitudes,   50
 Shouting and clapping with confusèd din,
 That makes a prince. No, Lucio, he's a king,
 A true right king, that dares do aught save wrong,
 Fears nothing mortal but to be unjust;
 Who is not blown up with the flattering puffs   55
 Of spongy sycophants; who stands unmoved
 Despite the jostling of opinion;
 Who can enjoy himself maugre the throng
 That strive to press his quiet out of him;
 Who sits upon Jove's footstool, as I do,   60
 Adoring, not affecting, majesty;
 Whose brow is wreathèd with the silver crown
 Of clear content. This, Lucio, is a king,
 And of this empire every man's possessed
 That's worth his soul.°   65
LUCIO My lord, the Genoese had wont to say—
ANDRUGIO Name not the Genoese. That very word
 Unkings me quite, makes me vile passion's slave.
 O you that wade upon the glibbery ice°
 Of vulgar favour, view Andrugio;   70
 Was never prince with more applause confirmed,
 With louder shouts of triumph launchèd out
 Into the surgy main of government;
 Was never prince with more despite cast out,

Left shipwrecked, banished, on more guiltless ground.°   75
O rotten props of the crazed multitude,
How you still double, falter under the lightest chance
That strains your veins! Alas, one battle lost,
Your whorish love, your drunken healths, your hoots and shouts,
Your smooth 'God save's', and all your devilish art°   80
That tempts our quiet to your hell of throngs—
Spit on me, Lucio, for I am turned slave;
Observe how passion domineers o'er me.

LUCIO No wonder, noble lord, having lost a son,
  A country, crown, and—   85

ANDRUGIO Ay, Lucio, having lost a son, a son,
  A country, house, crown, son. *O lares, miseri lares!*°
  Which shall I first deplore? My son, my son,
  My dear sweet boy, my dear Antonio.

ANTONIO Antonio?   90

ANDRUGIO Ay, echo, ay; I mean Antonio.

ANTONIO Antonio? Who means Antonio?

ANDRUGIO Where art? What art? Know'st thou Antonio?

ANTONIO Yes.

ANDRUGIO   Lives he?

ANTONIO   No.

ANDRUGIO   Where lies he dead?

ANTONIO   Here.

ANDRUGIO   Where?

ANTONIO [*starting up*] Here.

ANDRUGIO   Art thou Antonio?

ANTONIO   I think I am.   95

ANDRUGIO Dost thou but think? What, dost not know thyself?

ANTONIO He is a fool that thinks he knows himself.

ANDRUGIO Upon thy faith to heaven, give thy name.

ANTONIO I were not worthy of Andrugio's blood
  If I denied my name's Antonio.   100

ANDRUGIO I were not worthy to be called thy father
  If I denied my name, Andrugio.
  And dost thou live? O, let me kiss thy cheek
  And dew thy brow with trickling drops of joy.
  Now heaven's will be done, for I have lived   105
  To see my joy, my son Antonio.
  Give me thy hand.—Now, fortune, do thy worst.
  His blood, that lapped thy spirit in the womb,

Thus, in his love, will make his arms thy tomb.
    [*He embraces him*]

ANTONIO Bless not the body with your twining arms   110
    Which is accursed of heaven. O, what black sin
    Hath been committed by our ancient house,
    Whose scalding vengeance lights upon our heads,
    That thus the world and fortune casts us out
    As loathèd objects, ruin's branded slaves!   115

ANDRUGIO Do not expostulate the heavens' will.
    But O, remember to forget thyself;
    Forget remembrance what thou once hast been.
    Come, creep with me from out this open air;
    Even trees have tongues and will betray our life.   120
    I am a-raising of our house, my boy,°
    Which fortune will not envy, 'tis so mean,
    And like the world, all dirt. There shalt thou rip
    The inwards of thy fortunes in mine ears
    Whilst I sit weeping, blind with passion's tears.   125
    Then I'll begin, and we'll such order keep,
    That one shall still tell griefs, the other weep.

ANTONIO I'll follow you.
        Exeunt Andrugio [and Lucio], leaving Antonio and [Andrugio's]
        Page
                    —Boy, prithee, stay a little.
    Thou hast had a good voice, if this cold marsh
    Wherein we lurk have not corrupted it.   130
        Enter Mellida, standing out of sight, in her page's suit
    I prithee sing, but sirrah, mark you me,
    Let each note breathe the heart of passion,
    The sad extracture of extremest grief.
    Make me a strain; speak groaning like a bell
    That tolls departing souls.   135
    Breathe me a point that may enforce me weep,
    To wring my hands, to break my cursèd breast,
    Rave and exclaim, lie grovelling on the earth,
    Straight start up frantic, crying 'Mellida'.
    Sing but 'Antonio hath lost Mellida',   140
    And thou shalt see me, like a man possessed,
    Howl out such passion that even this brinish marsh
    Will squeeze out tears from out his spongy cheeks,
    The rocks even groan, and—

39

Prithee, prithee sing,   145
Or I shall ne'er ha' done; when I am in,
'Tis harder for me end than to begin.
    The Boy runs a note;° Antonio breaks it.°
For look thee, boy, my grief that hath no end
I may begin to plain, but—prithee sing.
    They sing°
MELLIDA *[coming forward]* Heaven keep you, sir.
ANTONIO   Heaven keep you
  from me, sir.   150
MELLIDA I must be acquainted with you, sir.
ANTONIO Wherefore? Art thou infected with misery,
  Seared with the anguish of calamity?
  Art thou true sorrow, hearty grief? Canst weep?
  I am not for thee if thou canst not rave,   155
    Antonio falls on the ground
  Fall flat on the ground, and thus exclaim on heaven:
  'O trifling nature, why inspir'dst thou breath?'
MELLIDA Stay, sir, I think you namèd Mellida.
ANTONIO Know'st thou Mellida?
MELLIDA Yes.   160
ANTONIO Hast thou seen Mellida?
MELLIDA Yes.
ANTONIO Then hast thou seen the glory of her sex,
  The music of nature, the unequalled lustre
  Of unmatched excellence, the united sweet   165
  Of heaven's graces, the most adorèd beauty
  That ever struck amazement in the world.
MELLIDA You seem to love her.
ANTONIO   With my very soul.
MELLIDA She'll not requite it; all her love is fixed
  Upon a gallant, one Antonio,   170
  The Duke of Genoa's son. I was her page,
  And often as I waited, she would sigh,
  'O dear Antonio', and to strengthen thought
  Would clip my neck and kiss, and kiss me thus.
    [Kisses him]
  Therefore leave loving her. Fa! Faith, methinks   175
  Her beauty is not half so ravishing
  As you discourse of. She hath a freckled face,
  A low forehead and a lumpish eye.

ANTONIO O heaven, that I should hear such blasphemy!
  Boy! Rogue! Thou liest, and—   180
       [*Recognizes Mellida*]
  Spavento del mio core, dole Mellida,
  Di grave morte ristoro vero, dolce Mellida,
  Celeste salvatrice, sovrana Mellida
  Del mio sperar; trofeo vero Mellida.
MELLIDA *Diletta e soave anima mia Antonio.*   185
  Godevole bellezza, cortese Antonio.
  Signor mio e virginal amore bell' Antonio,
  Gusto dei miei sensi, car' Antonio.
ANTONIO *O svanisce il cor in un soave bacio.*
MELLIDA *Muoiono i sensi nel desiato desio.*   190
ANTONIO *Nel cielo può esser beltà più chiara?*
MELLIDA *Nel mondo può esser beltà più chiara?*
ANTONIO *Dammi un bacio da quella bocca beata.*
  Lasciami coglier l'aura odorata
  Che in sù aleggia, in quelle dolci labbra.   195
MELLIDA *Dammi l'impero del tuo gradit' amore,*
  Che bea me, con sempiterno onore,
  Così così, mi converrà morir.°
  Good sweet, scout o'er the marsh, for my heart trembles
  At every little breath that strikes my ear.   200
  When thou returnest sit, and I'll discourse°
  How I deceived the court; then thou shalt tell
  How thou escap'dst the watch; we'll point our speech
  With amorous kissing, kissing commas, and even suck°
  The liquid breath from out each other's lips.   205
ANTONIO [*to himself*] Dull clod, no man but such sweet favour
    clips.°
  I go, and yet my panting blood persuades me stay.
  Turn coward in her sight? Away, away!
       [*Exit Antonio*]
PAGE [*aside*] I think confusion of Babel is fallen upon these lovers
    that they change their language; but I fear me my master, having   210
    but feigned the person of a woman, hath got their unfeigned
    imperfection and is grown double-tongued. As for Mellida, she
    were no woman if she could not yield strange language. But
    howsoever, if I should sit in judgement, 'tis an error easier to be
    pardoned by the auditors than excused by the authors; and yet   215
    some private respect may rebate the edge of the keener censure.°

Enter Piero, Castilio, Mazzagente, Forobosco, Felice, Galeazzo
[at one door]; Balurdo and his Page [Dildo], at another door

PIERO This way she took; search, my sweet gentlemen.—How now,
Balurdo, canst thou meet with anybody?

BALURDO As I am true gentleman, I made my horse sweat, that he
hath ne'er a dry thread on him, and I can meet with no living   220
creature but men and beasts. In good sadness, I would have sworn
I had seen Mellida even now; for I saw a thing stir under a hedge,
and I peeped, and I spied a thing; and I peered and I tweered°
underneath, and truly a right wise man might have been deceived,
for it was—   225

PIERO What, in the name of heaven?

BALURDO A dun cow.

FELICE Sh'ad ne'er a kettle° on her head?

PIERO [*to Mellida*] Boy, didst thou see a young lady pass this way?

GALEAZZO Why speak you not?   230

BALURDO God's nigs! proud elf, give the duke reverence;° stand
bare with a—[*He snatches off Mellida's hat.*] Whoa! Heavens bless
me!—Mellida! Mellida!

PIERO Where, man, where?

BALURDO Turned man, turned man; women wear the breeches. Lo,   235
here!
    [*Mellida kneels before Piero*]

PIERO Light and unduteous! Kneel not, peevish elf,°
Speak not, entreat not, shame unto my house,
Curse to my honour. Where's Antonio?
Thou traitress to my hate, what, is he shipped   240
For England° now? Well, whimpering harlot, hence!

MELLIDA Good father—

PIERO Good me no goods! Seest thou that sprightly youth?
    [*Indicates Galeazzo*]
Ere thou canst term tomorrow morning old,
Thou shalt call him thy husband, lord and love.   245

MELLIDA Ay me!

PIERO Blurt on your 'ay me's'!—Guard her safely hence.
Drag her away.—I'll be your guard tonight.—
[*To Galeazzo*] Young prince, mount up your spirits and prepare
To solemnize your nuptials' eve with pomp.   250

GALEAZZO The time is scant; now nimble wits appear;
Phoebus begins to gleam, the welkin's clear.
    Exeunt all but Balurdo and his Page [Dildo]

42

BALURDO 'Now nimble wits appear!' I'll myself appear;
   Balurdo's self, that in quick wit doth surpass,
   Will show the substance of a complete—
DILDO   Ass.   255
   Ass!
BALURDO I'll mount my courser and most gallantly prick—
DILDO 'Gallantly prick' is too long, and stands hardly in the verse,
   sir.
BALURDO I'll speak pure rhyme.—And will so bravely prank it,   260
   That I'll toss love like a . . . prank . . . it—a rhyme for 'prank it'?
DILDO 'Blanket.'
BALURDO —That I'll toss love like a dog in a blanket.
   Ha, ha, indeed, la! I think—ha, ha! I think—ha, ha! I think I shall
   tickle the Muses. An I strike it not dead, say, 'Balurdo, thou art an   265
   arrant sot'.
DILDO Balurdo, thou art an arrant sot.
       [*Exeunt Balurdo and Dilde. Andrugio's Page remains
       onstage*] *Enter Andrugio and Antonio wreathed together,* [*and*]
       Lucio
ANDRUGIO Now come, united force of chapfall'n death;
   Come, power of fretting anguish, leave distress.°
   O, thus enfolded, we have breasts of proof
   'Gainst all the venomed stings of misery.   270
ANTONIO Father, now I have an antidote
   'Gainst all the poison that the world can breathe.
   My Mellida, my Mellida doth bless
   This bleak waste with her presence.—How now, boy,
   Why dost thou weep? Alas, where's Mellida?   275
PAGE Ay me, my lord!
ANTONIO A sudden horror doth invade my blood;
   My sinews tremble, and my panting heart
   Scuds round about my bosom to go out,   280
   Dreading the assailant, horrid passion.
   O, be no tyrant! Kill me with one blow.
   Speak quickly, briefly, boy.
PAGE Her father found and seized her; she is gone.
ANDRUGIO Son, heat thy blood; be not froze up with grief.   285
   Courage, sweet boy; sink not beneath the weight
   Of crushing mischief. O, where's thy dauntless heart,
   Thy father's spirit? I renounce thy blood
   If thou forsake thy valour.

[*Exit Antonio as if in a daze*]

LUCIO See how his grief speaks in his slow-paced steps.   290
  Alas, 'tis more than he can utter; let him go;
  Dumb, solitary path best suiteth woe.

ANDRUGIO Give me my arms, my armour, Lucio.

LUCIO Dear lord, what means this rage? When lacking use
  Scarce saves your life, will you in armour rise?°   295

ANDRUGIO Fortune fears valour, presseth cowardice.

LUCIO Then valour gets applause when it hath place
  And means to blaze it.°

ANDRUGIO *Numquam potest non esse—*°

LUCIO Patience, my lord, may bring your ills some end.   300

ANDRUGIO What patience, friend, can ruined hopes attend?
  Come, let me die like old Andrugio,
  Worthy my birth. O, blood-true-honoured graves°
  Are far more blessèd than base life of slaves.
      Exeunt

5.1

Enter Balurdo, a Painter°, with two pictures,° and Dildo

BALURDO And are you a painter, sir? Can you draw, can you draw?

PAINTER Yes, sir.

BALURDO Indeed la! Now so can my father's fore-horse. And are these the workmanship of your hands?

PAINTER I did limn them.

BALURDO 'Limn' them? A good word, 'limn' them. Whose picture is this? [*Reads*] '*Anno Domini* 1599.' Believe me, Master Anno Domini was of a good settled age when you limned him. 1599 years old? Let's see the other. [*Reads*] '*Aetatis suae* 24'.° By'r lady, he is somewhat younger. Belike Master Aetatis Suae was Anno Domini's son.

PAINTER Is not your master a—°

DILDO He hath a little proclivity to him.

PAINTER 'Proclivity', good youth? I thank you for your courtly 'proclivity'.

BALURDO Approach, good sir. I did send for you to draw me a device, an *impresa*,° by synecdoche,° a mott. By Phoebus' crimson taffeta mantle, I think I speak as melodiously . . . Look you, sir, how think you on't? I would have you paint me for my device a good fat leg of ewe mutton swimming in stewed broth of plums.— Boy, keel your mouth,° it runs over.—And the word shall be: 'Hold my dish, whilst I spill my pottage'. Sure, in my conscience, 'twould be the most sweet device now.

PAINTER 'Twould scent of kitchen-stuff too much.°

BALURDO God's nigs, now I remember me, I ha' the rarest device in my head that ever breathed. Can you paint me a drivelling, reeling song, and let the word be 'Uh'?

PAINTER A belch?

BALURDO O, no, no! 'Uh'! Paint me 'Uh!' or nothing.

PAINTER It cannot be done, sir, but by a seeming kind of drunkenness.

BALURDO No? Well, let me have a good massy ring with your own posy graven in it, that must sing a small treble, word for word thus:

> '*And if you will my true lover be,*
> *Come follow me to the green wood*'.°

45

ANTONIO AND MELLIDA

PAINTER O lord, sir, I cannot make a picture sing.
BALURDO Why? 'Slid! I have seen painted things° sing as sweet. But
   I have't will tickle it for a conceit,° i'faith!
     Enter Felice and Alberto
ALBERTO O dear Felice, give me thy device;   40
   How shall I purchase love of Rosaline?
FELICE 'Swill, flatter her soundly.
ALBERTO Her love is such, I cannot flatter her;
   But with my utmost vehemence of speech
   I have adored her beauties.   45
FELICE Hast writ good moving unaffected rhymes to her?
ALBERTO O yes, Felice, but she scorns my writ.
FELICE Hast thou presented her with sumptuous gifts?
ALBERTO Alas, my fortunes are too weak to offer them.
FELICE O then I have it; I'll tell thee what to do.   50
ALBERTO What, good Felice?
FELICE Go and hang thyself, I say, go hang thyself;
   If that thou canst not give, go hang thyself.
   I'll rhyme thee dead, or verse thee to the rope.°
   How thinkst thou of a poet that sung thus: 55
   Munera sola pacant, sola addunt munera formam;
   Munere solicites Pallada, Cypris erit.
   Munera, munera.°
ALBERTO I'll go and breathe my woes unto the rocks,
   And spend my grief upon the deafest seas;   60
   I'll weep my passion to the senseless trees,
   And load most solitary air with plaints.
   For woods, trees, sea or rocky Appenine
   Is not so ruthless as my Rosaline.
   Farewell, dear friend, expect no more of me;   65
   Here ends my part in this love's comedy.°
     Exeunt Alberto [and the] Painter [separately]
FELICE Now, Master Balurdo, whither are you going, ha?
BALURDO Signor Felice, how do you, faith, and by my troth, how
   do you?
FELICE Whither art thou going, bully?   70
BALURDO And as heaven help me, how do you? How do you i'faith,
   heh?
FELICE Whither art going, man?
BALURDO O God, to the court. I'll be willing to give you grace and
   good countenance,° if I may but see you in the presence.   75

46

FELICE O, to court! Farewell.

BALURDO If you see one in a yellow taffeta doublet cut upon carnation velour, a green hat, a blue pair of velvet hose, a gilt rapier, and an orange-tawny pair of worsted silk stockings, that's I, that's I.   80

FELICE Very good. Farewell.

BALURDO Ho, you shall know me as easily; I ha' bought me a new green feather with a red sprig; you shall see my wrought shirt hang out at my breeches; you shall know me.

FELICE Very good, very good. Farewell.   85

BALURDO Marry, in the masque 'twill be somewhat hard. But if you hear anybody speak so wittily that he makes all the room laugh, that's I, that's I. Farewell, good
signor.
          [*Exeunt separately*]

5.2

          [*The Duke's state set out.*] *Enter Forobosco, Castilio, a Boy*
          carrying a gilt harp, Piero, Mellida in night apparel, Rosaline,
          Flavia, [and] two Pages. [Piero sits]

PIERO Advance the music's prize
          [*The Boy brings forward the harp*]
                                        —Now, cap'ring wits,°
     Rise to your highest mount; let choice delight
     Garland the brow of this triumphant night.

FOROBOSCO [*aside*] 'Sfoot! a sits like Lucifer himself.

ROSALINE Good sweet duke, first let their voices strain   5
     For music's prize. Give me the golden harp;
     Faith, with your favour, I'll be umpiress.

PIERO Sweet niece, content.—Boys, clear your voice and sing.
          First [Page] sings

ROSALINE By this gold, I had rather have a servant with a short nose
     and a thin hair than have such a high-stretched, minikin voice.   10

PIERO Fair niece, your reason?

ROSALINE By the sweets of love, I should fear extremely that he were an eunuch.

CASTILIO Spark spirit, how like you his voice?

47

ROSALINE 'Spark spirit, how like you his voice?'—So help me,   15
youth, thy voice squeaks like a dry cork shoe.—Come, come; let's
hear the next.
    Second [Page] sings

PIERO Trust me, a good strong mean.—Well sung, my boy.
    Enter Balurdo

BALURDO Hold, hold, hold! Are ye blind? Could you not see my
voice coming for the harp? An I knock not division on the head,°   20
take hence the harp, make me a slip, and let me go but for
ninepence.—Sir Mark, strike up for Master Balurdo.
    [Balurdo] sings
Judgement, gentlemen, judgement. Was't not above line?°
I appeal to your mouths that heard my song.
        [*Sings*] *Do me right*,   25
        And dub me knight,
        Balurdo.°

ROSALINE Kneel down, and I'll dub thee Knight of the Golden
Harp.

BALURDO Indeed la, do; and I'll make you Lady of the Silver   30
Fiddlestick.°

ROSALINE Come, kneel, kneel.
    Enter a Page to Balurdo°

BALURDO My troth, I thank you. It hath never a whistle in't.°

ROSALINE [*to Mellida*] Nay, good sweet coz, raise up your drooping
eyes. An I were at the point of 'To have and to hold, from this day   35
forward', I would be ashamed to look thus lumpish. What, my
pretty coz, 'tis but the loss of an odd maidenhead! Shall's dance?
Thou art so sad, hark in thine ear—I was about to say—but I'll
forbear.

BALURDO [*answering the Page's summons*] I come, I come. More than   40
most honeysuckle-sweet ladies, pine not for my presence;
I'll return in pomp.—Well spoke, Sir Jeffrey Balurdo. As I am
a true knight, I feel honourable eloquence begin to grope me
already.
    Exit [Balurdo]

PIERO Faith, mad niece, I wonder when thou wilt marry.   45

ROSALINE Faith, kind uncle, when men abandon jealousy, forsake
taking of tobacco, and cease to wear their beards so rudely long. O,
to have a husband with a mouth continually smoking, with a bush
of furze on the ridge of his chin, ready still to slop into his foaming
chaps; ah, 'tis more than most intolerable.   50

PIERO Nay, faith, sweet niece, I was mighty strong in thought we
   should have shut up night with an old comedy: the Prince of
   Milan° shall have Mellida and thou shouldst have—
ROSALINE Nobody, good sweet uncle. I tell you, sir, I have thirty-
   nine servants, and my monkey that makes the fortieth. Now I love 55
   all of them lightly for something, but affect none of them seriously
   for anything. One's a passionate fool and he flatters me above
   belief; the second's a testy ape and he rails at me beyond reason;
   the third's as grave as some censor and he strokes up his mous-
   tachios three times and makes six plots of set faces° before he 60
   speaks one wise word; the fourth's as dry as the bur of an arti-
   choke; the fifth paints° and hath always a good colour for what he
   speaks; the sixth—
PIERO Stay, stay, sweet niece! What makes you thus suspect young
   gallants' worth? 65
ROSALINE O, when I see one wear a periwig, I dread his hair;
   another wallow in a great slop, I mistrust the proportion of his
   thigh; and wears a ruffled boot, I fear the fashion of his leg. Thus
   something in each thing, one trick in everything, makes me mis-
   trust imperfection in all parts. And there's the full point of my 70
   addiction.
   The cornets sound a sennet. Enter Galeazzo, Mazzagente, and
   Balurdo in [masque costumes and masked]
PIERO The room's too scant.—Boys, stand in there close.°
MELLIDA [*to Galeazzo*] In faith, fair sir, I am too sad to dance.
PIERO How's that? how's that? Too sad? By heaven, dance,
   And grace him too, or—go to, I say no more. 75
MELLIDA [*reading Galeazzo's device*] A burning-glass, the word:
   'Splendente Phoebo'.°
   'Tis too curious; I conceit it not.
GALEAZZO Faith, I'll tell thee. I'll no longer burn
   Than you'll shine and smile upon my love.
   For look ye, fairest, by your pure sweets,
   I do not dote upon your excellence; 80
   And, faith, unless you shed your brightest beams
   Of sunny favour and acceptive grace
   Upon my tender love, I do not burn.
   Marry, but shine and I'll reflect your beams
   With fervent ardour. Faith, I would be loath 85
   To flatter thee, fair soul, because I love,
   Not dote, court like thy husband, which thy father

Swears tomorrow morn I must be. This is all,
And now from henceforth, trust me, Mellida,   90
I'll not speak one wise word to thee more.

MELLIDA I trust ye.

GALEAZZO By my troth, I'll speak pure fool to thee now.

MELLIDA You will speak the liker yourself.

GALEAZZO Good faith, I'll accept of the coxcomb, so you will not   95
refuse the bauble.°

MELLIDA Nay, good sweet, keep them both; I am enamoured of
neither.

GALEAZZO Go to! I must take you down° for this. Lend me your
ear.   100
    [*They walk aside*]

ROSALINE [*reading Mazzagente's device*] A glowworm. The word?
'*Splendescit tantum tenebris.*'°

MAZZAGENTE O lady, the glowworm figurates my valour which
shineth brightest in most dark, dismal and horrid achievements.

ROSALINE Or rather, your glowworm represents your wit, which   105
only seems to have fire in it, though indeed 'tis but an *ignis fatuus*°
and shines only in the dark, dead night of fools' admiration.

MAZZAGENTE Lady, my wit hath spurs, if it were disposed to ride°
you.

ROSALINE Faith, sir, your wits' spurs have but walking rowels; dull,   110
blunt, they will not draw blood. The gentlemen ushers may admit
them the presence° for any wrong they can do to ladies.
    [*They walk aside*]

BALURDO [*to Flavia*] Truly, I have strained a note above E la° for a
device. Look you, tis a fair-ruled singing book; the word: 'Perfect,
if it were pricked'.°   115

FLAVIA Though you are masked, I can guess who you are by your
wit. You are not the exquisite Balurdo, the most rarely shaped
Balurdo?

BALURDO Who, I? No, I am not Sir Jeffrey Balurdo. I am not as well
known by my wit as an alehouse by a red lattice.° I am not worthy   120
to love and be beloved of Flavia.

FLAVIA I will not scorn to favour such good parts as are applauded
in your rarest self.

BALURDO Truly, you speak wisely, and like a gentlewoman of fourteen years of age. You know the stone called *lapis*;° the nearer it   125
comes to the fire, the hotter it is. And the bird which the geomet-
ricians call *avis*,° the farther it is from the earth, the nearer it is to

the heaven. And love, the nigher it is to the flame, the more
remote—there's a word, 'remote'!—the more remote it is from
the frost. Your wit is quick. A little thing° pleaseth a young lady,   130
and a small favour contenteth an old courtier. And so, sweet
mistress, I truss my codpiece point.°
    [*A flourish sounds within.*] *Enter Felice*

PIERO What might import this flourish? Bring us word.

FELICE Stand away!—[*Aside*] Here's such a company of flyboats
lulling about this galliass of greatness that there's no boarding   135
him.°—Do you hear, you thing called duke?

PIERO How now, blunt Felice, what's the news?

FELICE Yonder's a knight hath brought Andrugio's head,
   And craves admission to your chair of state.
    Cornets sound a sennet. Enter Andrugio in armour

PIERO Conduct him with attendance sumptuous,   140
   Sound all the pleasing instruments of joy,
   Make triumph, stand on tiptoe whilst we meet.
   O sight most gracious! O revenge most sweet!

ANDRUGIO [*reading the proclamation*] 'We vow by the honour of our
   birth to recompense any man that bringeth Andrugio's head with   145
   twenty thousand double pistolets and the endearing to our choicest
   love.'

PIERO We still with most unmoved resolve confirm
   Our large munificence; and here breathe
   A sad and solemn protestation: 150
   When I recall this vow, O let our house
   Be even commanded, stained and trampled on
   As worthless rubbish of nobility.

ANDRUGIO Then here, Piero, is Andrugio's head,
    [*Raising his helmet*]
   Royally casquèd in a helm of steel.   155
   Give my thy love and take it. My dauntless soul
   Hath that unbounded vigour in his spirits
   That it can bear more rank indignity
   With less impatience than thy cankered hate
   Can sting and venom his untainted worth   160
   With the most viperous sound of malice. Strike!
   O, let no glimpse of honour light thy thoughts;
   If there be any heat of royal breath
   Creeping in thy veins, O stifle it.
   Be still thyself, bloody and treacherous.   165

Fame not thy house with an admirèd act
Of princely purity. Piero, I am come
To soil thy house with an eternal blot
Of savage cruelty. Strike, or bid me strike!
I pray my death, that thy ne'er-dying shame   170
Might live immortal to posterity.
Come, be a princely hangman, stop my breath.
O dread thou shame no more than I dread death.

PIERO We are amazed, our royal spirits numbed
In stiff astonished wonder at thy prowess,   175
Most mighty, valiant and high-tow'ring heart.
We blush, and turn our hate upon ourselves
For hating such an unpeered excellence.
I joy my state, him whom I loathed before
That now I honour, love, nay more, adore.°   180
      The still flutes° sound a mournful sennet. Enter [Attendants
      carrying] a coffin, [accompanied by Lucio]
But stay; what tragic spectacle appears?
Whose body bear you in that mournful hearse?

LUCIO The breathless trunk of young Antonio.

MELLIDA Antonio! Ay me! My lord, my love, my—

ANDRUGIO Sweet, precious issue of most honoured blood,   185
Rich hope, ripe virtue, O untimely loss!
[*To Lucio*] Come hither, friend. Prithee do not weep;
Why, I am glad he's dead; he shall not see
His father's vanquished by his enemy,
Even in princely honour. Nay, prithee speak;   190
How died the wretched boy?

LUCIO My lord—

ANDRUGIO I hope he died yet like my son, i'faith.

LUCIO Alas, my lord—

ANDRUGIO He died unforced, I trust, and valiantly.   195

LUCIO Poor gentleman, being—

ANDRUGIO Did his hand shake or his eye look dull,
His thoughts reel, fearful, when he struck the stroke?
And if they did, I'll rend them out the hearse,
Rip up his cerecloth, mangle his bleak face,   200
That when he comes to heaven, the powers divine
Shall ne'er take notice that he was my son.
I'll quite disclaim his birth. Nay, prithee speak.
An 'twere not hooped with steel, my breast would break.

MELLIDA O that my spirit in a sigh could mount   205
  Into the sphere where thy sweet soul doth rest!
PIERO O that my tears, bedewing thy wan cheek,
  Could make new spirit sprout in thy cold blood!
BALURDO Verily, he looks as pitifully as a poor John.° As I am true
  knight, I could weep like a stoned horse.   210
ANDRUGIO [*to Piero*] Villain, 'tis thou hast murderèd my son.
  Thy unrelenting spirit, thou black dog,
  That took'st no passion of his fatal love,
  Hath forced him give his life untimely end.
PIERO O that my life, her love, my dearest blood,   215
  Would but redeem one minute of his breath!
     [*Antonio rises from the coffin*]
ANTONIO I seise that breath. Stand not amazed, great states;
  I rise from death that never lived till now.—
  Piero, keep thy vow, and I enjoy
  More unexpressèd height of happiness   220
  Than power of thought can reach. If not, lo, here
  There stands my tomb, and here a pleasing stage,
  Most wished spectators of my tragedy;
  To this end have I feigned, that her fair eye
  For whom I lived might bless me ere I die.   225
MELLIDA Can breath depaint my unconceivèd thoughts?
  Can words describe my infinite delight
  Of seeing thee, my lord Antonio?
  O no; conceit, breath, passion, words be dumb,
  Whilst I instill the dew of my sweet bliss   230
  In the soft pressure of a melting kiss:
  Sic, sic iuvat ire sub umbras.°
PIERO Fair son—now I'll be proud to call thee son—
  Enjoy me thus: my very breast is thine.
     [*Piero embraces Antonio*]
  Possess me freely; I am wholly thine.   235
ANTONIO [*to Andrugio*] Dear father!
ANDRUGIO Sweet son, sweet son, I can speak no more;
  My joy's passion flows above the shore
  And chokes the current of my speech.
PIERO Young Florence' prince, to you my lips must beg   240
  For a remittance of your interest.
GALEAZZO In your fair daughter? With all my thought.
  So help me, faith, the naked truth I'll unfold:

He that was ne'er hot will soon be cold.

PIERO No man else makes claim unto her?   245

MAZZAGENTE The valiant speak truth in brief: no.

BALURDO Truly, for Sir Jeffrey Balurdo, he disclaims to have had
anything° in her.

PIERO Then here I give her to Antonio.

[*To Andrugio*] Royal, valiant, most respected prince,   250
Let's clip our hands. I'll thus observe my vow;
I promised twenty thousand double pistolets,
With the endearing to my dearest love,
To him that brought thy head; thine be the gold
To solemnize our houses' unity.   255
My love be thine, the all I have be thine.—
Fill us fresh wine.—The form we'll take by this:
We'll drink a health, while they two sip a kiss.
Now there remains no discord that can sound
Harsh accents to the ear of our accord,   260
So please you, niece, to match.

ROSALINE Troth, uncle, when my sweet-faced coz hath told me how
she likes the thing called wedlock, maybe I'll take a survey of the
checkroll° of my servants, and he that hath the best parts of—I'll
prick him down for my husband.   265

BALURDO For passion of love now, remember me to my mistress,
Lady Rosaline, when she is pricking down the good parts of her
servants. As I am true knight, I grow stiff;° I shall carry it.

PIERO I will.—
Sound Lydian wires, once make a pleasing note,°   270
On nectar streams of your sweet airs to float.

ANTONIO Here ends the comic crosses of true love;
O may the passage most successful prove.

[*Exeunt all save Andrugio*]

EPILOGUE

ANDRUGIO ([as] *the Epilogue*) Gentlemen, though I remain an armed
Epilogue,° I stand not as a peremptory challenger of desert, either
for him that composed the comedy or for us that acted it, but a
most submissive suppliant for both. What imperfection you have
seen in us, leave with us and we'll amend it; what hath pleased   5
you, take with you and cherish it. You shall not be more ready to
embrace anything commendable than we will endeavour to amend
all things reprovable. What we are, is by your favour. What we
shall be, rests all in your applausive encouragements.
    Exit

ANTONIO'S REVENGE

or

The Second Part of
the History of
Antonio and Mellida

THE PERSONS OF THE PLAY

Piero Sforza	Duke of Venice
Pandulfo Felice	father of dead Felice
Antonio	son of Andrugio
Galeazzo	son of the Duke of Florence
Mazzagente	son of the Duke of Milan
Jeffrey Balurdo	wealthy heir of Venice
Julio	son of Piero
Alberto	Venetian gentleman
Forobosco	the parasite
Castilio Balthazar	Venetian gentleman
Gaspar Strozzo°	servant to Piero
Ghost of Andrugio	late Duke of Genoa
Lucio	servant to Maria
Mellida	daughter of Piero, betrothed to Antonio
Maria	mother of Antonio
Nutrice°	nurse to Maria

Pages
Herald
Senators of Venice
Attendants
Ladies

Antonio's Revenge

PROLOGUE

[Enter] the Prologue

PROLOGUE The rawish dank of clumsy winter ramps°
The fluent summer's vein, and drizzling sleet
Chilleth the wan bleak cheek of the numbed earth,
Whilst snarling gusts nibble the juiceless leaves
From the naked shudd'ring branch, and peels the skin   5
From off the soft and delicate aspects.
O now, methinks, a sullen tragic scene
Would suit the time with pleasing congruence.
May we be happy in our weak devoir,°
And all part pleased in most wished content   10
—But sweat of Hercules can ne'er beget
So blest an issue. Therefore we proclaim,°
If any spirit breathes within this round
Uncapable of weighty passion°
(As from his birth being huggèd in the arms   15
And nuzzled 'twixt the breasts of happiness),
Who winks and shuts his apprehension up
From common sense of what men were and are,
Who would not know what men must be, let such
Hurry amain from our black-visaged shows;   20
We shall affright their eyes. But if a breast
Nailed to the earth with grief, if any heart
Pierced through with anguish, pant within this ring,
If there be any blood whose heat is choked
And stifled with true sense of misery,   25
If aught of these strains fill this consort up,
Th' arrive most welcome. O that our power
Could lackey or keep wing with our desires,
That with unusèd peise of style and sense
We might weigh massy in judicious scale!°   30
Yet here's the prop that doth support our hopes:
When our scenes falter, or invention halts,
Your favour will give crutches to our faults.

Exit

1.1

*Enter Piero unbraced, his arms bare, smeared in blood, a
poniard in one hand, bloody, and a torch in the other, Strozzo
following him with a cord*

PIERO Ho, Gaspar Strozzo, bind Felice's trunk
Unto the panting side of Mellida.
　　　Exit Strozzo
'Tis yet dead night, yet all the earth is clutched
In the dull leaden hand of snoring sleep;
No breath disturbs the quiet of the air,　　　　　　　　　　5
No spirit moves upon the breast of earth,
Save howling dogs, night-crows, and screeching owls,
Save meagre ghosts, Piero, and black thoughts.
　　　[Clock strikes]
One, two. Lord! in two hours what a topless mount
Of unpeered mischief have these hands cast up!　　　　10
　　　Enter Strozzo
I can scarce coop triumphing vengeance up
From bursting forth in braggart passion.
STROZZO My lord, 'tis firmly said that—
PIERO Andrugio sleeps in peace; this brain hath choked
The organ of his breast. Felice hangs°　　　　　　　　　　15
But as a bait upon the line of death
To 'tice on mischief. I am great in blood,
Unequalled in revenge. You horrid scouts°
That sentinel swart night, give loud applause
From your large palms. First know, my heart was raised　　20
Unto Andrugio's life upon this ground:—°
STROZZO Duke, 'tis reported—
PIERO —We both were rivals in our May of blood
Unto Maria, fair Ferrara's heir.
He won the lady, to my honour's death,　　　　　　　　　25
And from her sweets cropped this Antonio;
For which I burned in inward swelt'ring hate
And festered rankling malice in my breast,
Till I might belch revenge upon his eyes.
And now—O blessèd now!—'tis done! Hell, night,　　　30
Give loud applause to my hypocrisy.

60

When his bright valour even dazzled sense
In off'ring his own head, public reproach
Had blurred my name—speak, Strozzo, had it not?—
If then I had—   35
STROZZO It had, so please—
PIERO What had, so please? Unseasoned sycophant,
    Piero Sforza is no numbèd lord,
    Senseless of all true touch. Stroke not the head
    Of infant speech till it be fully born.   40
    Go to!
STROZZO How now? Fut! I'll not smother your speech.
PIERO Nay, right thine eyes; 'twas but a little spleen.—
    [*Aside*] Huge plunge!°
    Sin's grown a slave and must observe slight evils;   45
    Huge villains are enforced to claw all devils.—°
    [*To Strozzo*] Pish! sweet thy thoughts, and give me—
STROZZO 'Stroke not the head of infant speech! Go to!'
PIERO Nay, calm this storm. I ever held thy breast
    More secret and more firm in league of blood   50
    Than to be struck in heat with each slight puff.
    Give me thy ears. Huge infamy
    Press down my honour if even then, when
    His fresh act of prowess bloomed out full,°
    I had ta'en vengeance on his hated head—   55
STROZZO Why it had—
PIERO Could I avoid to give a seeming grant
    Unto fruition of Antonio's love?°
STROZZO No.
PIERO And didst thou ever see a Judas kiss°   60
    With a more covert touch of fleering hate?
STROZZO No.
PIERO And having clipped them with pretence of love,
    Have I not crushed them with a cruel wring?
STROZZO Yes.   65
PIERO Say, faith, didst thou e'er hear, or read, or see
    Such happy vengeance, unsuspected death?
    That I should drop strong poison in the bowl
    Which I myself caroused unto his health
    And future fortune of our unity;   70
    That it should work even in the hush of night
    And strangle him on sudden, that fair show

Of death for the excessive joy of his fate
Might choke the murder! Ha, Strozzo, is't not rare?
Nay, but weigh it! Then Felice stabbed,   75
Whose sinking thought frighted my conscious heart,
And laid by Mellida, to stop the match
And hale on mischief! This, all in one night!
Is't to be equalled, think'st thou? O, I could eat
Thy fumbling throat for thy lagged censure. Fut!°   80
Is't not rare?
STROZZO Yes.
PIERO No? Yes? Nothing but 'no' and 'yes', dull lump?
Canst thou not honey me with fluent speech
And even adore my topless villainy?   85
Will I not blast my own blood for revenge?
Must not thou straight be perjured for revenge?
And yet no creature dream 'tis my revenge?
Will I not turn a glorious bridal morn
Unto a Stygian night? Yet nought but 'no' and 'yes'?°   90
STROZZO I would have told you if the incubus
That rides your bosom would have patience.
It is reported that in private state
Maria, Genoa's duchess, makes to court,
Longing to see him whom she ne'er shall see,   95
Her lord, Andrugio. Belike she hath received
The news of reconciliation:°
Reconciliation with a death!
Poor lady, shall but find poor comfort in 't!
PIERO O, let me swoon for joy! By heaven, I think   100
I ha' said my prayers within this month at least,
I am so boundless happy. Doth she come?
By this warm reeking gore, I'll marry her.
Look I not now like an inamorate?
Poison the father, butcher the son, and marry the mother, ha! 105
Strozzo, to bed; snort in securest sleep;
For see the dapple-grey coursers of the morn
Beat up the light with their bright silver hooves
And chase it through the sky. To bed, to bed!
This morn my vengeance shall be amply fed.   110
     Exeunt

1.2

Enter Lucio, Maria, and Nutrice

MARIA Stay, gentle Lucio, and vouchsafe thy hand.

LUCIO O, madam!

MARIA Nay, prithee give me leave to say 'vouchsafe'.
Submiss entreats beseem my humble fate.
Here let us sit.
      [They sit, and Nutrice falls asleep]
                    O, Lucio, fortune's gilt   5
Is rubbed quite off from my slight tinfoiled state,
And poor Maria must appear ungraced
Of the bright fulgor of glossed majesty.

LUCIO Cheer up your spirits, madam; fairer chance
That that which courts your presence instantly°   10
Cannot be formed by the quick mould of thought.

MARIA Art thou assured the dukes are reconciled?
Shall my womb's honour wed fair Mellida?
Will heaven at length grant harbour to my head?
Shall I once more clip my Andrugio,   15
And wreathe my arms about Antonio's neck?
Or is glib rumour grown a parasite,
Holding a false glass to my sorrow's eyes,
Making the wrinkled front of grief seem fair,
Though 'tis much rivelled with abortive care?   20

LUCIO Most virtuous princess, banish straggling fear,
Keep league with comfort; for these eyes beheld
The dukes united. Yon faint glimmering light
Ne'er peepèd through the crannies of the east
Since I beheld them drink a sound carouse   25
In sparkling Bacchus unto each other's health,°
Your son assured to beauteous Mellida,
And all clouds cleared of threat'ning discontent.

MARIA What age is morning of?

LUCIO   I think 'bout five.

MARIA Nutrice, Nutrice!
      [She shakes Nutrice awake]   30

NUTRICE Beshrew your fingers! Marry, you have disturbed the
pleasure of the finest dream. O God, I was even coming to it, la!
O Jesu, 'twas coming of the sweetest! I'll tell you now: methought I

was married, and methought I spent—O Lord, why did you wake
me?—and methought I spent three spur-royals° on the fiddlers for   35
striking up a fresh hornpipe. Saint Ursula!° I was even going to
bed, and you—methought my husband was even putting out the
tapers, when you—Lord! I shall never have such a dream come
upon me as long as—

MARIA Peace, idle creature, peace!—When will the court rise?   40

LUCIO Madam, 'twere best you took some lodging up
And lay in private till the soil of grief
Were cleared your cheek, and new-burnished lustre
Clothed your presence, 'fore you saw the dukes
And entered 'mong the proud Venetian states.   45

MARIA No, Lucio, my dear lord's wise and knows
That tinsel glitter, or rich purfled robes,
Curled hairs hung full of sparkling carcanets,
Are not the true adornments of a wife.
So long as wives are faithful, modest, chaste,   50
Wise lords affect them. Virtue doth not waste
With each slight flam of crackling vanity.°
A modest eye forceth affection,
Whilst outward gayness light looks but entice.
Fairer than nature's fair is foulest vice.   55
She that loves art to get her cheek more lovers,
Much outward gauds, slight inward grace discovers.
I care not to seem fair but to my lord.
Those that strive most to please most strangers' sight,
Folly may judge most fair, wisdom most light.   60
       Music sounds a short strain
But hark, soft music gently moves the air;
I think the bridegroom's up. Lucio, stand close.—
O now, Maria, challenge grief to stay
Thy joy's encounter.—Look, Lucio, 'tis clear day.°
       [*They withdraw.*]° *Enter Antonio, Galeazzo, Mazzagente,*
       Balurdo, Pandulfo Felice, Alberto, Castilio, and a Page

ANTONIO Darkness is fled; look, infant morn hath drawn   65
Bright silver curtains 'bout the couch of night,
And now Aurora's horse trots azure rings,°
Breathing fair light about the firmament.
Stand! What's that?
       [*He starts in dismay*]°

MAZZAGENTE And if a hornèd devil should burst forth   70

64

I would pass on him with a mortal stock.°

ALBERTO O, a hornèd devil would prove ominous
Unto a bridegroom's eyes.°

MAZZAGENTE A hornèd devil? Good, good. Ha, ha, ha! Very good.

ALBERTO Good tanned prince, laugh not. By the joys of love,   75
When thou dost girn, thy rusty face doth look
Like the head of a roasted rabbit. Fie upon 't!

BALURDO By my troth, methinks his nose is just colour *de roi*.

MAZZAGENTE I tell thee, fool, my nose will abide no jest.

BALURDO No, in truth, I do not jest; I speak truth. Truth is the   80
touchstone of all things; and if your nose will not abide the truth,
your nose will not abide the touch;° and if your nose will not abide
the touch, your nose is a copper nose and must be nailed up for a
slip.

MAZZAGENTE I scorn to retort the obtuse jest of a fool.   85
    Balurdo draws out his writing tables° *and writes*

BALURDO 'Retort' and 'obtuse'—good words, very good words.

GALEAZZO [*to Antonio*] Young prince, look sprightly. Fie, a bridegroom sad!

BALURDO In truth, if he were retort and obtuse, no question he
would be merry. But, an't please my genius, I will be most retort
and obtuse ere night. I'll tell you what I'll bear soon at night in my   90
shield for my device.°

GALEAZZO What, good Balurdo?

BALURDO O, do me right: *Sir* Jeffrey Balurdo; *Sir, Sir*, as long as ye
live, *Sir*.

GALEAZZO What, good Sir Jeffrey Balurdo?   95

BALURDO Marry, forsooth, I'll carry for my device my grandfather's
great stone-horse flinging up his head and jerking out his left leg;
the word: 'Wehee Purt'.° As I am a true knight, will't not be most
retort and obtuse, ha?

ANTONIO Blow hence these sapless jests. I tell you, bloods,   100
My spirit's heavy, and the juice of life
Creeps slowly through my stiffened arteries.
Last sleep my sense was steeped in horrid dreams;
Three parts of night were swallowed in the gulf
Of ravenous time when to my slumb'ring powers   105
Two meagre ghosts made apparition.°
The one's breast seemed fresh paunched with bleeding wounds
Whose bubbling gore sprang in frighted eyes;
The other ghost assumed my father's shape;

Both cried 'Revenge!'; at which my trembling joints,   110
Icèd quite over with a frozed cold sweat,
Leaped forth the sheets. Three times I grasped at shades,
And thrice, deluded by erroneous sense,
I forced my thoughts make stand; when, lo, I oped°
A large bay window, through which the night   115
Struck terror to my soul. The verge of heaven
Was ringed with flames, and all the upper vault
Thick-laced with flakes of fire; in midst whereof
A blazing comet shot his threatn'ing train°
Just on my face. Viewing these prodigies,   120
I bowed my naked knee and pierced the star
With an outfacing eye, pronouncing thus:
Deus imperat astris. At which my nose straight bled;°
Then doubled I my word, so slunk to bed.°

BALURDO Verily, Sir Jeffrey had a monstrous strange dream the last   125
night; for methought I dreamed I was asleep, and methought the
ground yawned and belched up the abominable ghost of a mis-
shapen Simile, with two ugly pages, the one called Master Even-as
going before, and the other Monsieur Even-so following after,
whilst Signor Simile stalked most prodigiously in the midst. At   130
which I bewrayed° the fearfulness of my nature, and, being ready
to forsake the fortress of my wit, started up, called for a clean shirt,
ate a mass of broth, and with that I awaked.

ANTONIO I prithee peace.—I tell you, gentlemen,
The frightful shades of night yet shake my brain;   135
My gelid blood's not thawed, the sulphur damps°
That flow in wingèd lightning 'bout my couch
Yet stick within my sense; my soul is great
In expectation of dire prodigies.

PANDULFO Tut, my young prince, let not thy fortunes see   140
Their lord a coward. He that's nobly born
Abhors to fear; base fear's the brand of slaves.
He that observes, pursues, slinks back for fright,
Was never cast in mould of noble sprite.

GALEAZZO Tush, there's a sun will straight exhale these damps   145
Of chilling fear.
        [Indicates Mellida's window]
              Come, shall's salute the bride?
ANTONIO Castilio, I prithee mix thy breath with his;
Sing one of Signor Renaldo's airs°

To rouse the slumb'ring bride from gluttoning
In surfeit of superfluous sleep. Good signor, sing.   150
    [*Galeazzo and Castilio*] *sing.* [*There is no response from above*]
What means this silence and unmovèd calm?—
[*To the Page*] Boy, wind thy cornet; force the leaden gates
Of lazy sleep fly open with thy breath.—
    [*The Page sounds the cornet, but again there is no response from*
    above]
My Mellida not up? No stirring yet? Umh!

MARIA   That voice should be my son's, Antonio's.—   155
    Antonio!

ANTONIO   Here. Who calls? Here stands Antonio.

MARIA   [*coming forward*] Sweet son!

ANTONIO   Dear mother!

MARIA   Fair honour of a chaste and loyal bed,   160
    Thy father's beauty, thy sad mother's love,
    Were I as powerful as the voice of fate,
    Felicity complete should sweet thy state;
    But all the blessings that a poor banished wretch
    Can pour upon thy head, take, gentle son.   165
    Live, gracious youth, to close thy mother's eyes,
    Loved of thy parents till their latest hour.
    How cheers my lord, thy father? O, sweet boy,
    Part of him thus I clip, my dear, dear joy.
       [*She embraces him*]

ANTONIO   Madam, last night I kissed his princely hand   170
    And took a treasured blessing from his lips.
    O mother, you arrive in jubilee
    And firm atonement of all boist'rous rage;
    Pleasure, united love, protested faith,
    Guard my loved father as sworn pensioners.   175
    The dukes are leagued in firmest bond of love,
    And you arrive in the solsticy
    And highest point of sunshine happiness.
       One winds a cornet within
    Hark, madam, how yon cornet jerketh up
    His strained shrill accents in the capering air,   180
    As proud to summon up my bright-cheeked love.
    Now, mother, ope wide expectation;
    Let loose your amplest sense to entertain
    Th'impression of an object of such worth

That life's too poor to—   185
GALEAZZO Nay, leave hyperboles.
ANTONIO I tell thee, prince, that presence straight appears
  Of which thou canst not form hyperboles;
  The trophy of triumphing excellence,
  The heart of beauty, Mellida, appears.   190
  See, look, the curtain stirs.—Shine, nature's pride,
  Love's vital spirit, dear Antonio's bride!
        The curtain is drawn,° and the body of Felice, stabbed thick with
        wounds, appears hung up
  What villain bloods the window of my love?
  What slave hath hung yon gory ensign up
  In flat defiance of humanity?   195
  Awake, thou fair unspotted purity,
  Death's at thy window! Awake, bright Mellida!
  Antonio calls.
        Enter Piero as at first,° with Forobosco
PIERO Who gives these ill-befitting attributes
  Of 'chaste', 'unspotted', 'bright', to Mellida?   200
  He lies as loud as thunder; she's unchaste,
  Tainted, impure, black as the soul of hell.
        [Antonio] draws his rapier, offers to run at Piero; but Maria
        holds his arm and stays him
ANTONIO Dog, I will make thee eat thy vomit up,
  Which thou hast belched 'gainst taintless Mellida.
PIERO Ram 't quickly down, that it may not rise up   205
  To embraid my thoughts. Behold my stomach;°
  Strike me quite through with the relentless edge
  Of raging fury. Boy, I'll kill thy love.—
  Pandulfo, I have stabbed thy son;
  Look, yet his lifeblood reeks upon this steel.—   210
  Albert, yon hangs thy friend.—Have none of you
  Courage of vengeance? Forget I am your duke.
  Think Mellida is not Piero's blood.
  Imagine on slight ground I'll blast his honour.
  Suppose I saw not that incestuous slave   215
  Clipping the strumpet with luxurious twines.°
  O, numb my sense of anguish, cast my life
  In a dead sleep whilst law cuts off yon maim,
  Yon putrid ulcer of my royal blood.
FOROBOSCO Keep league with reason, gracious sovereign.   220

PIERO There glow no sparks of reason in the world;
　　All are raked up in ashy beastliness.
　　The bulk of man's as dark as Erebus;°
　　No branch of reason's light hangs in his trunk;
　　There lives no reason to keep league withal;　　　　225
　　I ha' no reason to be reasonable.
　　Her wedding eve, linked to the noble blood
　　Of my most firmly reconcilèd friend,
　　And found even clinged in sensuality!
　　O heaven! O heaven! Were she as near my heart　　230
　　As is my liver I would rend her off.
　　　　Enter Strozzo
STROZZO Whither, O whither shall I hurl vast grief?
PIERO Here, into my breast; 'tis a place built wide
　　By fate to give receipt to boundless woes.
STROZZO O, no; here throb those hearts which I must cleave　235
　　With my keen piercing news. Andrugio's dead.
PIERO Dead?
MARIA O me most miserable!
PIERO Dead? Alas, how dead? [*Aside to Strozzo*] Give seeming
　　passion;°
　　Fut! weep, act, feign.—Dead? Alas, how dead?　　240
STROZZO The vast delights of his large sudden joys
　　Opened his powers so wide that's native heat
　　So prodigally flowed t'exterior parts,
　　That th'inner citadel was left unmanned,
　　And so surprized on sudden by cold death.　　　　245
MARIA O fatal, disastrous, cursèd, dismal!
　　Choke breath and life. I breathe, I live too long.—
　　Andrugio, my lord, I come, I come.
　　　　[*She swoons*]
PIERO Be cheerful, princess.—Help, Castilio;
　　The lady's swooned; help to bear her in.　　　　250
　　Slow comfort to huge cares is swiftest sin.°
BALURDO Courage, courage, sweet lady! 'Tis Sir Jeffrey Balurdo
　　bids you courage.—Truly, I am as nimble as an elephant about a
　　lady.
　　　　[*Exeunt Piero, Forobosco, Castilio and Balurdo, Lucio and
　　　　Nutrice, bearing out Maria*]
PANDULFO Dead?　　　　　　　　　　　　　　　255
ANTONIO Dead?
ALBERTO Dead?

ANTONIO Why, now the womb of mischief is delivered
  Of the prodigious issue of the night.
PANDULFO Ha, ha, ha!   260
ANTONIO My father dead, my love attaint of lust—°
  That's a large lie, as vast as spacious hell!
  Poor guiltless lady! O accursèd lie!
  What, whom, whither, which shall I first lament?
  A dead father, a dishonoured wife? Stand!   265
  Methinks I feel the frame of nature shake.
  Cracks not the joints of earth to bear my woes?
ALBERTO Sweet prince, be patient.
ANTONIO 'Slid, sir, I will not, in despite of thee.
  Patience is slave to fools, a chain that's fixed   270
  Only to posts and senseless log-like dolts.
ALBERTO 'Tis reason's glory to command affects.
ANTONIO Lies thy cold father dead, his glossèd eyes
  New closèd up by thy sad mother's hands?
  Hast thou a love, as spotless as the brow   275
  Of clearest heaven, blurred with false defames?
  Are thy moist entrails crumpled up with grief
  Of parching mischiefs? Tell me, does thy heart
  With punching anguish spur thy gallèd ribs?
  Then come; let's sit and weep and wreathe our arms;°   280
  I'll hear thy counsel.
ALBERTO Take comfort—
ANTONIO Confusion to all comfort! I defy it.
  Comfort's a parasite, a flatt'ring Jack,
  And melts resolved despair. O boundless woe,   285
  If there be any black yet unknown grief,
  If there be any horror yet unfelt,
  Unthought-of mischief in thy fiend-like power,
  Dash it upon my miserable head;
  Make me more wretch, more cursèd if thou canst.   290
  O, now my fate is more than I could fear;
  My woes more weighty than my soul can bear.
      Exit [Antonio]
PANDULFO Ha, ha, ha!
ALBERTO Why laugh you, uncle? That's my coz, your son,
  Whose breast hangs casèd in his cluttered gore.   295
PANDULFO True, man, true. Why, wherefore should I weep?
  Come sit, kind nephew; come on. Thou and I

Will talk as chorus to this tragedy.
Entreat the music strain their instruments
With a slight touch whilst we—Say on, fair coz.°   300
    Music sounds softly°
ALBERTO He was the very hope of Italy,
    The blooming honour of your drooping age.
PANDULFO True, coz, true. They say that men of hope are crushed,
    Good are suppressed by base desertless clods
    That stifle gasping virtue. Look, sweet youth,   305
    How provident our quick Venetians are
    Lest hooves of jades should trample on my boy;
    Look how they lift him up to eminence,
    Heave him 'bove reach of flesh. Ha, ha, ha!
ALBERTO Uncle, this laughter ill becomes your grief.   310
PANDULFO Wouldst have me cry, run raving up and down
    For my son's loss? Wouldst have me turn rank mad,
    Or wring my face with mimic action?
    Stamp, curse, weep, rage, and then my bosom strike?
    Away! 'Tis apish action, player-like.   315
    If he is guiltless, why should tears be spent?
    Thrice-blessèd soul that dieth innocent.
    If he is lepered with so foul a guilt,
    Why should a sigh be lent, a tear be spilt?
    The grip of chance is weak to wring a tear   320
    From him that knows what fortitude should bear.
    Listen, young blood, 'tis not true valour's pride
    To swagger, quarrel, swear, stamp, rave and chide,
    To stab in fume of blood, to keep loud coil,
    To bandy factions in domestic broil,   325
    To dare the act of sins whose filth excels
    The blackest customs of blind infidels.
    No, my loved youth, he may of valour vaunt
    Whom fortune's loudest thunder cannot daunt;
    Whom fretful galls of chance, stern fortune's siege   330
    Makes not his reason slink, the soul's fair liege;°
    Whose well-peised action ever rests upon
    Not giddy humours, but discretion.
    This heart in valour even Jove out-goes;
    Jove is without, but this 'bove sense of woes;   335
    And such a one, eternity. Behold!—
    [*To Felice's corpse*] Good morrow, son; thou bidd'st a fig for cold.—°

Sound louder music; let my breath exact
You strike sad tones unto this dismal act.°

[*Exeunt, and the curtain is closed on Felice's corpse*]

2.1

[A dumbshow.] The cornets sound a sennet. Enter two Mourners with torches, two with streamers; Castilio and Forobosco with torches; a Herald bearing Andrugio's helm and sword; the coffin [borne by Attendants]; Maria supported by Lucio and Alberto; Antonio by himself; Piero and Strozzo talking; Galeazzo and Mazzagente; Balurdo and Pandulfo. The coffin [is] set down; helm, sword, and streamers [are] hung up, placed by the Herald; whilst Antonio and Maria wet their handkerchiefs with their tears, kiss them, and lay them on the hearse, kneeling.° All go out but Piero. Cornets cease and he speaks

PIERO Rot there, thou cerecloth that enfolds the flesh
Of my loathed foe; moulder to crumbling dust;
Oblivion choke the passage of thy fame.
Trophies of honoured birth drop quickly down;
Let nought of him but what was vicious live.°   5
Though thou art dead, think not my hate is dead;
I have but newly twone my arm in the curled locks
Of snaky vengeance. Pale beetle-browed hate°
But newly bustles up. Sweet wrong, I clap thy thoughts.
O, let me hug my bosom, rub my breast,   10
In hope of what may hap. Andrugio rots.
Antonio lives. Umh! How long? Ha, ha? How long?
Antonio packed hence, I'll his mother wed,
Then clear my daughter of supposèd lust,
Wed her to Florence' heir. O excellent!   15
Venice, Genoa, Florence at my beck,
At Piero's nod. *[Calls to offstage]—Balurdo, ho!—*
O 'twill be rare, all unsuspected done.
I have been nursed in blood, and still have sucked
The steam of reeking gore.—Balurdo, ho!   20
      Enter Balurdo with a beard half off, half on°

BALURDO When my beard is on, most noble prince, when my beard
is on!

PIERO Why, what dost thou with a beard?

BALURDO In truth, one told me that my wit was bald, and that a
mermaid was half fish and half conger;° and therefore to speak   25
wisely, like one of your council—as indeed it hath pleased you to

73

make me, not only, being a fool, of your counsel,° but also to make
me of your council, being a fool—if my wit be bald and a mermaid
be half fish and half conger, then I must be forced to conclude—
the tiring-man hath not glued on my beard half fast enough. God's   30
bores, it will not stick to fall off.

PIERO Dost thou know what thou has spoken all this while?

BALURDO O Lord, duke, I would be sorry of that. Many men can
utter that which no man but themselves can conceive; but, I thank
a good wit, I have the gift to speak that which neither any man else   35
nor myself understands.

PIERO Thou art wise. He that speaks he knows not what shall never
sin against his own conscience. Go to, thou art wise.

BALURDO Wise? O no. I have a little natural discretion or so; but for
wise—I am somewhat prudent; but for wise—O Lord!   40

PIERO Hold, take those keys, open the castle vault and put in Mellida.

BALURDO And put in Mellida? Well, let me alone.

PIERO Bid Forobosco and Castilio guard;
Endear thyself Piero's intimate.   45

BALURDO 'Endear' and 'intimate'—good, I assure you. I will endear
and intimate Mellida into the dungeon presently.

PIERO Will Pandulfo Felice wait on me?

BALURDO I will make him come, most retort and obtuse, to you
presently. I think Sir Jeffrey talks like a councillor. Go to, God's   50
nigs, I think I tickle it!
    [Exit Balurdo]

PIERO I'll seem to wind yon fool with kindest arm.
He that's ambitious-minded, and but man,
Must have his followers beasts, dubbed slavish sots,
Whose service is obedience and whose wit   55
Reacheth no further than to admire their lord
And stare in adoration of his worth.
I love a slave raked out of common mud
Should seem to sit in counsel with my heart;
High honoured blood's too squeamish to assent   60
And lend a hand to an ignoble act;
Poison from roses who could e'er abstract?
    Enter Pandulfo
How now, Pandulfo, weeping for thy son?

PANDULFO No, no, Piero, weeping for my sins;
Had I been a good father, he had been   65

A gracious son.

PIERO   Pollution must be purged.

PANDULFO   Why tain'st thou then the air with stench of flesh,
And human putrefaction's noisome scent?
I pray his body. Who less boon can crave
Than to bestow upon the dead his grave?   70

PIERO   Grave? Why? Think'st thou he deserves a grave
That hath defiled the temple of—

PANDULFO   Peace, peace!
Methinks I hear a humming murmur creep°
From out his gelid wounds. Look on those lips,°
Those now lawn pillows, on whose tender softness   75
Chaste modest speech, stealing from out his breast,
Had wont to rest itself, as loath to post
From out so fair an inn. Look, look, they seem to stir
And breathe defiance to black obloquy.

PIERO   Think'st thou thy son could suffer wrongfully?   80

PANDULFO   A wise man wrongfully but never wrong
Can take; his breast's of such well-tempered proof°
It may be rased, not pierced by savage tooth
Of foaming malice; showers of darts may dark
Heaven's ample brow, but not strike out a spark,   85
Much less pierce the sun's cheek. Such songs as these
I often dittied till my boy did sleep;
But now I turn plain fool, alas, I weep.

PIERO   [aside] 'Fore heaven, he makes me shrug; would a were dead;°
He is a virtuous man. What has our court to do   90
With virtue, in the devil's name!—Pandulfo, hark:
My lustful daughter dies. Start not; she dies.
I pursue justice, I love sanctity
And an undefilèd temple of pure thoughts.
Shall I speak freely? Good Andrugio's dead;   95
And I do fear a fetch; but—umh! would I durst speak—
I do mistrust; but—umh! Death!—[Aside] Is he all, all man?
Hath he no part of mother in him, ha?
No lickerish womanish inquisitiveness?

PANDULFO   Andrugio's dead!   100

PIERO   Ay, and I fear his own unnatural blood,
To whom he gave life, hath given death for life.—
[Aside] How coldly he comes on! I see false suspect
Is viced, wrung hardly in a virtuous heart.—

Well, I could give you reason for my doubts.   105
You are of honoured birth, my very friend;
You know how god-like 'tis to root out sin.
Antonio is a villain. Will you join
In oath with me against the traitor's life,
And swear you knew he sought his father's death?   110
I loved him well, yet I love justice more;
Our friends we should affect, justice adore.

PANDULFO My lord, the clapper of my mouth's not glibbed
  With court oil; 'twill not strike on both sides yet.°

PIERO 'Tis just that subjects act commands of kings.   115

PANDULFO Command then just and honourable things.

PIERO Even so; myself then will traduce his guilt.

PANDULFO Beware, take heed, less guiltless blood be spilt.

PIERO Where only honest deeds to kings are free
  It is no empire, but a beggary.   120

PANDULFO Where more than noble deeds to kings are free
  It is no empire, but a tyranny.

PIERO Tush, juiceless greybeard, 'tis immunity
  Proper to princes that our state exacts,
  Our subjects not alone to bear, but praise our acts.   125

PANDULFO O, but that prince that worthful praise aspires,
  From hearts, and not from lips, applause desires.

PIERO Pish! True praise the brow of common men doth ring,
  False only girts the temple of a king.°
  He that hath strength and's ignorant of power,   130
  He was not made to rule, but to be ruled.

PANDULFO 'Tis praise to do not what we can but should.

PIERO Hence, doting stoic! By my hope of bliss,
  I'll make thee wretched.

PANDULFO Defiance to thy power, thou rifted chawn!°   135
  Now, by the loved heaven, sooner thou shalt
  Rinse thy foul ribs from the black filth of sin
  That soots thy heart than make me wretched. Pish!
  Thou canst not coop me up. Hadst thou a gaol
  With treble walls like antique Babylon,   140
  Pandulfo can get out. I tell thee, duke,
  I have old Fortunatus' wishing-cap°
  And can be where I list, even in a trice.
  I'll skip from earth into the arms of heaven,
  And from triumphal arch of blessedness   145

Spit on thy frothy breast. Thou canst not slave
Or banish me; I will be free, at home,
Maugre the beard of greatness. The portholes
Of sheathèd spirit are ne'er corbèd up°
But still stand open, ready to discharge   150
Their precious shot into the shrouds of heaven.°

PIERO O torture! Slave, I banish thee the town,
Thy native seat of birth.

PANDULFO How proud thou speak'st! I tell thee, duke, the blasts
Of the swoll'n-cheeked winds, nor all the breath of kings,   155
Can puff me out my native seat of birth.
The earth's my body's, and the heaven's my soul's
Most native place of birth, which they will keep
Despite the menace of mortality.°
Why, duke,   160
That's not my native place where I was rocked;
A wise man's home is whereso'er he is wise.°
Now, that from man, not from the place, doth rise.

PIERO Would I were deaf! O plague!—Hence, dotard wretch,
Tread not in court! All that thou hast I seize.—   165
[Aside] His quiet's firmer than I can disease.

PANDULFO Go, boast unto thy flatt'ring sycophants
Pandulfo's slave Piero hath o'erthrown.°
Loose fortune's rags are lost; my own's my own.
        Piero going out looks back
'Tis true, Piero; thy vexed heart shall see   170
Thou hast but tripped my slave, not conquered me.
        Exeunt at several doors

2.2

*Enter Antonio with a book, Lucio, Alberto; Antonio in
black*°

ALBERTO Nay, sweet, be comforted, take counsel and—

ANTONIO Alberto, peace! That grief is wanton-sick
Whose stomach can digest and brook the diet
Of stale ill-relished counsel. Pigmy cares
Can shelter under patience' shield, but giant griefs   5

Will burst all covert.

LUCIO   My lord, 'tis supper time.°

ANTONIO Drink deep, Alberto.—Eat, good Lucio.
But my pined heart shall eat on nought but woe.

ALBERTO My lord, we dare not leave you thus alone.

ANTONIO You cannot leave Antonio alone.   10
The chamber of my breast is even thronged
With firm attendance that forswears to flinch.
I have a thing sits here; it is not grief,
'Tis not despair, nor the most plague
That the most wretched are infected with,   15
But the most grief-full, despairing, wretched,
Accursèd, miserable—O, for heaven's sake,
Forsake me now; you see how light I am,
And yet you force me to defame my patience.°

LUCIO Fair gentle prince—   20

ANTONIO Away, thy voice is hateful, thou dost buzz,
And beat my ears with intimations
That Mellida—that Mellida is light
And stainèd with adulterous luxury.
I cannot brook't. I tell thee, Lucio,   25
Sooner will I give faith that virtue's cant°
In princes' courts will be adorned with wreath
Of choice respect, and endeared intimate;°
Sooner will I believe that friendship's rein
Will curb ambition from utility,   30
Than Mellida is light. Alas, poor soul,
Didst e'er see her, good heart, hast heard her speak?
Kind, kind soul! Incredulity itself
Would not be so brass-hearted as suspect
So modest cheeks.   35

LUCIO My lord—

ANTONIO Away! A self-own guilt doth only hatch distrust;°
But a chaste thought's as far from doubt as lust.
I entreat you leave me.

ALBERTO Will you endeavour to forget your grief?   40

ANTONIO I'faith I will, good friend, i'faith I will.
I'll come and eat with you. Alberto, see,
I am taking physic; here's philosophy.
        [Shows book]°
Good honest, leave me; I'll drink wine anon.

ALBERTO Since you enforce us, fair prince, we are gone.   45
        Exeunt Alberto and Lucio
ANTONIO (*reading*) '*Ferte fortiter: hoc est quo deum antecedatis. Ille
    enim extra patientiam malorum; vos supra. Contemnite dolorem: aut
    solvetur, aut solvet. Contemnite fortunam: nullum telum, quo feriret
    animum habet*'.°
    Pish! thy mother was not lately widowed,   50
    Thy dear affièd love lately defamed
    With blemish of foul lust when thou wrot'st thus.
    Thou, wrapped in furs, beeking thy limbs 'fore fires,
    Forbid'st the frozen zone to shudder. Ha, ha! 'Tis nought
    But foamy bubbling of a phlegmy brain,°   55
    Nought else but smoke. O, what dank, marish spirit
    But would be firèd with impatience
    At my—
    No more, no more; he that was never blessed
    With height of birth, fair expectation   60
    Of mounted fortunes, knows not what it is
    To be the pitied object of the world.
    O poor Antonio, thou may'st sigh!
MELLIDA [*beneath the stage*]° Ay me!
ANTONIO   And curse—
PANDULFO [*within*]   Black powers!
ANTONIO   And cry—
MARIA [*within*]   O heaven!
ANTONIO And close laments with—
ALBERTO [*within*]   O me most miserable!   65
PANDULFO [*within*] Woe for my dear, dear son!
MARIA [*within*] Woe for my dear, dear husband!
MELLIDA [*beneath*] Woe for my dear, dear love!
ANTONIO Woe for me all; close all your woes in me,°
    In me, Antonio! Ha! Where live these sounds?   70
    I can see nothing; grief's invisible
    And lurks in secret angles of the heart.
    Come, sigh again; Antonio bears his part.
MELLIDA [*at a grating*] O here, here is a vent to pass my sighs.
    I have surcharged the dungeon with my plaints;   75
    Prison and heart will burst if void of vent.
    Ay, that is Phoebe, empress of the night,°
    That 'gins to mount. O chastest deity,
    If I be false to my Antonio,

If the least soil of lust smears my pure love,   80
Make me more wretched, make me more accursed
Than infamy, torture, death, hell and heaven
Can bound with amplest power of thought; if not,°
Purge my poor heart from defamation's blot.

ANTONIO 'Purge my poor heart from defamation's blot'!   85
Poor heart, how like her virtuous self she speaks.—
Mellida, dear Mellida, it is Antonio;
Slink not away, 'tis thy Antonio.

MELLIDA How found you out, my lord? Alas, I know
'Tis easy in this age to find out woe.   90
I have a suit to you.

ANTONIO   What is't, dear soul?

MELLIDA Kill me; i'faith, I'll wink, not stir a jot.
For God's sake, kill me. In sooth, lovèd youth,
I am much injured; look, see how I creep.
I cannot wreak my wrong, but sigh and weep.   95

ANTONIO May I be cursèd, but I credit thee.

MELLIDA Tomorrow I must die.

ANTONIO   Alas, for what?

MELLIDA For loving thee; 'tis true, my sweetest breast.
I must die falsely; so must thou, dear heart.
Nets are a-knitting to entrap thy life.   100
Thy father's death must make a paradise
To my—I shame to call him—father. Tell me, sweet,
Shall I die thine? Dost love me still, and still?

ANTONIO I do.

MELLIDA   Then welcome heaven's will.

ANTONIO   Madam,
I will not swell like a tragedian   105
In forcèd passion of affected strains.
If I had present power of aught but pitying you,
I would be as ready to redress your wrongs
As to pursue your love. Throngs of thoughts
Crowd for their passage; somewhat I will do.   110
Reach me thy hand; think this is honour's bent,
To live unslavèd, to die innocent.

MELLIDA Let me entreat a favour, gracious love:
Be patient, see me die. Good, do not weep.
Go sup, sweet chuck; drink and securely sleep.   115

ANTONIO I'faith, I cannot; but I'll force my face

To palliate my sickness.°

MELLIDA Give me thy hand. Peace on thy bosom dwell;
That's all my woe can breathe. Kiss; thus farewell.

ANTONIO Farewell.—My heart is great of thoughts—stay, dove—   120
And therefore I must speak. But what?—O love!
By this white hand, no more! Read in these tears
What crushing anguish thy Antonio bears.

> *Antonio kisseth Mellida's hand. Then Mellida goes from the
> grate*

MELLIDA Goodnight, good heart.

ANTONIO Thus heat from blood, thus souls from bodies part.   125

> [*Lies down and weeps.*] *Enter Piero and Strozzo*

PIERO He grieves! Laugh, Strozzo, laugh. He weeps!
Hath he tears? O pleasure! Hath he tears?
Now do I scourge Andrugio with steel whips
Of knotty vengeance. Strozzo, cause me straight
Some plaining ditty to augment despair.°   130

> [*Exit Strozzo*]

Triumph, Piero. Hark, he groans. O rare!

ANTONIO Behold a prostrate wretch laid on his tomb;
His epitaph thus: *Ne plus ultra*. Ho!°
Let none out-woe me; mine's Herculean woe.

> *A song is sung* [*off-stage*]. *Exit Piero at the end of the song.*
> *Enter Maria*

ANTONIO May I be more cursed than heaven can make me   135
If I am not more wretched than man can conceive me.
Sore forlorn orphan, what omnipotence
Can make thee happy?

MARIA   How now, sweet son?
Good youth, what dost thou?

ANTONIO   Weep, weep.

MARIA Dost nought but weep, weep?   140

ANTONIO Yes, mother, I do sigh and wring my hands,
Beat my poor breast and wreathe my tender arms.°
Hark ye; I'll tell you wondrous strange, strange news.

MARIA What, my good boy, stark mad?

ANTONIO   I am not.

MARIA Alas, is that strange news?   145

ANTONIO Strange news? Why mother, is't not wondrous strange
I am not mad, I run not frantic, ha?
Knowing my father's trunk scarce cold, your love

Is sought by him that doth pursue my life?
Seeing the beauty of creation,   150
Antonio's bride, pure heart, defamed, and stowed
Under the hatches of obscuring earth?
Heu quo labor, quo vota ceciderunt mea?°
      Enter Piero
PIERO Good evening to the fair Antonio,
Most happy fortune, sweet succeeding time,   155
Rich hope. Think not thy fate a bankrupt though—
ANTONIO [*aside*] Umh! The devil in his good time and tide forsake
thee!
PIERO How now? Hark ye, prince.
ANTONIO   God be with you.
PIERO Nay, noble blood, I hope ye not suspect—   160
ANTONIO Suspect? I scorn't. Here's cap and leg. Goodnight.°
[*Aside*] Thou that wants power, with dissemblance fight.
      Exit Antonio
PIERO Madam, O that you could remember to forget—
MARIA I had a husband and a happy son.
PIERO Most powerful beauty, that enchanting grace—   165
MARIA Talk not of beauty, nor enchanting grace;
My husband's dead, my son's distraught, accursed.
Come, I must vent my griefs, or heart will burst.
      Exit Maria
PIERO She's gone, and yet she's here; she hath left a print
Of her sweet graces fixed within my heart   170
As fresh as is her face. I'll marry her.
She's most fair, true; most chaste, false
Because most fair. 'Tis firm, I'll marry her.°
      Enter Strozzo
STROZZO My lord!
PIERO   Ha, Strozzo, my other soul, my life!
Dear, hast thou steeled the point of thy resolve?   175
Will't not turn edge in execution?
STROZZO No.
PIERO Do it with rare passion, and present thy guilt
As if 'twere wrung out with thy conscience' grip.
Swear that my daughter's innocent of lust   180
And that Antonio bribed thee to defame
Her maiden honour, on inveterate hate
Unto my blood; and that thy hand was fee'd

By his large bounty for his father's death.
Swear plainly that thou chok'dst Andrugio   185
By his son's only egging. Rush me in°
Whilst Mellida prepares herself to die,
Halter about thy neck, and with such sighs,
Laments and acclamations liven it,
As if impulsive power of remorse—   190
STROZZO I'll weep.
PIERO Ay, ay, fall on thy face and cry, 'Why suffer you
So lewd a slave as Strozzo is to breathe?'
STROZZO I'll beg a strangling, grow importunate—
PIERO As if thy life were loathsome to thee. Then I   195
Catch straight the cord's end, and, as much incensed
With thy damned mischiefs, offer a rude hand
As ready to gird in thy pipe of breath.
But on the sudden straight I'll stand amazed
And fall in exclamations of thy virtues.   200
STROZZO Applaud my agonies and penitence.
PIERO Thy honest stomach that could not digest
The crudities of murder, but, surcharged,
Vomited'st them up in Christian piety.
STROZZO Then clip me in your arms.   205
PIERO And call thee brother, mount thee straight to state,
Make thee of council. Tut, tut! what not, what not?
Think on 't, be confident, pursue the plot.
STROZZO Look, here's a trope: a true rogue's lips are mute;
I do not use to speak, but execute.   210
        He lays his finger on his mouth and draws his dagger. [Then exit
        Strozzo.]
PIERO So, so; run headlong to confusion,
Thou slight-brained mischief; thou art made as dirt
To plaster up the bracks of my defects.
I'll wring what may be squeezed from out his use,
And goodnight, Strozzo. Swell plump, bold heart,   215
For now thy tide of vengeance rolleth in.
O now *Tragoedia Cothurnata* mounts;°
Piero's thoughts are fixed on dire exploits.
Pell-mell confusion and black murder guides
The organs of my spirit. Shrink not, heart;   220
Capienda rebus in malis praeceps via est.°
        [Exit]

3.1

A dumbshow. The cornets sounding for the act. [A tomb is set out.] Enter Castilio and Forobosco, Alberto and Balurdo, with poleaxes. Strozzo [enters], talking with Piero [who] seemeth to send out Strozzo. Exit Strozzo. Enter Strozzo, with Maria, Nutrice, and Lucio. Piero passeth through his guard, and talks [with Maria] with seeming amorousness. She seemeth to reject his suit, flies to the tomb, kneels, and kisseth it. Piero bribes Nutrice and Lucio. They go to [Maria], seeming to solicit his suit. She riseth, offers to go out; Piero stayeth her, tears open his breast, embraceth and kisseth her, and so they go all out in state°

3.2

[The tomb set out as before.] Enter two Pages, the one with two tapers, the other with a chafing-dish, a perfume in it. Antonio, in his nightgown and a nightcap, unbraced, following after

ANTONIO The black jades of swart night trot foggy rings
'Bout heaven's brow.
   [Clock strikes twelve]
       'Tis now stark dead night.
Is this Saint Mark's Church?
1 PAGE It is, my lord.
ANTONIO   Where stands my father's hearse?
2 PAGE Those streamers bear his arms. Ay, that is it.   5
ANTONIO Set tapers to the tomb and lamp the church;
Give me the fire.
   [Page hands over the chafing-dish]
      Now depart and sleep.
   Exeunt Pages
I purify the air with odorous fume.
   [He swings the chafing-dish]
Graves, vaults and tombs, groan not to bear my weight;
Cold flesh, bleak trunks, wrapped in your half-rot shrouds, 10
I press you softly with a tender foot.

Most honoured sepulchre, vouchsafe a wretch
Leave to weep o'er thee. Tomb, I'll not be long
Ere I creep in thee, and with bloodless lips
Kiss my cold father's cheek. I prithee, grave,   15
Provide soft mould to wrap my carcass in.
Thou royal spirit of Andrugio,
Where'er thou hover'st, airy intellect,
I heave up tapers to thee—view thy son—
In celebration of due obsequies.   20
Once every night I'll dew thy funeral hearse
With my religious tears.
O, blessèd father of a cursèd son,
Thou died'st most happy since thou lived'st not
To see thy son most wretched and thy wife   25
Pursued by him that seeks my guiltless blood.
O, in what orb thy mighty spirit soars,
Stoop and beat down this rising fog of shame
That strives to blur thy blood and girt defame
About my innocent and spotless brows.   30
Non est mori miserum, sed misere mori.°
          [*Enter Andrugio's ghost from the tomb*]°
GHOST OF ANDRUGIO Thy pangs of anguish rip my cerecloth up,
And lo, the ghost of old Andrugio
Forsakes his coffin. Antonio, revenge!
I was empoisoned by Piero's hand;   35
Revenge my blood; take spirit, gentle boy;
Revenge my blood! Thy Mellida is chaste;
Only to frustrate thy pursuit in love
Is blazed unchaste. Thy mother yields consent
To be his wife and give his blood a son,   40
That made her husbandless and doth complot
To make her sonless; but before I touch
The banks of rest, my ghost shall visit her.°
Thou vigour of my youth, juice of my love,
Seize on revenge, grasp the stern-bended front   45
Of frowning vengeance with unpeisèd clutch.
Alarum Nemesis, rouse up thy blood,°
Invent some stratagem of vengeance
Which but to think on may like lightning glide
With horror through thy breast. Remember this: 50
Scelera non ulcisceris, nisi vincis.°

> *Exit Andrugio's ghost. Enter Maria, her hair about her ears,°*
> *Nutrice and Lucio with [the] Pages and torches*

MARIA Where left you him? Show me, good boys.
  [*They point to Antonio*]

                                          Away!

  [*Exeunt Pages*]

NUTRICE God's me, your hair!

MARIA   Nurse, 'tis not yet proud day;
  The neat gay mistress of the light's not up,
  Her cheeks not yet slurred over with the paint   55
  Of borrowed crimson; the unprankèd world
  Wears yet the night-clothes. Let flare my loosed hair;
  I scorn the presence of the night.
  Where's my boy? Run! I'll range about the church
  Like frantic Bacchanal or Jason's wife°   60
  Invoking all the spirits of the graves
  To tell me where.—[*Seeing Antonio*] Ha! O, my poor wretched
      blood,
  What dost thou up at midnight, my kind boy?
  Dear soul, to bed! O, thou hast struck a fright
  Unto thy mother's panting—   65

ANTONIO *O quisquis nova*
  Supplicia functis durus umbrarum arbiter
  Disponis, quisquis exeso iaces
  Pavidus sub antro, quisquis venturi times
  Montis ruinam, quisquis avidorum feros,   70
  Rictus leonum, et dira furiarum agmina
  Implicitus horres, Antonii vocem excipe
  Properantis ad vos: Ulciscar.°

MARIA Alas, my son's distraught.—Sweet boy, appease
  Thy mutining affections.°   75

ANTONIO By the astoning terror of swart night,
  By the infectious damps of clammy graves,
  And by the mould that presseth down
  My dead father's skull, I'll be revenged!

MARIA Wherefore? on whom? for what? Go, go to bed,   80
  Good, duteous son. Ho, but 'tis idle.°

ANTONIO So I may sleep tombed in an honoured hearse;
  So may my bones rest in that sepulchre.

MARIA Forget not duty, son; to bed, to bed.°

ANTONIO May I be cursèd by my father's ghost   85

And blasted with incensèd breath of heaven
If my heart beat on aught but vengeance!
May I be numbed with horror and my veins
Pucker with singeing torture, if my brain
Digest a thought but of dire vengeance!   90
May I be fettered slave to coward chance,
If blood, heart, brain, plot aught save vengeance!
MARIA Wilt thou to bed? I wonder when thou sleep'st.
  I'faith, thou look'st sunk-eyed; go couch thy head;
  Now, faith, 'tis idle; sweet, sweet son, to bed.   95
ANTONIO I have a prayer or two to offer up
  For the good, good prince, my most dear, dear lord,
  The Duke Piero, and your virtuous self;
  And then when those prayers have obtained success,
  In sooth I'll come—believe it now—and couch   100
  My head in downy mould. But first I'll see
  You safely laid. I'll bring ye all to bed,
  Piero, Maria, Strozzo, Lucio,°
  I'll see you all laid; I'll bring you all to bed,
  And then, i'faith, I'll come and couch my head   105
  And sleep in peace.
MARIA   Look then, we go before.°
    Exeunt all but Antonio
ANTONIO Ay, so you must, before we touch the shore
  Of wished revenge.—O you departed souls
  That lodge in coffined trunks which my feet press,
  If Pythagorean axioms be true°   110
  Of spirits' transmigration, fleet no more
  To human bodies; rather live in swine,
  Inhabit wolves' flesh, scorpions, dogs and toads,
  Rather than man. The curse of heaven rains
  In plagues unlimited through all his days;   115
  His mature age grows only mature vice,
  And ripens only to corrupt and rot
  The budding hopes of infant modesty;
  Still striving to be more than man, he proves
  More than a devil; devilish suspect,   120
  Devilish cruelty, all hell-strained juice
  Is pourèd to his veins, making him drunk
  With fuming surquedries, contempt of heaven,
  Untamed arrogance, lust, state, pride, murder.

[Pandulfo] from above and [the ghosts from] beneath°

GHOST OF ANDRUGIO Murder!   125

GHOST OF FELICE Murder!

PANDULFO Murder!

ANTONIO Ay, I will murder; graves and ghosts
Fright me no more; I'll suck red vengeance
Out of Piero's wounds.

GHOSTS *[under the stage]* Piero's wounds!°   130
*[Antonio withdraws.] Enter two Boys [with torches], with Piero
in his nightgown and nightcap*

PIERO Maria, love, Maria!—She took this aisle.
Left you her here? On, lights; away!
I think we shall not warm our beds today.
      Enter Julio, Forobosco, and Castilio

JULIO Ho, father! Father!

PIERO How now, Julio, my little pretty son?—   135
[To Forobosco] Why suffer you the child to walk so late?

FOROBOSCO He will not sleep, but calls to follow you,
Crying that bugbears and spirits haunted him.
      Antonio offers to come near and stab Piero

ANTONIO *[aside]* No, not so.
      Presently withdraws [again]
This shall be sought for; I'll force him feed on life   140
Till he shall loathe it. This shall be the close
Of vengeance' strain.°

PIERO Away there! Pages, lead on fast with light;
The church is full of damps; 'tis yet dead night.
      Exeunt all, saving Julio [and Antonio]

JULIO Brother Antonio, are you here, i'faith?   145
Why do you frown? Indeed, my sister said
That I should call you brother, that she did,
When you were married to her. Buss me; good truth,
I love you better than my father, 'deed.

ANTONIO Thy father?—Gracious, O bounteous heaven!   150
I do adore thy justice. *Venit in nostras manus
Tandem vindicta, venit et tota quidem.*°

JULIO 'Truth, since my mother died I loved you best.
Something hath angered you; pray you, look merrily.

ANTONIO I will laugh, and dimple my thin cheek   155
With cap'ring joy. Chuck, my heart doth leap

To grasp thy bosom.
    [*He clasps Julio*]
              —Time, place and blood,
How fit you close together! Heaven's tones°
Strike not such music to immortal souls
As your accordance sweets my breast withal.   160
Methinks I pass upon the front of Jove,
And kick corruption with a scornful heel,
Griping this flesh, disdain mortality.
O that I knew which joint, which side, which limb
Were father all and had no mother in't,   165
That I might rip it vein by vein and carve revenge
In bleeding rases! But since 'tis mixed together,
Have at adventure, pell-mell, no reverse!—
Come hither, boy. This is Andrugio's hearse.
    [*Antonio draws his dagger*]
JULIO O God! you'll hurt me. For my sister's sake,   170
Pray you, do not hurt me. An you kill me, 'deed,
I'll tell my father.
ANTONIO O, for thy sister's sake I flag revenge.
GHOST OF ANDRUGIO [*under the stage*]° Revenge!
ANTONIO Stay, stay, dear father; fright mine eyes no more.   175
Revenge as swift as lightning bursteth forth
And cleaves his heart.—Come, pretty, tender child,
It is not thee I hate, not thee I kill.
Thy father's blood that flows within thy veins
Is it I loathe, is that revenge must suck.   180
I love thy soul; and were thy heart lapped up
In any flesh but in Piero's blood,
I would thus kiss it; but being his, thus, thus,
And thus I'll punch it.
    [*He stabs Julio*]
              Abandon fears;
Whilst thy wounds bleed, my brows shall gush out tears.   185
JULIO So you will love me, do even what you will.
ANTONIO Now barks the wolf against the full-cheeked moon;
Now lions' half-clammed entrails roar for food;
Now croaks the toad, and night-crows screech aloud,
Fluttering 'bout casements of departing souls;   190
Now gapes the graves and through their yawns let loose
Imprisoned spirits to revisit earth;

And now, swart night, to swell thy hour out,
Behold I spurt warm blood in thy black eyes.
        From under the stage a groan
ANTONIO Howl not, thou putry mould, groan not, ye graves;   195
Be dumb, all breath. Here stands Andrugio's son,
Worthy his father.
        [*Checks to see that Julio is dead*]
                So, I feel no breath;
His jaws are fall'n, his dislodged soul is fled,
And now there's nothing but Piero left.
He is all Piero, father all; this blood,   200
This breast, this heart, Piero all,
Whom thus I mangle.——Sprite of Julio,
Forget this was thy trunk. I live thy friend.
May'st thou be twinèd with the soft'st embrace
Of clear eternity; but thy father's blood   205
I thus make incense of, to vengeance!
        [*Sprinkles the tomb with blood*]°
Ghost of my poisoned sire, suck this fume;
To sweet revenge, perfume thy circling air
With smoke of blood. I sprinkle round his gore,
And dew thy hearse with these fresh-reeking drops.   210
Lo, thus I heave my blood-dyed hands to heaven;
Even like insatiate hell still crying 'More!'
My heart hath thirsting dropsies after gore.
Sound peace and rest to church, night-ghosts and graves;
Blood cries for blood, and murder murder craves.°   215
        [*Exit, with Julio's body*]

3.3

        *Enter two Pages with torches, Maria, her hair loose [and
        weeping], and Nutrice*
NUTRICE Fie, fie! Tomorrow your wedding day and weep! God's my
    comfort, Andrugio could do well, Piero may do better. I have had
    four husbands myself. The first I called 'Sweet Duck'; the second
    'Dear Heart'; the third 'Pretty Pug'; but the fourth, most sweet,
    dear, pretty All-in-all, he was the very cockall of a husband. What,   5

lady? Your skin is smooth, your blood warm, your cheek fresh, your eye quick; change of pasture makes fat calves, choice of linen clean bodies, and—no question—variety of husbands perfect wives. I would you should know it, as few teeth as I have in my head, I have read Aristotle's *Problems,*° which saith that woman receiveth perfection by the man. What then by the men? Go to, to bed; lie on your back; dream not on Piero. I say no more; tomorrow is your wedding; do, dream not of Piero.

    Enter Balurdo with a bass viol

MARIA What an idle prate thou keep'st! Good nurse, go sleep.
    I have a mighty task of tears to weep.

BALURDO Lady, with a most retort and obtuse leg,
    I kiss the curled locks of your loose hair. [*Bows*]
    The duke hath sent you the most musical Sir Jeffrey, with his not base but most ennobled viol, to rock your baby thoughts in the cradle of sleep.

MARIA I give the noble duke respective thanks.

BALURDO 'Respective'—truly, a very pretty word. Indeed, madam, I have the most respective fiddle. [*Plucks it*] Did you ever smell a more sweet sound? My ditty must go thus—very witty, I assure you; I myself in an humorous passion made it, to the tune of my mistress Nutrice's beauty. Indeed, very pretty, very retort and obtuse, I'll assure you. 'Tis thus:

> *My mistress' eye doth oil my joints,*
>   *And makes my fingers nimble;*
> *O love, come on, untruss your points,*
>   *My fiddlestick wants rosin.*°
> *My lady's dugs are all so smooth,*
>   *That no flesh must them handle;*
> *Her eyes do shine, for to say sooth,*
>   *Like a new-snuffèd candle.*

MARIA Truly, very pathetical and unvulgar.

BALURDO 'Pathetical' and 'unvulgar'—words of worth, excellent words! In sooth, madam, I have taken a murr which makes my nose run most pathetically and unvulgarly. Have you any tobacco?°

MARIA Good signor, your song.

BALURDO Instantly, most unvulgarly, at your service. Truly, here's the most pathetical rosin. [*Clearing throat*] Umh!

    [*Balurdo*] sings [*the song and is accompanied by the Pages*]

MARIA In sooth, most knightly sung, and like Sir Jeffrey.

BALURDO Why, look you, lady, I was made a knight only for my
voice,° and a councillor only for my wit.   45

MARIA I believe it. Goodnight, gentle sir, goodnight.

BALURDO You will give me leave to take my leave of my mistress,
and I will do it most famously in rhyme.—
[*To Nutrice*]
         Farewell, adieu, saith thy love true,
            As to part loath;   50
         Time bids us part, mine own sweetheart,
            God bless us both.
    Exit Balurdo

MARIA Goodnight, Nutrice.—Pages, leave the room.
The life of night grows short, 'tis almost dead.
    Exeunt Pages and Nutrice
O thou cold widow-bed, sometime thrice blest   55
By the warm pressure of my sleeping lord,
Open thy leaves, and whilst on thee I tread
Groan out, 'Alas, my dear Andrugio's dead!'
    *Maria draweth the curtain, and the Ghost of Andrugio is
    displayed, sitting on the bed*°
Amazing terror! What portent is this?

GHOST OF ANDRUGIO Disloyal to our hymeneal rites,   60
What raging heat reigns in thy strumpet blood?
Hast thou so soon forgot Andrugio?
Are our love-bands so quickly cancellèd?
Where lives thy plighted faith unto this breast?°
O weak Maria! Go to, calm thy fears.   65
I pardon thee, poor soul. O, shed no tears.
Thy sex is weak. That black incarnate fiend
May trip thy faith that hath o'erthrown my life.
I was empoisoned by Piero's hand.
Join with my son to bend up strained revenge;   70
Maintain a seeming favour to his suit,
Till time may form our vengeance absolute
    *Enter Antonio, his arms bloody, [carrying] a torch and a
    poniard*°

ANTONIO [*to the Ghost*] See, unamazed I will behold thy face,
Outstare the terror of thy grim aspect,
Daring the horrid'st object of the night.   75
Look how I smoke in blood, reeking the steam

Of foaming vengeance. O, my soul's enthroned
In the triumphant chariot of revenge.
Methinks I am all air and feel no weight
Of human dirt clog. This is Julio's blood,   80
Rich music, father; this is Julio's blood.
Why lives that mother?
GHOST OF ANDRUGIO Pardon ignorance. Fly, dear Antonio.°
Once more assume disguise, and dog the court
In feignèd habit till Piero's blood°   85
May even o'erflow the brim of full revenge.
Peace and all blessèd fortunes to you both.
[*To Antonio*] Fly thou from court, be peerless in revenge.
 Exit Antonio
[*To Maria*] Sleep thou in rest. Lo, here I close thy couch.
 Exit Maria to her bed, Andrugio drawing the curtains°
And now, ye sooty coursers of the night,   90
Hurry your chariot into hell's black womb.
Darkness, make flight; graves, eat your dead again;°
Let's repossess our shrouds. Why lags delay?
Mount, sparkling brightness, give the world his day.
 Exit

4.1

Enter Antonio in a fool's habit, with a little toy of a
walnut shell and soap to make bubbles; Maria and Alberto
[follow]

MARIA Away with this disguise in any hand!

ALBERTO Fie, 'tis unsuiting to your elate spirit.
  Rather put on some trans-shaped cavalier,°
  Some habit of a spitting critic, whose mouth
  Voids nothing but genteel and unvulgar   5
  Rheum of censure. Rather assume—

ANTONIO Why, then should I put on the very flesh
  Of solid folly! No, this coxcomb is a crown
  Which I affect even with unbounded zeal.

ALBERTO 'Twill thwart your plot, disgrace your high resolve.   10

ANTONIO By wisdom's heart, there is no essence mortal
  That I can envy but a plump-cheeked fool.
  O, he hath a patent of immunities
  Confirmed by custom, sealed by policy,
  As large as spacious thought.°   15

ALBERTO You cannot press among the courtiers
  And have access to—

ANTONIO What? Not a fool? Why, friend, a golden ass,
  A baubled fool, are sole canonical,
  Whilst pale-cheeked wisdom and lean-ribbèd art   20
  Are kept in distance at the halberd's point,
  All held apocrypha, not worth survey.°
  Why, by the genius of that Florentine,
  Deep, deep-observing, sound-brained Machiavel,
  He is not wise that strives not to seem fool.°   25
  When will the duke hold fee'd intelligence,
  Keep wary observation in large pay,
  To dog a fool's act?

MARIA Ay, but such feigning, known, disgraceth much.

ANTONIO Pish!   30
  Most things that morally adhere to souls
  Wholly exist in drunk opinion,
  Whose reeling censure, if I value not,
  It values nought.

MARIA You are transported with too slight a thought,°   35

If you but meditate of what is past
And what you plot to pass.

ANTONIO   Even in that, note a fool's beatitude:
He is not capable of passion;
Wanting the power of distinction,   40
He bears an unturned sail with every wind;
Blow east, blow west, he steers his course alike.
I never saw a fool lean; the chub-faced fop
Shines sleek with full-crammed fat of happiness,
Whilst studious contemplation sucks the juice   45
From wizards' cheeks, who, making curious search
For nature's secrets, the first innating cause°
Laughs them to scorn, as man doth busy apes
When they will zany men. Had heaven been kind,°
Creating me an honest, senseless dolt,   50
A good, poor fool, I should want sense to feel
The stings of anguish shoot through every vein;
I should not know what 'twere to lose a father;
I should be dead of sense to view defame°
Blur my bright love; I could not thus run mad   55
As one confounded in a maze of mischief,
Staggered, stark felled with bruising stroke of chance;
I should not shoot mine eyes into the earth,
Poring for mischief that might counterpoise
Mischief, murder, and—
            Enter Lucio
                                How now, Lucio?   60
LUCIO   My lord, the duke with the Venetian states
Approach the great hall to judge Mellida.

ANTONIO   Asked he for Julio yet?

LUCIO   No motion of him. Dare you trust this habit?°

ANTONIO   Alberto, see you straight rumour me dead.—   65
Leave me, good mother.—Leave me, Lucio.
Forsake me all.
            Exeunt all, saving Antonio
                        Now patience hoop my sides
With steelèd ribs, lest I do burst my breast
With struggling passions. Now disguise stand bold.
Poor scornèd habits oft choice souls enfold.   70
            *The cornets sound a sennet. Enter Castilio, Forobosco, Balurdo,
            and Alberto with poleaxes; Lucio bare[headed];° Piero and*

95

Maria talking together; two Senators, Galeazzo and Mazza-
gente, Nutrice. [Piero takes the throne]

PIERO [*to Maria*] Entreat me not. There's not a beauty lives
Hath that imperial predominance
O'er my affects as your enchanting graces;
Yet give me leave to be myself—
ANTONIO [*aside*] A villain!   75
PIERO Just—
ANTONIO [*aside*] Most just!°
PIERO Most just and upright in our judgment seat.
Were Mellida mine eye, with such a blemish
Of most loathed looseness, I would scratch it out.—   80
Produce the strumpet in her bridal robes
That she may blush t'appear so white in show
And black in inward substance. Bring her in.
        Exeunt Forobosco and Castilio
I hold Antonio, for his father's sake,
So very dearly, so entirely choice,   85
That knew I but a thought of prejudice
Imagined 'gainst his high ennobled blood,
I would maintain a mortal feud, undying hate,
'Gainst the conceiver's life. And shall justice sleep
In fleshly lethargy for mine own blood's favour,   90
When the sweet prince hath so apparent scorn
By my—I will not call her 'daughter'?—Go,
Conduct in the loved youth, Antonio.
        Exit Alberto to fetch Antonio
He shall behold me spurn my private good;
Piero loves his honour more than's blood.   95
ANTONIO [*aside*] The devil he does, more than both!
BALURDO [*to Antonio*] Stand back there, fool.—I do hate a fool
most...most pathetically. O, these that have no sap of...of retort
and obtuse wit in them, faugh!
ANTONIO [*blowing bubbles*] Puff! hold, world! Puff! hold, bubble!   100
Puff! hold, world! Puff! break not behind! Puff! thou art full
of wind. Puff! keep up by wind. Puff! 'tis broke. And now I
laugh like a good fool at the breath of mine own lips. He, he, he,
he, he!
BALURDO You fool!   105
ANTONIO You fool! Puff!°

BALURDO I cannot digest thee, thou unvulgar° fool. Go, fool.
PIERO Forbear, Balurdo, let the fool alone.—
(*Affectedly*)° [*to Antonio*] Come hither.—[*To Maria*] Is he your fool?
MARIA Yes, my loved lord.   110
PIERO [*aside*] Would all the states in Venice were like thee;
  O, then I were secured!
  He that's a villain or but meanly souled
  Must still converse and cling to routs of fools
  That cannot search the leaks of his defects.   115
  O, your unsalted fresh fool is your only man;
  These vinegar-tart spirits are too piercing,
  Too searching in the unglued joints of shaken wits.°
  Find they a chink, they'll wriggle in and in,
  And eat like salt sea in his siddow ribs   120
  Till they have opened all his rotten parts
  Unto the vaunting surge of base contempt,
  And sunk the tossèd galliass in depth
  Of whirlpool scorn. Give me an honest fop.
  [*To Antonio*] Dud-a, dud-a. [*Gives present*]—Why, lo, sir, this takes   125
  he°
  As grateful now as a monopoly.°
      The still flutes° sound softly. Enter Forobosco and Castilio;
      [and] Mellida [in white], supported by two Waiting-Women
MELLIDA All honour to this royal confluence.
PIERO Forbear, impure, to blot bright honour's name
  With thy defilèd lips. The flux of sin
  Flows from thy tainted body; thou, so foul,   130
  So all-dishonoured, canst no honour give,
  No wish of good that can have good effect
  To this grave senate and illustrate bloods.—
  Why stays the doom of death?
1 SENATOR Who riseth up to manifest her guilt?   135
2 SENATOR You must produce apparent proof, my lord.
PIERO Why, where is Strozzo, he that swore he saw
  The very act, and vowed that Felice fled
  Upon his sight? on which I brake the breast
  Of the adulterous lecher with five stabs.—   140
  Go, fetch in Strozzo.—
     [*Exit Castilio*]
  [*To Mellida*]   Now, thou impudent,

If thou hast any drop of modest blood
Shrouded within thy cheeks, blush, blush for shame,
That rumour yet may say thou felt'st defame.

MELLIDA   Produce the devil, let your Strozzo come;   145
    I can defeat his strongest argument
    Which—

PIERO   With what?

MELLIDA   With tears, with blushes, sighs and claspèd hands,
    With innocent uprearèd arms to heaven;   150
    With my unnooked simplicity. These, these°
    Must, will, can only quit my heart of guilt;
    Heaven permits not taintless blood be spilt.
    If no remorse live in your savage breast—

PIERO   Then thou must die.

MELLIDA   Yet dying, I'll be blest.   155

PIERO   Accursed by me.

MELLIDA   Yet blest, in that I strove
    To live and die—

PIERO   My hate.

MELLIDA   —Antonio's love!

ANTONIO [aside] Antonio's love!

      Enter Strozzo, a cord about his neck, [and Castilio]

STROZZO   O what vast ocean of repentant tears
    Can cleanse my breast from the polluting filth   160
    Of ulcerous sin? Supreme Efficient,°
    Why cleav'st thou not my breast with thunderbolts
    Of winged revenge?

PIERO   What means this passion?

ANTONIO [aside] What villainy are they decocting now?
    Umh?   165

STROZZO   *In me convertite ferrum, O proceres.*
    Nihil iste, nec ista.°

PIERO   Lay hold on him. What strange portent is this?

STROZZO   I will not flinch. Death, hell, more grimly stare
    Within my heart than in your threat'ning brows.   170
    Record, thou threefold guard of dreadest power,°
    What I here speak is forcèd from my lips
    By the impulsive strain of conscience.
    I have a mount of mischief clogs my soul
    As weighty as the high-nolled Apennine,   175
    Which I must straight disgorge or breast will burst.
    I have defamed this lady wrongfully,

By instigation of Antonio,
Whose reeling love, tossed on each fancy's surge,
Began to loathe before it fully joyed. 180
PIERO Go seize Antonio! Guard him strongly in!
    Exit Forobosco
STROZZO By his ambition being only bribed,
Fee'd by his impious hand, I poisonèd
His agèd father, that his thirsty hopes
Might quench their dropsy of aspiring drought 185
With full unbounded quaff.
PIERO   Seize me Antonio!°
STROZZO O why permit you now such scum of filth
As Strozzo is to live and taint the air
With his infectious breath?
PIERO Myself will be thy strangler, unmatched slave. 190
    Piero comes from his chair, snatcheth the cord's end, and Castilio
    aideth him
STROZZO[*To Piero*] Now change your—
PIERO   Ay, pluck, Castilio.
    [*To Strozzo*] I change my humour?—Pluck, Castilio.—
    [*To Strozzo*] Die, with thy death's entreats even in thy jaws!—°
        [*Piero and Castilio*] strangle Strozzo
Now, now, now, now, now! [*Aside*] My plot begins to work.
Why, thus should statesmen do, 195
That cleave through knots of craggy policies,
Use men like wedges, one strike out another,
Till by degrees the tough and knurly trunk
Be rived in sunder.—Where's Antonio?
        Enter Alberto, running
ALBERTO O black accursèd fate! Antonio's drowned. 200
PIERO Speak, on thy faith; on thy allegiance, speak!
ALBERTO As I do love Piero, he is drowned.
ANTONIO [*aside*] In an inundation of amazement!
MELLIDA Ay, is this the close of all my strains in love?
O me, most wretched maid! 205
PIERO Antonio drowned? How, how? Antonio drowned?
ALBERTO Distraught and raving, from a turret's top
He threw his body in the high-swoll'n sea,
And as he headlong topsy-turvy dinged down,
He still cried 'Mellida!'
ANTONIO [*aside*]   My love's bright crown! 210

MELLIDA He still cried 'Mellida'!

PIERO Daughter, methinks your eyes should sparkle joy,
    Your bosom rise on tiptoe at this news.

MELLIDA Ay me!

PIERO How now? 'Ay me'? Why, art not great of thanks   215
    To gracious heaven for the just revenge
    Upon the author of thy obloquies?

MARIA [aside] Sweet beauty, I could sigh as fast as you,
    But that I know that which I weep to know:
    His fortunes should be such he dare not show   220
    His open presence.

MELLIDA I know he loved me dearly, dearly I;°
    And since I cannot live with him, I die.
        [Faints]

PIERO 'Fore heaven, her speech falters; look, she swoons.
    Convey her up into her private bed.   225
        Maria, Nutrice, and the Ladies bear out Mellida, as being
        swooned
    I hope she'll live. If not—

ANTONIO   Antonio's dead!
    The fool will follow too. He, he, he!
    [Aside] Now works the scene; quick observation scud
    To cote the plot or else the path is lost.
    My very self am gone, my way is fled;   230
    Ay, all is lost if Mellida is dead.
        Exit Antonio

PIERO Alberto, I am kind, Alberto, kind;
    I am sorry for thy coz, i'faith I am.
    Go, take him down and bear him to his father;
    Let him be buried, look ye; I'll pay the priest.   235

ALBERTO Please you to admit his father to the court?

PIERO No.

ALBERTO Please you to restore his lands and goods again?

PIERO No.

ALBERTO Please you vouchsafe him lodging in the city?   240

PIERO God's foot! no, thou odd uncivil fellow!
    I think you do forget, sir, where you are.

ALBERTO I know you do forget, sir, where you must be.°

FOROBOSCO You are too malapert, i'faith you are.
    Your honour might do well to—   245

ALBERTO Peace, parasite, thou bur that only sticks

Unto the nap of greatness.

PIERO Away with that same yelping cur, away!

ALBERTO Ay, I am gone. But mark, Piero, this:
There is a thing called scourging Nemesis.   250

    Exit Alberto

BALURDO God's nigs, he has wrong, that he has! And 'sfoot! an I
were as he, I would bear no coals,° la, I. I begin to swell. Puff!

PIERO How now, fool, fop, fool!

BALURDO Fool, fop, fool? Marry-muff!° I pray you, how many fools
have you seen go in a suit of satin? I hope yet I do not look a fool,   255
i'faith. A fool? God's bores! I scorn't with my heel. 'Snigs, an I
were worth but three hundred pound a year more, I could swear
richly; nay, but as poor as I am, I will swear the fellow hath wrong.

PIERO [*aside*] Young Galeazzo? Ay, a proper man;
Florence, a goodly city; it shall be so.   260
I'll marry her to him instantly.
Then Genoa mine by my Maria's match,
Which I'll solemnize ere next setting sun;
Thus Venice, Florence, Genoa, strongly leagued.
Excellent, excellent! I'll conquer Rome,   265
Pop out the light of bright religion;
And then helter-skelter, all cocksure!

BALURDO Go to, 'tis just; the man hath wrong. Go to.

PIERO Go to, thou shalt have right.—Go to, Castilio,
Clap him into the palace dungeon,   270
Lap him in rags, and let him feed on slime
That smears the dungeon cheek. Away with him!

BALURDO In very good truth now, I'll ne'er do so more; this one
time and—

PIERO Away with him; observe it strictly. Go!   275

BALURDO   Why then, O wight,
                     Alas poor knight,
                     O welladay, Sir Jeffrey!
                     Let poets roar,
                     And all deplore,
                     For I now bid you goodnight.°   280

    Exit Balurdo with Calisto. [Enter Maria]

MARIA O piteous end of love! O too, too rude hand
Of unrespective death! Alas, sweet maid!

PIERO Forbear me, heaven! What intend these plaints?

MARIA The beauty of admired creation,   285

The life of modest, unmixed purity,
Our sex's glory, Mellida, is—
PIERO What? O heaven, what?
MARIA Dead!
PIERO May it not sad your thoughts, how?°   290
MARIA Being laid upon her bed, she grasped my hand,
  And kissing it spake thus: 'Thou very poor,
  Why dost not weep? The jewel of thy brow,
  The rich adornment that enchased thy breast,
  Is lost; thy son, my love, is lost, is dead.   295
  And do I live to say Antonio's dead?
  And have I lived to see his virtues blurred
  With guiltless blots? O world, thou art too subtle°
  For honest natures to converse withal.
  Therefore I'll leave thee. Farewell, mart of woe;   300
  I fly to clip my love, Antonio'.
  With that her head sunk down upon her breast,
  Her cheek changed earth, her senses slept in rest;°
  Until my fool that pressed unto the bed
  Screeched out so loud that he brought back her soul,   305
  Called her again, that her bright eyes 'gan ope
  And stared upon him. He, audacious fool,
  Dared kiss her hand, wished her, 'Soft rest, loved bride!'
  She fumbled out, 'Thanks, good', and so she died.
PIERO And so she died! I do not use to weep,   310
  But by thy love, out of whose fertile sweet
  I hope for as fair fruit, I am deep sad.
  I will not stay my marriage for all this.—
  Castilio, Forobosco, all,
  Strain all your wits, wind up invention   315
  Unto his highest bent, to sweet this night;
  Make us drink Lethe by your quaint conceits,°
  That for two days oblivion smother grief;
  But when my daughter's exequies approach,
  Let's all turn sighers. Come, despite of fate,   320
  Sound loudest music; let's pass out in state.
         The cornets sound. Exeunt

4.2

Enter Antonio alone, in fool's habit

ANTONIO Ay, heaven, thou may'st; thou may'st, Omnipotence.°
What vermin bred of putrefacted slime
Shall dare to expostulate with thy decrees?
O heaven, thou may'st indeed; she was all thine,
All heavenly; I did but humbly beg   5
To borrow her of thee a little time.
Thou gav'st her me as some weak-breasted dame
Giveth her infant, puts it out to nurse,
And, when it once goes high-lone, takes it back.°
She was my vital blood; and yet, and yet,   10
I'll not blaspheme. Look here, behold!
       Antonio puts off his cap and lieth just upon his back
I turn my prostrate breast upon thy face,
And vent a heaving sigh. O hear but this:
I am a poor, poor orphan; a weak, weak child,
The wreck of splitted fortune, the very ooze,   15
The quicksand that devours all misery.
Behold the valiant'st creature that doth breathe!
For all this, I dare live, and I will live,
Only to numb some others' cursèd blood
With the dead palsy of like misery.   20
Then death, like to a stifling incubus,
Lie on my bosom. Lo, sir, I am sped;
My breast is Golgotha, grave for the dead.°
       Enter Pandulfo, Alberto, and a Page, carrying Felice's trunk
       [i.e. corpse] in a winding sheet, and lay it thwart Antonio's
       breast

PANDULFO Antonio, kiss my foot; I honour thee
In laying thwart my blood upon thy breast.   25
I tell thee, boy, he was Pandulfo's son,
And I do grace thee with supporting him.°
Young man,
The domineering monarch of the earth,°
He who hath nought that fortune's gripe can seize,   30
He who is all impregnably his own,
He whose great heart heaven cannot force with force,
Vouchsafes his love. *Non servio Deo, sed assentio.*°

ANTONIO I ha' lost a good wife.

PANDULFO Didst find her good, or didst thou make her good?   35
  If found, thou may'st re-find because thou hadst her;
  If made, the work is lost; but thou that mad'st her
  Liv'st yet as cunning. Hast lost a good wife?°
  Thrice-blessèd man that lost her whilst she was good,
  Fair, young, unblemished, constant, loving, chaste.   40
  I tell thee, youth, age knows young loves seem graced
  Which with grey cares' rude jars are oft defaced.°

ANTONIO But she was full of hope.

PANDULFO May be, may be; but that which 'may be' stood,
  Stands now without all 'may'. She died good,°   45
  And dost thou grieve?

ALBERTO   I ha' lost a true friend.

PANDULFO I live encompassed with two blessèd souls!
  Thou lost a good wife, thou lost a true friend, ha?
  Two of the rarest lendings of the heavens;
  But lendings, which, at the fixed day of pay   50
  Set down by fate, thou must restore again.
  O what unconscionable souls are here!
  Are you all like the spokeshaves of the church?°
  Have you no maw to restitution?°
  [To Alberto] Hast lost a true friend, coz? Then thou hadst one.   55
  I tell thee, youth, 'tis all as difficult
  To find true friend in this apostate age,
  That balks all right affiance 'twixt two hearts,
  As 'tis to find a fixèd, modest heart
  Under a painted breast. Lost a true friend?   60
  O happy soul that lost him whilst he was true.
  Believe it, coz, I to my tears have found,
  Oft dirt's respect makes firmer friends unsound.°

ALBERTO You have lost a good son.

PANDULFO Why there's the comfort on't, that he was good.   65
  Alas, poor innocent!

ALBERTO   Why weeps mine uncle?

PANDULFO Ha? dost ask me why? Ha? ha?
  Good coz, look here.
            He shows him his son's breast
  Man will break out, despite philosophy.
  Why, all this while I ha' but played a part   70
  Like to some boy that acts a tragedy,

Speaks burly words and raves out passion;
But when he thinks upon his infant weakness,
He droops his eye. I spake more than a god,
Yet am less than a man.   75
I am the miserablest soul that breathes.
     Antonio starts up
ANTONIO 'Slid, sir, ye lie! By th'heart of grief, thou liest!
  I scorn't that any wretched should survive
  Outmounting me in that superlative:
  Most miserable, most unmatched in woe.   80
  Who dare assume that, but Antonio?
PANDULFO Will 't still be so? And shall yon bloodhound live?
ANTONIO Have I an arm, a heart, a sword, a soul?
ALBERTO Were you but private unto what we know—
PANDULFO I'll know it all. First, let's inter the dead;   85
  Let's dig his grave with that shall dig the heart,
  Liver and entrails of the murderer.
     They strike the stage with their daggers, and the grave openeth°
ANTONIO [*to Page*] Wilt sing a dirge, boy?°
PANDULFO No, no song; 'twill be vile out of tune.
ALBERTO Indeed he's hoarse; the poor boy's voice is cracked.   90
PANDULFO Why, coz, why should it not be hoarse and cracked,
  When all the strings of nature's symphony
  Are cracked and jar? Why should his voice keep tune,
  When there's no music in the breast of man?
  I'll say an honest, antique rhyme I have.   95
  Help me, good sorrow-mates, to give him grave.
     They all help to carry Felice to his grave
        Death, exile, plaints and woe
        Are but man's lackeys, not his foe.
        No mortal 'scapes from fortune's war
        Without a wound, at least a scar.
        Many have led these to the grave,   100
        But all shall follow, none shall save.°
        Blood of my youth, rot and consume;
        Virtue in dirt doth life assume.°
        With this old saw, close up this dust: 105
        Thrice-blessèd man that dieth just.°
    [*The grave is closed*]
ANTONIO The gloomy wing of night begins to stretch
  His lazy pinion over all the air.

We must be stiff and steady in resolve.
Let's thus our hands, our hearts, our arms involve.   110
   They wreathe their arms
PANDULFO Now swear we by this Gordian knot of love,°
By the fresh turned-up mould that wraps my son,
By the dread brow of triple Hecate,°
Ere night shall close the lids of yon bright stars
We'll sit as heavy on Piero's heart   115
As Etna doth on groaning Pelorus.°
ANTONIO Thanks, good old man.—We'll cast at royal chance.°
Let's think a plot; then pell-mell vengeance!
   Exeunt, their arms wreathed. The cornets sound for the act

5.1

*The dumbshow. Enter at one door Castilio and Forobosco, with
halberds; four Pages with torches; Lucio bare[headed]; Piero,
Maria, and Alberto, talking. Alberto draws out his dagger,
Maria her knife, aiming to menace the Duke. Then [enter]
Galeazzo betwixt two Senators, reading a paper to them; at
which they all make semblance of loathing Piero, and knit their
fists at him; [then enter] two Ladies and Nutrice. All these go
softly over the stage, whilst at the other door enters the Ghost of
Andrugio, who passeth by them, tossing his torch about his head
in triumph.° All forsake the stage, saving Andrugio who,
speaking, begins the act*

GHOST OF ANDRUGIO *Venit dies, tempusque, quo reddat suis
Animam squallentem sceleribus.*°
The fist of strenuous vengeance is clutched,
And stern Vindicta tow'reth up aloft°
That she may fall with a more weighty peise   5
And crush life's sap from out Piero's veins.
Now 'gins the lep'rous cores of ulcered sins
Wheel to a head. Now is his fate grown mellow,°
Instant to fall into the rotten jaws
Of chap-fall'n death. Now down looks providence   10
T'attend the last act of my son's revenge.
Be gracious, observation, to our scene;
For now the plot unites his scattered limbs
Close in contracted bands. The Florence prince,
Drawn by firm notice of the duke's black deeds,   15
Is made a partner in conspiracy.
The states of Venice are so swoll'n in hate
Against the duke for his accursèd deeds,
Of which they are confirmed by some odd letters
Found in dead Strozzo's study which had passed   20
Betwixt Piero and the murd'ring slave,
That they can scare retain from bursting forth
In plain revolt. O, now triumphs my ghost,
Exclaiming, 'Heaven's just!' for I shall see
The scourge of murder and impiety.   25
    Exit

5.2

Balurdo [speaks] from under the stage,° [as in prison]

BALURDO Ho! Who's above there? Ho!—A murrain on all proverbs!
They say hunger breaks through stone walls,° but I am as gaunt as
lean-ribbed famine, yet I can burst through no stone walls. O now,
Sir Jeffrey, show thy valour; break prison and be hanged.
Nor shall the darkest nook of hell contain   5
The discontented Sir Balurdo's ghost.°
        [He climbs through a trap door]
Well, I am out well! I have put off the prison to put on the rope.° O
poor shotten herring, what a pickle art thou in! O hunger, how
thou domineerest in my guts! O for a fat leg of ewe mutton in
stewed broth, or drunken song to feed on. I could belch rarely, for   10
I am all wind. O cold, cold, cold, cold, cold! O poor knight, O poor
Sir Jeffrey! Sing like an unicorn before thou dost dip thy horn in
the water of death.° O cold! O sing! O cold! O poor Sir Jeffrey,
sing, sing!
        *He sings. Enter Antonio and Alberto at several doors, their
        rapiers drawn, in their masquing attire*

ANTONIO *Vindicta!*   15
ALBERTO Mellida!
ANTONIO Alberto!
ALBERTO Antonio!
ANTONIO Hath the duke supped?
ALBERTO Yes, and triumphant revels mount aloft;   20
The duke drinks deep to overflow his grief.
The court is racked to pleasure, each man strains
To feign a jocund eye. The Florentine—
ANTONIO Young Galeazzo?
ALBERTO Even he—is mighty on our part.   25
The states of Venice—
        Enter Pandulfo running, in masquing attire, [hearing Antonio]
PANDULFO —Like high-swoll'n floods, drive down the muddy
    dams
Of pent allegiance! O, my lusty bloods,
Heaven sits clapping of our enterprise.
I have been labouring general favour firm,°   30
And I do find the citizens grown sick
With swallowing the bloody crudities

Of black Piero's acts; they fain would cast
And vomit him from off their government.
Now is the plot of mischief ripped wide ope;   35
Letters are found 'twixt Strozzo and the duke
So clear apparent, yet more firmly strong
By suiting circumstance, that as I walked
Muffled, to eavesdrop speech, I might observe
The graver statesmen whispering fearfully.   40
Here one gives nods and hums what he would speak;
The rumour's got 'mong troop of citizens
Making loud murmur with confusèd din.
One shakes his head and sighs, 'O ill-used power!'
Another frets and sets his grinding teeth   45
Foaming with rage, and swears, 'This must not be!'
Here one complots and on a sudden starts
And cries, 'O monstrous, O deep villainy!'
All knit their nerves and from beneath swoll'n brows
Appears a gloating eye of much mislike;   50
Whilst swart Piero's lips reek steam of wine,
Swallows lust-thoughts, devours all pleasing hopes
With strong imagination of—what not?
O now, '*Vindicta!*' that's the word we have;
A royal vengeance, or a royal grave!   55

ANTONIO *Vindicta!*

BALURDO I am a-cold.

PANDULFO Who's there? Sir Jeffrey!

BALURDO A poor knight, God wot. The nose of my knighthood is
bitten off with cold. O poor Sir Jeffrey, cold, cold!   60

PANDULFO What chance of fortune hath tripped up his heels
And laid him in the kennel? Ha?

ALBERTO I will discourse it all.—Poor, honest soul,
Hadst thou a beaver to clasp up thy face,
Thou shouldst associate us in masquery   65
And see revenge.

BALURDO Nay, an you talk of revenge, my stomach's up, for I am
most tyrannically hungry. A beaver? I have a headpiece, a skull, a
brain of proof, I warrant ye.

ALBERTO Slink to my chamber then and 'tire thee.   70

BALURDO Is there a fire?

ALBERTO Yes.

BALURDO Is there a fat leg of ewe mutton?

ALBERTO Yes.

BALURDO And a clean shirt?   75

ALBERTO Yes.

BALURDO Then am I for you, most pathetically and unvulgarly, la!
    Exit [Balurdo]

ANTONIO Resolved hearts, time curtails night, opportunity shakes
  us his foretop.° Steel your thoughts, sharp your resolve, embolden
  your spirit, grasp your swords, alarum mischief, and with an   80
  undaunted brow out-scowl the grim opposition of most menacing
  peril.
    [Sounds of revelry offstage]
  Hark here! Proud pomp shoots mounting triumph up,
  Borne in loud accents to the front of Jove.

PANDULFO O now, he that wants soul to kill a slave,   85
  Let him die slave and rot in peasant's grave.

ANTONIO *[to Alberto]* Give me thy hand.—*[To Pandulfo]*
                        And thine, most noble heart.
Thus will we live and, but thus, never part.
    Exeunt twined together

5.3

    Cornets sound a sennet. Enter Castilio and Forobosco, two Pages
    with torches, Lucio bare[headed], Piero and Maria, Galeazzo,
    two Senators, and Nutrice

PIERO *(to Maria)* Sit close unto my breast, heart of my love;
  Advance thy drooping eyes; thy son is drowned
  (Rich happiness that such a son is drowned),
  Thy husband's dead. Life of my joys, most blessed
  In that the sapless log that pressed thy bed   5
  With an unpleasing weight, being lifted hence,
  Even I, Piero, live to warm his place.
  I tell you, lady, had you viewed us both
  With an unpartial eye when first we wooed
  Your maiden beauties, I had borne the prize.   10
  'Tis firm I had; for, fair, I ha' done that—

MARIA *[aside]* Murder!

PIERO Which he would quake to have adventurèd.
  Thou know'st I have—

MARIA [*aside*] Murdered my husband! 15

PIERO —Borne out the shock of war, and done, what not,
That valour durst. Dost love me, fairest? Say!

MARIA As I do hate my son, I love thy soul.

PIERO Why then, *Io* to Hymen! Mount a lofty note.°
Fill red-cheeked Bacchus, let Lyaeus float° 20
In burnished goblets; force the plump-lipped god
Skip light lavoltas in your full-sapped veins!
      [*Goblets are filled with wine*]
'Tis well, brim-full. Even I have glut of blood.
Let quaff carouse; I drink this Bordeaux wine°
Unto the health of dead Andrugio, 25
Felice, Strozzo, and Antonio's ghosts.
[*Aside*] Would I had some poison to infuse it with,
That, having done this honour to the dead,
I might send one to give them notice on't!
I would endear my favour to the full.—° 30
[*To a Page*] Boy, sing aloud, make heaven's vault to ring
With thy breath's strength. I drink. Now loudly sing.
      [*The Page*] *sings. The song ended, the cornets sound a sennet.*
      Enter Antonio, Pandulfo, and Alberto in masquery, Balurdo,
      and a Torchbearer

PIERO Call Julio hither; where's the little soul?
I saw him not today. Here's sport alone
For him, i'faith; for babes and fools, I know, 35
Relish not substance but applaud the show.
      [*Galeazzo speaks*] *to the Conspirators as they stand in rank for*
      the measure

GALEAZZO (*to Antonio*) All blessèd fortune crown your brave
      attempt.
(*To Pandulfo*) I have a troop to second your attempt.
(*To Alberto*) The Venice states join hearts unto your hands.

PIERO By the delights in contemplation 40
Of coming joys, 'tis magnificent.
You grace my marriage eve with sumptuous pomp.—
Sound still, loud music. O, your breath gives grace
To curious feet that in proud measure pace.

ANTONIO [*aside*] Mother, is Julio's body— 45

MARIA [*aside*] Speak not, doubt not; all is above all hope.

ANTONIO [*aside*] Then will I dance and whirl about the air.
Methinks I am all soul, all heart, all spirit.

Now murder shall receive his ample merit.
>   *The measure. While the measure is dancing, Andrugio's Ghost is*
>   *placed betwixt the music-houses*°

PIERO   Bring hither suckets, candied delicates.—   50
We'll taste some sweetmeats, gallants, ere we sleep.
>   [*A curtain is drawn to reveal a table with sweetmeats set in the*
>   *discovery space*]°

ANTONIO   [*aside*] We'll cook your sweetmeats, gallants, with tart
sour sauce!

GHOST OF ANDRUGIO   [*aside*] Here will I sit, spectator of revenge,°
And glad my ghost in anguish of my foe.   55
>   *The Masquers whisper with Piero*

PIERO   Marry, and shall; i'faith, I were too rude
If I gainsaid so civil fashion.—
[*To the courtiers, etc.*] The masquers pray you to forbear the room
Till they have banqueted. Let it be so;
No man presume to visit them, on death.   60
>   [*Exeunt Courtiers.*] *The Masquers whisper [with Piero] again*
Only myself? O why, with all my heart,
I'll fill your consort; here Piero sits.
Come on, unmask; let's fall to.

ANTONIO   Murder and torture!
>   *The Conspirators [unmask and, during the following lines,] bind*
>   *Piero, pluck out his tongue,*° *and triumph over him*
>   No prayers, no entreats.

PANDULFO   We'll spoil your oratory.—Out with his tongue!   65

ANTONIO   I have't, Pandulfo; the veins panting bleed,
Trickling fresh gore about my fist. Bind fast! So, so.

GHOST OF ANDRUGIO   Blessed be thy hand! I taste the joys of
heaven,
Viewing my son triumph in his black blood.°

BALURDO   Down to the dungeon with him! I'll dungeon with him!—   70
I'll fool you! Sir Jeffrey will be Sir Jeffrey. I'll tickle you!

ANTONIO   Behold, black dog!

PANDULFO   Grinn'st thou, thou snarling cur?

ALBERTO   Eat thy black liver!

ANTONIO   To thine anguish see
A fool triumphant in thy misery.—
Vex him, Balurdo.   75

PANDULFO   He weeps! Now do I glorify my hands;
I had no vengeance if I had no tears.

ANTONIO Fall to, good duke. [*Indicating the banquet*] O, these are
    worthless cates,
    You have no stomach to them. Look, look here;
    Here lies a dish to feast thy father's gorge;°   80
    Here's flesh and blood which I am sure thou lov'st.
        [*He uncovers the dish containing Julio's limbs.*] *Piero seems to*
        condole his son
PANDULFO Was he thy flesh, thy son, thy dearest son?
ANTONIO So was Andrugio my dearest father.
PANDULFO So was Felice my dearest son.
        Enter Maria
MARIA So was Andrugio my dearest husband.   85
ANTONIO My father found no pity in thy blood.
PANDULFO Remorse was banished when thou slew'st my son.
MARIA When thou empoisonèd'st my loving lord,
    Exiled was piety.
ANTONIO Now, therefore, pity, piety, remorse,   90
    Be aliens to our thoughts; grim fire-eyed rage
    Possess us wholly.
        [*Piero again seems to condole his son*]
PANDULFO Thy son? True; and which is my most joy,
    I hope no bastard but thy very blood,
    Thy true-begotten, most legitimate   95
    And lovèd issue. There's the comfort on't!
ANTONIO Scum of the mud of hell!
ALBERTO   Slime of all filth!
MARIA Thou most detested toad!
BALURDO Thou most retort and obtuse rascal!
ANTONIO Thus charge we death at thee. Remember hell,   100
    And let the howling murmurs of black spirits,
    The horrid torments of the damnèd ghosts
    Affright thy soul as it descendeth down
    Into the entrails of the ugly deep.
PANDULFO Sa, sa! No, let him die and die, and still be dying.°   105
        They offer to run all at Piero, and on a sudden stop
    And yet not die till he hath died and died
    Ten thousand deaths in agony of heart.
ANTONIO Now pell-mell! Thus the hand of heaven chokes
    The throat of murder. This for my father's blood!
        He stabs Piero

PANDULFO This for my son!
> [*Stabs him*]

ALBERTO   This for them all!   110
> [*Stabs him*]

And this, and this! Sink to the heart of hell!
> *They run all at Piero with their rapiers.* [*He dies*]

PANDULFO Murder for murder, blood for blood doth yell.

GHOST OF ANDRUGIO 'Tis done, and now my soul shall sleep in
rest.

Sons that revenge their father's blood are blest.
> *The curtains* [*above*] *being drawn, exit* [*the Ghost of*]
> *Andrugio.*° *Enter Galeazzo, two Senators, Lucio, Forobosco,*
> *Castilio, and Ladies*

1 SENATOR Whose hand presents this gory spectacle?   115

ANTONIO Mine.

PANDULFO No, mine!

ALBERTO No, mine!

ANTONIO I will not lose the glory of the deed
Were all the tortures of the deepest hell   120
Fixed to my limbs. I pierced the monster's heart
With an undaunted hand.

PANDULFO By yon bright-spangled front of heaven, 'twas I;
'Twas I sluiced out his life-blood.

ALBERTO Tush! To say truth, 'twas all.   125

2 SENATOR Blessed be you all, and may your honours live
Religiously held sacred, even for ever and ever.

GALEAZZO (*to Antonio*) Thou art another Hercules to us
In ridding huge pollution from our state.°

1 SENATOR Antonio, belief is fortified   130
With most invincible approvements of much wrong
By this Piero to thee. We have found
Bead-rolls of mischief, plots of villainy
Laid 'twixt the duke and Strozzo; which we found
Too firmly acted.

2 SENATOR   Alas, poor orphan!   135

ANTONIO Poor? Standing triumphant over Beelzebub?
Having large interest for blood, and yet deemed poor?°

1 SENATOR What satisfaction outward pomp can yield,
Or chiefest fortunes of the Venice state,
Claim freely. You are well-seasoned props   140
And will not warp or lean to either part;°

Calamity gives man a steady heart.

ANTONIO We are amazed at your benignity;
    But other vows constrain another course.

PANDULFO We know the world, and did we know no more   145
    We would not live to know.° But since constraint
    Of holy bands forceth us keep this lodge
    Of dirt's corruption till dread power calls°
    Our souls' appearance, we will live enclosed
    In holy verge of some religious order,   150
    Most constant votaries.

      The curtains are drawn; Piero departeth°

ANTONIO First let's cleanse our hands,
    Purge hearts of hatred, and entomb my love;
    Over whose hearse I'll weep away my brain
    In true affection's tears.   155
    For her sake, here I vow a virgin bed;
    She lives in me, with her my love is dead.

2 SENATOR We will attend her mournful exequies;
    Conduct you to your calm sequestered life,
    And then—   160

MARIA Leave us to meditate on misery,
    To sad our thought with contemplation
    Of past calamities. If any ask
    Where lives the widow of the poisoned lord,
    Where lies the orphan of a murdered father,   165
    Where lies the father of a butchered son,
    Where lives all woe, conduct him to us three,
    The downcast ruins of calamity.

ANTONIO Sound doleful tunes, a solemn hymn advance
    To close the last act of my vengeance;   170
    And when the subject of your passion's spent,
    Sing 'Mellida is dead'; all hearts will relent
    In sad condolement at that heavy sound.
    Never more woe in lesser plot was found.
    And O, if ever time create a muse   175
    That to th'immortal fame of virgin faith
    Dares once engage his pen to write her death,
    Presenting it in some black tragedy,
    May it prove gracious, may his style be decked
    With freshest blooms of purest elegance;   180
    May it have gentle presence, and the scenes sucked up

By calm attention of choice audience;
And when the closing Epilogue appears,
Instead of claps may it obtain but tears.°
            They sing [an exequy]. Exeunt

THE MALCONTENT

THE PERSONS OF THE PLAY

Giovanni Altofronto°	disguised Malevole, sometime Duke of Genoa
Pietro Jacomo	Duke of Genoa
Mendoza	a minion to the Duchess of Pietro Jacomo
Celso°	a friend to Altofronto
Bilioso°	an old choleric marshal
Prepasso°	a gentleman-usher
Ferneze°	a young courtier, and enamoured on the Duchess
Ferrard°	a minion to Duke Pietro Jacomo
Equato° ⎫ Guerrino° ⎭	two courtiers
Aurelia	duchess to Duke Pietro Jacomo
Maria	duchess to Duke Altofronto
Emilia ⎫ Bianca° ⎭	two ladies attending the Duchess [to Pietro Jacomo]
Maquerelle°	an old panderess
[Captain]	[of the citadel]
[Mercury]	[presenter of the masque]
[Suitors] [Pages] [Guards]	

The Malcontent

1.1

*The vilest out-of-tune music° being heard, enter Bilioso and
Prepasso*

BILIOSO [*addressing offstage*] Why, how now? Are ye mad? or drunk?
or both? or what?

PREPASSO [*addressing offstage*] Are ye building Babylon° there?

BILIOSO Here's a noise° in court! [*Addressing offstage*] You think you
are in a tavern, do you not?   5

PREPASSO [*addressing offstage*] You think you are in a brothel-house,
do you not?—This room is ill-scented.

Enter one with a perfume

So perfume, perfume! Some upon me, I pray thee. The duke is
upon instant entrance; so, make place there!

[*Exit the one with the perfume.*] *Enter the Duke Pietro, [with]
Ferrard, Count Equato, [and] Count Celso before, and
Guerrino°*

PIETRO Where breathes° that music?   10

BILIOSO The discord, rather than the music, is heard from the
malcontent Malevole's chamber.

FERRARD [*calling*] Malevole!

Malevole [enters above, as] out of his chamber°

MALEVOLE Yaugh, God o'man, what dost thou there? Duke's
Ganymede,° Juno's jealous of thy long stockings. Shadow of a   15
woman, what wouldst, weasel? Thou lamb a'court, what dost thou
bleat for? Ah, you smooth-chinned catamite!

PIETRO Come down, thou rugged cur, and snarl here. I give thy
dogged° sullenness free liberty. Trot about and bespurtle whom
thou pleasest.   20

MALEVOLE I'll come among you, you goatish-blooded° totterers, as
gum into taffeta, to fret, to fret.° I'll fall like a sponge into water to
suck up, to suck up. [*To the musicians*] Howl again!° I'll go to
church and come to you.

[*Exit Malevole above*]

PIETRO This Malevole is one of the most prodigious affections° that   25
ever conversed with nature; a man, or rather a monster, more
discontent than Lucifer when he was thrust out of the presence.

His appetite is unsatiable as the grave; as far from any content as
from heaven. His highest delight is to procure others' vexation,
and therein he thinks he truly serves heaven; for 'tis his position, 30
whosoever in this earth can be contented is a slave and damned;
therefore does he afflict all in that to which they are most affected.
The elements struggle within him;° his own soul is at variance
within herself; his speech is halter-worthy at all hours. I like him,
faith; he gives good intelligence to my spirit, makes me understand 35
those weaknesses which others' flattery palliates.—Hark, they
sing.

A song [within]. Enter Malevole [below] after the song

PIETRO See, he comes! Now shall you hear the extremity of a
malcontent. He is as free as air; he blows over every man.—And
sir, whence come you now?   40

MALEVOLE From the public place of much dissimulation, the
church.

PIETRO What didst there?

MALEVOLE Talk with a usurer; take up at interest.

PIETRO I wonder what religion thou art?   45

MALEVOLE Of a soldier's religion.

PIETRO And what dost thou think makes most infidels now?

MALEVOLE Sects, sects. I have seen seeming piety change her robe
so oft, that sure none but some arch-devil can shape her a new
petticoat.   50

PIETRO O, a religious policy.°

MALEVOLE But damnation on a politic religion! I am weary.
Would I were one of the duke's hounds now.

PIETRO But what's the common news abroad, Malevole? Thou
dogg'st rumour still.   55

MALEVOLE Common news? Why, common words are 'God save ye',
'Fare ye well'; common actions, flattery and cozenage; common
things, women and cuckolds.—And how does my little Ferrard?
Ah, ye lecherous animal!—My little ferret, he goes sucking up and
down the palace into every hen's nest like a weasel.—And to what 60
dost thou addict thy time to now, more than to those antique
painted drabs that are still affected of young courtiers, Flattery,
Pride, and Venery?

FERRARD I study languages. Who dost think to be the best linguist
of our age?   65

MALEVOLE Phew, the devil! Let him possess thee, he'll teach thee to
speak all languages most readily and strangely;° and great reason,
marry, he's travelled greatly i'the world and is everywhere.

FERRARD Save i'th' court.

MALEVOLE Ay, save i'th' court.—(*To Bilioso*) And how does my old   70
muckhill overspread with fresh snow? Thou half a man, half a
goat, all a beast, how does thy young wife, old huddle?

BILIOSO Out, you improvident rascal! [*Kicks at him*]

MALEVOLE Do, kick, thou hugely-horned, old duke's ox,° good
Master Make-please.   75

PIETRO How dost thou live nowadays, Malevole?

MALEVOLE Why, like the knight Sir Patrick Penlolians,° with killing
o' spiders for my lady's monkey.

PIETRO How dost spend the night? I hear thou never sleep'st.

MALEVOLE O no, but dream the most fantastical...O heaven! O   80
fubbery, fubbery!

PIETRO Dream? What dream'st?

MALEVOLE Why, methinks I see that signor pawn his footcloth; that
metreza her plate; this madam takes physic that t'other *monsieur*
may minister to her; here is a pander jewelled; there is a fellow in   85
shift of satin this day that could not shift a shirt t'other night; here
a Paris supports that Helen; there's a Lady Guinevere bears up
that Sir Lancelot.° Dreams, dreams, visions, fantasies, chimeras,
imaginations, tricks, conceits!— (*To Prepasso*) Sir Tristram Trimtram, come aloft Jackanapes with a whim-wham.° Here's a knight   90
of the land of Catito shall play at trap with any page in Europe, do
the sword-dance with any morris-dancer in Christendom, ride at
the ring° till the fin of his eyes look as blue as the welkin,° and run
the wild-goose-chase even with Pompey the Huge.°

PIETRO You run—°   95

MALEVOLE To the devil.—Now Signor Guerrino,° that thou from a
most pitied prisoner shouldst grow a most loathed flatterer!°—
Alas, poor Celso, thy star's oppressed, thou art an honest lord, 'tis
pity.

EQUATO Is't pity?   100

MALEVOLE Ay, marry is't, philosophical Equato; and 'tis pity that
thou, being so excellent a scholar by art, shouldst be so ridiculous
a fool by nature.—I have a thing to tell you, duke. Bid 'em avaunt,
bid 'em avaunt.

PIETRO Leave us, leave us.—   105
        Exeunt all saving Pietro and Malevole
Now sir, what is't?

MALEVOLE Duke, thou art a *becco*, a *cornuto*.°

PIETRO How?

MALEVOLE Thou art a cuckold.

PIETRO Speak! Unshale him quick.   110

MALEVOLE With most tumbler-like nimbleness.

PIETRO Who? By whom? I burst with desire.

MALEVOLE Mendoza is the man makes thee a horned beast; duke,
'tis Mendoza cornutes thee.

PIETRO What conformance? Relate; short, short!   115

MALEVOLE As a lawyer's beard.

        There is an old crone in the court,
        Her name is Maquerelle;°
        She is my mistress, sooth to say,
        And she doth ever tell me—   120

Blurt o'rhyme,° blurt o'rhyme! Maquerelle is a cunning bawd, I am
an honest villain,° thy wife is a close drab, and thou art a notorious
cuckold. Farewell, duke.

PIETRO Stay, stay!

MALEVOLE Dull, dull duke, can lazy patience make lame revenge? O   125
God, for a woman to make a man that which God never created,
never made!

PIETRO What did God never make?

MALEVOLE A cuckold. To be made a thing that's hoodwinked with
kindness whilst every rascal fillips his brows;° to have a coxcomb   130
with egregious horns pinned to a lord's back, every page sporting
himself with delightful laughter, whilst he must be the last must
know it! Pistols and poniards, pistols and poniards!

PIETRO Death and damnation!

MALEVOLE Lightning and thunder!   135

PIETRO Vengeance and torture!

MALEVOLE *Cazzo!*

PIETRO O, revenge!

MALEVOLE Nay, to select among ten thousand fairs
A lady far inferior to the most   140
In fair proportion both of limb and soul;°
To take her from austerer check of parents
To make her his by most devoutful rites,
Make her commandress of a better essence
Than is the gorgeous world, even of a man;   145
To hug her with as raised an appetite
As usurers do their delved-up treasury,
Thinking none tells it but his private self;
To meet her spirit in a nimble kiss,
Distilling panting ardour to her heart;   150

True to her sheets, nay, diets strong his blood,
To give her height of hymeneal sweets—
PIETRO O God!
MALEVOLE Whilst she lisps, and gives him some court *quelquechose*,
  Made only to provoke, not satiate;   155
  And yet even then the thaw of her delight
  Flows from lewd heat of apprehension,°
  Only from strange imagination's rankness,
  That forms the adulterer's presence in her soul
  And makes her think she clips the foul knave's loins. 160
PIETRO Affliction to my blood's root!
MALEVOLE Nay, think, but think what may proceed of this:
  Adultery is often the mother of incest.
PIETRO Incest?
MALEVOLE Yes, incest. Mark! Mendoza of his wife begets per- 165
chance a daughter; Mendoza dies; his son° marries this daughter.
Say you? Nay, 'tis frequent, not only probable, but no question
often acted, whilst ignorance, fearless ignorance, clasps his own
seed.
PIETRO Hideous imagination!   170
MALEVOLE Adultery? Why, next to the sin of simony,° 'tis the most
horrid transgression under the cope of salvation.°
PIETRO Next to simony?
MALEVOLE Ay, next to simony, in which our men in next age shall
not sin.   175
PIETRO Not sin? Why?
MALEVOLE Because, thanks to some churchmen, our age will leave
them nothing to sin with. But adultery! O dullness! Show shrewd°
exemplary punishment, that intemperate bloods may freeze but to
think it. I would damn° him and all his generation; my own hands 180
should do it. Ha! I would not trust heaven with my vengeance
anything.
PIETRO Anything, anything, Malevole! Thou shalt see instantly
what temper my spirit holds. Farewell; remember, I forget thee
not; farewell.   185
    Exit Pietro
MALEVOLE Farewell.
  Lean thoughtfulness, a sallow meditation,
  Suck thy veins dry, distemperance rob thy sleep!
  The heart's disquiet is revenge most deep.
  He that gets blood the life of flesh but spills, 190

But he that breaks heart's peace the dear soul kills.—
Well, this disguise doth yet afford me that
Which kings do seldom hear or great men use,
Free speech. And though my state's usurped,
Yet this affected strain gives me a tongue°   195
As fetterless as is an emperor's.
I may speak foolishly, ay, knavishly,
Always carelessly, yet no-one thinks it fashion
To poise my breath; for he that laughs and strikes
Is lightly felt or seldom struck again.—°   200
Duke, I'll torment thee. Now my just revenge
From thee than crown a richer gem shall part;
Beneath God, nought's so dear as a calm heart.
        Enter Celso
CELSO My honoured lord—
MALEVOLE Peace, speak low, peace! O Celso, constant lord,   205
Thou to whose faith I only rest discovered,
Thou one of full ten millions of men
That lovest virtue only for itself,
Thou in whose hands old Ops may put her soul;°
Behold forever-banished Altofront,   210
This Genoa's last year's duke. O truly noble!
I wanted those old instruments of state,
Dissemblance and suspect. I could not time it, Celso;°
My throne stood like a point in midst of a circle,
To all of equal nearness; bore with none,°   215
Reigned all alike; so slept in fearless virtue,
Suspectless, too suspectless; till the crowd,
Still lickerous of untried novelties,
Impatient with severer government,
Made strong with Florence, banished Altofront.   220
CELSO Strong with Florence! Ay, thence your mischief rose,
For when the daughter of the Florentine
Was matched once with this Pietro, now duke,
No stratagem of state untried was left,
Till you of all—
MALEVOLE   Of all was quite bereft.   225
Alas, Maria, too, close prisonèd,
My true-faithed duchess, i'the citadel!
CELSO I'll still adhere; let's mutiny and die.
MALEVOLE O no, climb not a falling tower, Celso;

'Tis well held desperation, no zeal,   230
Hopeless to strive with fate. Peace! Temporise.
Hope, hope, that never forsak'st the wretched'st man,
Yet bidd'st me live and lurk in this disguise.
What? play I well the free-breathed discontent?
Why, man, we are all philosophical monarchs   235
Or natural fools. Celso, the court's afire;
The duchess' sheets will smoke for't ere it be long;
Impure Mendoza, that sharp-nosed lord, that made°
The cursèd match linked Genoa with Florence,
Now broad-horns the duke, which he now knows.   240
Discord to malcontents is very manna;
When the ranks are burst, then scuffle Altofront.°

CELSO Ay, but durst?

MALEVOLE 'Tis gone; 'tis swallowed like a mineral.
Some way 'twill work. Phew't, I'll not shrink;   245
He's resolute who can no lower sink.

> *Bilioso entering, Malevole shifteth his speech*°

O the father of maypoles!° Did you never see a fellow whose
strength consisted in his breath, respect in his office, religion in
his lord, and love in himself? Why then, behold.

BILIOSO Signor—   250

MALEVOLE My right worshipful lord, your court nightcap makes
you have a passing high forehead.°

BILIOSO I can tell you strange news, but I am sure you know them
already: the duke speaks much good of you.

MALEVOLE Go to, then; and shall you and I now enter into a strict   255
friendship?

BILIOSO Second one another?

MALEVOLE Yes.

BILIOSO Do one another good offices?

MALEVOLE Just. What though I called thee old ox, egregious wittol,   260
broken-bellied coward, rotten mummy? Yet since I am in favour—

BILIOSO Words of course, terms of disport. His grace presents you
by me a chain,° as his grateful remembrance for . . . I am ignorant
for what. Marry, ye may impart.° [*Presents chain*] Yet, howso-
ever—come, dear friend. Dost know my son?   265

MALEVOLE Your son?

BILIOSO He shall eat woodcocks, dance jigs, make possets, and play
at shuttlecock with any young lord about the court. He has as
sweet a lady, too. Dost know her little bitch?

MALEVOLE 'Tis a dog, man.   270

BILIOSO Believe me, a she-bitch! O, 'tis a good creature! Thou shalt
be her servant. I'll make thee acquainted with my young wife,°
too. What, I keep her not at court for nothing. 'Tis grown to
suppertime; come to my table: that, anything I have, stands open
to thee.   275

MALEVOLE (to Celso) How smooth to him that is in state of grace,°
How servile is the rugged'st courtier's face!
What profit, nay, what nature would keep down,
Are heaved to them are minions to a crown.°
Envious ambition never states his thirst,   280
Till, sucking all, he swells and swells, and bursts.

BILIOSO I shall now leave you with my always-best wishes; only let's
hold betwixt us a firm correspondence, a mutual-friendly-reci-
procal kind of steady-unanimous-heartily-leagued—

MALEVOLE Did your signorship ne'er see a pigeon-house that was   285
smooth, round, and white without, and full of holes and stink
within? Ha' ye not, old courtier?

BILIOSO O yes, 'tis the form, the fashion of them all.

MALEVOLE Adieu, my true court-friend; farewell, my dear Castilio.°
        *Exit Bilioso. [Celso] descries Mendoza [who] enters with three or
        four Suitors*

CELSO Yonder's Mendoza.

MALEVOLE   True, the privy key.°   290

CELSO I take my leave, sweet lord.

MALEVOLE   'Tis fit; away!
        Exit Celso

MENDOZA Leave your suits with me; I can and will. Attend my
secretary, leave me.°
        [*Exeunt Suitors*]

MALEVOLE Mendoza, hark ye, hark ye. You are a treacherous villain, God b' wi' ye!   295

MENDOZA Out, you base-born rascal!

MALEVOLE We are all the sons of heaven, though a tripe-wife were
our mother. Ah, you whoreson, hot-reined he-marmoset! Aegisthus—didst ever hear of one Aegisthus?

MENDOZA Gisthus?   300

MALEVOLE Ay, Aegisthus. He was a filthy, incontinent fleshmonger,
such a one as thou art.

MENDOZA Out, grumbling rogue!

MALEVOLE Orestes!° beware Orestes!

MENDOZA Out, beggar!   305
MALEVOLE I once shall rise.
MENDOZA Thou rise?
MALEVOLE Ay, at the resurrection.
  No vulgar seed but once may rise, and shall;
  No king so huge, but 'fore he die may fall.   310
      Exit
MENDOZA Now, good Elysium! What a delicious heaven is it for a
  man to be in a prince's favour! O sweet God! O pleasure! O
  fortune! O all thou best of life! What should I think? What say?
  What do? To be a favourite! A minion! To have a general, timor-
  ous respect observe a man, a stateful silence in his presence,   315
  solitariness in his absence, a confused hum and busy murmur of
  obsequious suitors training° him, the cloth° held up and way
  proclaimed before him; petitionary vassals licking the pavement
  with their slavish knees, whilst some odd palace lampreys that
  engender with snakes and are full of eyes on both sides,° with a   320
  kind of insinuated humbleness, fix all their delights upon his brow!
  O blessed state! What a ravishing prospect doth the Olympus of
  favour yield! Death, I cornute the duke!—Sweet women, most
  sweet ladies, nay, angels, by heaven! he is more accursed than a
  devil that hates you or is hated by you, and happier than a god that 325
  loves you or is beloved by you. You preservers of mankind, life-
  blood of society, who would live, nay, who can live without you? O
  paradise, how majestical is your austerer presence! How
  imperiously chaste is your more modest face! But O how full of
  ravishing attraction is your pretty, petulant, languishing, lasci-   330
  viously-composed countenance! These amorous smiles, those
  soul-warming, sparkling glances, ardent as those flames that singed
  the world by heedless Phaeton!° In body how delicate, in soul how
  witty, in discourse how pregnant, in life how wary, in favours how
  judicious, in day how sociable, and in night how—? O pleasure   335
  unutterable!° Indeed, it is most certain, one man cannot deserve
  only° to enjoy a beauteous woman. But a duchess! In despite of
  Phoebus,° I'll write a sonnet instantly in praise of her.
      Exit

1.2

*Enter Ferneze ushering Aurelia, Emilia and Maquerelle bearing
up her train, Bianca attending. All go out but Aurelia,
Maquerelle, and Ferneze*

AURELIA And is't possible? Mendoza slight me? Possible?

FERNEZE Possible!
What can be strange in him that's drunk with favour,
Grows insolent with grace?—Speak, Maquerelle, speak.

*Ferneze privately feeds Maquerelle's hands with jewels during
[the following] speech*°

MAQUERELLE To speak feelingly, more, more richly in solid sense   5
than worthless words, give me those jewels of your ears to receive
my enforced duty. As for my part, 'tis well known I can put up
anything, can bear patiently with any man. But when I heard he
wronged your precious sweetness, I was enforced to take deep
offence. 'Tis most certain he loves Emilia with high appetite; and,   10
as she told me—as you know we women impart our secrets one to
another—when she repulsed his suit, in that he was possessed with
your endeared grace, Mendoza most ingratefully renounced all
faith to you.

FERNEZE Nay, called you—speak, Maquerelle, speak.   15

MAQUERELLE By heaven, 'witch', 'dried biscuit', and contested
blushlessly he loved you but for a spurt or so.

FERNEZE For maintenance.

MAQUERELLE Advancement and regard.

AURELIA O villain! O impudent Mendoza!   20

MAQUERELLE Nay, he is the rustiest-jawed, the foulest-mouthed
knave in railing against our sex. He will rail against women—

AURELIA How, how?

MAQUERELLE I am ashamed to speak't, I.

AURELIA I love to hate him; speak!   25

MAQUERELLE Why, when Emilia scorned his base unsteadiness, the
black-throated rascal scolded and said—

AURELIA What?

MAQUERELLE Troth, 'tis too shameless.

AURELIA What said he?   30

MAQUERELLE Why, that at four women were fools, at fourteen,
drabs, at forty, bawds, at fourscore, witches, and at a hundred,
cats.

AURELIA   O unlimitable impudency!

FERNEZE   But as for poor Ferneze's fixèd heart,   35
Was never shadeless meadow drier parched
Under the scorching heat of heaven's dog°
Than is my heart with your enforcing eyes.°

MAQUERELLE   A hot simile!

FERNEZE   Your smiles have been my heaven, your frowns my hell;   40
O pity, then; grace should with beauty dwell.

MAQUERELLE   Reasonable perfect, by'r Lady.

AURELIA   I will love thee, be it but in despite
Of that Mendoza. 'Witch', Ferneze, 'witch'!
Ferneze, thou art the duchess' favourite;   45
Be faithful, private; but 'tis dangerous.

FERNEZE   His love is lifeless that for love fears breath;
The worst that's due to sin, O would 'twere death!

AURELIA   Enjoy my favour. I will be sick instantly and take physic.
Therefore in depth of night visit—   50

MAQUERELLE   Visit her chamber, but conditionally you shall not
offend her bed—by this diamond!

FERNEZE   By this diamond. (*Gives [a diamond] to Maquerelle*)

MAQUERELLE   Nor tarry longer than you please—by this ruby!

FERNEZE   By this ruby. (*Gives again*)   55

MAQUERELLE   And that the door shall not creak—

FERNEZE   And that the door shall not creak.

MAQUERELLE   Nay, but swear.°

FERNEZE   By this purse. (*Gives her his purse*)

MAQUERELLE   Go to! I'll keep your oaths for you. Remember, visit. 60
      Enter Mendoza, reading a sonnet

AURELIA   'Dried biscuit'?—Look where the base wretch comes.°

MENDOZA [*reading*]   'Beauty's life, heaven's model, love's queen'—

MAQUERELLE   That's his Emilia.

MENDOZA [*reading*]   'Nature's triumph, best on earth'—

MAQUERELLE   Meaning Emilia.   65

MENDOZA [*reading*]   'Thou only wonder that the world hath seen'—

MAQUERELLE   That's Emilia.

AURELIA   Must I then hear her praised?—Mendoza!

MENDOZA   Madam, your excellency is graciously encountered.
      Exit Ferneze
I have been writing passionate flashes in honour of—   70

AURELIA   Out, villain, villain!
O judgement, where have been my eyes?

What bewitched election made me dote on thee?°
What sorcery made me love thee? But begone,
Bury thy head. O that I could do more   75
Than loathe thee. Hence, worst of ill;
No reason ask; our reason is our will.

    Exit [Aurelia] with Maquerelle

MENDOZA Women? Nay, furies! Nay, worse, for they torment only
the bad, but women good and bad. Damnation of mankind!
Breath, hast thou praised them for this? And is't you, Ferneze,   80
are wriggled into smock-grace?° Sit sure! O, that I could rail
against these monsters in nature, models of hell, curse of the earth,
women that dare attempt anything, and what they attempt they
care not how they accomplish; without all premeditation or prevention; rash in asking, desperate in working, impatient in suffer-   85
ing, extreme in desiring, slaves unto appetite, mistresses in
dissembling, only constant in unconstancy, only perfect in coun-
terfeiting; their words are feigned, their eyes forged, their sighs
dissembled, their looks counterfeit, their hair false, their given
hopes° deceitful, their very breath artificial. Their blood is their   90
only god; bad clothes and old age are only the devils they tremble
at. That I could rail now!

    Enter Pietro, his sword drawn

PIETRO A mischief fill thy throat, thou foul-jawed slave! Say thy
prayers.
MENDOZA I ha' forgot 'em.   95
PIETRO Thou shalt die!
MENDOZA So shalt thou. I am heart-mad.
PIETRO I am horn-mad.
MENDOZA Extreme mad.
PIETRO Monstrously mad.   100
MENDOZA Why?
PIETRO Why? Thou, thou hast dishonourèd my bed.
MENDOZA I? Come, come, sir. Here's my bare heart to thee,°
As steady as is this centre to the glorious world.°
And yet, hark, thou art a *cornuto*—but by me?   105
PIETRO Yes, slave, by thee.
MENDOZA Do not, do not with tart and spleenful breath
Lose him can loose thee. I offend my duke?—°
Bear record, O ye dumb and raw-aired nights,
How vigilant my sleepless eyes have been   110
To watch the traitor. Record, thou spirit of truth,

With what debasement I ha' thrown myself
To under-offices, only to learn
The truth, the party, time, the means, the place,
By whom, and when, and where thou wert disgraced.   115
And am I paid with 'slave'? Hath my intrusion
To places private and prohibited
Only to observe the closer passages—°
Heaven knows with vows of revelation—°
Made me suspected, made me deemed a villain?   120
What rogue hath wronged us?

PIETRO   Mendoza, I may err.

MENDOZA Err? 'Tis too mild a name. But err and err,
    Run giddy with suspect 'fore through me thou know
    That which most creatures save thyself do know.
    Nay, since my service hath so loathed reject,°   125
    'Fore I'll reveal, shalt find them clipped together.

PIETRO Mendoza, thou know'st I am a most plain-breasted man.

MENDOZA The fitter to make a cuckold. Would your brows were
    most plain too!

PIETRO Tell me; indeed, I heard thee rail.   130

MENDOZA At women, true. Why, what cold phlegm° could choose,
    knowing a lord so honest, virtuous, so boundless-loving, boun-
    teous, fair-shaped, sweet, to be contemned, abused, defamed, made
    cuckold? Heart, I hate all women for't: sweet sheets, wax lights,
    antic bedposts, cambric smocks, villainous curtains, arras pictures,° 135
    oiled hinges,° and all the tongue-tied, lascivious witnesses of great
    creatures' wantonness!—What salvation can you expect?

PIETRO Wilt thou tell me?

MENDOZA Why, you may find it yourself; observe, observe.

PIETRO I ha' not the patience. Wilt thou deserve me?° Tell, give it. 140

MENDOZA Take't. Why, Ferneze is the man, Ferneze. I'll prove't.
    This night you shall take him in your sheets. Will't serve?

PIETRO It will. My bosom's in some peace. Till night—

MENDOZA What?

PIETRO   Farewell.

MENDOZA   God, how weak a lord are you!
    Why, do you think there is no more but so?   145

PIETRO Why?

MENDOZA Nay, then will I presume to counsel you.
    It should be thus: you with some guard upon the sudden
    Break into the princess' chamber; I stay behind,

Without the door through which he needs must pass.   150
Ferneze flies; let him. To me he comes; he's killed
By me—observe, by me! You follow; I rail,
And seem to save the body. Duchess comes,
On whom, respecting her advancèd birth°
And your fair nature, I know—nay, I do know!—   155
No violence must be used. She comes; I storm,
I praise, excuse Ferneze, and still maintain
The duchess' honour; she for this loves me;
I honour you, shall know her soul, you mine.
Then nought shall she contrive in vengeance—   160
As women are most thoughtful in revenge—
Of her Ferneze but you shall sooner know't
Than she can think't.—Thus shall his death come sure,
Your duchess brain-caught, so your life secure.

PIETRO It is too well, my bosom and my heart.   165
  When nothing helps, cut off the rotten part.
      Exit [Pietro]

MENDOZA Who cannot feign friendship can ne'er produce the
  effects of hatred. Honest fool duke, subtle lascivious duchess, silly
  novice Ferneze—I do laugh at ye. My brain is in labour till it
  produce mischief, and I feel sudden throes, proofs sensible the   170
  issue is at hand.
  As bears shape young, so I'll form my device,°
  Which grown proves horrid: vengeance makes men wise.
      [Exit]

2.1

Enter Mendoza with a sconce to observe Ferneze's entrance,
who, whilst the act is playing,° enters unbraced, two Pages
before him with lights; is met by Maquerelle and conveyed in.
The Pages are sent away

MENDOZA He's caught! The woodcock's head is i'th' noose!
Now treads Ferneze in dangerous path of lust,
Swearing his sense is merely deified.
The fool grasps clouds and shall beget centaurs;°
And now, in strength of panting faint delight,
The goat bids heaven envy him.—Good goose,   5
I can afford thee nothing but the poor
Comfort of calamity, pity.
Lust's like the plummets hanging on clock-lines;°
Will ne'er ha' done till all is quite undone.
Such is the course salt sallow lust doth run,°   10
Which thou shalt try. I'll be revenged.
Duke, thy suspect, duchess, thy disgrace,
Ferneze, thy rivalship, shall have swift vengeance.
Nothing so holy, no band of nature so strong,
No law of friendship so sacred,   15
But I'll profane, burst, violate
'Fore I'll endure disgrace, contempt and poverty.
Shall I, whose very 'hum' struck all heads bare,
Whose face made silence, creaking of whose shoe   20
Forced the most private passages fly ope,
Scrape like a servile dog at some latched door?
Learn now to make a leg, and cry, 'Beseech ye,
Pray ye, is such a lord within?', be awed
At some odd usher's scoffed formality?   25
First sear my brains! *Unde cadis, non quo refert.*°
My heart cries 'Perish all!' How, how? What fate
Can once avoid revenge that's desperate?
I'll to the duke. If all should ope—if? Tush!
Fortune still dotes on those who cannot blush.   30
      [*Exit*]

2.2

Enter Malevole at one door, Bianca, Emilia, and Maquerelle at the other door

MALEVOLE Bless ye, cast o'ladies!—Ha, Dipsas,° how dost thou, old coal?

MAQUERELLE Old coal?

MALEVOLE Ay, old coal. Methinks thou liest like a brand under these billets of green wood. He that will inflame a young wench's   5
heart, let him lay close to her an old coal that hath first been fired, a pandress, my half-burnt lint, who, though thou canst not flame thyself, yet art able to set a thousand virgins' tapers afire. (*To Bianca*) And how does Janivere° thy husband, my little periwinkle? Is 'a troubled with the cough o'the lungs still? Does he   10
hawk a-nights still? He will not bite!

BIANCA No, by my troth, I took him with his mouth empty of old teeth.

MALEVOLE And he took thee with thy belly full of young bones. Marry, he took his maim by the stroke of his enemy.   15

BIANCA And I mine by the stroke of my friend.

MALEVOLE The close stock!° O mortal wench! [*To Maquerelle*] Lady, ha' ye now no restoratives for your decayed Jasons?° Look ye, crab's guts baked, distilled ox-pith, the pulverised hairs of a lion's upper lip, jelly of cock-sparrows, he-monkey's marrow, or   20
powder of fox-stones?°—And whither are all you ambling now?

BIANCA Why, to bed, to bed.

MALEVOLE Do your husbands lie with ye?

BIANCA That were country fashion,° i'faith!

MALEVOLE Ha' ye no foregoers about you? Come, whither in good   25
deed, la now?

MAQUERELLE In good indeed, la now, to eat the most miraculously, admirably, astonishable-composed posset with three curds, without any drink.° Will ye help me with a he-fox?—Here's the duke.

Exeunt [Bianca, Emilia, and Maquerelle]

MALEVOLE ([*calling after*] *Bianca*) Fried frogs are very good, and   30
French-like, too!

Enter Duke Pietro, Count Celso, Count Equato, Bilioso, Ferrard, and Mendoza

PIETRO The night grows deep and foul. What hour is't?

CELSO Upon the stroke of twelve.

MALEVOLE Save ye, duke!

PIETRO From thee! Begone, I do not love thee. Let me see thee no   35
more. We are displeased.

MALEVOLE Why, God b' wi' thee! Heaven hear my curse:
May thy wife and thee live long together!

PIETRO Begone, sirrah!

MALEVOLE [sings] 'When Arthur first in court began'—Agamem-   40
non, Menelaus!°—Was ever any duke a *cornuto*?

PIETRO Begone, hence!

MALEVOLE What religion wilt thou be of next?

MENDOZA Out with him!

MALEVOLE With most servile patience. Time will come   45
When wonder of thy error will strike dumb
Thy bezzled sense.
Slaves i'favour? Ay! Marry, shall he rise?°
Good God! how subtle hell doth flatter vice,
Mounts him aloft and makes him seem to fly,   50
As fowl the tortoise mocked, who to the sky
Th'ambitious shell-fish raised. Th'end of all
Is only that from height he might dead fall.°

BILIOSO Why when? Out, ye rogue! Begone, ye rascal!

MALEVOLE 'I shall now leave ye with all my best wishes.'   55

BILIOSO Out, ye cur!

MALEVOLE 'Only let's hold together a firm correspondence.'

BILIOSO Out!

MALEVOLE 'A mutual-friendly-reciprocal-perpetual kind of steady-
unanimous-heartily-leagued—'°   60

BILIOSO Hence, ye gross-jawed peasantly—out, go!

MALEVOLE Adieu, pigeon-house, thou bur, that only stickest to
nappy fortunes. The serpigo, the strangury, an eternal uneffectual
priapism seise° thee!

BILIOSO Out, rogue!   65

MALEVOLE Mayest thou be a notorious wittolly pander to thine own
wife, and yet get no office but live to be the utmost misery of
mankind, a beggarly cuckold.
Exit [Malevole]

PIETRO It shall be so.°

MENDOZA It must be so, for where great states revenge,   70
'Tis requisite the parts which piety
And loft respect forbears be closely dogged.°
Lay one into his breast shall sleep with him,

Feed in the same dish, run in self-faction,°
Who may discover any shape of danger;   75
For once disgraced, displayèd in offence,
It makes man blushless, and man is (all confess)
More prone to vengeance than to gratefulness.
Favours are writ in dust, but stripes we feel;
Depravèd nature stamps in lasting steel.   80

PIETRO You shall be leagued with the duchess.

EQUATO The plot is very good.

BILIOSO° You shall both kill and seem the corpse to save.

FERRARD A most fine brain-trick.

CELSO (*aside*)° Of a most cunning knave!   85

PIETRO My lords, the heavy action we intend
Is death and shame, two of the ugliest shapes
That can confound a soul. Think, think of it;
I strike, but yet, like him that 'gainst stone walls
Directs his shafts, rebounds in his own face,   90
My lady's shame is mine, O God, 'tis mine!
Therefore I do conjure all secrecy;
Let it be as very little as may be,
Pray ye, as may be.
Make frightless entrance, salute her with soft eyes,   95
Stain nought with blood; only Ferneze dies,
But not before her brows.—O gentlemen,
God knows I love her! Nothing else, but this:
I am not well; if grief that sucks veins dry,
Rivels the skin, casts ashes in men's faces,   100
Bedulls the eye, unstrengthens all the blood,
Chance to remove me to another world,
As sure I once must die, let him succeed.
        [*He indicates Mendoza*]
I have no child; all that my youth begot
Hath been your loves, which shall inherit me;   105
Which as it ever shall, I do conjure it,
Mendoza may succeed; he's nobly born,
With me of much desert.

CELSO (*aside*) Much!

PIETRO Your silence answers, 'Ay';   110
I thank you. Come on now. O, that I might die
Before her shame's displayed. Would I were forced
To burn my father's tomb, unhele his bones

And dash them in the dirt, rather than this!
This both the living and the dead offends;   115
Sharp surgery where nought but death amends.
    Exit [Pietro] with the others

2.3

Enter Maquerelle, Emilia and Bianca, [Maquerelle] with the
posset [in a dish]

MAQUERELLE Even here it is, three curds in three regions individu-
    ally distinct, most methodically according to art composed, with-
    out any drink.°

BIANCA Without any drink?

MAQUERELLE Upon my honour! Will ye sit and eat?   5

EMILIA Good, the composure, the receipt, how is't?

MAQUERELLE 'Tis a pretty pearl! [*Emilia gives Maquerelle a pearl*]
    By this pearl—how does't with me?°—thus it is: seven and thirty
    yolks of Barbary hens' eggs; eighteen spoonfuls and a half of the
    juice of cock-sparrow bones; one ounce, three drams, four scruples   10
    and one quarter of the syrup of Ethiopian dates; sweetened with
    three quarters of a pound of pure candied Indian eryngoes;°
    strewed over with the powder of pearl of America, amber of
    Cathaia° and lamb-stones° of Muscovia.

BIANCA Trust me, the ingedients are very cordial and, no question,   15
    good and most powerful in restoration.

MAQUERELLE I know not what you mean by 'restoration', but this it
    doth: it purifieth the blood, smootheth the skin, enliveneth the
    eye, strengtheneth the veins, mundifieth the teeth, comforteth the
    stomach, fortifieth the back,° and quickeneth the wit; that's all.   20

EMILIA By my troth, I have eaten but two spoonfuls, and methinks I
    could discourse most swiftly and wittily already.

MAQUERELLE Have you the art to seem honest?°

BIANCA I thank advice and practice.

MAQUERELLE Why then, eat me o'this posset, quicken your blood,   25
    and preserve your beauty. Do you know Doctor Plaster-face? By
    this curd, he is the most exquisite in forging of veins,° sprighten-
    ing of eyes, dyeing of hair, sleeking of skins, blushing of cheeks,
    surfling of breasts, blanching and bleaching of teeth, that ever
    made an old lady gracious by torchlight; by this curd, la.   30

BIANCA Well, we are resolved; what God has given us we'll cherish.

MAQUERELLE Cherish anything saving your husband; keep him not too high lest he leap the pale.° But for your beauty, let it be your saint; bequeath two hours to it every morning in your closet. I ha' been young, and yet, in my conscience, I am not above five and twenty; but believe me, preserve and use your beauty, for youth and beauty once gone, we are like beehives without honey, out-o'-fashion apparel that no man will wear. Therefore, use me your beauty.   35

EMILIA Ay, but men say—   40

MAQUERELLE Men say! Let men say what they will. Life o'woman! they are ignorant of our wants. The more in years, the more in perfection they grow; if they lose youth and beauty, they gain wisdom and discretion. But when our beauty fades, goodnight with us. There cannot be an uglier thing to see than an old woman,° from which, O pruning, pinching and painting deliver all sweet beauties!°   45

    [*Music within*]°

BIANCA Hark, music.

MAQUERELLE Peace! 'Tis i'the duchess' bedchamber. Good rest, most prosperously-graced ladies.   50

EMILIA Goodnight, sentinel.°

BIANCA 'Night, dear Maquerelle.

    Exeunt all but Maquerelle

MAQUERELLE May my posset's operation send you my wit and honesty, and me your youth and beauty. The pleasing'st rest!

    Exit Maquerelle

2.4

    A song [within]. Whilst the song is singing, enter Mendoza with his sword drawn, standing ready to murder Ferneze as he flies from the Duchess' chamber. Tumult within

ALL [*within*] Strike, strike!

AURELIA [*within*] Save my Ferneze! O, save my Ferneze!

    Enter Ferneze in his shirt, and is received upon Mendoza's sword°

ALL [*within*] Follow, pursue!

AURELIA [*within*] O, save Ferneze!

MENDOZA Pierce, pierce!
        Thrusts his rapier in Ferneze
                        Thou shallow fool, drop there!   5
    He that attempts a prince's lawless love°
    Must have broad hands, close heart, with Argus' eyes,
    And back of Hercules, or else he dies.°
        *Enter Aurelia, Duke Pietro, Ferrard, Bilioso, Celso, and
        Equato*
ALL Follow, follow!
        *Mendoza bestrides the wounded body of Ferneze and seems to
        save him*
MENDOZA Stand off, forbear, ye most uncivil lords!   10
PIETRO Strike!
MENDOZA Do not! Tempt not a man resolved.
    Would you, inhuman murderers, more than death?
AURELIA O poor Ferneze!
MENDOZA Alas, now all defence too late!
AURELIA   He's dead!   15
PIETRO I am sorry for our shame. Go to your bed.
    Weep not too much, but leave some tears to shed
    When I am dead.
AURELIA What, weep for thee? My soul no tears shall find.
PIETRO Alas, alas, that women's souls are blind!   20
MENDOZA Betray such beauty?
    Murder such youth? Contemn civility!
    He loves him not that rails not at him.°
PIETRO Thou canst not move us; we have blood enough.—
    An't please you, lady, we have quite forgot
    All your defects; if not, why then—   25
AURELIA   Not.
PIETRO   Not.
        —The best of rest, goodnight.
        Exit Pietro with other Courtiers
AURELIA   Despite go with thee!
MENDOZA Madam, you ha' done me foul disgrace;
    You have wronged him much loves you too much.°
    Go to! Your soul knows you have.   30
AURELIA I think I have.
MENDOZA   Do you but think so?
AURELIA Nay, sure I have; my eyes have witnessed thy love;
    Thou hast stood too firm for me.

MENDOZA Why, tell me, fair-cheeked lady, who even in tears
  Art powerfully beauteous, what unadvised passion   35
  Struck ye into such a violent heat against me?
  Speak, what mischief wronged us? What devil injured us?
  Speak!
AURELIA That thing ne'er worthy of the name of man, Ferneze.
  Ferneze swore thou lov'st Emilia,   40
  Which to advance, with most reproachful breath
  Thou both didst blemish and denounce my love.
MENDOZA Ignoble villain, did I for this bestride
  Thy wounded limbs? For this, rank opposite
  Even to my sovereign? For this—O God—for this   45
  Sunk all my hopes, and with my hopes my life?
  Ripped bare my throat unto the hangman's axe?
  Thou most dishonoured trunk! [Kicks Ferneze]—Emilia?
  By life, I know her not.—Emilia?
  Did you believe him?
AURELIA   Pardon me, I did   50
MENDOZA Did you? And thereupon you graced him?
AURELIA I did.
MENDOZA Took him to favour? Nay, even clasped with him?
AURELIA Alas, I did.
MENDOZA This night?   55
AURELIA This night.
MENDOZA And in your lustful twines the duke took you?
AURELIA A most sad truth.
MENDOZA O God, O God! How we dull honest souls,
  Heavy-brained men, are swallowed in the bogs   60
  Of a deceitful ground, whilst nimble bloods,
  Light-joined spirits, pent, cut good men's throats°
  And 'scape! Alas, I am too honest for this age,
  Too full of phlegm and heavy steadiness;°
  Stood still whilst this slave cast a noose about me.   65
  Nay, then, to stand in honour of him and her°
  Who had even sliced my heart!
AURELIA Come, I did err, and am most sorry I did err.
MENDOZA Why, we are both but dead; the duke hates us;
  And those whom princes do once groundly hate,   70
  Let them provide to die. As sure as fate,
  Prevention is the heart of policy.
AURELIA Shall we murder him?

MENDOZA   Instantly!°

AURELIA   Instantly! Before he casts a plot,
   Or further blaze my honour's much-known blot,   75
   Let's murder him.

MENDOZA   I would do much for you; will ye marry me?

AURELIA   I'll make thee duke; we are of Medicis,°
   Florence our friend, in court my faction
   Not meanly strengthful. The duke then dead,   80
   We well prepared for change; the multitude
   Irresolutely reeling, we in force;
   Our party seconded, the kingdom mazed:
   No doubt of swift success, all shall be graced.

MENDOZA   You do confirm me; we are resolute.   85
   Tomorrow look for change; rest confident.
   'Tis now about the immodest waist of night;°
   The mother of moist dew with pallid light°
   Spreads gloomy shades about the numbèd earth.
   Sleep, sleep, whilst we contrive our mischief's birth.   90
   This man I'll get inhumed. Farewell, to bed;
   Ay, kiss thy pillow, dream; the duke is dead!
   So, so, good night.

     Exit Aurelia

How fortune dotes on impudence! I am in private the adopted
son of yon good prince. I must be duke; why, if I must, I must.
Most silly lord, name me? O heaven! I see God made honest   95
fools to maintain crafty knaves. The duchess is wholly mine
too; must kill her husband to quit her shame. Much! Then marry
her, ay!
O, I grow proud in prosperous treachery!
As wrestlers clip, so I'll embrace you all,   100
Not to support, but to procure your fall.

     Enter Malevole

MALEVOLE   God arrest thee!°

MENDOZA   At whose suit?

MALEVOLE   At the devil's. Ha, you treacherous, damnable monster!
How dost? How dost, thou treacherous rogue! Ha, ye rascal! I am   105
banished the court, sirrah.

MENDOZA   Prithee, let's be acquainted; I do love thee, faith!

MALEVOLE   At your service, by the Lord, la. Shall's go to supper?
Let's be once drunk together, and so unite a most virtuously
strengthened friendship. Shall's, Huguenot,° shall's?   110

MENDOZA Wilt fall upon my chamber tomorrow morn?

MALEVOLE As a raven to a dunghill! They say there's one dead here, pricked for the pride of the flesh.

MENDOZA Ferneze. There he is; prithee, bury him.

MALEVOLE O, most willingly. I mean to turn pure Rochelle° 115
churchman, I.

MENDOZA Thou churchman? Why, why?

MALEVOLE Because I'll live lazily, rail upon authority, deny king's supremacy in things indifferent, and be a pope in mine own parish.° 120

MENDOZA Wherefore dost thou think churches were made?

MALEVOLE To scour ploughshares; I ha' seen oxen plough up altars. *Et nunc seges ubi Sion fuit.*°

MENDOZA Strange!

MALEVOLE Nay, monstrous! I ha' seen a sumptuous steeple turned 125
to a stinking privy; more beastly, the sacredest place° made a dog's kennel; nay, most inhuman, the stoned coffins of long-dead Christians burst up and made hogs' troughs. *Hic finis Priami.*° Shall I ha' some sack and cheese at thy chamber? Goodnight, good mischievous incarnate devil! Goodnight, Mendoza. Ha, ye inhuman 130
villain, goodnight, 'night, fub!

MENDOZA Goodnight. Tomorrow morn.

Exit Mendoza

MALEVOLE Ay, I will come, friendly damnation, I will come. I do descry cross-points;° honesty and courtship straddle as far asunder as a true Frenchman's legs.° 135

FERNEZE O!

MALEVOLE Proclamations, more proclamations!

Ferneze stirs

FERNEZE O, a surgeon!

MALEVOLE Hark! lust cries for a surgeon.—What news from limbo?° How does the grand cuckold, Lucifer? 140

FERNEZE O help, help! Conceal and save me.

MALEVOLE Thy shame more than thy wounds do grieve me far;
Thy wounds but leave upon thy flesh some scar,
But fame ne'er heals, still rankles worse and worse;
Such is of uncontrollèd lust the curse. 145
Think what it is in lawless sheets to lie,
But O, Ferneze, what in lust to die!
Then thou that shame respects, O fly converse
With women's eyes and lisping wantonness.

Stick candles 'gainst a virgin wall's white back;   150
If they not burn, yet at the least they'll black.
    Malevole helps [Ferneze] up and conveys him away
Come, I'll convey thee to a private port,
Where thou shalt live, O happy man, from court.
The beauty of the day begins to rise,
From whose bright form night's heavy shadow flies.   155
Now 'gins close plots to work; the scene grows full,
And craves his eyes who hath a solid skull.°
    Exeunt

3.1

Enter Duke Pietro, Mendoza, Count Equato, and Bilioso

PIETRO 'Tis grown to youth of day; how shall we waste this light?°
My heart's more heavy than a tyrant's crown.
Shall we go hunt? Prepare for field.
Exit Equato

MENDOZA Would ye could be merry.

PIETRO Would God I could! Mendoza, bid 'em haste.   5
Exit Mendoza
I would fain shift place. O vain relief!
Sad souls may well change place, but not change grief;
As deer, being struck, fly thorough many soils,
Yet still the shaft sticks fast.°

BILIOSO A good old simile, my honest lord.   10

PIETRO I am not much unlike to some sick man
That long desirèd hurtful drink; at last
Swills in and drinks his last, ending at once
Both life and thirst. O, would I ne'er had known°
My own dishonour! Good God, that men should desire   15
To search out that which being found kills all
Their joy of life; to taste the tree of knowledge
And then be driven from out paradise!
Canst give me some comfort?

BILIOSO My lord, I have some books which have been dedicated to   20
my honour and I ne'er read 'em, and yet they had very fine names:
Physic for Fortune, Lozenges of Sanctified Sincerity;° very pretty
works of curates, scriveners and schoolmasters. Marry, I remember one Seneca, Lucius Annaeus Seneca—

PIETRO Out upon him! He writ of temperance and fortitude, yet   25
lived like a voluptuous epicure and died like an effeminate cow-
ard.°
Haste thee to Florence.
Here, take our letters; see 'em sealed. Away!
Report in private to the honoured duke   30
His daughter's forced disgrace; tell him at length
We know too much; due compliments advance.°
There's nought that's safe and sweet but ignorance.
*Exit Pietro. Enter Malevole in some frieze gown, whilst Bilioso
reads his patent*°

144

MALEVOLE I cannot sleep; my eyes' ill-neighbouring lids
   Will hold no fellowship. O thou pale sober night,   35
   Thou that in sluggish fumes all sense dost steep,
   Thou that gives all the world full leave to play,
   Unbend'st the feebled veins of sweaty labour;
   The galley-slave, that all the toilsome day
   Tugs at his oar against the stubborn wave,   40
   Straining his rugged veins, snores fast;
   The stooping scythe-man, that doth barb the field,
   Thou mak'st wink sure. In night all creatures sleep;
   Only the malcontent, that 'gainst his fate
   Repines and quarrels, alas! he's goodman tell-clock;   45
   His sallow jawbones sink with wasting moan;
   Whilst others' beds are down, his pillow's stone.

BILIOSO Malevole!

MALEVOLE (*to Bilioso*) Elder of Israel,° thou honest defect of wicked
   nature and obstinate ignorance, when did thy wife let thee lie with   50
   her?

BILIOSO I am going ambassador to Florence.

MALEVOLE Ambassador! Now, for thy country's honour, prithee, do
   not put up mutton and porridge i'thy cloak-bag. Thy young lady
   wife goes to Florence with thee too, does she not?   55

BILIOSO No, I leave her at the palace.

MALEVOLE At the palace? Now discretion shield man! For God's
   love, let's ha' no more cuckolds! Hymen begins to put off his
   saffron robe.° Keep thy wife i'the state of grace. Heart o'truth, I
   would sooner leave my lady singled in a bordello than in the   60
   Genoa palace.
   Sin there appearing in her sluttish shape°
   Would soon grow loathsome, even to blushless sense;
   Surfeit would choke intemperate appetite,
   Make the soul scent the rotten breath of lust.   65
   When in an Italian lascivious palace,°
   A lady guardianless,
   Left to the push of all allurement,
   The strongest incitements to immodesty,
   To have her bound, incensed with wanton sweets,°   70
   Her veins filled high with heating delicates,°
   Soft rest, sweet music, amorous masquerers,
   Lascivious banquets, sin itself gilt o'er,
   Strong fantasy tricking up strange delights,
   Presenting it dressed pleasingly to sense,   75

Sense leading it unto the soul, confirmed
With potent example, impudent custom,
Enticed by that great bawd, Opportunity;
Thus being prepared, clap to her easy ear
Youth in good clothes, well-shaped, rich,   80
Fair-spoken, promising-noble, ardent, blood-full,
Witty, flattering—Ulysses absent,
O Ithaca, can chastest Penelope hold out?°

BILIOSO Mass, I'll think on't. Farewell.

MALEVOLE Farewell. Take thy wife with thee! Farewell.   85

    Exit Bilioso

To Florence, um? It may prove good, it may,
And we may once unmask our brows.

    Enter Count Celso

CELSO My honoured lord—

MALEVOLE Celso, peace! How is't? Speak low; pale fears
Suspect that hedges, walls and trees have ears.   90
Speak, how runs all?

CELSO I'faith, my lord, that beast with many heads,
The staggering multitude, recoils apace.
Though through great men's envy, most men's malice,
Their much intemperate heat hath banished you,   95
Yet, now they find envy and malice near,°
Produce faint reformation.
The duke, the too soft duke, lies as a block,
For which two tugging factions seem to saw;
But still the iron through the ribs they draw.°   100

MALEVOLE I tell thee, Celso, I have ever found
Thy breast most far from shifting cowardice
And fearful baseness; therefore I'll tell thee, Celso,
I find the wind begins to come about.
I'll shift my suit of fortune.°   105
I know the Florentine, whose only force,°
By marrying his proud daughter to this prince,
Both banished me and made this weak lord duke,
Will now forsake them all; be sure he will.
I'll lie in ambush for conveniency,°   110
Upon their severance to confirm myself,°

CELSO Is Ferneze interred?

MALEVOLE Of that at leisure; he lives.

146

CELSO But how stands Mendoza? How is't with him?

MALEVOLE Faith, like a pair of snuffers: snibs° filth in other men   115
and retains it in himself.

CELSO He does fly from public notice, methinks, as a hare does from
hounds: the feet whereon he flies betrays him.

MALEVOLE I can track him, Celso.
O, my disguise fools him most powerfully!   120
For that I seem a desperate malcontent
He fain would clasp with me. He is the true slave
That will put on the most affected grace
For some vile second cause.°

    Enter Mendoza

CELSO He's here.   125

MALEVOLE Give place.—

    Exit Celso

Illo, ho, ho, ho!° Art there, old truepenny?° Where hast thou spent
thyself this morning? I see flattery in thine eyes and damnation
i'thy soul. Ha, ye huge rascal!

MENDOZA Thou art very merry,   130

MALEVOLE As a scholar, *futuens gratis.*° How does the devil go with
thee now?

MENDOZA Malevole, thou art an arrant knave.

MALEVOLE Who, I? I have been a sergeant,° man.

MENDOZA Thou art very poor.   135

MALEVOLE As Job, an alchemist, or a poet.

MENDOZA The duke hates thee.

MALEVOLE As Irishmen do bum-cracks.°

MENDOZA Thou has lost his amity.

MALEVOLE As pleasing as maids lose their virginity.   140

MENDOZA Would thou wert of a lusty spirit! would thou wert noble!

MALEVOLE Why, sure my blood gives me I am noble, sure I am° of
noble kind, for I find myself possessed with all their qualities: love
dogs, dice and drabs, scorn wit in stuff clothes, have beat my
shoemaker, knocked my sempstress, cuckold' my 'pothecary, and   145
undone my tailor. Noble? Why not? Since the stoic said, *Neminem
servum non ex regibus, neminem regem non ex servis esse oriundum,*°
only busy Fortune touses, and the provident Chances blends them
together. I'll give you a simile: did you e'er see a well with two
buckets? Whilst one comes up full to be emptied, another goes   150
down empty to be filled. Such is the state of all humanity. Why

look you, I may be the son of some duke, for believe me, intemperate lascivious bastardy makes nobility doubtful. I have a lusty, daring heart, Mendoza.

MENDOZA Let's grasp! I do like thee infinitely. Wilt enact one thing   155
for me?

MALEVOLE Shall I get by it?
        [*Mendoza*] *gives him his purse*
Command me; I am thy slave beyond death and hell.

MENDOZA Murder the duke!

MALEVOLE My heart's wish, my soul's desire, my fantasy's dream,   160
my blood's longing, the only height of my hopes! How? O God,
how? O, how my united spirits throng together! So strengthen my
resolve!

MENDOZA The duke is now a-hunting.

MALEVOLE Excellent! Admirable! As the devil would have it! Lend   165
me ... Lend me ... rapier, pistol, crossbow! So, so!° I'll do it!

MENDOZA Then we agree.

MALEVOLE As Lent and fishmongers. Come, *cap-à-pie?*° How?
Inform.

MENDOZA Know that this weak-brained duke, who only stands on   170
Florence' stilts, hath out of witless zeal made me his heir and
secretly confirmed the wreath to me after his life's full point.

MALEVOLE Upon what merit?

MENDOZA Merit? By heaven, I horn him! Only Ferneze's death gave
me state's life.° Tut! we are politic; he must not live now.   175

MALEVOLE No reason, marry.° But how must he die now?

MENDOZA My utmost project is to murder the duke that I might
have his state, because he makes me his heir; to banish the duchess
that I might be rid of a cunning Lacedaemonian,° because I know
Florence will forsake her; and then to marry Maria, the banished   180
Duke Altofront's wife, that her friends might strengthen me and
my faction. This is all, la.

MALEVOLE Do you love Maria?

MENDOZA Faith, no great affection, but as wise men do love great
women, to ennoble their blood and augment their revenue. To   185
accomplish this now, thus now: the duke is in the forest next the
sea; single him, kill him, hurl him i'the main, and proclaim thou
saw'st wolves eat him.

MALEVOLE Um, not so good. Methinks when he is slain
        To get some hypocrite, some dangerous wretch   190
        That's muffled o'er with feignèd holiness,

148

To swear he heard the duke on some steep cliff
Lament his wife's dishonour and, in an agony
Of his heart's torture, hurled his groaning sides
Into the swollen sea. This circumstance,   195
Well made, sounds probable; and hereupon
The duchess—
MENDOZA   May well be banished.
O unpeerable invention! Rare!
Thou god of policy! It honeys me.
MALEVOLE Then fear not for the wife of Altofront;   200
I'll close to her.
MENDOZA Thou shalt, thou shalt! Our excellency is pleased.°
Why wert not thou an emperor? When we°
Are duke, I'll make thee some great man, sure!
MALEVOLE Nay, make me some rich knave, and I'll make myself   205
Some great man.
MENDOZA   In thee be all my spirit.
Retain ten souls, unite thy virtual powers.
Resolve; ha, remember greatness! Heart, farewell.°
The fate of all my hopes in thee doth dwell.
          Exit [Mendoza.] Enter Celso
MALEVOLE Celso, didst hear?—O heaven, didst hear?   210
Such devilish mischief? Sufferest thou the world
Carouse damnation even with greedy swallow
And still dost wink, still does thy vengeance slumber?
If now thy brows are clear, when will they thunder?
          Exeunt

3.2

          Enter Pietro, Ferrard, Prepasso, and three Pages. Cornets like
          horns [within]
FERRARD The dogs are at a fault.°
PIETRO Would God nothing but the dogs were at it! Let the deer
pursue safety, the dogs follow the game, and do you follow the
dogs. As for me, 'tis unfit one beast should hunt another. I ha' one
chaseth me. An't please you, I would be rid of ye a little.   5
FERRARD Would your grief would, as soon as we, leave you to
quietness.

PIETRO I thank you.—
    Exeunt [Ferrard and Prepasso]
  Boy, what dost thou dream of now?

1 PAGE Of a dry summer, my lord, for here's a hot world towards.   10
But, my lord, I had a strange dream last night.

PIETRO What strange dream?

1 PAGE Why, methought I pleased you with singing, and then I
dreamt you gave me that short sword.

PIETRO Prettily begged. Hold thee, I'll prove thy dream true; take't.   15
  [Gives him the sword]

1 PAGE My duty! But still I dreamt on, my lord, and methought,
an't shall please your excellency, you would needs out of your
royal bounty give me that jewel in your hat.

PIETRO O, thou didst but dream, boy; do not believe it. Dreams
prove not always true; they may hold in a short sword, but not in a   20
jewel. But now, sir, you dreamt you had pleased me with singing;
make that true, as I ha' made the other.

1 PAGE Faith, my lord, I did but dream, and dreams you say prove
not always true; they may hold in a good sword, but not in a good
song. The truth is, I ha' lost my voice.   25

PIETRO Lost thy voice? How?

1 PAGE With dreaming, faith! But here's a couple of sirenical° rascals shall enchant ye. What shall they sing, my good lord?

PIETRO Sing of the nature of women, and then the song shall be
surely full of variety, old crotchets,° and most sweet closes.° It   30
shall be humorous, grave, fantastic, amorous, melancholy,
sprightly, one in all, and all in one.

1 PAGE All in one?°

PIETRO By 'r Lady, too many! Sing! My speech grows culpable of
unthrifty idleness. Sing!   35
    [The] song [is sung by Pages 2 and 3]

PIETRO Ah, so, so, sing. I am heavy. Walk off; I shall talk in my
sleep. Walk off.
    [Pietro settles down to sleep.] Exeunt Pages. Enter Malevole,
    with cross-bow and pistol

MALEVOLE Brief, brief! Who? The duke? Good heaven, that fools
should stumble upon greatness!—Do not sleep, duke. *[He wakes
Pietro]* Give ye good morrow. Must be brief, duke; I am fee'd to   40
murder thee. Start not! Mendoza, Mendoza hired me. Here's his
gold, his pistol, cross-bow, sword; 'tis all as firm as earth. O fool,
fool, choked with the common maze of easy idiots, credulity! Make
him thine heir? What, thy sworn murderer?

PIETRO O, can it be?   45

MALEVOLE Can!

PIETRO Discovered he not Ferneze?

MALEVOLE Yes, but why, but why? For love to thee? Much, much!
To be revenged upon his rival, who had thrust his jaws awry; who
being slain, supposed by thine own hands, defended by his sword,   50
made thee most loathsome, him most gracious, with thy loose
princess. Thou, closely yielding egress and regress to her, madest
him heir, whose hot unquiet lust straight toused thy sheets, and
now would seize thy state. Politician! Wise man! Death, to be led
to the stake like a bull by the horns!° To make even kindness cut a   55
gentle throat! Life, why art thou numbed? Thou foggy dullness,
speak! Lives not more faith in a home-thrusting tongue than in
these fencing tip-tap° courtiers?

    Enter Celso, with a hermit's gown and beard

PIETRO Lord! Malevole, if this be true—

MALEVOLE If? Come, shade thee with this disguise. If? Thou shalt   60
handle it; he shall thank thee for killing thyself. Come, follow my
directions, and thou shalt see strange sleights.

PIETRO World, whither wilt thou?

MALEVOLE Why, to the devil. Come, the morn grows late.
    A steady quickness is the soul of state.   65

    Exeunt

4.1

Enter Maquerelle, knocking at the [chamber] door of the ladies
[Bianca and Emilia]

MAQUERELLE Medam,° medam, are you stirring, medam? If you be
stirring, medam—if I thought I should disturb ye—

[Enter a Page from the chamber]

PAGE My lady is up, forsooth.

MAQUERELLE A pretty boy, faith!—How old art thou?

PAGE I think fourteen.   5

MAQUERELLE Nay, an ye be in the teens—are ye a gentleman born?
Do you know me? My name is Medam Maquerelle. I lie in the old
Cunnycourt.°

Enter Bianca and Emilia

See, here the ladies.

Exit Page

BIANCA A fair day to ye, Maquerelle.   10

EMILIA Is the duchess up yet, sentinel?

MAQUERELLE O ladies, the most abominable mischance! O dear
ladies, the most piteous disaster! Ferneze was taken last night in
the duchess' chamber. Alas, the duke catched him and killed him.

BIANCA Was he found in bed?   15

MAQUERELLE O, no, but the villainous certainty is, the door was not
bolted, the tongue-tied hatch° held his peace; so the naked truth
is, he was found in his shirt, whilst I like an arrant beast lay in the
outward chamber, heard nothing; and yet they came by me in the
dark, and yet I felt them not, like a senseless creature as I was. O   20
beauties, look to your busk-points, if not chastely, yet charily. Be
sure the door be bolted.—*[To Bianca]* Is your lord gone to Florence?

BIANCA Yes, Maquerelle.

MAQUERELLE I hope you'll find the discretion to purchase a fresh   25
gown 'fore his return.—Now by my troth, beauties, I would ha' ye
once wise. He loves ye—pish! He is witty—bubble! Fair-propor-
tioned—miaow! Nobly born—wind! Let this be still your fixed
position: esteem me every man according to his good gifts, and so
ye shall ever remain 'most dear, and most worthy to be most dear, 30
ladies'.°

EMILIA Is the duke returned from hunting yet?

MAQUERELLE They say not yet.

BIANCA 'Tis now in midst of day.

EMILIA How bears the duchess with this blemish now? 35

MAQUERELLE Faith, boldly; strongly defies defame, as one that has a duke to her father. And there's a note to you: be sure of a stout friend in a corner, that may always awe your husband. Mark the 'haviour of the duchess now; she dares defame; cries, 'Duke, do what thou canst; I'll 'quit° mine honour'. Nay, as one confirmed in 40 her own virtue against ten thousand mouths that mutter her disgrace, she's presently for dances.

Enter Ferrard

BIANCA For dances?

MAQUERELLE Most true.

EMILIA Most strange. See, here's my servant, young Ferrard. How 45 many servants thinkest thou I have, Maquerelle?

MAQUERELLE The more the merrier! 'Twas well said, use your servants as you do your smocks; have many, use one, and change often,° for that's most sweet and courtlike.

FERRARD Save ye, fair ladies. Is the duke returned? 50

BIANCA Sweet sir, no voice of him as yet in court.

FERRARD 'Tis very strange.

EMILIA° And how like you my servant, Maquerelle?

MAQUERELLE I think he could hardly draw Ulysses' bow,° but, by my fidelity, were his nose narrower, his eyes broader, his hands 55 thinner, his lips thicker, his legs bigger, his feet lesser, his hair blacker, and his teeth whiter, he were a tolerable sweet youth, i'faith. An he will come to my chamber, I will read him the fortune of his beard.

Cornets sound [offstage]

FERRARD Not yet returned, I fear; but the duchess approacheth. 60

Enter Mendoza supporting the Duchess [Aurelia], [and]
Guerrino. The Ladies that are on the stage rise. Ferrard ushers
in the Duchess, and then takes a Lady to tread a measure.
[Music sounds]

AURELIA We will dance.—Music!—We will dance.

GUERRINO *Les quanto*, lady, *Pensez bien, Passa regis*, or *Bianca's brawl?*°

AURELIA We have forgot the brawl.

FERRARD So soon? 'Tis wonder! 65

GUERRINO Why, 'tis but two singles on the left, two on the right, three doubles forward, a traverse of six round; do this twice, three

singles side, galliard trick-of-twenty, coranto-pace; a figure of
eight, three singles broken down, come up, meet, two doubles,
fall back, and then honour.°   70
AURELIA O Daedalus, thy maze!° I have quite forgot it.
MAQUERELLE Trust me, so have I, saving the falling back and then
    honour!°
        Enter Prepasso
AURELIA Music, music!
PREPASSO Who saw the duke? the duke?   75
        Enter Equato
AURELIA Music!
EQUATO The duke? is the duke returned?
AURELIA Music!
        Enter Celso
CELSO The duke is either quite invisible or else is not.
AURELIA We are not pleased with your intrusion upon our private   80
    retirement. We are not pleased; you have forgot yourselves.
        Enter a Page
CELSO Boy, thy master? Where's the duke?
PAGE Alas, I left him burying the earth with his spread, joyless
    limbs. He told me he was heavy, would sleep; bade me walk off,
    for that the strength of fantasy oft made him talk in his dreams. I 85
    straight obeyed, nor ever saw him since. But wheresoe'er he is,
    he's sad.
AURELIA Music, sound high, as is our heart; sound high!
        Enter Malevole, and Pietro disguised like a hermit
MALEVOLE The duke—peace! [*Music ceases*]—the duke is dead.
AURELIA Music!   90
MALEVOLE Is't music?
MENDOZA Give proof.
FERRARD How?
CELSO Where?
PREPASSO When?   95
MALEVOLE Rest in peace, as the duke does; quietly sit. For my own
    part, I beheld him but dead, that's all. Marry, here's one can give
    you a more particular account of him.
MENDOZA [*to Pietro*] Speak, holy father, nor let any brow
    Within this presence fright thee from the truth.   100
    Speak confidently and freely.
AURELIA   We attend.
PIETRO Now had the mounting sun's all-ripening wings

Swept the cold sweat of night from earth's dank breast,
When I, whom men call Hermit of the Rock,
Forsook my cell and clambered up a cliff, 105
Against whose base the heady Neptune dashed
His high-curled brows. There 'twas I eased my limbs,
When, lo, my entrails melted with the moan
Someone, who far 'bove me was climbed, did make—
I shall offend. 110
MENDOZA Not.
AURELIA On.
PIETRO Methinks I hear him yet: 'O female faith!
Go sow the ingrateful sand, and love a woman!
And do I live to be the scoff of men, 115
To be their wittol-cuckold, even to hug my poison?
Thou knowest, O truth,
Sooner hard steel will melt with southern wind,
A seaman's whistle calm the ocean,
A town on fire be extinct with tears, 120
Than women, vowed to blushless impudence,
With sweet behaviour and soft minioning,
Will turn from that where appetite is fixed.
O powerful blood, how thou dost slave their soul!
I washed an Ethiop, who, for recompense,° 125
Sullied my name. And must I then be forced
To walk, to live thus black? Must, must! Fie!
He that can bear with "must", he cannot die'.
With that he sighed so passionately deep
That the dull air even groaned. At last he cries, 130
'Sink shame in seas, sink deep enough!', so dies.
For then I viewed his body fall and souse
Into the foamy main. O then I saw
That which methinks I see: it was the duke,
Whom straight the nicer-stomached sea belched up. 135
But then—
MALEVOLE Then came I in; but, 'las, all was too late,
For even straight he sunk.
PIETRO   Such was the duke's sad fate.
CELSO A better fortune to our Duke Mendoza!
ALL Mendoza! 140
        Cornets flourish
MENDOZA A guard, a guard!

Enter a Guard

We, full of hearty tears
For our good father's loss,
For so we well may call him
Who did beseech your loves for our succession,
Cannot so lightly over-jump his death   145
As leave his woes revengeless.—(*To Aurelia*) Woman of shame,
We banish thee forever to the place
From whence this good man comes; nor permit, on death,
Unto thy body any ornament;°
But base as was thy life, depart away.   150

AURELIA Ungrateful!

MENDOZA Away!

AURELIA Villain, hear me!

MENDOZA Begone!

Prepasso and Guerrino lead away the Duchess
                    —My lords,
Address to public council; 'tis most fit°   155
The train of fortune is borne up by wit.
Away! Our presence shall be sudden; haste.°

All depart saving Mendoza, Malevole, and Pietro

MALEVOLE Now, you egregious devil! Ha, ye murdering politician!
How dost, duke? How dost look now? Brave duke, i'faith!

MENDOZA How did you kill him?   160

MALEVOLE Slatted his brains out, then soused him in the briny sea.

MENDOZA Brained him and drowned him too?

MALEVOLE O, 'twas best, sure work; for he that strikes a great man,
let him strike home, or else 'ware he'll prove no man. Shoulder not
a huge fellow, unless you may be sure to lay him in the kennel.   165

MENDOZA A most sound brain-pan! I'll make you both emperors.

MALEVOLE Make us Christians, make us Christians!

MENDOZA I'll hoist ye, ye shall mount!

MALEVOLE [*aside*] To the gallows, say ye? Come: *praemium incertum
petit certum scelus*.°—How stands the progress?   170

MENDOZA Here, take my ring unto the citadel;
Have entrance to Maria, the grave duchess
Of banished Altofront. Tell her we love her;
Omit no circumstance to grace our person. Do't.°

MALEVOLE I'll make an excellent pander. Duke, farewell; due   175
adieu,° duke.

MENDOZA Take Maquerelle with thee, for 'tis found

None cuts a diamond but a diamond.
    Exit Malevole
Hermit, thou art a man for me, my confessor.
O thou selected° spirit, born for my good,   180
Sure thou wouldst make an excellent elder
In a deformed° church. Come,
We must be inward, thou and I all one.

PIETRO I am glad I was ordained° for ye.

MENDOZA Go to, then; thou must know that Malevole is a strange   185
  villain, dangerous, very dangerous; you see how broad a speaks, a
  gross-jawed rogue. I would have thee poison him. He's like a corn
  upon my great toe; I cannot go for him.° He must be cored out, he
  must. Wilt do't, ha?

PIETRO Anything, anything.   190

MENDOZA Heart of my life! Thus then to the citadel.
  Thou shalt consort with this Malevole;
  There being at supper, poison him.
  It shall be laid upon Maria, who yields love or dies.
  Scud quick!   195

PIETRO Like lightning. Good deeds crawl, but mischief flies.
    Exit Pietro. Enter Malevole

MALEVOLE Your devilship's ring° has no virtue. The buff-captain,
  the sallow Westphalian gammon-faced zaza,° cries, 'Stand out';
  must have a stiffer warrant, or no pass into the Castle of Comfort.°

MENDOZA Command our sudden letter.° Not enter? Sha't! What   200
  place is there in Genoa but thou shalt? Into my heart, into my very
  heart. Come, let's love; we must love, we two, soul and body.

MALEVOLE How didst like the hermit? A strange hermit, sirrah.

MENDOZA A dangerous fellow, very perilous. He must die.

MALEVOLE Ay, he must die.   205

MENDOZA Thou'st° kill him. We are wise; we must be wise.

MALEVOLE And provident.

MENDOZA Yea, provident. Beware an hypocrite;
  A churchman once corrupted, O avoid!
  A fellow that makes religion his stalking-horse,
  Shoots under his belly, he breeds a plague.°   210
  Thou shalt poison him.

MALEVOLE Ho, 'tis wondrous necessary. How?

MENDOZA You both go jointly to the citadel;
  There sup, there poison him. And Maria,
  Because she is our opposite, shall bear   215

The sad suspect, on which she dies or loves us.

MALEVOLE I run.

    Exit Malevole

MENDOZA We that are great, our sole self-good still moves us.
They shall die both, for their deserts craves more   220
Than we can recompense, their presence still
Imbraids our fortunes with beholdingness,
Which we abhor; like deed, not doer. Then conclude,
They live not to cry out 'ingratitude!'
One stick burns t'other, steel cuts steel alone.   225
'Tis good trust few, but O, 'tis best trust none!

    Exit

4.2

Enter Malevole and Pietro still disguised, at several doors

MALEVOLE How do you? How dost, duke?

PIETRO O, let the last day fall, drop, drop on our cursed heads! Let
heaven unclasp itself, vomit forth flames!

MALEVOLE O, do not rant, do not turn player. There's more of
them than can well live one by another already. What, art an   5
infidel still?

PIETRO I am amazed, struck in a swoon with wonder! I am commanded to poison thee.

MALEVOLE I am commanded to poison thee, at supper.

PIETRO At supper!   10

MALEVOLE In the citadel.

PIETRO In the citadel!

MALEVOLE Cross-capers, tricks!° Truth o'heaven! he would discharge us as boys do eldern guns,° one pellet to strike out another!
Of what faith art now?   15

PIETRO All is damnation, wickedness extreme. There is no faith in
man.

MALEVOLE In none but usurers and brokers; they deceive no man;
men take 'em for bloodsuckers, and so they are. Now God deliver
me from my friends!   20

PIETRO Thy friends?

MALEVOLE Yes, from my friends, for from mine enemies I'll deliver
myself. O, cut-throat friendship is the rankest villainy. Mark this

Mendoza, mark him for a villain; but heaven will send a plague
upon him for a rogue.   25

PIETRO O world!

MALEVOLE World? 'Tis the only region of death, the greatest shop
of the devil, the cruell'st prison of men, out of the which none pass
without paying their dearest breath for a fee. There's nothing
perfect in it, but extreme, extreme calamity, such as comes yonder.   30

> *Enter Aurelia, two [Guards with] halberds before and two after,*
> *supported by Celso and Ferrard, Aurelia in base mourning attire*

AURELIA To banishment! Lead on to banishment!

PIETRO Lady, the blessedness of repentance to you!

AURELIA Why, why? I can desire nothing
But death, nor deserve anything but hell.
If heaven should give sufficiency of grace   35
To clear my soul, it would make heaven graceless;
My sins would make the stock of mercy poor;
O, they would tire heaven's goodness to reclaim them.
Judgement is just yet from that vast villain;
But sure he shall not miss sad punishment   40
'Fore he shall rule.—On to my cell of shame.

PIETRO My cell 'tis, lady, where instead of masques,
Music, tilts, tourneys, and such courtlike shows,
The hollow murmur of the checkless winds
Shall groan again, whilst the unquiet sea   45
Shakes the whole rock with foamy battery;
There usherless the air comes in and out;
The rheumy vault will force your eyes to weep,
Whilst you behold true desolation;
A rocky barrenness shall pierce your eyes,   50
Where all at once one reaches where he stands,
With brows the roof, both walls with both his hands.

AURELIA It is too good.—Blessed spirit of my lord,
O, in what orb soe'er thy soul is throned,
Behold me worthily most miserable.   55
O let the anguish of my contrite spirit
Entreat some reconciliation.
If not, O joy triumph in my just grief:
Death is the end of woes, and tears' relief.

PIETRO Belike your lord not loved you, was unkind.   60

AURELIA O heaven!
As the soul loves the body, so loved he;

'Twas death to him to part my presence,
Heaven to see me pleased.
Yet I, like to a wretch given o'er to hell,   65
Brake all the sacred rites of marriage,
To clip a base, ungentle, faithless villain,
O God, a very pagan reprobate—
What should I say?—ungrateful, throws me out,
For whom I lost soul, body, fame and honour.   70
But 'tis most fit; why should a better fate
Attend on any who forsake chaste sheets,
Fly the embrace of a devoted heart
Joined by a solemn vow 'fore God and man,
To taste the brackish blood of beastly lust   75
In an adulterous touch? O ravenous immodesty,
Insatiate impudence of appetite!
Look, here's your end; for mark what sap in dust,
What sin in good, even so much love in lust.
Joy to thy ghost, sweet lord, pardon to me.   80

CELSO It is the duke's pleasure this night you rest in court.

AURELIA Soul, lurk in shades; run, shame, from brightsome skies;
In night the blind man misseth not his eyes.

Exit [Aurelia with Celso, Ferrardo, and Guards]

MALEVOLE Do not weep, kind cuckold; take comfort, man; thy
betters have been *beccos*: Agamemnon,° emperor of all the merry   85
Greeks, that tickled all the true Trojans, was a *cornuto;* Prince
Arthur,° that cut off twelve kings' beards, was a *cornuto;* Hercules,° whose back bore up heaven and got forty wenches with
child in one night—

PIETRO Nay, 'twas fifty.   90

MALEVOLE Faith, forty's enough o'conscience—yet was a *cornuto*.
Patience; mischief grows proud; be wise.

PIETRO Thou pinchest too deep, art too keen upon me.

MALEVOLE Tut! a pitiful surgeon makes a dangerous sore;° I'll tent
thee to the ground. Think'st I'll sustain myself by flattering thee   95
because thou art a prince? I had rather follow a drunkard, and live
by licking up his vomit, than by servile flattery.

PIETRO Yet great men ha' done't.

MALEVOLE Great slaves fear better than love, born naturally for a
coal-basket,° though the common usher of princes' presence, For-   100
tune, ha' blindly given them better place.
I am vowed to be thy affliction.

PIETRO   Prithee be;

I love much misery, and be thou so° to me.
 Enter Bilioso
MALEVOLE Because you are an usurping duke.—
 (*To Bilioso*) Your lordship's well returned from Florence. 105
BILIOSO Well returned, I praise my horse.
MALEVOLE What news from the Florentines?
BILIOSO I will conceal the great duke's° pleasure; only this was his
 charge: his pleasure is that his daughter die, Duke Pietro be
 banished for banishing his blood's dishonour,° and that Duke 110
 Altofront be re-accepted. This is all. But I hear Duke Pietro is
 dead.
MALEVOLE Ay, and Mendoza is duke. What will you do?
BILIOSO Is Mendoza strongest?
MALEVOLE Yet he is. 115
BILIOSO Then yet I'll hold with him.
MALEVOLE But if that Altofront should turn straight again?°
BILIOSO Why, then I would turn straight again.°
 'Tis good run still with him that has most might;
 I had rather stand with wrong than fall with right. 120
MALEVOLE What religion will you be of now?
BILIOSO Of the duke's religion, when I know what it is.
MALEVOLE O Hercules!
BILIOSO Hercules? Hercules was the son of Jupiter and Alcmena.°
MALEVOLE Your lordship is a very wittol. 125
BILIOSO Wittol?
MALEVOLE Ay, all-wit.
BILIOSO Amphitryo° was a cuckold.
MALEVOLE Your lordship sweats; your young lady will get you a
 cloth for your old worship's brows. 130
 Exit Bilioso
 Here's a fellow to be damned! This is his inviolable maxim: flatter
 the greatest and oppress the least. A whoreson flesh-fly that still
 gnaws upon the lean galled backs.
PIETRO Why dost then salute him?
MALEVOLE Faith, as bawds go to church, for fashion sake. Come, be 135
 not confounded; thou'rt but in danger to lose a dukedom. Think
 this: this earth is the only grave and Golgotha° wherein all things
 that live must rot; 'tis but the draught wherein the heavenly bodies
 discharge their corruption; the very muckhill on which the sub-
 lunary orbs cast their excrements. Man is the slime of this dung- 140
 pit, and princes are the governors of these men; for, for our souls,

they are as free as emperors', all of one piece;° there goes but a
pair of shears betwixt an emperor and the son of a bagpiper, only
the dyeing, dressing, pressing, glossing makes the difference. Now,
what art thou like to lose?   145
A jailer's office to keep men in bonds,
Whilst toil and treason all life's good confounds.

PIETRO I here renounce forever regency.—
O Altofront, I wrong thee to supplant thy right,
To trip thy heels up with a devilish sleight;   150
For which I now from throne am thrown, world-tricks abjure;
For vengeance, though 't comes slow, yet it comes sure.
O, I am changed; for here, 'fore the dread power,
In true contrition I do dedicate
My breath to solitary holiness,   155
My lips to prayer, and my breast's care shall be
Restoring Altofront to regency.

MALEVOLE Thy vows are heard, and we accept thy faith.
        [*Malevole/Altofronto*] *undisguiseth himself. Enter Ferneze and*
        Celso°
Banish amazement.—Come, we four must stand
Full shock of fortune.—Be not so wonder-stricken!   160

PIETRO Doth Ferneze live?

FERNEZE   For your pardon.

PIETRO Pardon and love. Give leave to recollect°
My thoughts dispersed in wild astonishment.
My vows stand fixed in heaven, and from hence
I crave all love and pardon.

MALEVOLE   Who doubts of providence   165
That sees this change? A hearty faith to all!°
He needs must rise who can no lower fall;
For still impetuous vicissitude
Touseth the world. Then let no maze intrude
Upon your spirits; wonder not I rise,   170
For who can sink that close can temporise?°
The time grows ripe for action. I'll detect
My privat'st plot, lest ignorance fear suspect.°
Let's close to counsel, leave the rest to fate;
Mature discretion is the life of state.   175
        Exeunt

5.1

Enter Altofronto [as Malevole] and Maquerelle, at several doors
opposite,° singing

MALEVOLE   'The Dutchman for a drunkard,'
MAQUERELLE   'The Dane for golden locks;'
MALEVOLE   'The Irishman for usquebaugh,'
MAQUERELLE   'The Frenchman for the pox.'°

MALEVOLE O, thou art a blessed creature! Had I a modest woman to   5
conceal, I would put her to thy custody, for no reasonable creature
would ever suspect her to be in thy company. Ha, thou art a
melodious Maquerelle, thou picture of a woman and substance
of a beast! And how dost thou think o'this transformation of state
now?   10

MAQUERELLE Verily, very well; for we women always note the falling of the one is the rising of the other;° some must be fat, some
must be lean; some must be fools, and some must be lords; some
must be knaves, and some must be officers;° some must be beggars, some must be knights; some must be cuckolds, and some   15
must be citizens.° As, for example, I have two court dogs, the most
fawning curs, the one called Watch, th'other Catch. Now I, like
Lady Fortune, sometimes love this dog, sometimes raise that dog;
sometimes favour Watch, most commonly fancy Catch. Now that
dog which I favour I feed, and he's so ravenous that what I give he   20
never chews it, gulps it down whole without any relish of what he
has but with a greedy expectation of what he shall have. The other
dog now—

MALEVOLE No more dog, sweet Maquerelle, no more dog! And
what hope hast thou of the Duchess Maria? Will she stoop to the   25
duke's lure? Will she come, think'st?

MAQUERELLE Let me see, where's the sign° now? Ha' ye e'er a
calendar? Where's the sign, trow you?

MALEVOLE Sign! Why, is there any moment in that?

MAQUERELLE O, believe me, a most secret power. Look ye, a Chal-   30
dean° or an Assyrian, I am sure 'twas a most sweet Jew, told me:
court any woman in the right sign, you shall not miss. But you
must take her in the right vein then, as when the sign is in Pisces,
a fishmonger's wife is very sociable; in Cancer, a precisian's wife is
very flexible; in Capricorn, a merchant's wife hardly holds out; in   35

Libra, a lawyer's wife is very tractable, especially if her husband be at the term;° only in Scorpio, 'tis very dangerous meddling. Has the duke sent any jewel, any rich stones?°

Enter Captain

MALEVOLE Ay, I think those are the best signs to take a lady in.— [*To Captain*] By your favour, signor, I must discourse with the Lady Maria, Altofront's duchess; I must enter for the duke.   40

CAPTAIN She here shall give you interview. I received the guardship of this citadel from the good Altofront, and for his use I'll keep't till I am of no use.

MALEVOLE Wilt thou? O heavens, that a Christian should be found in a buff-jerkin!° Captain Conscience! I love thee, captain. We attend.   45

Exit Captain

—And what hope hast thou of this duchess' easiness?°

MAQUERELLE 'Twill go hard. She was a cold creature ever; she hated monkeys, fools, jesters and gentlemen-ushers extremely. She had the vile trick on't not only to be truly modestly honourable in her own conscience, but she would avoid the least wanton carriage that might incur suspect, as, God bless me, she had almost brought bed-pressing out of fashion. I could scarce get a fine° for the lease of a lady's favour once in a fortnight.   50   55

MALEVOLE Now, in the name of immodesty, how many maiden-heads hast thou brought to the block?

MAQUERELLE Let me see—Heaven forgive us our misdeeds! Here's the duchess.

Enter Maria and Captain

MALEVOLE God bless thee, lady.   60

MARIA Out of thy company!

MALEVOLE We have brought thee tender of a husband.

MARIA I hope I have one already.

MAQUERELLE Nay, by mine honour, madam, as good ha' ne'er a husband as a banished husband; he's in another world now. I'll tell ye, lady, I have heard of a sect that maintained, when the husband was asleep, the wife might lawfully entertain another man, for then her husband was as dead;° much more when he is banished.   65

MARIA Unhonest creature!

MAQUERELLE Pish! Honesty is but an art to seem so. Pray ye, what's honesty? what's constancy? but fables feigned, odd old fools' chat, devised by jealous fools to wrong our liberty.   70

MALEVOLE Mully,° he that loves thee is a duke, Mendoza. He will
maintain thee royally, love thee ardently, defend thee powerfully,
marry thee sumptuously, and keep thee in despite of Rosicleer or   75
Donzel del Phoebo.° There's jewels. [*Offers jewels*] If thou wilt, so;
if not, so.

MARIA Captain, for God's love, save poor wretchedness
From tyranny of lustful insolence;
Enforce me in the deepest dungeon dwell   80
Rather than here; here round about is hell.—
O, my dear'st Altofront, where'er thou breathe,
Let my soul sink into the shades beneath
Before I stain thine honour; 'tis thou has't;
And long as I can die, I will live chaste.   85

MALEVOLE 'Gainst him that can enforce, how vain is strife!

MARIA She that can be enforced has ne'er a knife.
She that through force her limbs with lust enrolls
Wants Cleopatra's° asps and Portia's° coals.
God amend you!   90
Exit [Maria] with Captain

MALEVOLE Now the fear of the devil for ever go with thee!—
Maquerelle, I tell thee, I have found an honest woman. Faith, I
perceive when all is done, there is of women as of all other things,
some good, most bad; some saints, some sinners. For as nowadays
no courtier but has his mistress, no captain but has his cockatrice,°   95
no cuckold but has his horns, and no fool but has his feather,°
even so, no woman but has her weakness and feather too, no sex
but has his . . . I can hunt the letter no further. [*Aside*] O God, how
loathsome this toying is to me! That a duke should be forced to
fool it! Well, *Stultorum plena sunt omnia*:° better play the fool lord   100
than be the fool lord.—Now, where's your sleights, Madam
Maquerelle?

MAQUERELLE Why, are ye ignorant that 'tis said a squeamish
affected niceness is natural to women, and that the excuse of their
yielding is only, forsooth, the difficult obtaining? You must put   105
her to 't.° Women are flax and will fire in a moment.°

MALEVOLE Why, was the flax put into thy mouth, and yet thou—
thou set fire? thou inflame her?

MAQUERELLE Marry, but I'll tell ye now, you were too hot.

MALEVOLE The fitter to have inflamed the flaxwoman.   110

MAQUERELLE You were too boisterous, spleeny, for indeed—

MALEVOLE Go, go, thou art a weak pand'ress; now I see,°
Sooner earth's fire heaven itself shall waste
Than all with heat can melt a mind that's chaste.
Go thou, the duke's lime-twig! I'll make the duke turn thee out of   115
thine office. What, not get one touch of hope, and had her at such
advantage?

MAQUERELLE Now o' my conscience, now I think in my discretion
we did not take her in the right sign; the blood was not in the true
vein, sure.   120

　　　　　　Exit [Maquerelle.] Enter Bilioso

BILIOSO Make way there! The duke returns from the enthrone-
ment.—Malevole!

MALEVOLE Out, rogue!

BILIOSO Malevole—

MALEVOLE 'Hence, ye gross-jawed peasantly—out, go!'°   125

BILIOSO Nay, sweet Malevole, since my return I hear you are
become the thing I always prophesied would be: an advanced
virtue, a worthily-employed faithfulness, a man o' grace, dear
friend. Come, what? *Si quoties peccant homines*° . . . If as often as
courtiers play the knaves, honest men should be angry—why, look   130
ye, we must collogue sometimes, forswear sometimes.

MALEVOLE Be damned sometimes.

BILIOSO Right. *Nemo omnibus horis sapit,*° no man can be honest at
all hours; necessity often depraves virtue.

MALEVOLE I will commend thee to the duke.   135

BILIOSO Do; let us be friends, man.

MALEVOLE And knaves, man.

BILIOSO Right! Let us prosper and purchase. Our lordships shall
live and our knavery be forgotten.

MALEVOLE He that by any ways gets riches, his means never shames   140
him.

BILIOSO True!

MALEVOLE For impudency and faithlessness are the mainstays to
greatness.

BILIOSO By the Lord, thou art a profound lad!   145

MALEVOLE By the Lord, thou art a perfect knave! Out, ye ancient
damnation!

BILIOSO Peace, peace! An thou wilt not be a friend to me as I am a
knave, be not a knave to me as I am thy friend, and disclose me.
Peace! Cornets!   150

[*Cornets sound.*] *Enter Prepasso and Ferrard, two Pages with lights, Celso and Equato, Mendoza in Duke's robes, and Guerrino*

MENDOZA On, on; leave us, leave us.—
  Exeunt all saving Malevole [and Mendoza]
  Stay! Where is the hermit?

MALEVOLE With Duke Pietro, with Duke Pietro.

MENDOZA Is he dead? Is he poisoned?

MALEVOLE Dead as the duke is.   155

MENDOZA Good, excellent; he will not blab. Secureness lives in secrecy. Come hither, come hither.

MALEVOLE Thou hast a certain strong villainous scent about thee my nature cannot endure.

MENDOZA Scent, man! What returns Maria? What answer to our   160
  suit?

MALEVOLE Cold, frosty; she is obstinate.

MENDOZA Then she's but dead; 'tis resolute, she dies.
  Black deed only through black deeds safely flies.

MALEVOLE Pooh! *Per scelera semper sceleribus tutum est iter.*°   165

MENDOZA What, art a scholar? Art a politician? Sure thou art an arrant knave!

MALEVOLE Who, I? I ha' been twice an undersheriff, man.

MENDOZA Canst thou empoison? Canst thou empoison?

MALEVOLE Excellently; no Jew, 'pothecary or politician better.   170
  Look ye, here's a box. Whom wouldst thou empoison? Here's a box which, opened and the fume ta'en up in conduits° through which the brain purges itself, doth instantly for twelve hours' space bind up all show of life in a deep senseless sleep. Here's another which, being opened under the sleeper's nose, chokes all   175
  the power of life, kills him suddenly.
  [*Mendoza takes the two boxes*]

MENDOZA [*aside*] I'll try experiments. 'Tis good not to be deceived.
  Seems to poison Altofronto [who falls]
  So, so. *Cazzo!*°
      Who would fear that may destroy?
        Death hath no teeth nor tongue;   180
      And he that's great, to him are slaves
        Shame, murder, fame and wrong.
  Celso!
      Enter Celso

CELSO My honoured lord?

MENDOZA The good Malevole, that plain-tongued man,   185
    Alas, is dead on sudden, wondrous strangely.
    He held in our esteem good place.
    Celso, see him buried, see him buried.

CELSO I shall observe ye.

MENDOZA And Celso, prithee let it be thy care tonight   190
    To have some pretty show to solemnize
    Our high instalment; some music, masquery.
    We'll give fair entertain unto Maria,
    The duchess to the banished Altofront.
    Thou shalt conduct her from the citadel   195
    Unto the palace. Think on some masquery.

CELSO Of what shape, sweet lord?

MENDOZA What shape? Why, any quick-done fiction,
    As some brave spirits of the Genoan dukes
    To come out of Elysium, forsooth,   200
    Led in by Mercury, to 'gratulate°
    Our happy fortune; some such anything,
    Some far-fet trick, good for ladies,°
    Some stale toy or other,
    No matter, so't be of your devising.°   205
    Do thou prepare 't; 'tis but for fashion sake.
    Fear not, it shall be graced, man, it shall take.

CELSO All service.

MENDOZA All thanks. Our hand shall not be close to thee.
    Farewell.   210
    [Aside] Now is my treachery secure, nor can we fall.
    Mischief that prospers, men do virtue call.
    I'll trust no man; he that by tricks gets wreaths
    Keeps them with steel; no man securely breathes
    Out of deservèd ranks; the crowd will mutter, 'fool';°   215
    Who cannot bear with spite, he cannot rule.
    The chiefest secret for a man of state
    Is to live senseless of a strengthless hate.
        Exit Mendoza. [Malevole] starts up and speaks

MALEVOLE Death of the damned thief! I'll make one i'the masque.
    Thou shalt ha' some brave spirits of the antique° dukes!   220

CELSO My lord, what strange delusion?

MALEVOLE Most happy, dear Celso; poisoned with an empty box!
    I'll give thee all anon. My lady comes to court. There is a whirl of
    fate comes tumbling on: the castle's captain stands for me, the

people pray for me, and the Great Leader of the just stands for
me. Then courage, Celso!   225
For no disastrous chance can ever move him
That leaveth nothing but a God above him.°
Exeunt

5.2

*Enter Prepasso and Bilioso, two Pages before them, Maquerelle,
Bianca, and Emilia*

BILIOSO Make room there, room for the ladies. Why, gentlemen,
will not ye suffer the ladies to be entered in the great chamber?
Why, gallants! And you, sir, to drop your torch° where the beauties must sit, too!

PREPASSO And there's a great fellow plays the knave; why dost not   5
strike him?

BILIOSO Let him play the knave, i' God's name; think'st thou I have
no more wit than to strike a great fellow?—The music! More
lights! Revelling-scaffolds!° Do you hear? Let there be oaths
enough° ready at the door; swear out the devil himself. Let's leave   10
the ladies and go see if the lords be ready for them.

All save the Ladies depart

MAQUERELLE And by my troth, beauties, why do you not put you
into the fashion? This is a stale cut; you must come in fashion.
Look ye, you must be all felt, felt and feather,° a felt upon your
bare hair. Look ye, these tiring-things are justly out of request   15
now. And, do ye hear? you must wear falling-bands,° you must
come into the falling fashion. There is such a deal o' pinning these
ruffs, when the fine clean fall is worth all. And again, if you should
chance to take a nap in the afternoon, your falling-band requires
no poting-stick° to recover his form. Believe me, no fashion to the   20
falling, I say.

BIANCA And is not Signor St. Andrew Jaques° a gallant fellow now?

MAQUERELLE By my maidenhead, la, honour and he agrees as well
together as a satin suit and woollen stockings.

EMILIA But is not Marshal Make-room,° my servant in reversion, a   25
proper gentleman?

MAQUERELLE Yes, in reversion; as he had his office; as, in truth, he
hath all things in reversion: he has his mistress in reversion, his
clothes in reversion, his wit in reversion, and indeed is a suitor to

me for my dog in reversion. But, in good verity, la, he is as proper   30
a gentleman in reversion as—and, indeed, as fine a man as may be,
having a red beard and a pair of warped legs.°

BIANCA But i'faith, I am most monstrously in love with Count Quidlibet-in-Quodlibet.° Is he not a pretty, dapper, wimble gallant?

MAQUERELLE He is even one of the most busy-fingered lords. He   35
will put the beauties to the squeak most hideously.

    [Enter Bilioso]

BILIOSO Room! Make a lane there! The duke is entering. Stand
handsomely, for beauty's sake.—Take up the ladies there. So,
cornets, cornets!

    [Cornets sound.] Enter [at one door] Prepasso [who] joins to
    Bilioso, two Pages with lights, Ferrard, Mendoza; at the other
    door two Pages with lights, and the Captain leading in Maria.
    The Duke meets Maria and closeth with her; the rest fall back

MENDOZA Madam, with gentle ear receive my suit;   40
A kingdom's safety should o'erpoise slight rites;°
Marriage is merely nature's policy.
Then since, unless our royal beds be joined,
Danger and civil tumult frights the state,
Be wise as you are fair, give way to fate.   45

MARIA What wouldst thou, thou affliction to our house?
Thou ever devil, 'twas thou that banishedst
My truly noble lord.

MENDOZA I?

MARIA Ay, by thy plots, by thy black stratagems.   50
Twelve moons have suffered change since I beheld
The lovèd presence of my dearest lord.
O thou far worse than death! He parts but soul
From a weak body, but thou soul from soul
Dissever'st, that which God's own hand did knit;   55
Thou scant of honour, full of devilish wit!

MENDOZA We'll check your too-intemperate lavishness.
I can and will.

MARIA What canst?

MENDOZA Go to! In banishment thy husband dies.   60

MARIA He ever is at home that's ever wise.

MENDOZA You'st never meet more; reason should love control.°

MARIA Not meet?
She that dear loves, her love's still in her soul.

MENDOZA You are but a woman, lady; you must yield.   65

MARIA O save me, thou innated bashfulness;
    Thou only ornament of woman's modesty!
MENDOZA Modesty? Death, I'll torment thee!
MARIA Do, urge all torments, all afflictions try;
    I'll die my lord's as long as I can die.   70
MENDOZA Thou obstinate, thou shalt die.—Captain,
    That lady's life is forfeited to justice.
    We have examined her,
    And we do find she hath empoisonèd
    The reverend hermit. Therefore we command   75
    Severest custody.—Nay, if you'll do 's no good,
    You'st do 's no harm. A tyrant's peace is blood.
MARIA O, thou art merciful! O gracious devil,
    Rather by much let me condemnèd be
    For seeming murder than be damned for thee.   80
    I'll mourn no more; come, girt my brows with flowers;
    Revel and dance, soul, now thy wish thou hast;
    Die like a bride, poor heart, thou shalt die chaste.
       Enter Aurelia in mourning habit
AURELIA 'Life is a frost of cold felicity,
    And death the thaw of all our vanity.'°   85
    Was't not an honest priest that wrote so?
MENDOZA Who let her in?
BILIOSO   Forbear!
PREPASSO   Forbear!
AURELIA (*to Maria*) Alas, calamity is everywhere.
    Sad misery, despite your double doors,
    Will enter even in court.   90
BILIOSO Peace!
AURELIA I ha' done. One word: take heed! I ha' done.
       Enter Mercury with loud music
MERCURY Cyllenian Mercury, the god of ghosts,°
    From gloomy shades that spread the lower coasts,
    Calls four high-famèd Genoan dukes to come
    And make this presence their Elysium,   95
    To pass away this high triumphal night
    With song and dances, court's more soft delight.
AURELIA Are you god of ghosts? I have a suit depending in hell
    betwixt me and my conscience; I would fain have thee help me to   100
    an advocate.
BILIOSO Mercury shall be your lawyer,° lady.

AURELIA Nay, faith, Mercury has too good a face to be a right
lawyer.°

PREPASSO Peace! Forbear! Mercury presents the masque.   105
    Cornets. The song to the cornets; which playing, the masque
    enters: Altofronto, Pietro, Ferneze, and Celso in white robes
    [and masked], with Dukes' crowns upon laurel wreathes,
    pistolets, and short swords [concealed] under their robes

MENDOZA Celso, Celso, court Maria for our love.——Lady, be gracious, yet grace.
    Altofronto takes his wife to dance

MARIA With me, sir?

MALEVOLE   Yes, more lovèd than my breath;
With you I'll dance.

MARIA   Why then, you dance with death.
But come, sir, I was ne'er more apt for mirth.   110
Death gives eternity a glorious birth;°
O, to die honoured, who would fear to die?

MALEVOLE They die in fear who live in villainy.

MENDOZA Yes, believe him, lady, and be ruled by him.
    Pietro takes his wife Aurelia to dance

PIETRO Madam, with me?

AURELIA   Wouldst then be miserable?   115

PIETRO I need not wish.

AURELIA O yet forbear my hand; away, fly, fly!
O seek not her that only seeks to die.

PIETRO Poor lovèd soul!

AUELIA   What, wouldst court misery?

PIETRO Yes.   120

AURELIA She'll come too soon. O my grieved heart!

PIETRO Lady, ha' done, ha' done.
Come, let's dance; be once from sorrow free.

AURELIA Art a sad man?

PIETRO   Yes, sweet.

AURELIA   Then we'll agree.°
    Ferneze takes Maquerelle, and Celso, Bianca [to dance]; then
    the cornets sound the measure; one change° and rest

FERNEZE (*to Bianca*) Believe it, lady; shall I swear? Let me enjoy you 125
in private, and I'll marry you, by my soul.

BIANCA I had rather you would swear by your body. I think that
would prove the more regarded oath with you.

FERNEZE I'll swear by them both, to please you.

BIANCA O, damn them not both to please me, for God's sake!   130

FERNEZE Faith, sweet creature, let me enjoy you tonight, and I'll
marry you tomorrow fortnight, by my troth, la.

MAQUERELLE On his troth, la! Believe him not; that kind of cony-
catching is as stale as Sir Oliver Anchovy's perfumed jerkin.
Promise of matrimony by a young gallant to bring a virgin lady   135
into a fool's paradise, make her a great woman, and then cast her
off: 'tis as common, as natural to a courtier, as jealousy to a
citizen,° gluttony to a puritan, wisdom to an alderman, pride to
a tailor, or an empty handbasket to one of these sixpenny damnations.° Of his troth, la! Believe him not; traps to catch polecats!   140

MALEVOLE (to Maria) Keep your face constant. Let no sudden
    passion
    Speak in your eyes. [Reveals himself]

MARIA   O, my Altofront!

PIETRO (to Aurelia) A tyrant's jealousies
    Are very nimble; you receive it all. [Reveals himself]

AURELIA (to Pietro) My heart, though not my knees, doth humbly
    fall   145
    Low as the earth to thee.

PIETRO   Peace! Next change. No words.

AURELIA° Speech to such, ay, O, what will affords!°
    Cornets sound the measure over again; which danced they
    unmask°

MENDOZA Malevole?
    They environ Mendoza, bending their pistols on him

MALEVOLE No.°

MENDOZA Altofront, Duke Pietro, Ferneze, ha!   150

ALL Duke Altofront! Duke Altofront!
    Cornets, a flourish

MENDOZA Are we surprised? What strange delusions mock
    Our senses? Do I dream? Or have I dreamt
    This two days' space? Where am I?
    They seize upon Mendoza

MALEVOLE Where an arch-villain is.   155

MENDOZA O, lend me breath till I am fit to die;
    For peace with heaven, for your own souls' sake,
    Vouchsafe me life.

PIETRO Ignoble villain, whom neither heaven nor hell,
    Goodness of God or man, could once make good!   160

MALEVOLE Base, treacherous wretch, what grace canst thou expect,

That hast grown impudent in gracelessness?
MENDOZA O life!
MALEVOLE Slave, take thy life.
　　Wert thou defencèd, through blood and wounds,　　165
　　The sternest horror of a civil fight,
　　Would I achieve thee; but prostrate at my feet,
　　I scorn to hurt thee; 'tis the heart of slaves
　　That deigns to triumph over peasants' graves.
　　For such thou art, since birth doth ne'er enrol　　170
　　A man 'mong monarchs, but a glorious soul.
　　O, I have seen strange accidents of state:
　　The flatterer like the ivy clip the oak
　　And waste it to the heart; lust so confirmed
　　That the black act of sin itself not shamed　　175
　　To be termed courtship.
　　O, they that are as great as be their sins,
　　Let them remember that th'inconstant people
　　Love many princes merely for their faces
　　And outward shows; and they do covet more　　180
　　To have a sight of these than of their virtues.
　　Yet thus much let the great ones still conceit:°
　　When they observe not heaven's imposed conditions,
　　They are no kings but forfeit their commissions.
MAQUERELLE O, good my lord, I have lived in the court this twenty　　185
　　year; they that have been old courtiers and come to live in the city,
　　they are spitted at and thrust to the walls like apricots,° good my
　　lord.
BILIOSO My lord, I did know your lordship in this disguise; you
　　heard me ever say, if Altofront did return, I would stand for him.　　190
　　Besides, 'twas your lordship's pleasure to call me wittol and cuck-
　　old; you must not think, but that I knew you, I would have put it
　　up° so patiently.
MALEVOLE [to the Courtiers] You o'er-joyed spirits, wipe your
　　long-wet eyes.—
　　Hence with this man; an eagle takes not flies.—　　195
　　　　Kicks out Mendoza
　　(To Pietro and Aurelia) You to your vows.—(To Maquerelle)
　　　　And thou unto the suburbs.—°
　　(To Bilioso) You to my worst friend I would hardly give;
　　Thou art a perfect old knave.—(To Celso and the Captain) All-
　　　　pleased, live,

You two, unto my breast.—(*To Maria*) Thou to my heart.—
The rest of idle actors idly part.°   200
And as for me, I here assume my right,
To which I hope all's pleased. To all, goodnight.

    Cornets, a flourish. Exeunt

EPILOGUE

Enter the Epilogue

EPILOGUE Your modest silence, full of heedy stillness,
  Makes me thus speak: a voluntary illness
  Is merely 'scuseless, but unwilling error,
  Such as proceeds from too rash youthful fervour,
  May well be called a fault, but not a sin.   5
  Rivers take names from founts where they begin.
  Then let not too severe an eye peruse
  The slighter breaks of our reformèd Muse,°
  Who could herself herself of faults detect,
  But that she knows 'tis easy to correct,   10
  Though some men's labour. Troth, to err is fit,°
  As long as wisdom's not professed, but wit.
  Then till another's happier Muse appears,
  Till his Thalia feast your learnèd ears,°
  To whose desertful lamps pleased fates impart°   15
  Art above Nature, Judgement above Art,
  Receive this piece, which hope nor fear yet daunteth;
  He that knows most, knows most how much he wanteth.
    [*Exit*]

THE DUTCH COURTESAN

THE PERSONS OF THE PLAY

Franceschina°	a Dutch courtesan
Mary Faugh°	an old woman, [Franceschina's bawd]
Sir Lionel Freevill° ⎫ Sir Hubert Subboys ⎭	two old knights
Young Freevill	Sir Lionel's son
Beatrice° ⎫ Crispinella° ⎭	Sir Hubert's daughters
Putifer°	their nurse
Tysefew°	a blunt gallant
Caqueteur°	a prattling gull
Malheureux°	young Freevill's unhappy friend
Cocledemoy°	a knavishly witty, city companion
Master Mulligrub°	a vintner
Mistress Mulligrub°	the vintner's wife
Master Burnish	a goldsmith
Lionel	his man
Holifernes Reinscure°	a barber's boy
[Christian]	[a servant to Mulligrub]
3 Watchmen [Constables]	
[Pages]	
[Gentlemen]	
Halberdiers	
[Servants]	
[Officers]	
[Musicians]	

The Dutch Courtesan

PROLOGUE

[Enter the] Prologue

PROLOGUE Slight hasty labours in this easy play
    Present not what you would, but what we may.
    For this vouchsafe to know, the only end
    Of our now study is not to offend.
    Yet think not but, like others, rail we could;   5
    Best art presents not what it can but should;
    And if our pen in this seem over-slight
    We strive not to instruct but to delight.°
    As for some few we know of purpose here
    To tax and scout, know firm art cannot fear   10
    Vain rage; only the highest grace we pray
    Is, you'll not tax until you judge our play.
    Think, and then speak; 'tis rashness, and not wit,
    To speak what is in passion, and not judgement fit.
    Sit, then, with fair expectance, and survey   15
    Nothing but passionate man in his slight play,°
    Who hath this only ill, to some deemed worst:
    A modest diffidence and self-mistrust.
       [Exit]

1.1

Enter three Pages with lights,° Mulligrub, Freevill,
Malheureux, Tysefew, and Caqueteur

FREEVILL Nay, comfort, my good host Shark, my good Mulligrub.

MALHEUREUX Advance thy snout; do not suffer thy sorrowful nose°
to drop on thy Spanish leather jerkin, most hardly-honest Mulligrub.

FREEVILL What, cogging Cocledemoy is run away with a nest of   5
goblets?° True, what then? They will be hammered out° well
enough, I warrant you.

MULLIGRUB Sure, some wise man would find them out presently.

FREEVILL Yes, sure, if we could find out some wise man presently.

MALHEUREUX How was the plate lost? How did it vanish?   10

FREEVILL In most sincere prose, thus:° that man of much money,
some wit, but less honesty, cogging Cocledemoy, comes this night
late into mine host's Mulligrub's tavern here, calls for a room. The
house being full, Cocledemoy, consorted with his movable chattel,
his instrument of fornication, the bawd Mistress Mary Faugh, are   15
imparloured next the street.° Good poultry was their food, black-
bird, lark, woodcock; and mine host here comes in, cries, 'God
bless you!' and departs. A blind harper° enters, craves audience,
uncaseth,° plays. The drawer, for female privateness' sake, is
nodded out, who, knowing that whosoever will hit the mark of   20
profit must, like those that shoot in stone-bows, wink with one
eye, grows blind o'the right side and departs.

CAQUETEUR He shall answer for that winking with one eye at the
last day.°

MALHEUREUX Let him have day° till then, and he will wink with   25
both his eyes.

FREEVILL Cocledemoy, perceiving none in the room but the blind
harper, whose eyes heaven had shut up from beholding wickedness, unclasps a casement to the street very patiently, pockets up
three bowls unnaturally, thrusts his wench forth the window, and   30
himself most preposterously,° with his heels forward, follows. The
unseeing harper plays on, bids the empty dishes and the treacherous candles much good do them.° The drawer returns; but out
alas, not only the birds, but also the nest of goblets, were flown
away. Laments are raised—   35

TYSEFEW Which did not pierce the heavens.°

FREEVILL —The drawers moan, mine host doth cry, the bowls are gone.

MULLIGRUB *Hic finis Priami!*°

MALHEUREUX Nay, be not jaw-fallen, my most sharking Mulligrub.   40

FREEVILL 'Tis your just affliction; remember the sins of the cellar° and repent, repent!

MULLIGRUB I am not jaw-fallen, but I will hang the cony-catching Cocledemoy, and there's an end of't.
  Exit [Mulligrub]

CAQUETEUR [*indicating Tysefew's ring*] Is it a right stone? It shows   45
well by candlelight.

TYSEFEW So do many things that are counterfeit, but I assure you this is a right diamond.

CAQUETEUR Might I borrow it of you? It will not a little grace my finger in visitation of my mistress.   50

TYSEFEW Why, use it, most sweet Caqueteur, use it.
  [*Gives the ring to him*]

CAQUETEUR Thanks, good sir.—'Tis grown high night. Gentles, rest to you.
  [*Exit Caqueteur with a Page*]

TYSEFEW [*to Page*] A torch!—Sound wench, soft sleep, and sanguine dreams to you both!—On, boy!   55
  [*Exit Tysefew with a Page*]

FREEVILL Let me bid you good rest.

MALHEUREUX Not so, trust me, I must bring my friend home. I dare not give you up to your own company; I fear the warmth of wine and youth will draw you to some common house of lascivious entertainment.   60

FREEVILL Most necessary buildings, Malheureux. Ever since my intention of marriage, I do pray for their continuance.

MALHEUREUX Loved sir, your reason?

FREEVILL Marry, lest my house should be made one. I would have married men love the stews as Englishmen love the Low Coun-   65
tries:° wish war should be maintained there lest it should come home to their own doors. What, suffer a man to have a hole to put his head in,° though he go to the pillory for it! Youth and appetite are above the club of Hercules.°

MALHEUREUX This lust is a most deadly sin, sure.   70

FREEVILL Nay, 'tis a most lively sin, sure.

MALHEUREUX Well, I am sure 'tis one of the head sins.

FREEVILL Nay, I am sure it is one of the middle° sins.

MALHEUREUX Pity 'tis grown a most daily vice.

FREEVILL But a more nightly vice, I assure you.   75

MALHEUREUX Well, 'tis a sin.

FREEVILL Ay, or else few men would wish to go to heaven. And, not
to disguise with my friend, I am now going the way of all flesh.

MALHEUREUX Not to a courtesan?

FREEVILL A courteous one.   80

MALHEUREUX What, to a sinner?

FREEVILL A very publican.°

MALHEUREUX Dear my loved friend, let me be full with you.
Know, sir, the strongest argument that speaks
Against the soul's eternity is lust,   85
That wise man's folly and the fool's wisdom;
But to grow wild in loose lasciviousness,
Given up to heat and sensual appetite,
Nay, to expose your health, and strength, and name,
Your precious time, and with that time the hope   90
Of due preferment, advantageous means
Of any worthy end, to the stale use,
The common bosom, of a money-creature,
One that sells human flesh, a mangonist!

FREEVILL Alas, good creatures, what would you have them do?   95
Would you have them get their living by the curse of man, the
sweat of their brows? So they do. Every man must follow his trade,
and every woman her occupation. A poor, decayed, mechanical
man's wife, her husband is laid up; may not she lawfully be laid
down when her husband's only rising is by his wife's falling? A   100
captain's wife wants means, her commander lies in open field
abroad; may not she lie in civil° arms at home? A waiting-gentle-
woman, that had wont to take say° to her lady, miscarries or so,
the court misfortune throws her down; may not the city courtesy
take her up? Do you know no alderman would pity such a   105
woman's case?° Why, is charity grown a sin? or relieving the poor
and impotent an offence? You will say beasts take no money for
their fleshly entertainment. True, because they are beasts, therefore beastly. Only men give to lose,° because they are men, therefore manly. And indeed, wherein should they bestow their money   110
better? In land? The title may be cracked. In houses? They may be
burned. In apparel? 'Twill wear. In wine? Alas for pity, our throat
is but short. But employ your money upon women, and a thousand

to nothing some one of them will bestow that on you which shall
stick by you as long as you live. They are no ingrateful persons; 115
they will give *quid* for *quo*. Do ye protest, they'll swear; do you
rise, they'll fall; do you fall, they'll rise; do you give them the
French crown,° they'll give you the French°—*O justus, justa,
justum!*° They sell their bodies; do not better persons sell their
souls? Nay, since all things have been sold—honour, justice, faith, 120
nay, even God himself!—ay me, what base ignobleness is it to sell
the pleasure of a wanton bed?
Why do men scrape, why heap to full heaps join?
But for his mistress, who would care for coin?
For this I hold to be denied of no man: 125
All things are made for man, and man for woman.
Give me my fee!°

MALHEUREUX Of ill you merit well. My heart's good friend,
Leave yet at length, at length, for know this ever:
'Tis no such sin to err, but to persever.   130

FREEVILL Beauty is woman's virtue, love the life's music, and
woman the daintiness or second course of heaven's curious workmanship. Since, then, beauty, love and woman are good, how can
the love of woman's beauty be bad? And, *Bonum, quo communius,
eo melius.*° Wilt then go with me?   135

MALHEUREUX Whither?

FREEVILL To a house of salvation.

MALHEUREUX Salvation?

FREEVILL Yes, 'twill make thee repent. Wilt go to the Family of
Love?° I will show thee my creature, a pretty, nimble-eyed Dutch 140
Tannakin;° an honest, soft-hearted impropriation; a soft, plump,
round-cheeked *frau,* that has beauty enough for her virtue, virtue
enough for a woman, and woman enough for any reasonable man
in my knowledge. Wilt pass along with me?

MALHEUREUX What, to a brothel? to behold an impudent prostitu- 145
tion? Fie on't! I shall hate the whole sex to see her. The most
odious spectacle the earth can present is an immodest, vulgar
woman.

FREEVILL Good, still; my brain shall keep't. You must go, as you
love me.   150

MALHEUREUX Well! I'll go to make her loathe the shame she's in;
The sight of vice augments the hate of sin.

FREEVILL 'The sight of vice augments the hate of sin.'
Very fine, perdy!
        Exeunt

1.2

Enter Cocledemoy and Mary Faugh

COCLEDEMOY Mary, Mary° Faugh!

MARY Hem!

COCLEDEMOY Come, my worshipful, rotten, rough-bellied bawd.
Ha! my blue-toothed patroness of natural wickedness, give me the
goblets.   5

MARY By yea and by nay, Master Cocledemoy, I fear you'll play the
knave and restore them.

COCLEDEMOY No, by the Lord, aunt; restitution is Catholic,° and
thou know'st we love—

MARY What?   10

COCLEDEMOY Oracles are ceased; *tempus praeteritum.*° Dost hear,
my worshipful clyster-pipe, thou ungodly fire that burned Diana's
temple?° Dost hear, bawd?

MARY In very good truthness, you are the foulest-mouthed, profane,
railing brother! call a woman the most ungodly names! I must   15
confess we all eat of the forbidden fruit; and for mine own part,
though I am one of the Family of Love and, as they say, a bawd
that covers the multitude of sins, yet I trust I am none of the
wicked that eat fish o' Fridays.°

COCLEDEMOY Hang toasts!° I rail at thee? my worshipful organ-   20
bellows that fills the pipes, my fine, rattling, phlegmy cough o'the
lungs and cold with a pox. I rail at thee? What, my right precious
panderess, supportress of barber-surgeons° and enhanceress of
lotium and diet-drink?° I rail at thee, necessary damnation? I'll
make an oration, I, in praise of thy most courtly-in-fashion and   25
most pleasurable function, I.

MARY I prithee do. I love to hear myself praised, as well as any old
lady, I.

COCLEDEMOY List, then. A bawd. First for her profession or vocation: it is most worshipful of all the twelve companies;° for as that 30
trade is most honourable that sells the best commodities—as the
draper is more worshipful than the pointmaker, the silkman more
worshipful than the draper, and the goldsmith more honourable
than both, little Mary—so the bawd above all: her shop has the
best ware, for where these sell but cloth, satins and jewels, she sells 35
divine virtues, as virginity, modesty and such rare gems, and those
not like a petty chapman, by retail, but like a great merchant, by

wholesale. Wahahowe!° And who are her customers? Not base
corncutters or sowgelders, but most rare wealthy knights and most
rare bountiful lords are her customers. Again, whereas no trade or   40
vocation profiteth but by the loss and displeasure of another—as
the merchant thrives not but by the licentiousness of giddy and
unsettled youth, the lawyer but by the vexation of his client, the
physician but by the maladies of his patient—only my smooth-
gummed bawd lives by others' pleasure and only grows rich by   45
others' rising. O merciful gain! O righteous income! So much for
her vocation, trade and life. As for their death, how can it be bad
since their wickedness is always before their eyes and a death's
head° most commonly on their middle finger? To conclude, 'tis
most certain they must needs both live well and die well, since   50
most commonly they live in Clerkenwell and die in Bridewell.°
Dixi,° Mary.

>   *Enter Freevill and Malheureux [preceded by a Page with a*
>   *light]*

FREEVILL Come along; yonder's the preface or exordium to my
wench, the bawd.—Fetch, fetch!

>   [*Exit Mary Faugh*]

—What, Master Cocledemoy, is your knaveship yet stirring? Look   55
to it; Mulligrub lies for° you.

COCLEDEMOY The more fool he. I can lie for myself, worshipful
friend. Hang toasts! I vanish? Ha, my fine boy, thou art a scholar
and hast read Tully's *Offices,*° my fine knave! Hang toasts!

FREEVILL The vintner will toast you an he catch you.   60

COCLEDEMOY I will draw the vintner to the stoup, and when
he runs low, tilt him.° Ha, my fine knave, art going to thy recreation?

FREEVILL Yes, my capricious rascal.

COCLEDEMOY Thou wilt look like a fool then, by and by.   65

FREEVILL Look like a fool? Why?

COCLEDEMOY Why, according to the old saying, a beggar when he
is lousing of himself looks like a philosopher, a hard-bound philosopher when he is on the stool looks like a tyrant, and a wise man
when he is in his belly-act looks like a fool. God give your worship   70
good rest! Grace and mercy keep your syringe straight and your
lotium° unspilled!

>   [*Exit Cocledemoy.*] *Enter Franceschina*

FREEVILL See, sir, this is she.

MALHEUREUX This?

FREEVILL This.   75

MALHEUREUX A courtesan? [*Aside*] Now cold blood defend me!
What a proportion° afflicts me!

FRANCESCHINA O mine aderliver° love, vat sall me do to requit dis
your mush affection?

FREEVILL Marry, salute my friend, clip his neck and kiss him wel-   80
come.

FRANCESCHINA O' mine art, sir, you bin very velcome.
        [*She kisses Malheureux*]

FREEVILL Kiss her, man, with a more familiar affection.
        [*Malheureux kisses Franceschina*]
So.—Come, what entertainment? Go to your lute.
        [*Exit Franceschina*]
—And how dost approve my sometimes elected? She's none of   85
your ramping cannibals that devour man's flesh, nor any of your
Curtian gulfs° that will never be satisfied until the best thing a
man has be thrown into them. I loved her with my heart until my
soul showed me the imperfection of my body and placed my
affection on a lawful love, my modest Beatrice, which if this   90
short-heels knew, there were no being for me with eyes before
her face. But faith, dost thou not somewhat excuse my sometimes
incontinency with her enforcive beauties? Speak!

MALHEUREUX Ha, she is a whore, is she not?

FREEVILL Whore? Fie, whore! You may call her a courtesan, a   95
cockatrice,° or—as that worthy spirit of an eternal happiness
said—a suppository.° But whore! Fie! 'Tis not in fashion to call
things by their right names. Is a great merchant a cuckold? You
must say he is one of the livery.° Is a great lord a fool? You must
say he is weak. Is a gallant pocky? You must say he has the court   100
scab. Come, she's your mistress, or so.
        [*Enter Franceschina with her lute*]
—Come, siren, your voice!

FRANCESCHINA Vill you not stay in mine bosom tonight, love?

FREEVILL By no means, sweet breast. This gentleman has vowed to
see me chastely laid.   105

FRANCESCHINA He shall have a bed, too, if dat it please him.

FREEVILL Peace! you tender him offence. He is one of a professed
abstinence. Siren, your voice, and away.

FRANCESCHINA (*singing the song to her lute*)
        The dark is my delight,
        So 'tis the nightingale's.   110

>*My music's in the night,*
>*So is the nightingale's.*
>*My body is but little,*
>*So is the nightingale's.*
>*I love to sleep 'gainst prickle,*   115
>*So doth the nightingale.°*

FREEVILL Thanks. Buss! [*Kisses her*] So. The night grows old; good
rest.

FRANCESCHINA Rest to mine dear love; rest, and no long absence.

FREEVILL Believe me, not long.   120

FRANCESCHINA Sall ick not believe you long?
Exit Franceschina

FREEVILL O yes.—[*To Page*] Come, *via!* Away, boy! On!
Exit [Freevill], his Page lighting him. [Then] enter
Freevill and seems to overhear° Malheureux

MALHEUREUX Is she unchaste? Can such a one be damned?
Of love and beauty, ye two eldest seeds
Of the vast chaos, what strong right you have   125
Even in things divine, our very souls!

FREEVILL [*aside*] Wahahowe! Come, bird, come! Stand, peace!

MALHEUREUX Are strumpets, then, such things so delicate?
Can custom spoil what nature made so good?
Or is their custom bad? Beauty's for use.   130
I never saw a sweet face vicious;
It might be proud, inconstant, wanton, nice,
But never tainted with unnatural vice.
Their worst is, their best art is love to win;
O that to love should be or shame or sin!   135

FREEVILL [*aside*] By the Lord, he's caught! Laughter eternal!

MALHEUREUX Soul, I must love her!
Destiny is weak to my affection.
A common love! Blush not, faint breast;
That which is ever loved of most is best.
Let colder eld the strong'st objections move;   140
No love's without some lust, no life without some love.

FREEVILL [*to Malheureux*] Nay, come on, good sir; what though 'the
most odious spectacle the world can present be an immodest,
vulgar woman'? Yet, sir, for my sake—   145

MALHEUREUX Well, sir, for your sake I'll think better of them.

FREEVILL Do, good sir, and pardon me that have brought you in.
You know 'the sight of vice augments the hate of sin'.

MALHEUREUX Ha, will you go home, sir? 'Tis high bedtime.

FREEVILL With all my heart, sir; only do not chide me;   150
I must confess.

MALHEUREUX   A wanton lover you have been.

FREEVILL 'O that to love should be or shame or sin!'

MALHEUREUX Say ye?

FREEVILL 'Let colder eld the strong'st objections move!'

MALHEUREUX How's this?   155

FREEVILL 'No love's without some lust, no life without some love!'
Go your ways for an *apostata*! I believe my cast garment must be
let out in the seams for you when all is done.
Of all the fools that would all man out-thrust
He that 'gainst nature would seem wise is worst.   160

　　Exeunt

2.1

Enter Freevill, Pages with torches, and Gentlemen with music°

FREEVILL The morn is yet but young. Here, gentlemen,
This is my Beatrice' window, this the chamber
Of my betrothèd dearest, whose chaste eyes,
Full of loved sweetness and clear cheerfulness,
Have gaged my soul to her enjoyings,   5
Shredding away all those weak under-branches
Of base affections and unfruitful heats.
Here bestow your music to my voice.

   He sings. [Exeunt Gentlemen and Pages.] Enter Beatrice [at the
   window]° *above*

Always a virtuous name to my chaste love!

BEATRICE Loved sir,   10
The honour of your wish return to you.
I cannot with a mistress' compliment,
Forcèd discourses, or nice art of wit
Give entertain to your dear wishèd presence;
But safely thus: what hearty gratefulness,   15
Unsullen silence, unaffected modesty,
And an unignorant shamefastness can express,
Receive as your protested due. Faith, my heart,°
I am your servant.
O let not my secure simplicity   20
Breed your mislike, as one quite void of skill;
'Tis grace enough in us not to be ill.
I can some good and, faith, I mean no hurt;
Do not then, sweet, wrong sober ignorance.
I judge you all of virtue, and our vows   25
Should kill all fears that base distrust can move.
My soul, what say you? Still you love?

FREEVILL   Still!
My vow is up above me and, like time,
Irrevocable. I am sworn all yours;
No beauty shall untwine our arms, no face   30
In my eyes can or shall seem fair;
And would to God only to me you might
Seem only fair! Let others disesteem

Your matchless graces, so might I safer seem.
Envy I covet not; far, far be all ostent,   35
Vain boasts of beauties, soft joys, and the rest;
He that is wise pants on a private breast.
So could I live in desert most unknown,
Yourself to me enough were populous.
Your eyes shall be my joys, my wine that still   40
Shall drown my often cares. Your only voice
Shall cast a slumber on my list'ning sense.
You with soft lip shall only ope mine eyes
And suck their lids asunder; only you
Shall make me wish to live, and not fear death,   45
So on your cheeks I might yield latest breath.
O he that thus may live and thus shall die
May well be envied of a deity.

BEATRICE Dear my loved heart, be not so passionate;
Nothing extreme lives long.

FREEVILL   Nothing in love's extreme,°   50
But not to be extreme. My love receives no mean.

BEATRICE I give you faith; and prithee, since, poor soul,°
I am so easy to believe thee,
Make it much more pity to deceive me.
Wear this slight favour in my remembrance.   55
        Throweth down a ring to him

FREEVILL Which when I part from, hope the best of life,
Ever part from me.

BEATRICE I take you and your word, which may ever live your
servant. See, day is quite broke up—the best of hours.

FREEVILL Good morrow, graceful mistress. Our nuptial day holds. 60

BEATRICE With happy constancy, a wishèd day.
        Exit [Beatrice from above]

FREEVILL Myself and all content rest with you.
        Enter Malheureux

MALHEUREUX [*aside*] The studious morn with paler cheek draws on
The day's bold light. Hark how the free-born birds
Carol their unaffected passions.   65
        The nightingales sing°
Now sing they sonnets; thus they cry, 'We love!'
O breath of heaven! Thus they, harmless souls,
Give entertain to mutual affects.
They have no bawds, no mercenary beds,

No politic restraints, no artificial heats,   70
No faint dissemblings; no custom makes them blush;
No shame afflicts their name.—O, you happy beasts
In whom an inborn heat is not held sin,
How far transcend you wretched, wretched man,
Whom national custom, tyrannous respects   75
Of slavish order, fetters, lames his power,
Calling that sin in us which in all things else
Is nature's highest virtue!
O miseri quorum gaudia crimen habent!°
Sure nature against virtue cross doth fall,°   80
Or virtue's self is oft unnatural.
That I should love a strumpet, I, a man of snow!
Now shame forsake me! Whither am I fallen?
A creature of a public use! My friend's love, too!
To live to be a talk to men, a shame   85
To my professèd virtue! O accursèd reason,
How many eyes hast thou to see thy shame,
And yet how blind once to prevent defame!

FREEVILL *Diaboli virtus in lumbis est!*° Morrow, my friend. Come, I
could make a tedious scene of this now, but what? Pah! thou art in   90
love with a courtesan. Why, sir, should we loathe all strumpets,
some men should hate their own mothers or sisters; a sin against
kind, I can tell you.

MALHEUREUX May it beseem a wise man to be in love?

FREEVILL Let wise men alone; 'twill beseem thee and me well   95
enough.

MALHEUREUX Shall I not offend the vow-band of our friendship?

FREEVILL What, to affect that which thy friend affected? By heaven,
I resign her freely. The creature and I must grow off. By this time
she has assuredly heard of my resolved marriage, and, no question,   100
swears, 'God's sacrament, ten tousand divels!' I'll resign, i'faith.

MALHEUREUX I would but embrace her, hear her speak, and at the
most but kiss her.

FREEVILL O friend, he that could live with the smoke of roast meat
might live at a cheap rate!   105

MALHEUREUX I shall ne'er prove heartily received;
A kind of flat ungracious modesty,
An insufficient dullness, stains my 'haviour.

FREEVILL No matter, sir. Insufficiency and sottishness are much
commendable in a most discommendable action. Now could I   110

swallow thee! Thou hadst wont to be so harsh and cold, I'll tell
thee.
Hell and the prodigies of angry Jove
Are not so fearful to a thinking mind
As a man without affection. Why, friend,   115
Philosophy and nature are all one;
Love is the centre in which all lines close,
The common bond of being.

MALHEUREUX O, but a chaste, reservèd privateness,
A modest continence—   120

FREEVILL I'll tell thee what, take this as firmest sense:
Incontinence will force a continence;
Heat wasteth heat, light defaceth light;
Nothing is spoiled but by his proper might.
This is something too weighty for thy floor!°   125

MALHEUREUX But howsoe'er you shade it, the world's eye°
Shines hot and open on 't.
Lying, malice, envy are held but slidings,
Errors of rage, when custom and the world
Calls lust a crime spotted with blackest terrors.   130

FREEVILL Where errors are held crimes, crimes are but errors.
Along, sir, to her! She is an arrant strumpet, and a strumpet is a
serpigo, venomed gonorrhoea to man, things actually possessed!
Yet since thou art in love—
          Offers to go out and suddenly draws back
And again, as good make use of a statue, a body without a soul, a   135
carcass three months dead! Yet since thou art in love—

MALHEUREUX Death, man, my destiny I cannot choose!

FREEVILL Nay, I hope so. Again, they sell but only flesh, no jot
affection, so that even in the enjoying, *Absentem marmoreamque*
putes.° Yet since you needs must love—   140

MALHEUREUX Unavoidable though folly, worse than madness!

FREEVILL It's true.
But since you needs must love, you must know this:
He that must love, a fool and he must kiss.
          Enter Cocledemoy
—Master Cocledemoy, *ut vales, domine!*°   145

COCLEDEMOY *Ago tibi gratias,*° my worshipful friend. How does
your friend?

FREEVILL Out, you rascal!

COCLEDEMOY Hang toasts, you are an ass! Much o'your worship's
brain lies in your calves. Bread o' God, boy, I was at supper last   150
night with a new-weaned bulchin.° Bread o' God, drunk, horribly
drunk, horribly drunk! There was a wench, one Frank Frailty,° a
punk, an honest polecat, of a clean instep, sound leg, smooth
thigh, and the nimble devil in her buttock. Ah, fist o' grace! When
saw you Tysefew or Master Caqueteur, that prattling° gallant of a   155
good draught, common customs, fortunate impudence, and sound
fart?

FREEVILL Away, rogue!

COCLEDEMOY Hang toasts, my fine boy, my companions are worshipful.   160

MALHEUREUX Yes, I hear you are taken up with scholars and
churchmen.

Enter Holifernes, the barber['s boy]

COCLEDEMOY *Quamquam te Marce fili,* my fine boy.—°[*To Freevill*]
Does your worship want a barber-surgeon?°

FREEVILL Farewell, knave. Beware the Mulligrubs!   165

Exeunt Freevill and Malheureux

COCLEDEMOY Let the Mulligrubs beware the knave.—What, a barber-surgeon, my delicate boy?

HOLIFERNES Yes, sir, an apprentice to surgery.

COCLEDEMOY 'Tis my fine boy. To what bawdy house doth your
master belong? What's thy name?   170

HOLIFERNES Holifernes Reinscure. [*He takes off his hat*]

COCLEDEMOY Reinscure? Good Master Holifernes, I desire your
further acquaintance. Nay, pray ye be covered,° my fine boy; kill
thy itch and heal thy scabs. Is thy master rotten?

HOLIFERNES My father, forsooth, is dead.

COCLEDEMOY   '—And laid in his grave.   175
Alas, what comfort shall Peggy then have?'°

HOLIFERNES None but me, sir, that's my mother's son, I assure you.

COCLEDEMOY Mother's son? A good, witty boy; would live to read
an homily well. And to whom are you going now?

HOLIFERNES Marry, forsooth, to trim Master Mulligrub, the vint-   180
ner.

COCLEDEMOY Do you know Master Mulligrub?

HOLIFERNES My godfather, sir.

COCLEDEMOY Good boy, hold up thy chops. I pray thee do one
thing for me. My name is Gudgeon.   185

HOLIFERNES Good Master Gudgeon.

COCLEDEMOY Lend me thy basin, razor and apron.

HOLIFERNES O Lord, sir!

COCLEDEMOY Well spoken, good English. But what's thy furniture
worth?   190

HOLIFERNES O Lord sir, I know not.

COCLEDEMOY Well spoken; a boy of good wit. Hold this pawn.
Where dost dwell?

HOLIFERNES At the sign of the Three Razors, sir.

COCLEDEMOY A sign of good shaving, my catastrophonical° fine   195
boy. I have an odd jest to trim° Master Mulligrub for a wager, a
jest, boy, a humour. I'll return thy things presently. Hold.

HOLIFERNES What mean you, good Master Gudgeon?

COCLEDEMOY Nothing, faith, but a jest, boy. Drink that. [*Gives
money*] I'll recoil presently.   200

HOLIFERNES You'll not stay long?

COCLEDEMOY As I am an honest man. The Three Razors?

HOLIFERNES Ay, sir.

Exit Holifernes

COCLEDEMOY Good. And if I shave not Master Mulligrub, my wit
has no edge and I may go cack in my pewter! Let me see—a   205
barber. My scurvy tongue will discover me. Must dissemble, must
disguise. For my beard, my false hair; for my tongue,
Spanish, Dutch, or Welsh? No, a Northern barber;° very good.
Widow Reinscure's man; well. Newly entertained; right. So.
Hang toasts! All cards have white backs, and all knaves would   210
seem to have white breasts.° So proceed now, worshipful Cocledemoy!

Exit Cocledemoy in his barber's furniture

2.2

*Enter Mary Faugh and Franceschina with her hair loose,°
chafing*

MARY Nay, good sweet daughter, do not swagger so. You hear your
love is to be married. True, he does cast you off; right, he will
leave you to the world. What then? Though blue and white, black
and green leave you, may not red and yellow entertain you? Is
there but one colour in the rainbow?   5

FRANCESCHINA Grand grincome on your sentences! God's sacrament, ten tousand devils take you! You ha' brought mine love, mine honour, mine body, all to noting.

MARY To nothing? I'll be sworn I have brought them to all the things I could. I ha' made as much o'your maidenhead; an you had been mine own daughter, I could not ha' sold your maidenhead oftener that I ha' done. I ha' sworn for you, God forgive me! I have made you acquainted with the Spaniard, Don Skirtoll; with the Italian, Master Beieroane; with the Irish Lord, Sir Patrick; with the Dutch merchant, Hans Herkin Glukin Skellam Flapdragon; and especially with the greatest French; and now lastly with this English—yet, in my conscience, an honest gentleman. And am I now grown one of the accursed with you for my labour? Is this my reward? Am I called bawd?—Well, Mary Faugh, go thy ways, Mary Faugh; thy kind heart will bring thee to the hospital.

FRANCESCHINA Nay, good naunt, you'll help me to anoder love, vill you not?

MARY Out, thou naughty belly! Wouldst thou make me thy bawd? Thou'st best make me thy bawd; I ha' kept counsel for thee.° Who paid the apothecary? Was't not honest Mary Faugh? Who redeemed thy petticoat and mantle? Was't not honest Mary Faugh? Who helped thee to thy custom, not of swaggering Ireland captains, nor of two-shilling Inns o' Court men,° but with honest flat-caps,° wealthy flat-caps, that pay for their pleasure the best of any men in Europe, nay, which is more, in London? And dost thou defy me, vile creature?

FRANCESCHINA Foutra 'pon you, vitch, bawd, polecat! Paugh! did you not praise Freevill to mine love?

MARY I did praise, I confess, I did praise him. I said he was a fool, an unthrift, a true whoremaster, I confess; a constant drab-keeper, I confess. But what, the wind is turned!

FRANCESCHINA It is, it is, vile woman, reprobate woman, naughty woman, it is! Vat sall become of mine poor flesh now? Mine body must turn Turk for twopence.° O divila, life o' mine art! Ick sall be revenged! Do ten tousand hell damn me, ick sall have the rogue troat cut; and his love, and his friend, and all his affinity sall smart, sall die, sall hang! Now legion of devil seize him! De gran' pest, St. Anthony's fire, and de hot Neapolitan pock° rot him!

Enter Freevill and Malheureux

FREEVILL Franceschina!

195

FRANCESCHINA O mine seet, dear'st, kindest, mine loving! O mine tousand, ten tousand, delicated, petty seet'art! Ah, mine aderlievest affection!

FREEVILL Why, monkey, no fashion in you? Give entertain to my friend.°

FRANCESCHINA Ick sall make de most of you dat courtesy may.—   50
Aunt Mary! Mettre Faugh! Stools, stools for dese gallants!

> [*Mary Faugh places stools and they sit. Franceschina*
> *sings in the French style*]

> *Mine mettre sing non oder song—*

[*to Malheureux*] Frolic, frolic, sir!—

> *But still complain me do her wrong—*   55

Lighten your heart, sir!—

> *For me did but kiss her,*
> *For me did but kiss her,*
> *And so let go.*°

[*To Freevill*] Your friend is very heavy. Ick sall ne'er like such sad   60
company.

FREEVILL No, thou delightest only in light company.

FRANCESCHINA By mine trot, he been very sad.—Vat ail you, sir?

MALHEUREUX A toothache, lady, a paltry rheum.

FRANCESCHINA De diet is very goot for de rheum.   65

FREEVILL How far off dwells the house-surgeon,° Mary Faugh?

MARY You are a profane fellow, i'faith. I little thought to hear such ungodly terms come from your lips.

> [*Franceschina attempts to take Beatrice's ring from Freevill*]

FRANCESCHINA Pridee now, 'tis but a toy, a very trifle.

FREEVILL I care not for the value, Frank, but i'faith—   70

FRANCESCHINA I'fait, me must needs have it.—[*Aside*] Dis is Beatrice's ring. O could I get it!—Seet, pridee now, as ever you have embraced me with a hearty arm, a warm thought, or a pleasing touch, as ever you will profess to love me, as ever you do wish me life, give me dis ring, dis little ring.   75

FREEVILL Prithee, be not uncivilly importunate. Sha' not ha't. Faith, I care not for thee nor thy jealousy. Sha' not ha't, i'faith.

FRANCESCHINA You do not love me. I hear of Sir Hubert Subboys' daughter, Mistress Beatrice. God's sacrament! Ick could scratch out her eyes and suck the holes!   80

FREEVILL Go! Y'are grown a punk rampant!

FRANCESCHINA So? Get thee gone! Ne'er more behold min eyes, by
thee made wretched!

FREEVILL Mary Faugh, farewell.——Farewell, Frank.

FRANCESCHINA Sall I not ha' de ring?   85

FREEVILL No, by the Lord!

FRANCESCHINA By te Lord?

FREEVILL By the Lord!

FRANCESCHINA Go to your new blowze, your unproved sluttery,°
your modest mettre, forsooth!   90

FREEVILL Marry, will I, forsooth.

FRANCESCHINA Will you marry, forsooth?

FREEVILL Do not turn witch before thy time.——[*To Malheureux*]
With all my heart, sir, you will stay.

MALHEUREUX I am no whit myself. *Video meliora proboque,*°   95
But raging lust my fate all strong doth move;
The gods themselves cannot be wise and love.

FREEVILL Your wishes to you.

    Exit Freevill

MALHEUREUX Beauty entirely choice—

FRANCESCHINA Pray ye, prove a man of fashion and neglect the   100
neglected.

MALHEUREUX [*aside*] Can such a rarity be neglected? Can there be
measure or sin in loving such a creature?

FRANCESCHINA O, min poor forsaken heart!

MALHEUREUX [*aside*] I cannot contain!—   105
[*To Franceschina*] He saw thee not that left thee.—
If there be wisdom, reason, honour, grace
Or any foolishly esteemèd virtue°
In giving o'er possession of such beauty,
Let me be vicious, so I may be loved.   110
Passion, I am thy slave.——Sweet, it shall be my grace,
That I account thy love my only virtue.
Shall I swear I am thy most vowed servant?

FRANCESCHINA Mine vowed? Go, go, go! I can no more of love
No, no, no! You bin all unconstant. O unfaithful men, tyrants,   115
betrayers! De very enjoying us loseth us, and when you only ha'
made us hateful, you only hate us. O mine forsaken heart!

MALHEUREUX [*aside*] I must not rave. Silence and modesty, two
customary virtues. [*To Franceschina*] Will you be my mistress?

FRANCESCHINA Mettres? Ha, ha, ha!   120

MALHEUREUX Will you lie with me?

FRANCESCHINA Lie with you? O, no! You men will out-lie any woman. Fait, me no more can love.

MALHEUREUX No matter. Let me enjoy your bed.

FRANCESCHINA O vile man, vat do you tink on me? Do you 125 take me to be a beast, a creature that for sense only will entertain love, and not only for love, love? O brutish abomination!

MALHEUREUX Why then, I pray thee love, and with thy love enjoy me.

FRANCESCHINA Give me reason to affect you. Will you swear you 130 love me?

MALHEUREUX So seriously, that I protest no office so dangerous, no deed so unreasonable, no cost so heavy, but I vow to the utmost temptation of my best being to effect it.

FRANCESCHINA Sall I or can I trust again? O fool, 135
How natural 'tis for us to be abused!
Sall ick be sure that no satiety,
No enjoying, not time, shall languish your affection?

MALHEUREUX If there be aught in brain, heart or hand
Can make you doubtless, I am your vowed servant. 140

FRANCESCHINA Will you do one ting for me?

MALHEUREUX Can I do it?

FRANCESCHINA Yes, yes; but ick do not love dis same Freevill.

MALHEUREUX Well?

FRANCESCHINA Nay, I do hate him. 145

MALHEUREUX So.

FRANCESCHINA By this kiss, I hate him. [*Kisses him*]

MALHEUREUX I love to feel such oaths. Swear again.

FRANCESCHINA No, no. Did you ever hear of any that loved at the first sight? 150

MALHEUREUX A thing most proper.

FRANCESCHINA Now, fait, I judge it all incredible, until this hour I saw you, pretty fair-eyed yout. Would you enjoy me?

MALHEUREUX Rather than my breath; even as my being!

FRANCESCHINA Vell, had ick not made a vow— 155

MALHEUREUX What vow?

FRANCESCHINA O let me forget it; it makes us both despair.

MALHEUREUX Dear soul, what vow?

FRANCESCHINA Ha! good morrow, gentle sir. Endeavour to forget me, as I must be enforced to forget all men. Sweet mind rest in 160 you! [*Offers to go*]

MALHEUREUX Stay! Let not my desire burst me. O my impatient
heat endures no resistance, no protraction. There is no being for
me but your sudden enjoying.°
FRANCESCHINA I do not love Freevill.   165
MALHEUREUX But what vow, what vow?
FRANCESCHINA So long as Freevill lives, I must not love.
MALHEUREUX Then he—
FRANCESCHINA Must—
MALHEUREUX Die!   170
FRANCESCHINA Ay.—No, there is no such vehemence in your
affects. Would I were anything, so he were not!
MALHEUREUX Will you be mine when he is not?
FRANCESCHINA Will I? Dear, dear breast, by this most zealous
kiss—but I will not persuade you. But if you hate him that I   175
loathe most deadly—yet, as you please; I'll persuade noting.
MALHEUREUX Will you be only mine?
FRANCESCHINA Vill I? How hard 'tis for true love to dissemble. I
am only yours.
MALHEUREUX 'Tis as irrevocable as breath: he dies!   180
Your love!
FRANCESCHINA My vow, not until he be dead,
Which that I may be sure not to infringe,
Dis token of his death sall satisfy:
He has a ring, as dear as the air to him,
His new love's gift. Tat got and brought to me,   185
I shall assurèd your professèd rest.
MALHEUREUX To kill a man!
FRANCESCHINA O, done safely: a quarrel sudden picked, with an
advantage strike; then bribe, a little coin; all's safe, dear soul. But
I'll not set you on.   190
MALHEUREUX Nay, he is gone. The ring? Well. Come, little more
liberal of thy love. [Tries to kiss her]
FRANCESCHINA Not yet; my vow.
MALHEUREUX   O heaven, there is no hell
But love's prolongings! Dear, farewell.
FRANCESCHINA   Farewell.
[Aside] Now does my heart swell high, for my revenge   195
Has birth and form. First friend sall kill his friend;
He dat survives, I'll hang; besides, de chaste
Beatrice I'll vex. Only de ring!

Dat got, the world sall know the worst of evils;
Woman corrupted is the worst of devils.   200
    Exit Franceschina [with Mary Faugh]
MALHEUREUX To kill my friend! O, 'tis to kill myself!
Yet man's but man's excrement, man breeding man
As he does worms. Or this.
    He spits
                      To spoil this, nothing.
The body of a man is of the selfsame soil
As ox or horse; no murder to kill these.   205
As for that only part which makes us man,°
Murder wants power to touch 't.—O wit, how vile,
How hellish art thou when thou raisest nature
'Gainst sacred faith! Think more, to kill a friend
To gain a woman, to lose a virtuous self   210
For appetite and sensual end, whose very having
Loseth all appetite and gives satiety—
That corporal end, remorse and inward blushings,
Forcing us loathe the steam of our own heats,
Whilst friendship closed in virtue, being spiritual,   215
Tastes no such languishings and moment's pleasure
With much repentance, but like rivers flow,
And further that they run, they bigger grow.
Lord, how was I misgone! How easy 'tis to err
When passion will not give us leave to think!   220
A learn'd, that is an honest, man may fear,
And lust, and rage, and malice, and anything
When he is taken uncollected suddenly:
'Tis sin of cold blood, mischief with waked eyes,
That is the damnèd and the truly vice.   225
Not he that's passionless, but he 'bove passion's wise.
My friend shall know it all.
    Exit

2.3

Enter Master Mulligrub and Mistress Mulligrub, she with a bag of money
MISTRESS MULLIGRUB It is right, I assure you, just fifteen pounds.

MULLIGRUB Well, Cocledemoy, 'tis thou putt'st me to this charge, but an I catch thee, I'll charge thee with as many irons.°—Well, is the barber come? I'll be trimmed and then to Cheapside° to buy a fair piece of plate to furnish the loss.° Is the barber come?

MISTRESS MULLIGRUB Truth, husband, surely heaven is not pleased with our vocation. We do wink at the sins of our people, our wines are Protestants,° and, I speak it to my grief and to the burden of my conscience, we fry our fish with salt butter.°

MULLIGRUB Go, look to your business; mend the matter, and score false with a vengeance.—

    Exit [Mistress Mulligrub]. Enter Cocledemoy like a barber
Welcome, friend. Whose man?

COCLEDEMOY Widow Reinscure's man, an't shall please your good worship; my name's Andrew Shark.°

MULLIGRUB How does my godson, good Andrew?

COCLEDEMOY Very well. He's gone to trim Master Quicquid,° our parson. Hold up your head.

MULLIGRUB How long have you been a barber, Andrew?

COCLEDEMOY Not long, sir; this two year.°

MULLIGRUB What, and a good workman already? I dare scarce trust my head to thee.

COCLEDEMOY O, fear not; we ha' polled° better men than you. We learn the trade very quickly. Will your good worship be shaven or cut?

MULLIGRUB As you will. What trade didst live by before thou turned'st barber, Andrew?

COCLEDEMOY I was a pedlar in Germany, but my countrymen thrive better by this trade.

MULLIGRUB What's the news, barber? Thou art sometimes at court.°

COCLEDEMOY Sometimes poll° a page or so, sir.

MULLIGRUB And what's the news? How do all my good lords and all my good ladies, and all the rest of my acquaintance?

COCLEDEMOY [*aside*] What an arrogant knave's this! I'll acquaintance ye! (*He spieth the bag*) 'Tis cash!—[*To Mulligrub*] Say ye, sir?

MULLIGRUB And what news? What news, good Andrew?

COCLEDEMOY Marry, sir, you know the conduit at Greenwich and the under-holes that spouts up water?

MULLIGRUB Very well; I was washed there one day and so was my wife; you might have wrung her smock, i'faith. But what o' those holes?

COCLEDEMOY   Thus, sir: out of those little holes in the midst of the night crawled out twenty-four huge, horrible, monstrous, fearful, devouring—

MULLIGRUB   Bless us!   45

COCLEDEMOY   —Serpents, which no sooner were beheld but they turned to mastiffs, which howled; those mastiffs instantly turned to cocks, which crowed; those cocks in a moment were changed to bears, which roared; which bears are at this hour to be yet seen in Paris Garden,° living upon nothing but toasted cheese and green   50 onions.°

MULLIGRUB   By the Lord, and this may be! My wife and I will go see them; this portends something.

COCLEDEMOY   [aside] Yes, worshipful fist, thou'st feel what portends by and by.   55

MULLIGRUB   And what more news? You shave the world; especially you barber-surgeons; you know the ground of many things; you are cunning privy searchers;° by the mass, you scour all! What more news?

COCLEDEMOY   They say, sir, that twenty-five couple of Spanish   60 jennets are to be seen hand-in-hand dance the old measures, whilst six goodly Flanders mares play to them on a noise of flutes.

MULLIGRUB   O monstrous! This is a lie, o' my word. Nay, an this be not a lie—I am no fool, I warrant!—nay, make an ass of me once—

COCLEDEMOY   Shut your eyes close, wink! Sure, sir, this ball° will   65 make you smart.

MULLIGRUB   I do wink.

COCLEDEMOY   Your head will take cold.

I will put on your good worship's nightcap whilst I shave you.

Cocledemoy puts on a coxcomb on Mulligrub's head

So, mum! [*Aside*] Hang toasts! Faugh! *Via!* Sparrows must peck   70 and Cocledemoy munch.

[*Exit Cocledemoy with the bag of money*]

MULLIGRUB   Ha, ha, ha! Twenty-five couple of Spanish jennets to dance the old measures! Andrew makes my worship laugh, i'faith. Dost take me for an ass, Andrew? Dost know one Cocledemoy in town? He made me an ass last night, but I'll ass him! Art thou   75 free,° Andrew? Shave me well; I shall be one of the Common Council° shortly, and then, Andrew—Why, Andrew?—Andrew, dost leave me in the suds?

He sings°

Why, Andrew, I shall be blind with winking. Ha, Andrew! Wife!
Andrew! What means this? Wife! My money! Wife! 80
Enter Mistress Mulligrub

MISTRESS MULLIGRUB What's the noise with you? What ail you?

MULLIGRUB Where's the barber?

MISTRESS MULLIGRUB Gone. I saw him depart long since. Why,
are not you trimmed?

MULLIGRUB Trimmed! O wife, I am shaved! Did you take hence 85
the money?

MISTRESS MULLIGRUB I touched it not, as I am religious.

MULLIGRUB O Lord, I have winked fair!
Enter Holifernes

HOLIFERNES I pray, godfather, give me your blessing. [*He kneels*]

MULLIGRUB O, Holifernes! O, where's thy mother's Andrew? 90

HOLIFERNES Blessing, godfather!

MULLIGRUB The devil choke thee! Where's Andrew, thy mother's
man?

HOLIFERNES My mother hath none such, forsooth.

MULLIGRUB My money—fifteen pounds! Plague of all Andrews! 95
Who was't trimmed me?

HOLIFERNES I know not, godfather, only one met me as I was
coming to you and borrowed my furniture, as he said for a jest'
sake.

MULLIGRUB What kind of fellow?

HOLIFERNES A thick, elderly, stub-bearded fellow. 100

MULLIGRUB Cocledemoy! Cocledemoy! Raise all the wise men in the
street! I'll hang him with mine own hands. O wife, some *rosa solis*!°

MISTRESS MULLIGRUB Good husband, take comfort in the Lord;
I'll play the devil, but I'll recover it. Have a good conscience; 'tis 105
but a week's cutting in the term.°

MULLIGRUB O wife, O wife!—O Jack, how does thy mother?—Is
there any fiddlers in the house?

MISTRESS MULLIGRUB Yes, Master Creak's noise.°

MULLIGRUB Bid 'em play. Laugh, make merry! Cast up my 110
accounts, for I'll go hang myself presently. I will not curse, but
a pox on Cocledemoy! He has polled and shaved me; he has
trimmed me!
Exeunt

3.1

Enter Beatrice, Crispinella, and Nurse Putifer°

PUTIFER Nay, good child o' love, once more Master Freevill's sonnet o'the kiss you gave him!

BEATRICE Sh'a 't,° good nurse. [*Reads*]
'Purest lips, soft banks of blisses,
Self alone, deserving kisses,   5
O give me leave to—'

CRISPINELLA Pish! sister Beatrice, prithee read no more! My stomach o' late stands against kissing extremely.

BEATRICE Why, good Crispinella?

CRISPINELLA By the faith and trust I bear to my face, 'tis grown   10
one of the most unsavoury ceremonies. Body o' beauty! 'tis one of
the most unpleasing, injurious customs to ladies. Any fellow that
has but one nose on his face, and standing collar and skirts also
lined with taffeta sarcenet, must salute us on the lips as familiarly—Soft skins save us! There was a stub-bearded John-a-Stile°   15
with a ployden's° face saluted me last day and struck his bristles
through my lips. I ha' spent ten shillings in pomatum since to skin
them again. Marry, if a nobleman or a knight with one lock visit
us, though his unclean goose-turd-green teeth ha' the palsy, his
nostrils smell worse than a putrefied marrowbone, and his loose   20
beard drops into our bosom, yet we must kiss him with a cur'sy.°
A curse! For my part, I had as lief they would break wind in my
lips.

BEATRICE Fie, Crispinella, you speak too broad!

CRISPINELLA No jot, sister. Let's ne'er be ashamed to speak what   25
we be not ashamed to think. I dare as boldly speak venery as think
venery.

BEATRICE Faith, sister, I'll be gone if you speak so broad.

CRISPINELLA Will you so? Now bashfulness seize you! We pro-
nounce boldly robbery, murder, treason, which deeds must needs   30
be far more loathsome than an act which is so natural, just and
necessary as that of procreation. You shall have an hypocritical
vestal virgin speak that with close teeth publicly which she will
receive with open mouth privately. For my own part, I consider
nature without apparel; without disguising of custom or compli-   35
ment, I give thoughts words, and words truth, and truth boldness.

She whose honest freeness makes it her virtue to speak what she thinks, will make it her necessity to think what is good. I love no prohibited things, and yet I would have nothing prohibited by policy but by virtue; for as in the fashion of the time° those books that are called in° are most in sale and request, so in nature those actions that are most prohibited are most desired.

BEATRICE Good quick sister, stay your pace. We are private, but the world would censure you; for truly, severe modesty is women's virtue.

CRISPINELLA Fie, fie! Virtue is a free, pleasant, buxom quality.° I love a constant countenance well; but this froward, ignorant coyness, sour, austere, lumpish, uncivil privateness that promises nothing but rough skins and hard stools—ha, fie on't! good for nothing but for nothing.—Well, nurse, and what do you conceive of all this?

PUTIFER Nay, faith, my conceiving days be done! Marry, for kissing, I'll defend that; that's within my compass. But for my own part, here's Mistress Beatrice is to be married, with the grace of God. A fine gentleman he is shall have her, and I warrant a strong; he has a leg like a post, a nose like a lion, a brow like a bull, and a beard of most fair expectation.—This week you must marry him, and I now will read a lecture to you both, how you shall behave yourselves to your husbands the first month of your nuptial. I ha' broke my skull° about it, I can tell you, and there is much brain in it.

CRISPINELLA Read it to my sister, good nurse, for I assure you I'll ne'er marry.

PUTIFER Marry, God forfend! What will you do then?

CRISPINELLA Faith, strive against the flesh. Marry? No, faith; husbands are like lots in the lottery: you may draw forty blanks before you find one that has any prize° in him. A husband generally is a careless, domineering thing that grows like coral, which as long as it is under water is soft and tender, but as soon as it has got his branch above the waves is presently hard, stiff, not to be bowed but burst; so, when your husband is a suitor and under your choice, Lord! how supple he is, how obsequious, how at your service, sweet lady; once married, got up his head above, a stiff, crooked, knobby, inflexible, tyrannous creature he grows. Then they turn like water: more you would embrace, the less you hold. I'll live my own woman, and if the worst come to the worst, I had rather prove a wag than a fool.

BEATRICE O, but a virtuous marriage—

CRISPINELLA Virtuous marriage? There is no more affinity betwixt
virtue and marriage than betwixt a man and his horse. Indeed,   80
virtue gets up upon marriage sometimes and manageth it in the
right way, but marriage is of another piece; for as a horse may be
without a man, and a man without a horse, so marriage, you know,
is often without virtue, and virtue, I am sure, more oft without
marriage. But thy match, sister, by my troth, I think 'twill do well.   85
He's a well-shaped, clean-lipped gentleman, of a handsome but
not affected fineness, a good faithful eye, and a well-humoured
cheek. Would he did not stoop in the shoulders, for thy sake!

> *Enter Freevill and Tysefew*

See, here he is.

FREEVILL Good day, sweet.   90

CRISPINELLA Good morrow, brother. Nay, you shall have my lip.
[*Kisses him.*]—Good morrow, servant.

TYSEFEW Good morrow, sweet life.

CRISPINELLA Life? Dost call thy mistress life?

TYSEFEW Life, yes, why not life?   95

CRISPINELLA How many mistresses has thou?

TYSEFEW Some nine.

CRISPINELLA Why then, thou hast nine lives like a cat.

TYSEFEW Mew! You would be taken up for that.

CRISPINELLA Nay, good, let me still sit; we low statures love still to   100
sit, lest when we stand we may be supposed to sit.

TYSEFEW Dost not wear high cork shoes, chopines?

CRISPINELLA Monstrous ones. I am as many other are, pieced
above° and pieced beneath.

TYSEFEW Still the best part in the—°   105

CRISPINELLA And yet all will scarce make me so high as one of the
giant's stilts that stalks before my Lord Mayor's pageant.°

TYSEFEW By the Lord, so; I thought 'twas for something Mistress
Joyce jested at thy high insteps.

CRISPINELLA She might well enough, and long enough, before I   110
would be ashamed of my shortness. What I made or can mend
myself I may blush at; but what nature put upon me, let her be
ashamed for me, I ha' nothing to do with it. I forget my beauty.

TYSEFEW Faith, Joyce is a foolish, bitter creature.

CRISPINELLA A pretty mildewed wench she is.   115

TYSEFEW And fair.

CRISPINELLA As myself.

TYSEFEW O, you forget your beauty now!

CRISPINELLA Troth, I never remember my beauty but as some men
    do religion, for controversy's sake.   120

BEATRICE A motion,° sister—

CRISPINELLA *Nineveh, Julius Caesar, Jonah,* or *The Destruction of*
    Jerusalem?

BEATRICE My love here—

CRISPINELLA Prithee, call him not 'love'; 'tis the drab's phrase: nor   125
    'sweet honey', nor 'my cony', nor 'dear duckling'; 'tis the citizen
    terms. But call me him—

BEATRICE What?

CRISPINELLA Anything. What's the motion?

BEATRICE You know this night our parents have intended solemnly   130
    to contract us; and my love, to grace the feast, hath promised a
    masque.

FREEVILL You'll make one, Tysefew, and Caqueteur shall fill up a
    room.°

TYSEFEW 'Fore heaven, well remembered! He borrowed a diamond   135
    of me last night to grace his finger in your visitation.° The lying
    creature will swear some strange thing on it now.

    Enter Caqueteur

CRISPINELLA Peace! he's here. Stand close, lurk.

    [*Freevill and Tysefew withdraw*]

CAQUETEUR Good morrow, most dear and worthy to be most wise.
    How does my mistress?   140

CRISPINELLA Morrow, sweet servant. You glister; prithee, let's see
    that stone.

CAQUETEUR A toy, lady, I bought to please my finger.

CRISPINELLA Why, I am more precious to you than your finger.

CAQUETEUR Yes, or than all my body, I swear.   145

CRISPINELLA Why then, let it be bought to please me. Come, I am
    no professed beggar. [*She tries to take the ring*]

CAQUETEUR Troth, mistress! Zounds! Forsooth, I protest—

CRISPINELLA Nay, if you turn Protestant for such a toy!

CAQUETEUR In good deed, la! Another time I'll give you a—   150

CRISPINELLA Is this yours to give?

CAQUETEUR O God! Forsooth, mine, quoth you? Nay, as for that—

CRISPINELLA Now I remember, I ha' seen this on my servant
    Tysefew's finger.

CAQUETEUR Such another.   155

CRISPINELLA Nay, I am sure this is it.

CAQUETEUR Troth, 'tis, forsooth. The poor fellow wanted money to pay for supper last night and so pawned it to me. 'Tis a pawn, i'faith, or else you should have it.

TYSEFEW [*coming forward; to Caqueteur*] Hark ye, thou base, lying— 160 How dares thy impudence hope to prosper? Were't not for the privilege of this respected company, I would so bang thee!

CRISPINELLA Come hither, servant. What's the matter betwixt you two?

CAQUETEUR Nothing.—[*Aside to Crispinella*] But, hark you, he did 165 me some uncivil discourtesies last night, for which, because I should not call him to account, he desires to make me any satisfaction. The coward trembles at my very presence, but I ha' him on the hip;° I'll take the forfeit on his ring.°

TYSEFEW What's that you whisper to her?   170

CAQUETEUR Nothing, sir, but satisfy her that the ring was not pawned, but only lent by you to grace my finger; and so told her I craved your pardon for being too familiar or, indeed, over-bold with your reputation.

CRISPINELLA Yes, indeed he did. He said you desired to make him 175 any satisfaction for an uncivil discourtesy you did him last night, but he said he had you o'the hip and would take the forfeit of your ring.

TYSEFEW How now, ye base poltroon!

CAQUETEUR Hold, hold! My mistress speaks by contraries.   180

TYSEFEW Contraries?

CAQUETEUR She jests, faith, only jests.

CRISPINELLA Sir, I'll no more o' your service; you are a child; I'll give you to my nurse.

PUTIFER An he come to me, I can tell you, as old as I am, what to do 185 with him.

CAQUETEUR I offer my service, forsooth.

TYSEFEW Why, so; now every dog has his bone to gnaw on.

FREEVILL The masque holds, Master Caqueteur.

CAQUETEUR I am ready, sir.—[*To Putifer*] Mistress, I'll dance with 190 you, ne'er fear; I'll grace you.

PUTIFER I tell you, I can my singles and my doubles and my trick o' twenty, my coranto pace, my traverse forward, and my falling back° yet, i'faith.

BEATRICE [*to Freevill*] Mine, the provision for the night is ours.°   195 Much must be our care; till night we leave you. I am your servant; be not tyrannous.

Your virtue won me; faith, my love's not lust.
Good, wrong me not; my most fault is much trust.

FREEVILL Until night only; my heart be with you!—Farewell, sister.   200

CRISPINELLA Adieu, brother.—Come on, sister, for these sweetmeats.

FREEVILL [to Tysefew] Let's meet and practise presently.

TYSEFEW Content; we'll but fit our pumps.—[To Caqueteur] Come,
ye pernicious vermin!   205

        Exeunt [all but Freevill]. Enter Malheureux

FREEVILL My friend, wished hours! What news from Babylon?°
How does the woman of sin and natural concupiscence?

MALHEUREUX The eldest child of nature ne'er beheld°
So damned a creature.

FREEVILL What? *In nova fert animus mutatas dicere formas.*° Which   210
way bears the tide?

MALHEUREUX Dear loved sir, I find a mind courageously vicious
may put on a desperate security, but can never be blessed with a
firm enjoying and self-satisfaction.

FREEVILL What passion is this, my dear Lindabrides?°   215

MALHEUREUX 'Tis well; we both may jest. I ha' been tempted to
your death.

FREEVILL What, is the rampant cockatrice grown mad for the loss of
her man?

MALHEUREUX Devilishly mad.   220

FREEVILL As most assured of my second love?

MALHEUREUX Right.

FREEVILL She would have had this ring.

MALHEUREUX Ay, and this heart; and in true proof you were slain, I
should bring her this ring, from which she was assured you would   225
not part until from life you parted. For which deed, and only for
which deed, I should possess her sweetness.

FREEVILL O bloody villainess! Nothing is defamed but by his proper
self. Physicians abuse remedies, lawyers spoil the law, and women
only shame women. You ha' vowed my death?   230

MALHEUREUX My lust, not I, before my reason would; yet I must
use her. That I, a man of sense, should conceive endless pleasure
in a body whose soul I know to be so hideously black!

FREEVILL That a man at twenty-three should cry, 'O sweet pleasure!' and at forty-three should sigh, 'O sharp pox!' But consider   235
man furnished with omnipotency, and you overthrow him. Thou
must cool thy impatient appetite. 'Tis fate, 'tis fate.

MALHEUREUX I do malign my creation that I am subject to passion.
    I must enjoy her!

FREEVILL I have it; mark! I give a masque tonight   240
    To my love's kindred. In that thou shalt go;
    In that we two make show of falling out,
    Give seeming challenge, instantly depart
    With some suspicion to present fight.
    We will be seen as going to our swords;   245
    And after meeting, this ring only lent,
    I'll lurk in some obscure place till rumour,
    The common bawd to loose suspicions,
    Have feigned me slain, which, in respect myself
    Will not be found, and our late seeming quarrel,   250
    Will quickly sound to all as earnest truth.
    Then to thy wench; protest me surely dead,
    Show her this ring, enjoy her, and, blood cold,
    We'll laugh at folly.

MALHEUREUX   O, but think of it!

FREEVILL Think of it! Come away! Virtue, let sleep thy passions;   255
    What old times held as crimes are now but fashions.
       Exeunt

3.2

    Enter [at one door] Master Burnish and Lionel, Master
    Mulligrub with a standing cup in his hand and an obligation in
    the other. Cocledemoy stands at the other door,° *disguised like a*
    French pedlar, and overhears them

MULLIGRUB I am not at this time furnished, but there's my bond
    for your plate. [*Gives bond to Burnish*]

BURNISH Your bill had been sufficient; you're a good° man. [*Reads*]°
    'A standing cup, parcel-gilt, of thirty-two ounces, eleven pounds,
    seven shillings, the first of July.'—Good plate, good man, good   5
    day, good all!

MULLIGRUB 'Tis my hard fortune; I will hang the knave! No, first
    he shall half rot in fetters in the dungeon, his conscience made
    despairful. I'll hire a knave o'purpose shall assure him he is
    damned, and after see him with mine own eyes hanged without   10
    singing any psalm.° Lord, that he has but one neck!°

BURNISH You are too tyrannous! You'll use me no further?

MULLIGRUB No, sir. Lend me your servant only to carry the plate home. I have occasion of an hour's absence.

BURNISH With easy consent, sir.—[*To Lionel*] Haste and be careful.   15
   Exit Burnish

MULLIGRUB Be very careful, I pray thee; to my wife's own hands.
   [*Hands him the cup*]

LIONEL Secure yourself,° sir.

MULLIGRUB To her own hand!

LIONEL Fear not; I have delivered greater things° than this to a woman's own hand.   20
   [*Exit Lionel*]

COCLEDEMOY [*coming forward*] Monsieur, please you to buy a fine delicate ball, sweet ball, a camphor ball?

MULLIGRUB Prithee, away!

COCLEDEMOY Or a ball to scour, a scouring ball, a ball to be shaved?°   25

MULLIGRUB For the love of God, talk not of shaving! I have been shaved! Mischief and a thousand devils seize him! I have been shaved!
   Exit Mulligrub

COCLEDEMOY The fox grows fat when he is cursed!° I'll shave ye smoother yet. Turd on a tile-stone! My lips have a kind of rheum°   30
at this bowl;° I'll have't! I'll gargalize my throat with this vintner, and when I have done with him, spit him out. I'll shark. Con-science does not repine. Were I to bite an honest gentleman, a poor grogram poet, or a penurious parson that had but ten pigs' tails in a twelvemonth, and for want of learning had but one good   35
stool in a fortnight,° I were damned beyond the works of super-erogation!° But to wring the withers of my gouty, barmed, spigot-frigging jumbler of elements,° Mulligrub, I hold it as lawful as sheep-shearing, taking eggs from hens, caudles from asses, or buttered shrimps from horses: they make no use of them, were   40
not provided for them. And therefore, worshipful Cocledemoy, hang toasts! On, in grace and virtue to proceed! Only beware, beware degrees. There be rounds in a ladder and knots in a halter; 'ware carts!° Hang toasts! The Common Council has decreed it. I must draw a lot for the great goblet.   45
   Exit

3.3

Enter Mistress Mulligrub and Lionel, with [the] goblet

MISTRESS MULLIGRUB Nay, I pray you, stay and drink. And how
does your mistress? I know her very well; I have been inward with
her, and so has many more. She was ever a good, patient creature,
i'faith. With all my heart, I'll remember your master, an honest
man. He knew me° before I was married. An honest man he is,   5
and a crafty. He comes forward in the world well, I warrant him.
And his wife is a proper woman, that she is. Well, she has been as
proper a woman as any in Cheap.° She paints now, and yet she
keeps her husband's old customers to him still. In troth, a fine-
faced wife in a wainscot carved seat is a worthy ornament to a   10
tradesman shop, and an attractive, I warrant. Her husband shall
find it in the custom of his ware, I'll assure him. God be with you,
good youth. I acknowledge the receipt.

Exit Lionel

I acknowledge all the receipt! Sure, 'tis very well spoken! 'I
acknowledge the receipt!' Thus 'tis to have good education and   15
to be brought up in a tavern. I do keep as gallant and as good
company, though I say it, as any she in London. Squires, gentlemen and knights diet at my table, and I do lend some of them
money; and full many fine men go upon my score,° as simple as I
stand here, and I trust them; and truly they very knightly and   20
courtly promise fair, give me very good words, and a piece of flesh
when time of year serves.° Nay, though my husband be a citizen
and's cap's made of wool,° yet I ha' wit and can see my good as
soon as another, for I have all the thanks. My silly husband, alas,
he knows nothing of it; 'tis I that bear, 'tis I that must bear a brain 25
for all.

*[Enter Cocledemoy, carrying the head and shoulder-parts of a
fish]*

COCLEDEMOY Fair hour to you, mistress!

MISTRESS MULLIGRUB *[aside]* 'Fair hour'! Fine term; faith, I'll
score it up° anon.—A beautiful thought to you, sir.

COCLEDEMOY Your husband and my master, Master Burnish, has   30
sent you a jowl of fresh salmon; and they both will come to dinner
to season your new cup with the best wine, which cup your
husband entreats you to send back by me that his arms may be
graved o'the side, which he forgot before it was sent.

MISTRESS MULLIGRUB By what token are you sent? By no token? 35
Nay, I have wit.

COCLEDEMOY He sent me by the same token that he was dry-
shaved this morning.

MISTRESS MULLIGRUB A sad token, but true. Here sir. [*Hands over
the goblet*] I pray you to commend me to your master, but espe- 40
cially to your mistress. Tell them they shall be most sincerely
welcome.

    Exit [Mistress Mulligrub with the salmon]

COCLEDEMOY 'Shall be most sincerely welcome'! Worshipful
Cocledemoy, lurk close. Hang toasts! Be not ashamed of
thy quality. Every man's turd smells well in's own nose. Vanish, 45
foist!

    *Exit [Cocledemoy]. Enter Mistress Mulligrub, with Servants
and furniture for the table, [including the salmon]*

MISTRESS MULLIGRUB Come, spread these table diaper napkins,
and—do you hear?—perfume! This parlour does so smell of profane tobacco. I could never endure this ungodly tobacco since one
of our elders assured me, upon his knowledge, tobacco was not 50
used in the congregation of the Family of Love. Spread, spread
handsomely.—Lord, these boys do things arsy-versy!—You show
your bringing up. I was a gentlewoman by my sister's side; I can
tell ye so methodically.—'Methodically'! I wonder where I got that
word? O, Sir Aminadab Ruth° bade me kiss him methodically. I 55
had it somewhere, and I had it indeed.

    Enter Master Mulligrub

MULLIGRUB Mind, be not desperate; I'll recover all. All things with
me shall seem honest that can be profitable.
  He must ne'er wince, that would or thrive or save,
  To be called niggard, cuckold, cut-throat, knave. 60

MISTRESS MULLIGRUB Are they come, husband?

MULLIGRUB Who? What? How now? What feast towards in my
private parlour?

MISTRESS MULLIGRUB Pray leave your foolery. What, are they
come? 65

MULLIGRUB Come? Who come?

MISTRESS MULLIGRUB You need not make't so strange.

MULLIGRUB Strange?

MISTRESS MULLIGRUB Ay, strange. You know no man that sent me
word that he and his wife would come to dinner to me, and sent 70
this jowl of fresh salmon beforehand?

MULLIGRUB Peace, not I! Peace! The messenger hath mistaken the
house. Let's eat it up quickly before it be inquired for. Sit to it.
    [*Mulligrub and Mistress Mulligrub sit at the table*]
—Some vinegar, quick!—Some good luck yet! Faith, I never
tasted salmon relished better. O, when a man feeds at other men's   75
cost!

MISTRESS MULLIGRUB Other men's cost? Why, did not you send
this jowl of salmon?

MULLIGRUB No.

MISTRESS MULLIGRUB By Master Burnish' man?   80

MULLIGRUB No.

MISTRESS MULLIGRUB Sending me word that he and his wife
would come to dinner to me?

MULLIGRUB No, no!

MISTRESS MULLIGRUB To season my new bowl?   85

MULLIGRUB Bowl?

MISTRESS MULLIGRUB And withal willed me to send the bowl
back?

MULLIGRUB Back?

MISTRESS MULLIGRUB That you might have your arms graved on   90
the side?

MULLIGRUB Ha?

MISTRESS MULLIGRUB By the same token you were dry-shaven this
morning before you went forth?

MULLIGRUB Pah! How this salmon stinks!   95

MISTRESS MULLIGRUB And thereupon sent the bowl back, prepared dinner—nay, an I bear not a brain!

MULLIGRUB Wife, do not vex me. Is the bowl gone? Is it delivered?

MISTRESS MULLIGRUB Delivered? Yes, sure 'tis delivered.

MULLIGRUB I will never more say my prayers! Do not make me   100
mad! 'Tis common. Let me not cry like a woman. Is it gone?

MISTRESS MULLIGRUB Gone! God is my witness, I delivered it
with no more intention to be cozened on't° than the child new-
born; and yet—

MULLIGRUB Look to my house! I am haunted with evil spirits. Hear   105
me, do! Hear me. If I have not my goblet again, heaven, I'll to the
devil; I'll to a conjuror. Look to my house! I'll raise all the wise
men i'the street.
    [*Exit Mulligrub*]

MISTRESS MULLIGRUB Deliver us! What words are these? I trust in
God he is but drunk, sure.   110

Enter Cocledemoy

COCLEDEMOY [*aside*] I must have the salmon, too. Worshipful
Cocledemoy, now for the masterpiece! God bless thy neck-
piece, and foutra!—[*To Mistress Mulligrub*] Fair Mistress, my
master—

MISTRESS MULLIGRUB Have I caught you?—What, Roger!° 115

COCLEDEMOY Peace, good mistress; I'll tell you all. A jest, a very
mere jest! Your husband only took sport to fright you. The bowl's
at my master's; and there is your husband, who sent me in all
haste lest you should be over-frighted with his feigning, to come to
dinner to him. 120

MISTRESS MULLIGRUB Praise heaven it is no worse!

COCLEDEMOY And desired me to desire you to send the jowl of
salmon before, and yourself to come after to them; my mistress
would be right glad to see you.

MISTRESS MULLIGRUB I pray, carry it. Now thank them entirely. 125
Bless me! I was never so out of my skin° in all my life! Pray thank
your mistress most entirely.

COCLEDEMOY [*aside*] So now, figo! Worshipful Moll Faugh and I
will munch. Cheaters and bawds go together like washing and
wringing. 130

Exit [*Cocledemoy with the salmon*]

MISTRESS MULLIGRUB Beshrew his heart for his labour! How
everything about me quivers.—[*To servant*] What, Christian, my
hat and apron. Here, take my sleeves.°—And how I tremble! So,
I'll gossip it now for 't,° that's certain. Here has been revolutions
and false fires indeed! 135

Enter Mulligrub

MULLIGRUB Whither now? What's the matter with you now?
Whither are you a-gadding?

MISTRESS MULLIGRUB Come, come, play the fool no more. Will
you go?

MULLIGRUB Whither, in the rank name of madness? Whither? 140

MISTRESS MULLIGRUB Whither? Why, to Master Burnish, to eat
the jowl of salmon! Lord, how strange you make it!

MULLIGRUB Why so, why so?

MISTRESS MULLIGRUB Why so? Why, did you not send the selfsame fellow for the jowl of salmon that had the cup?

MULLIGRUB 'Tis well, 'tis very well! 145

MISTRESS MULLIGRUB And willed me to come and eat it with you
at the goldsmith's?

MULLIGRUB O, ay, ay, ay! Art thy in thy right wits?

MISTRESS MULLIGRUB Do you hear? Make a fool of somebody else.   150
An you make an ass of me, I'll make an ox of you,° do ye see?

MULLIGRUB Nay wife, be patient; for look you, I may be mad, or
drunk, or so; for my own part, though you can bear more than I,
yet I can do well. I will not curse nor cry, but heaven knows what I
think. Come, let's go hear some music;° I will never more say my   155
prayers. Let's go hear some doleful music. Nay, if heaven forget to
prosper knaves, I'll go no more to the synagogue. Now I am
discontented, I'll turn sectary; that is fashion.

    Exeunt

4.1

Enter Sir Hubert Subboys, Sir Lionel Freevill, Crispinella,
[other Ladies and Gentlemen, and] Servants with lights

SIR HUBERT More lights!—Welcome, Sir Lionel Freevill, brother
  Freevill shortly.—Look to your lights!

SERVANT The masquers are at hand.

SIR HUBERT Call down our daughter.—Hark, they are at hand.
  Rank handsomely.°   5

Enter the Masquers [including Freevill, Tysefew, and
Caqueteur. Enter Beatrice]. They dance, [Freevill with
Beatrice]. Enter Malheureux and takes Beatrice from Freevill.°
They draw [their swords]

FREEVILL Know, sir, I have the advantage of the place;
  You are not safe; I would deal even with you.°

MALHEUREUX So.

FREEVILL So.

They exchange gloves as pledges

BEATRICE I do beseech you, sweet, do not for me   10
  Provoke your fortune.

SIR LIONEL What sudden flaw is risen?

SIR HUBERT   From whence comes this?

FREEVILL An ulcer long time lurking now is burst.

SIR HUBERT [*to Freevill*] Good sir, the time and your designs are
  soft.°

BEATRICE Ay, dear sir, counsel him, advise him! 'Twill relish   15
  well from your carving.—[*To Freevill*] Good my sweet, rest safe

FREEVILL All's well, all's well. This shall be ended straight.

SIR HUBERT The banquet stays; there we'll discourse more large.

FREEVILL Marriage must not make men cowards.

SIR LIONEL   Nor rage fools.

SIR HUBERT 'Tis valour not where heat but reason rules.   20

Exeunt [all except] Tysefew and Crispinella

TYSEFEW But do you hear, lady, you proud ape, you,
  What was the jest you brake of me even now?

CRISPINELLA Nothing. I only said you were all mettle:° that you
  had a brazen face, a leaden brain, and a copper° beard.

TYSEFEW Quicksilver!° thou little more than a dwarf, and something   25
  less than a woman.

CRISPINELLA A wisp,° a wisp, a wisp! Will you go to the banquet?

TYSEFEW By the Lord, I think thou wilt marry shortly, too; thou growest somewhat foolish already.

CRISPINELLA O, i'faith, 'tis a fair thing to be married, and a necessary. To hear this word 'must'! If our husband be proud, we must bear his contempt; if noisome, we must bear with the goat under his armholes; if a fool, we must bear his babble;° and, which is worse, if a loose liver, we must live upon unwholesome reversions.° Where, on the contrary side, our husbands, because they may and we must, care not for us. Things hoped with fear and got with strugglings are men's high pleasures, when duty pales and flats their appetite.

TYSEFEW What a tart monkey is this! By heaven, if thou hadst not so much wit, I could find in my heart to marry thee. Faith, bear with me for all this.

CRISPINELLA Bear with thee! I wonder how thy mother could bear thee ten months in her belly, when I cannot endure thee two hours in mine eye.

TYSEFEW Alas for you, sweet soul! By the Lord, you are grown a proud, scurvy, apish, idle, disdainful, scoffing—God's foot! because you have read *Euphues and his England, Palmerin de Oliva,* and *The Legend of Lies!*°

CRISPINELLA Why i'faith, yet, servant, you of all others should bear with my known unmalicious humours. I have always in my heart given you your due respect; and, heaven may be sworn, I have privately given fair speech of you, and protested—

TYSEFEW Nay, look you, for my own part, if I have not as religiously vowed my heart to you, been drunk to your health, swallowed flap-dragons,° ate glasses, drunk urine, stabbed arms,° and done all the offices of protested gallantry for your sake. And yet you tell me I have a brazen face, a leaden brain, and a copper beard! Come, yet, an it please you.

CRISPINELLA No, no, you do not love me!

TYSEFEW By—,° but I do now; and whosoever dares say that I do not love you, nay, honour you, and if you would vouchsafe to marry—

CRISPINELLA Nay, as for that, think on 't as you will, but God's my record, and my sister knows I have taken drink° and slept upon 't, that if ever I marry it shall be you, and I will marry, and yet I hope I do not say it shall be you neither.

TYSEFEW By heaven, I shall be as soon weary of health as of your
enjoying! Will you cast a smooth cheek upon me?

CRISPINELLA I cannot tell. I have no crumped shoulders, my back   70
needs no mantle;° and yet marriage is honourable. Do you think ye
shall prove a cuckold?

TYSEFEW No, by the Lord, not I!

CRISPINELLA Why, I thank you, i'faith. Heigh-ho! I slept on my
back this morning and dreamt the strangest dreams. Good Lord,   75
how things will come to pass! Will you go to the banquet?

TYSEFEW If you will be mine, you shall be your own. My purse, my
body, my heart is yours. Only be silent in my house, modest at my
table, and wanton in my bed, and the Empress of Europe cannot
content, and shall not be contented, better.   80

CRISPINELLA Can any kind heart speak more discreetly affectionately? My father's consent, and as for mine—
     [*She offers herself to be kissed, which he does*]

TYSEFEW Then thus—and thus—. So Hymen° should begin;
Sometimes a falling out proves falling in.
     Exeunt

4.2

*Enter Freevill, speaking to some within; Malheureux at the
other door*

FREEVILL As you respect my virtue, give me leave
To satisfy my reason, though not blood.—
[*To Malheureux*] So, all runs right. Our feignèd rage hath ta'en
To fullest life; they are much possessed°
Of force must we still quarrel. Now, my right friend,°   5
Resolve me with open breast, free and true heart,
Cannot thy virtue, having space to think
And fortify her weakened powers with reason,
Discourses, meditations, discipline,
Divine ejaculatories, and all those aids against devils—   10
Cannot all these curb thy low appetite
And sensual fury?

MALHEUREUX There is no god in blood, no reason in desire.
Shall I but live? Shall I not be forced to act
Some deed whose very name is hideous?   15

FREEVILL No.

MALHEUREUX Then I must enjoy Franceschina.

FREEVILL You shall. I'll lend this ring; show it
    To that fair devil; it will resolve me dead;
    Which rumour, with my artificial absence,   20
    Will make most firm. Enjoy her suddenly.

MALHEUREUX But if report go strong that you are slain,
    And that by me, whereon I may be seized,
    Where shall I find your being?

FREEVILL At Master Shatewe's the jeweller's, to whose breast   25
    I'll trust our secret purpose.

MALHEUREUX   Ay, rest yourself;
    Each man hath follies.

FREEVILL   But those worst of all
    Who with a willing eye do, seeing, fall.

MALHEUREUX 'Tis true, but truth seems folly in madness' spec-
    tacles.
    I am not now myself, no man. Farewell.

FREEVILL   Farewell.   30

MALHEUREUX When woman's in the heart, in the soul hell.
    Exit Malheureux

FREEVILL Now repentance, the fool's whip, seize thee!
    Nay, if there be no means I'll be thy friend,
    But not thy vice's; and with greatest sense,
    I'll force thee feel thy errors to the worst.   35
    The vilest of dangers thou shalt sink into.
    No jeweller shall see me; I will lurk
    Where none shall know or think; close I'll withdraw,
    And leave thee with two friends, a whore and knave.°
    But is this virtue in me? No, not pure;   40
    Nothing extremely best with us endures;
    No use in simple purities; the elements
    Are mixed for use. Silver without alloy
    Is all too eager to be wrought for use;
    Nor precise virtues ever purely good   45
    Holds useful size with temper of weak blood.°
    Then let my course be borne, though with side wind;°
    The end being good, the means are well assigned.
    Exit

4.3

Enter Franceschina melancholy, Cocledemoy leading her [and bearing the goblet]

COCLEDEMOY Come, cacafuego,° Frank o' Frank Hall! Wahahowe! Excellent! Ha, here's a plump-rumped wench with a breast softer than a courtier's tongue, an old lady's gums, or an old man's mentula.° My fine rogue—

FRANCESCHINA Pah! you poltroon! 5

COCLEDEMOY Goody fist, flumpum pumpum! Ah, my fine wagtail,° thou art as false, as prostituted, and adulterate as some translated manuscript. Buss, fair whore, buss!

FRANCESCHINA God's sacrament! Pox!

COCLEDEMOY *Hadamoy key*, dost thou frown, *medianthon teukey*? 10 Nay, look here. [*Shows her the goblet*] *Numeron key*, silver *blithefor cany os cany* goblet. *Us key ne moy blegefoy oteeston*° pox on you, gosling!

FRANCESCHINA By me fait, dis bin very fine langage. Ick sall bush° ye now. Hah, be garzon, vare had you dat plate? 15

COCLEDEMOY *Hedemoy key*, get you gone, punk rampant, *key*, common up-tail!

Enter Mary Faugh, in haste

MARY O daughter, cousin, niece, servant, mistress!

COCLEDEMOY Humpum plumpum squat, I am gone!

Exit Cocledemoy

MARY There is one Master Malheureux at the door desires to see 20 you. He says he must not be denied, for he hath sent you this ring, and withal says 'tis done.

[*Gives Beatrice's ring*]

FRANCESCHINA Vat sall me do now? God's sacrament! Tell him two hours hence he sall be most affectionately velcome. Tell him—vat sall me do?—tell him ick am bin in my bate,° and ick 25 sall perfume my seets,° mak-a mine body so delicate for his arm, two hours hence.

MARY I shall satisfy him; two hours hence; well.

Exit Mary Faugh

FRANCESCHINA Now ick sall revange. Hay, begar,° me sal tartar° de whole generation! Mine brain vork it. Freevill is dead; 30 Malheureux sall hang; and mine rival, Beatrice, ick sall make run mad.

Enter Mary Faugh

MARY He's gone, forsooth, to eat a caudle of cock-stones,° and will
return within this two hours.

FRANCESCHINA Very vell. Give monies to some fellow to squire me;   35
ick sall go abroad.

MARY There's a lusty bravo beneath, a stranger, but a good stale°
rascal. He swears valiantly, kicks a bawd right virtuously,
and protests with an empty pocket right desperately. He'll squire
you.   40

FRANCESCHINA Very velcome! Mine fan! Ick sall retorn presantly.
[*Exit Mary Faugh*]
Now sall me be revange. Ten tousant devla! Dere sall be no Got in
me but passion, no tought but rage, no mercy but blood, no spirit
but devla in me. Dere sall noting tought good for me, but dat is
mischievous for others.   45
Exit

4.4

*Enter Sir Hubert, Sir Lionel, Beatrice, Crispinella, and
Nurse [Putifer], Tysefew following*

SIR LIONEL Did no-one see him since? Pray God—nay, all is well.
A little heat, what? He is but withdrawn. And yet I would to
God—but fear you nothing.

BEATRICE Pray God that all be well, or would I were not!

TYSEFEW He's not to be found, sir, anywhere.   5

SIR LIONEL You must not make a heavy face presage an ill event. I
like your sister well; she's quick and lively. Would she would
marry, faith!

CRISPINELLA Marry! Nay, an I would marry, methinks an old
man's a quiet thing.   10

SIR LIONEL Ha, mass! and so he is.

CRISPINELLA You are a widower?

SIR LIONEL That I am, i'faith, fair Crispinella;° and I can tell you,
would you affect me, I have it in me yet, i'faith.

CRISPINELLA Troth, I am in love. Let me see your hand. Would   15
you cast yourself away upon me willingly?

SIR LIONEL Will I? Ay, by the—°

222

CRISPINELLA Would you be a cuckold willingly? By my troth, 'tis a
comely, fine and handsome sight for one of my years to marry an
old man! Truth, 'tis restorative. What a comfortable thing it is to   20
think of her husband, to hear his venerable cough o'the everlastings,° to feel his rough skin, his summer hands and winter legs, his
almost no eyes, and assuredly no teeth; and then to think what she
must dream of when she considers others' happiness and her own
want—'tis a worthy and notorious comfortable match!   25

SIR LIONEL Pish, pish! Will you have me?

CRISPINELLA Will you assure me—

SIR LIONEL Five-hundred pound jointure.

CRISPINELLA That you will die within this fortnight?

SIR LIONEL No, by my faith, Crispinella.   30

CRISPINELLA Then Crispinella, by her faith, assures you, she'll
have none of you.

Enter Freevill, disguised like a pander, and Franceschina

FREEVILL B'y'r leave, gentles and men of nightcaps,° I would speak,
but that here stands one is able to express her own tale best.

FRANCESCHINA [*to Sir Lionel*] Sir, mine speech is to you. You had   35
a son, Matre° Freevill.

SIR LIONEL Had! Ha! And have.

FRANCESCHINA No point;° me am come to assure you dat one
Mestre° Malheureux hath killed him.

BEATRICE O me! Wretched, wretched!   40

SIR HUBERT Look to our daughter.

SIR LIONEL How art thou informed?

FRANCESCHINA If dat it please you to go vid me, ick sall bring you
where you sall hear Malheureux vid his own lips confess it; and dere
ye may apprehend him and revenge your and mine love's blood.   45

SIR HUBERT Your love's blood, mistress? Was he your love?

FRANCESCHINA He was so, sir; let your daughter hear it.—Do not
veep, lady. De yong man dat be slain did not love you, for he still
lovit me ten tousant, tousant times more dearly.

BEATRICE O my heart! I will love you the better; I cannot hate what   50
he affected. O passion! O my grief! which way wilt break, think,
and consume?

CRISPINELLA Peace!

BEATRICE Dear woes cannot speak.

FRANCESCHINA For look you, lady, dis your ring he gave me, vid   55
most bitter jests at your scorned kindness.

BEATRICE He did not ill not to love me, but sure he did not well to
mock me; gentle minds will pity though they cannot love. Yet
peace and my love sleep with him!—Unlace, good nurse.°—Alas, I
was not so ambitious of so supreme an happiness that he should   60
only love me; 'twas joy enough for me, poor soul, that I only might
only love him.

FRANCESCHINA O, but to be abused, scorned, scoffed at! O ten
tousand divla! By such a one, and unto such a one!

BEATRICE I think you say not true.—Sister, shall we know one   65
another in the other world?

CRISPINELLA What means my sister?

BEATRICE I would fain see him again. O my tortured mind!
Freevill is more than dead; he is unkind.

> *Exeunt Beatrice, and Crispinella and Nurse*

SIR HUBERT Convey her in, and so, sir, as you said,   70
Set a strong watch.

SIR LIONEL   Ay, sir, and so pass along
With this same common woman.°—[*To Franceschina*] You must
make it good.

FRANCESCHINA Ick sall, or let me pay for his, mine blood.

SIR HUBERT Come, then, along all, with quiet speed.

SIR LIONEL O fate!   75

TYSEFEW O sir, be wisely sorry, but not passionate.

> *Exeunt all except Freevill*

FREEVILL I will go and reveal myself.—Stay! No, no!
Grief endears love. Heaven! to have such a wife
Is happiness to breed pale envy in the saints.
Thou worthy, dove-like virgin without gall,°   80
Cannot that woman's evil, jealousy,
Despite disgrace, nay, which is worst, contempt,
Once stir thy faith? O truth, how few sisters hast thou!
Dear memory!
With what a suffring sweetness, quiet modesty,   85
Yet deep affection, she received my death!
And then with what a patient yet oppressèd kindness
She took my lewdly intimated wrongs!
O, the dearest of heaven!
Were there but three such women in the world,   90
Two might be saved. Well, I am great°
With expectation to what devilish end

This woman of foul soul will drive her plots;
But Providence all wicked art o'ertops,
And Impudence must know, though stiff as ice,   95
That Fortune doth not alway dote on vice.
  Exit

4.5

  [*The stocks are set out.*] *Enter Sir Hubert, Sir Lionel, Tysefew,*
  Franceschina, and three [*Constables*] *with halberds*
SIR HUBERT [*to Constables*] Plant a watch there. Be very careful,
  sirs.—
  The rest with us.
TYSEFEW The heavy night grows to her depth of quiet;
  'Tis about mid-darkness.
FRANCESCHINA Mine shambre is hard by. Ick sall bring you to it   5
  presantment.°
SIR LIONEL Deep silence! On!
  Exeunt [*all*], [*except the Constables*°]
COCLEDEMOY (*within*) Wahahowe!°
  Enter Mulligrub
MULLIGRUB It was his voice; 'tis he. He sups with his cupping-
  glasses.° 'Tis late; he must pass this way. I'll ha' him, I'll ha' my   10
  fine boy, my 'worshipful' Cocledemoy! I'll moy him! He shall be
  hanged in lousy linen. I'll hire some sectary to make him an
  heretic before he die, and when he is dead, I'll piss on his grave.
  Enter Cocledemoy
COCLEDEMOY [*speaking to off-stage*] Ah, my fine punks,
  goodnight, Frank Frailty, Frail o' Frail-Hall! *Bonus noches,*° my 15
  ubiquitari.°
MULLIGRUB 'Ware polling and shaving, sir!
COCLEDEMOY A wolf, a wolf, a wolf!
  Exit Cocledemoy, leaving his cloak behind him
MULLIGRUB Here's something yet. A cloak, a cloak! Yet I'll after; he
  cannot 'scape the watch. I'll hang him if I have any mercy!° I'll   20
  slice him!
  Exit [*Mulligrub with the cloak*]. *Enter Cocledemoy.* [*The*
  Constables step forward]

1 CONSTABLE Who goes there? Come before the constable.

COCLEDEMOY Bread o' God, constable, you are a watch for the devil! Honest men are robbed under your nose. There's a false knave in the habit of a vintner set upon me. He would have had   25
my purse, but I took me to my heels. Yet he got my cloak, a plain stuff cloak, poor, ye 'twill serve to hang him! 'Tis my loss, poor man that I am.

    [*Exit Cocledemoy*]

2 CONSTABLE Masters, we must watch better. Is't not strange that knaves, drunkards and thieves should be abroad, and yet we of the   30
watch, scriveners, smiths, and tailors,° never stir?

    Enter Mulligrub running, with Cocledemoy's cloak

1 CONSTABLE Hark!—Who goes there?

MULLIGRUB An honest man and a citizen.

2 CONSTABLE Appear, appear! What are you?

MULLIGRUB A simple vintner.   35

1 CONSTABLE A vintner, ha! and simple? Draw nearer—nearer!—Here's the cloak!

2 CONSTABLE Ay, Master Vintner, we know you. A plain stuff cloak—'tis it.

1 CONSTABLE [*apprehending Mulligrub*] Right, come! O thou varlet,   40
dost not thou know that the wicked cannot 'scape the eyes of the constable?

MULLIGRUB What means this violence? As I am an honest man, I took the cloak—

1 CONSTABLE As you are a knave you took the cloak! We are your   45
witnesses for that.

MULLIGRUB But hear me, hear me! I'll tell you what I am.

2 CONSTABLE A thief you are.

MULLIGRUB I tell you my name is Mulligrub.

1 CONSTABLE I will grub° you!—In with him to the stocks!   50

    [*They put Mulligrub in the stocks*]

There let him sit till tomorrow morning, that Justice Quodlibet° may examine him.

MULLIGRUB Why, but I tell thee—

2 CONSTABLE Why, but I tell thee! We'll tell thee now.

MULLIGRUB Am I not mad? Am I not an ass? Why, scabs!—God's   55
foot, let me out!

2 CONSTABLE Ay, ay, let him prate. He shall find matter in us scabs,° I warrant. God's-so, what good members of the commonwealth do we prove!

1 CONSTABLE Prithee peace! Let's remember our duties, and let's   60
go sleep in the fear of God.

    Exeunt [Constables], having left Mulligrub in the stocks

MULLIGRUB [*calling*] Who goes there? Illo, ho, ho!°—Zounds, shall I
run mad, lose my wits? Shall I be hanged?—Hark, who goes
there?—Do not fear to be poor, Mulligrub. Thou hast a sure
stock° now.   65

    Enter Cocledemoy like a bellman

COCLEDEMOY [*sings*] *The night grows old,*
              And many a cuckold
              Is now—Wahahahowe!
              Maids on their backs
              Dream of sweet smacks,   70
              And warm—Wohohohowe!

I must go comfort my venerable Mulligrub; I must fiddle him till
he fist.° Fough! [*Sings*]

              Maids in your night-rails,
              Look well to your light—;°   75
              Keep close your locks,
              And down your smocks;
              Keep a broad eye,
              And a close thigh.

Excellent, excellent!—Who's there? Now, Lord, Lord! Master   80
Mulligrub! Deliver us! What does your worship in the stocks? I
pray come out, sir.

MULLIGRUB Zounds, man, I tell thee I am locked!

COCLEDEMOY Locked! O world! O men! O time! O night! that canst
not discern virtue and wisdom, and one of the Common Council!°   85
What is your worship in for?

MULLIGRUB For—a plague on't!—suspicion of felony.

COCLEDEMOY Nay, an it be such a trifle, Lord! I could weep to
see your good worship in this taking. Your worship has been a
good friend to me; and though you have forgot me, yet I knew   90
your wife before she was married; and, since, I have found
your worship's door open, and I have knocked, and God
knows what I have saved.° And do I live to see your worship
stocked?

MULLIGRUB Honest bellman, I perceive thou knowest me. I prithee   95
call the watch. Inform the constable of my reputation, that I may

no longer abide in this shameful habitation. And hold thee—all I have about me.

Gives him his purse

COCLEDEMOY 'Tis more than I deserve, sir. Let me alone for your   100
delivery.

MULLIGRUB Do, and then let me alone with Cocledemoy. I'll moy him!

COCLEDEMOY [*sings*] *Maids in your*—
      [*Enter the Constables. Mulligrub does not hear the following exchange*]
Master Constable, who's that i'the stocks?

1 CONSTABLE One for a robbery; one Mulligrub he calls himself.   105

COCLEDEMOY Mulligrub?

1 CONSTABLE Bellman, know'st thou him?

COCLEDEMOY Know him? O Master Constable, what good service have you done! Know him? He's a strong thief; his house has been suspected for a bawdy tavern a great while, and a receipt for   110
cutpurses,° 'tis most certain. He has been long in the black book,° and he is ta'en now?

2 CONSTABLE By'r Lady, my masters, we'll not trust the stocks with him; we'll have him to the justices, get a *mittimus*° to New-gate° presently.—Come sir, come on, sir!   115
      [*They take Mulligrub out of the stocks*]

MULLIGRUB Ha, does your rascalship yet know my worship in the end?

1 CONSTABLE Ay, the end of your worship° we know.

MULLIGRUB Ha, goodman constable, here's an honest fellow can tell you what I am.
      [*He indicates Cocledemoy*]

2 CONSTABLE 'Tis true, sir; you're a strong thief, he says, on his   120
own knowledge.—Bind fast, bind fast.—We know you. We'll trust no stocks with you.—Away with him to the gaol instantly!

MULLIGRUB Why, but dost hear?—Bellman? Rogue! Rascal! God's—Why, but—
      The Constable drags away Mulligrub

COCLEDEMOY Why, but! Wahahowe! Excellent, excellent! Ha, my   125
fine Cocledemoy, my vintner fists! I'll make him fart crackers before I ha' done with him. Tomorrow is the day of judgement. Afore the Lord God, my knavery grows unperegal! 'Tis time to take a nap, until half an hour hence. God give your worship music,° content and rest!   130

      Exit

5.1

*Enter Franceschina, Sir Lionel, Tysefew, with Officers [and
Freevill disguised as before]*

FRANCESCHINA You bin very velcome to mine shambra.

SIR LIONEL But how know ye, how are ye assured,
Both of the deed, and of his sure return?

FRANCESCHINA O, mynheer, ick sall tell you. Mettre Malheureux
came all breatless, running a my shambra, his sword all bloody. He   5
tell-a me he had kill Freevill, and pred-a° me to conceal him. Ick
flatter him, bid bring monies, he should live and lie vid me. He
went, whilst ick, me hope vidout sins, out of mine mush love to
Freevill betray him.

SIR LIONEL Fear not, 'tis well; good works get grace for sin.   10
She conceals them behind the curtain°

FRANCESCHINA Dere, peace, rest dere; so, softly, all go in.
[*Aside*] De net is lay; now sall ick be revenge.
If dat me knew a dog dat Freevill love,
Me would puisson him, for know de deepest hell°
As a revenging woman's nought so fell.   15
Enter Mary Faugh

MARY Ho! cousin Frank, the party you wot of, Master Malheureux.

FRANCESCHINA Bid him come up, I pridee.
She sings and dances to the cittern. Enter Malheureux
O mynheer man, aderliver love,
Mine ten tousant times velcome love,
Ha, by mine trat, you bin de just—vat sall me say?°   20
Vat seet honey name sall I call you?

MALHEUREUX   Any from you
Is pleasure. Come, my loving prettiness,
Where's thy chamber? I long to touch your sheets.

FRANCESCHINA No, no, not yet, mine seetest, soft-lipped love;
You sall not gulp down all delights at once.   25
Be min trat, dis all-fles-lovers, dis ravenous wenches
Dat sallow all down whole, vill have all at one bit!
Fie, fie, fie!
Be min fait, dey do eat comfits vid spoons.
No, no, I'll make you chew your pleasure vit love.   30
De more degrees and steps, de more delight;

De more endearèd is de pleasure height.

MALHEUREUX What, you're a learned wanton, and proceed by art!

FRANCESCHINA Go, little vag! Pleasure should have a crane's long
neck, to relish de ambrosia of delight. And ick pridee tell me, for   35
me loves to hear of manhood very mush, i' fait, ick pridee—vat vas
me a-saying?—O, ick pridee tell-a me, how did you kill-a Mettre
Freevill?

MALHEUREUX Why, quarrelled o' set purpose, drew him out,
Singled him, and having th'advantage   40
Of my sword and might, ran him through and through.

FRANCESCHINA Vat did you vid him van he was sticken?

MALHEUREUX I dragged him by the heels to the next wharf
And spurned him in the river.

Those in ambush rush forth and take him

SIR LIONEL Seize, seize him! O monstrous! O ruthless villain!   45

MALHEUREUX What mean you, gentlemen? By heaven—

TYSEFEW Speak not of anything that's good.

MALHEUREUX Your errors gives you passion; Freevill lives.

SIR LIONEL Thy own lips say thou liest.

MALHEUREUX   Let me die
If at Shatewe's the jeweller he lives not safe untouched.   50

TYSEFEW Meantime to strictest guard, to sharpest prison.

MALHEUREUX No rudeness, gentlemen. I'll go undragged.—
[*To Franceschina*] O wicked, wicked devil!

Exit [Malheureux with Officers]

SIR LIONEL   Sir, the day
Of trial is this morn. Let's prosecute
The sharpest rigour and severest end;   55
Good men are cruel when they're vice's friend.

SIR HUBERT Woman,
We thank thee with no empty hand.
[*Gives money*]
                                        Farewell.
Strumpets are fit for something.

All save Freevill depart

FREEVILL   Ay, for hell!°
O thou unreprievable, beyond all   60
Measure of grace, damned immediately!
That things of beauty created for sweet use,
Soft comfort, and as the very music of life,
Custom should make so unutterably hellish!

O heaven! What difference is in women and their life!   65
What man, but worthy name of man, would leave
The modest pleasures of a lawful bed,
The holy union of two equal hearts,
Mutually holding either dear as health,
The undoubted issues, joys of chaste sheets,   70
The unfeigned embrace of sober ignorance,
To twine the unhealthful loins of common loves,
The prostituted impudence of things
Senseless like those by cataracts of Nile,
Their use so vile takes away sense? How vile   75
To love a creature made of blood and hell,
Whose use makes weak, whose company doth shame,
Whose bed doth beggar, issue doth defame!
    Enter Franceschina

FRANCESCHINA Mettre Freevill live! Ha, ha! live at Mestre
Shatewe's! Mush at Mettre Shatewe's! Freevill is dead; Malheur-   80
eux sall hang; and sweet divel! dat Beatrice would but run mad,
dat she would but run mad, den me would dance and sing.—[*To
Freevill*] Mettre Don Dubon, me pre ye now go to Mestress
Beatrice; tell her Freevill is sure dead, and dat he curse herself
especially, for dat he was sticked in her quarrel, swearing in his   85
last gasp dat if it had bin in mine quarrels 'twould never have
grieved him.

FREEVILL I will.

FRANCESCHINA Pridee do, and say anything dat vill vex her.

FREEVILL Let me alone to vex her.   90

FRANCESCHINA Vill you? Vill you mak-a her run mad? Here, take
dis ring. [*Gives Freevill the ring*] Say me scorn to wear anyting dat
was hers or his. I pridee torment her. Ick cannot love her; she
honest and virtuous, forsooth!

FREEVILL Is she so? O vile creature! Then let me alone with her.   95

FRANCESCHINA Vat? Vill you mak-a her mad? Seet, by min trat, be
pretta servan! Bush! Ick sall go to bet now.
    [*Exit Franceschina*]

FREEVILL Mischief, whither wilt thou?
O thou tearless woman! How monstrous is thy devil,
The end of hell as thee!° How miserable   100
Were it to be virtuous if thou couldst prosper!
I'll to my love, the faithful Beatrice;
She has wept enough, and, faith, dear soul, too much.

But yet how sweet it is to think how dear
One's life was to his love, how mourned his death!   10
'Tis joy not to be expressed with breath.
But, O, let him that would such passion drink
Be quiet of his speech, and only think.
    Exit

5.2

Enter Beatrice and Crispinella

BEATRICE Sister, cannot a woman kill herself? Is it not lawful to die
when we should not live?

CRISPINELLA O sister, 'tis a question not for us; we must do what
God will.

BEATRICE What God will? Alas, can torment be his glory, or our
grief his pleasure? Does not the nurse's nipple, juiced over with
wormwood,° bid the child it should not suck? And does not
heaven, when it hath made our breath bitter unto us, say we
should not live? O my best sister,
To suffer wounds when one may 'scape this rod   1
Is against nature, that is, against God.

CRISPINELLA Good sister, do not make me weep. Sure, Freevill was
not false;
I'll gage my life that strumpet, out of craft
And some close second end, hath maliced him.   1

BEATRICE O sister, if he were not false, whom have I lost!
If he were, what grief to such unkindness!
From head to foot I am all misery.
Only in this, some justice I have found:
My grief is like my love, beyond all bound.   2
    Enter Nurse [Putifer]

PUTIFER My servant, Master Caqueteur, desires to visit you.

CRISPINELLA For grief's sake, keep him out! His discourse is like
the long word *Honorificabilitudinitatibus*:° a great deal of sound and
no sense. His company is like a parenthesis to a discourse; you may
admit it or leave it out, it makes no matter.   2
    Enter Freevill in his disguise

FREEVILL By your leave, sweet creatures.

CRISPINELLA Sir, all I can yet say of you is you are uncivil.

FREEVILL You must deny it.—[*To Beatrice*] By your sorrow's leave,
I bring some music to make sweet your grief.
BEATRICE Whate'er you please.—O break, my heart.   30
Canst thou yet pant? O dost thou yet survive?
Thou didst not love him if thou now canst live.
FREEVILL (*sings*) *O love, how strangely sweet*
Are thy weak passions,
That love and joy should meet   35
In selfsame fashions!
O who can tell
The cause why this should move?
But only this,
No reason ask of love!   40
[*Beatrice*] *swoons*
CRISPINELLA Hold, peace! The gentlest soul is swooned.—
O my best sister!
FREEVILL Ha! get you gone, close the doors.—
[*Exit Nurse. Freevill*] *discovers himself°*

My Beatrice,
Cursed be my indiscreet trials! O my immeasurably loving!
CRISPINELLA She stirs; give air! she breathes.   45
BEATRICE Where am I, ha? [*Seeing Freevill*] How, have I slipped
off life?
Am I in heaven? O my lord, though not loving,
By our eternal being, yet give me leave
To rest by thy dear side. Am I not in heaven?
FREEVILL O eternally much loved, recollect your spirits!   50
BEATRICE Ha, you do speak? I do see you; I do live!
I would not die now; let me not burst with wonder!
FREEVILL Call up your blood; I live to honour you
As the admirèd glory of your sex.
Nor ever hath my love been false to you;
Only I presumed to try your faith too much,   55
For which I most am grieved.
CRISPINELLA   Brother, I must
Be plain with you; you have wronged us.
FREEVILL I am not so covetous to deny it;
But yet, when my discourse hath stayed your quaking,
You will be smoother-lipped; and the delight   60
And satisfaction which we all have got
Under these strange disguisings, when you know,

You will be mild and quiet, forget at last.
It is much joy to think on sorrows past.   65
BEATRICE Do you then live? And are you not untrue?
Let me not die with joy! Pleasure's more extreme
Than grief; there's nothing sweet to man but mean.°
FREEVILL Heaven cannot be too gracious to such goodness.
I shall discourse to you the several chances.   70
    [*Noises offstage*]
But hark, I must yet rest disguised.
The sudden close of many drifts now meet;
Where pleasure hath some profit, art is sweet.
    [*Freevill re-adopts his disguise.*] *Enter Tysefew*
TYSEFEW News, news, news, news!
CRISPINELLA Oysters, oysters, oysters, oysters!°   75
TYSEFEW Why, is not this well now? Is not this better than louring
    and pouting and puling, which is hateful to the living and vain to
    the dead? Come, come, you must live by the quick, when all is
    done; and for my own part, let my wife laugh at me when I am
    dead, so she'll smile upon me whilst I live. But to see a woman   80
    whine, and yet keep her eyes dry; mourn, and yet keep her cheeks
    fat; nay, to see a woman claw her husband by the feet when he is
    dead, that would have scratched him by the face when he was
    living: this now is somewhat ridiculous.
CRISPINELLA Lord, how you prate!   85
TYSEFEW And yet I was afraid, i'faith, that I should ha' seen a
    garland on this beauty's hearse; but time, truth, experience, and
    variety are great doers with women.
CRISPINELLA But what's the news? The news, I pray you!
TYSEFEW I pray you? Ne'er pray me, for by your leave you may   90
    command me. This 'tis:
The public sessions, which this day is past,
Hath doomed to death ill-fortuned Malheureux.°
CRISPINELLA But, sir, we heard he offered to make good
That Freevill lived at Shatewe's the jewellers.   95
BEATRICE And that 'twas but a plot betwixt them two.
TYSEFEW O ay, ay, he gaged his life with it; but know,
When all approached the test, Shatewe denied
He saw or heard of any such complot,
Or of Freevill; so that his own defence   100
Appeared so false, that like a madman's sword,
He struck his own heart. He hath the course of law

And instantly must suffer. But the jest—
If hanging be a jest, as many make it—
Is to take notice of one Mulligrub,
A sharking vintner.   105

FREEVILL What of him, sir?

TYSEFEW Nothing but hanging. The whoreson slave is mad before
he hath lost his senses.

FREEVILL Was his fact clear and made apparent, sir?   110

TYSEFEW No, faith, suspicious; for 'twas thus protested:
A cloak was stol'n; that cloak he had; he had it,
Himself confessed, by force. The rest of his defence
The choler of a justice wronged in wine,°
Joined with malignance of some hasty jurors,   115
Whose wit was lighted by the justice' nose;°
The knave was cast.
But, Lord, to hear his moan, his prayers, his wishes,
His zeal ill-timed, and his words unpitièd,
Would make a dead man rise and smile,   120
Whilst he observed how fear can make men vile.

CRISPINELLA Shall we go meet the execution?

BEATRICE I shall be ruled by you.

TYSEFEW By my troth, a rare motion! You must haste,°
For malefactors goes like the world, upon wheels.°   125

BEATRICE (to Freevill) Will you man us? You shall be our guide.

FREEVILL I am your servant.

TYSEFEW Ha, servant! Zounds, I am no companion for panders!
You're best make him your love.

BEATRICE So will I, sir; we must live by the quick, you say.   130

TYSEFEW 'Sdeath o' virtue! What a damned thing's this!
Who'll trust fair faces, tears, and vows? 'Sdeath, not I!
She is a woman; that is, she can lie.

CRISPINELLA Come, come, turn not a man of time, to make all ill°
Whose goodness you conceive not, since the worst of chance   135
Is to crave grace for heedless ignorance.

        Exeunt

5.3

Enter Cocledemoy like a sergeant°

COCLEDEMOY So, I ha' lost my sergeant in an ecliptic mist. Drunk,
horrible drunk! He is fine! So now will I fit myself. I hope this
habit will do me no harm. I am an honest man already. Fit, fit, fit
as a punk's tail,° that serves everybody. By this time my vintner
thinks of nothing but hell and sulphur; he farts fire and brimstone   5
already. Hang toasts! the execution approacheth.

Enter Sir Lionel, Sir Hubert, Malheureux pinioned, Tysefew,
Beatrice, Freevill [disguised], Crispinella, Franceschina, and
[Officers with] halberds

MALHEUREUX I do not blush, although condemned by laws;
No kind of death is shameful, but the cause,
Which I do know is none; and yet my lust
Hath made the one, although not cause, most just.   10
May I not be reprieved? Freevill is but mislodged;
Some lethargy hath seized him—no, much malice.
Do not lay blood upon your souls with good intents;
Men may do ill, and law sometime repents.

Cocledemoy picks Malheureux' pocket of his purse

SIR LIONEL Sir, sir, prepare; vain is all lewd defence.   15

MALHEUREUX Conscience was law, but now law's conscience.
My endless peace is made, and to the poor—
My purse, my purse!

COCLEDEMOY Ay, sir, an it shall please you, the poor has your
purse already.   20

MALHEUREUX You are a wily man!
[*To Franceschina*] But now, thou source of devils, O how I loathe
The very memory of that I adored!
He that's of fair blood, well-miened, of good breeding,
Best famed, of sweet acquaintance and true friends,   25
And would with desperate impudence lose all these,
And hazard landing at this fatal shore,
Let him ne'er kill, nor steal, but love a whore!

FRANCESCHINA De man does rave.—Tink o' Got, tink o' Got, and
bid de flesh, de world and the dibil farewell.   30

MALHEUREUX Farewell.

FREEVILL (*discovering himself*) Farewell.

FRANCESCHINA Vat is't you say? Ha!

FREEVILL [*to Malheureux*] Sir, your pardon; with my this defence,
    Do not forget protested violence
    Of your low affections; no requests,   35
    No arguments of reason, no known danger,
    No assurèd wicked bloodiness,
    Could draw your heart from this damnation.
MALHEUREUX Why, stay!
FRANCESCHINA Unprosperous divel! Vat sall me do now?   40
FREEVILL Therefore, to force you from the truer danger,
    I wrought the feigned, suffering this fair devil
    In shape of woman to make good her plot;
    And, knowing that the hook was deeply fast,
    I gave her line at will, till with her own vain strivings   45
    See here she's tired.—O thou comely damnation!°
    Does think that vice is not to be withstood?
    O, what is woman merely made of blood!°
SIR LIONEL You 'maze us all; let us not be lost in darkness.   50
FREEVILL All shall be lighted, but this time and place
    Forbids longer speech; only what you can think
    Has been extremely ill is only hers.
SIR LIONEL To severest prison with her!—
    With what heart canst live? What eyes behold a face?   55
FRANCESCHINA Ick vill not speak; torture, torture your fill;
    For me am worse than hanged; me ha' lost my will.
SIR LIONEL To the extremest whip and gaol!
       Exit Franceschina with the guard
FREEVILL Frolic! How is it, sir?
MALHEUREUX I am myself. How long was't ere I could   60
    Persuade my passion to grow calm to you!
    Rich sense makes good bad language, and a friend
    Should weigh no action but the action's end.
    I am now worthy yours, when, before,
    The beast of man, loose blood, distempered us.   65
    He that lust rules cannot be virtuous.
       Enter Mulligrub, Mistress Mulligrub, and Officers
OFFICER On afore, there! Room for the prisoners!
MULLIGRUB I pray you, do not lead me to execution through
    Cheapside. I owe Master Burnish, the goldsmith, money, and I
    fear he'll set a sergeant on my back for it.   70
COCLEDEMOY Trouble not your sconce, my Christian brother,
    but have an eye unto the main chance. I will warrant your

shoulders; as for your neck, Plinius Secundus, or Marcus Tullius
Cicero, or somebody it is, ° says that a three-fold cord is hardly
broken.°   75

MULLIGRUB Well, I am not the first honest man that hath been cast
away, and I hope shall not be the last.

COCLEDEMOY O sir, have a good stomach and maws; you shall have
a joyful supper.

MULLIGRUB In troth, I have no stomach to it; an it please you, take   80
my trencher; I use to fast at nights.

MISTRESS MULLIGRUB O husband, I little thought you should have
come to think on God thus soon. Nay, an you had been hanged
deservedly, it would never have grieved me; I have known of many
honest, innocent men have been hanged deservedly; but to be cast   85
away for nothing!

COCLEDEMOY Good woman, hold your peace, your prittles and
your prattles, your bibbles and your babbles; for I pray you
hear me in private. I am a widower, and you are almost a widow;
shall I be welcome to your houses, to your tables, and your other   90
things?

MISTRESS MULLIGRUB I have a piece of mutton° and a featherbed
for you at all times.—[To Mulligrub] I pray make haste.

MULLIGRUB I do here make my confession: if I owe any man anything, I do heartily forgive him; if any man owe me anything, let   95
him pay my wife.

COCLEDEMOY I will look to your wife's payment, I warrant you!

MULLIGRUB And now, good yoke-fellow, leave thy poor Mulligrub.

MISTRESS MULLIGRUB Nay, then I were unkind, i'faith; I will not
leave you until I have seen you hang.   100

COCLEDEMOY But brother, brother, you must think of your sins
and iniquities. You have been a broacher of profane vessels;° you
have made us drink of the juice of the Whore of Babylon;° for
whereas good ale, perries, braggets, ciders and metheglins was the
true ancient British and Trojan° drinks, you ha' brought in   105
Popish wines, Spanish wines, French wines, *tam Marti quam
Mercurio*,° both muscadine and malmsey,° to the subversion, staggering, and sometimes overthrow of many a good Christian. You
ha' been a great jumbler. O, remember the sins of your nights, for
your night works ha' been unsavoury in the taste of your custo-   110
mers.

MULLIGRUB I confess, I confess, and I forgive as I would be forgiven. Do you know one Cocledemoy?

COCLEDEMOY O, very well. Know him? An honest man he is and a
　　comely, an upright° dealer with his neighbours, and their wives   115
　　speak good things of him.

MULLIGRUB Well, wheresoe'er he is, or whatsoe'er he is, I'll take it
　　on my death he's the cause of my hanging. I heartily forgive him;
　　and if he would come forth he might save me, for he only knows
　　the why and the wherefore.   120

COCLEDEMOY You do, from your hearts and midriffs and entrails,
　　forgive him then? You will not let him rot in rusty irons, procure
　　him to be hanged in lousy linen without a song, and after he is
　　dead piss on his grave?

MULLIGRUB That hard heart of mine has procured all this, but I   125
　　forgive as I would be forgiven.

COCLEDEMOY Hang toasts, my worshipful Mulligrub! Behold thy
　　Cocledemoy, my fine vintner, my catastrophonical, fine boy!
　　Behold and see! [Discovers himself]

TYSEFEW Bliss o'the blessed! Who would but look for two knaves   130
　　here!

COCLEDEMOY No knave, worshipful friend, no knave; for observe,
　　honest Cocledemoy restores whatsoever he has got, to make you
　　know that whatsoe'er he has done has been only euphoniae gratia,°
　　for wit's sake.—I acquit this vintner as he has acquitted me. All   135
　　has been done for emphasis of wit, my fine boy, my worshipful
　　friends.

TYSEFEW Go, you are a flattering knave.

COCLEDEMOY I am so; 'tis a good thriving trade. It comes forward
　　better than the seven liberal sciences° or the nine cardinal virtues;°   140
　　which may well appear in this: you shall never have flattering
　　knave turn courtier, and yet I have read of many courtiers that
　　have turned flattering knaves.

SIR HUBERT Was't even but so? Why, then, all's well!

MULLIGRUB I could even weep for joy!   145

MISTRESS MULLIGRUB I could weep, too, but God knows for what!

TYSEFEW Here's another tack to be given—your son and daughter.

SIR HUBERT Is't possible? Heart, ay, all my heart, will you be joined
　　here?

TYSEFEW Yes, faith, father; marriage and hanging are spun both in   150
　　one hour.

COCLEDEMOY Why then, my worshipful good friends, I bid myself
　　most heartily welcome to your merry nuptials and wanton jigga-
　　joggies.—

[*Coming forward and addressing the audience, as the Epilogue*]
And now, my very fine Heliconian gallants,°   155
And you, my worshipful friends in the middle region,°
If with content our hurtless mirth hath been,
Let your pleased minds at our much care be seen;
For he shall find, that slights such trivial wit,
'Tis easier to reprove than better it.   160
We scorn to fear, and yet, we fear to swell;
We do not hope 'tis best; 'tis all, if well.
     Exeunt

SOPHONISBA

or

The Wonder of Women

THE PERSONS OF THE PLAY

Masinissa ⎱
Syphax   ⎰   kings in Libya, rivals for Sophonisba

Hasdrubal   father to Sophonisba

Gelosso° ⎱
Bytheas ⎰   senators of Carthage

Hanno Magnus   captain of Carthage

Jugurth°   Masinissa's nephew

Scipio ⎱
Laelius ⎰   generals of Rome

Vangue   an Ethiopian [negro,] slave to Syphax

Carthalon   a senator of Carthage

Gisco°   a surgeon of Carthage

Messenger°

Sophonisba   daughter of Hasdrubal of Carthage

Zanthia   her maid, [a negress]

Erichtho°   an enchantress

Arcathia ⎱
Nycea   ⎰   waiting women to Sophonisba

[Prologue]
[A Chorus of Singers]
[Pages]
[Attendants]
[Guard]
[Ushers]

Sophonisba

1.1

*[A dumbshow.]° Cornets sound a march. Enter at one door the
Prologue, two Pages with torches, Hasdrubal and Jugurth, two
Pages with lights, Masinissa leading Sophonisba, Zanthia
bearing Sophonisba's train, Arcathia and Nycea, Hanno and
Bytheas; at the other door two Pages with target and
javelins, two Pages with lights,° Syphax armed from top to toe.
Vangue follows [him]. These, thus entered, stand still, whilst the
Prologue [enters, and,] resting between both troops, speaks*

PROLOGUE The scene is Libya, and the subject thus:
Whilst Carthage stood the only awe of Rome,°
As most imperial seat of Libya,
Governed by statesmen each as great as kings
(For seventeen kings were Carthage' feodars);   5
Whilst thus she flourished, whilst her Hannibal
Made Rome to tremble, and the walls yet pale;
Then in this Carthage Sophonisba lived,
The far-famed daughter of great Hasdrubal;
For whom, 'mongst others, potent Syphax sues,   10
And well-graced Masinissa rivals him,
Both princes of proud sceptres; but the lot
Of doubtful favour Masinissa graced,
At which Syphax grows black; for now the night°
Yields loud resoundings of the nuptial pomp: 15
Apollo strikes his harp, Hymen his torch,°
Whilst louring Juno, with ill-boding eye,°
Sits envious at too forward Venus. Lo,°
The instant night; and now ye worthier minds,
To whom we shall present a female glory   20
(The wonder of a constancy so fixed,
That fate itself might well grow envious),
Be pleased to sit, such as may merit oil
And holy dew stilled from diviner heat;°
For rest thus knowing: what of this you hear,   25
The author lowly hopes, but must not fear.°

For just worth never rests on popular frown;
To have done well is fair deeds' only crown.
    Cornets sound a march; the Prologue leads Masinissa's troops
    over the stage, and departs; Syphax' troops only stay

SYPHAX Syphax, Syphax, why wast thou cursed a king?
What angry god made thee so great, so vile   30
Contemned, disgraced? Think, wert thou a slave,
Though Sophonisba did reject thy love,
Thy low neglected head unpointed at,
Thy shame unrumoured and thy suit unscoffed,
Might yet rest quiet.—Reputation!   35
Thou awe of fools and great men, thou that chok'st
Freest addictions and mak'st mortals sweat
Blood and cold drops in fear to lose or hope
To gain thy never-certain seldom-worthy gracings;
Reputation!   40
Were't not for thee, Syphax could bear this scorn,
Not spouting up his gall among his blood
In black vexations; Masinissa might°
Enjoy the sweets of his preferrèd graces
Without my dangerous envy or revenge;   45
Were't not for thy affliction all might sleep
In sweet oblivion. But—O greatness' scourge!—
We cannot without envy keep high name,
Nor yet disgraced can have a quiet shame.

VANGUE Scipio—   50

SYPHAX Some light in depth of hell. Vangue, what hope?

VANGUE I have received assured intelligence
That Scipio, Rome's sole hope, hath raised up men,
Drawn troops together for invasion—

SYPHAX Of this same Carthage!

VANGUE   With this policy,   55
To force wild Hannibal from Italy—°

SYPHAX And draw the war to Afric!

VANGUE   Right.

SYPHAX   And strike
This secure country with unthought-of arms.

VANGUE My letters bear he is departed Rome,
Directly setting course and sailing up—   60

SYPHAX To Carthage, Carthage!—O thou eternal youth,
Man of large fame, great and abounding glory,

Renownful Scipio, spread thy two-necked eagles,°
Fill full thy sails with a revenging wind,
Strike through obedient Neptune, till thy prows   65
Dash up our Libyan ooze, and thy just arms
Shine with amazeful terror on these walls!
O now record thy father's honoured blood
Which Carthage drunk, thy uncle Publius' blood°
Which Carthage drunk, thirty thousand souls   70
Of choice Italians Carthage set on wing.
Remember Hannibal, yet Hannibal,
The consul-queller. O then enlarge thy heart,
Be thousand souls in one; let all the breath,
The spirit of thy name and nation, be mixed strong   75
In thy great heart! O fall like thunder-shaft,
The wingèd vengeance of incensèd Jove,
Upon this Carthage; for Syphax here flies off
From all allegiance, from all love or service
His now free'd sceptre once did yield this city.   80
Ye universal gods, light, heat and air,
Prove all unblessing Syphax, if his hands°
Once rear themselves for Carthage but to curse it.
It had been better they had changed their faith,
Denied their gods, than slighted Syphax' love,   85
So fearfully will I take vengeance.
I'll interleague with Scipio.—Vangue,
Dear Ethiopian negro, go wing a vessel°
And fly to Scipio; say his confederate,
Vowed and confirmed, is Syphax; bid him haste   90
To mix our palms and arms; will him make up,°
Whilst we are in the strength of discontent,
Our unsuspected forces well in arms,°
For Sophonisba, Carthage, Hasdrubal
Shall feel their weakness in preferring weakness,   95
And one less great than we. To our dear wishes,
Haste, gentle negro, that this heap may know
Me and their wrong.°
VANGUE Wrong?
SYPHAX Ay, though 'twere not, yet know, while kings are strong,   100
What they'll but think, and not what is, is wrong.
I am disgraced in and by that which hath
No reason: love and woman. My revenge

Shall therefore bear no argument of right;°
Passion is reason when it speaks from might.   105
I tell thee, man, nor kings nor gods exempt,
But they grow pale if once they find contempt.
Haste!

Exeunt

1.2

*Enter Arcathia, Nycea with tapers, Sophonisba in her night
attire, followed by Zanthia*

SOPHONISBA [*to Arcathia and Nycea*] Watch at the doors; and till
    we be reposed
    Let no-one enter.—Zanthia, undo me.
ZANTHIA With this motto I undo your girdle:°
    'You had been undone if you had not been undone'.°
    Humblest service!   5
SOPHONISBA I wonder, Zanthia, why the custom is
    To use such ceremony, such strict shape°
    About us women. Forsooth, the bride must steal
    Before her lord to bed; and then delays
    Long expectations, all against known wishes.   10
    I hate these figures in locution,
    These about-phrases forced by ceremony.°
    We must still seem to fly what we most seek,
    And hide ourselves from that we fain would find us.
    Let those that think and speak and do just acts   15
    Know form can give no virtue to their acts
    Nor detract vice.°
ZANTHIA 'Las, fair princess, those that are strongly formed
    And truly shaped may naked walk, but we,
    We things called women, only made for show   20
    And pleasure, created to bear children
    And play at shuttlecock, we imperfect mixtures,°
    Without respective ceremony used
    And ever compliment, alas, what are we?
    Take from us formal custom and the courtesies   25
    Which civil fashion hath still used to us,
    We fall to all contempt.—O women, how much,

246

How much are you beholding to ceremony!

SOPHONISBA You are familiar. Zanthia, my shoe.
    [Zanthia removes Sophonisba's shoes]

ZANTHIA 'Tis wonder, madam, you tread not awry.   30

SOPHONISBA Your reason, Zanthia.

ZANTHIA   You go very high.°
    [The sound of cornets]

SOPHONISBA Hark, music, music!
    The Ladies lay the Princess in a fair bed and close the curtains°
    whilst Masinissa [seeks to] enter°

NYCEA The bridegroom!

ARCATHIA   The bridegroom!

SOPHONISBA Haste, good Zanthia!—Help, keep yet the doors.

ZANTHIA Fair fall you, lady.—*[To Arcathia and Nycea]* So, admit,
    admit!   35
    Enter four Boys anticly attired, with bows and quivers,°
    dancing to the cornets a fantastic measure; Masinissa in his
    night-gown, led by Hasdrubal and Hanno, followed by
    Bytheas and Jugurth. The Boys draw the curtains, discovering
    Sophonisba, to whom Masinissa speaks

MASINISSA You powers of joy, gods of a happy bed,
  Show you are pleased; sister and wife of Jove,
  High-fronted Juno, and thou Carthage' patron,
  Smooth-chinned Apollo, both give modest heat°
  And temperate graces!—
    Masinissa draws a white ribbon° forth of the bed, as from the
    waist of Sophonisba
               Lo, I unloose thy waist.   40
  She that is just in love is godlike chaste.—
  Io to Hymen!°

CHORUS *[with cornets, organ and voices]*° *Io* to Hymen!

SOPHONISBA A modest silence, though't be thought
  A virgin's beauty and her highest honour,   45
  Though bashful feignings nicely wrought
  Grace her that virtue takes not in, but on her,°
  What I dare think I boldly speak;
  After my word my well-bold action rusheth.
  In open flame then passion break!   50
  Where virtue prompts, thought, word, act never blusheth.
  Revenging gods, whose marble hands
  Crush faithless men with a confounding terror,

Give me no mercy if these bands°
I covet not with an unfeigned fervour;   55
Which zealous vow when aught can force me t'lame,
Load with that plague Atlas would groan at, shame.°
Io to Hymen!

CHORUS   *Io* to Hymen!

HASDRUBAL   Live both high parents of so happy birth,   60
Your stems may touch the skies and shadow earth;
Most great in fame, more great in virtue shining.
Prosper, O powers, a just, a strong divining.
Io to Hymen!

CHORUS   *Io* to Hymen!   65
Enter Carthalon, his sword drawn, his body wounded, his shield
struck full of darts; Masinissa being ready for bed

CARTHALON   To bold hearts, fortune! Be not you amazed;
Carthage, O Carthage, be not you amazed.

MASINISSA   Jove made us not to fear; resolve, speak out;
The highest misery of man is doubt.
Speak, Carthalon.   70

CARTHALON   The stooping sun, like to some weaker prince,
Let his shades spread to an unnatural hugeness,
When we, the camp that lay at Utica,
From Carthage distant but five easy leagues,
Descried from off the watch three hundred sail,   75
Upon whose tops the Roman eagles stretched
Their large-spread wings, which fanned the evening air,
To us cold breath, for well we might discern
Rome swam to Carthage.

HASDRUBAL   Hannibal, our anchor is come back; thy sleight,° 80
Thy stratagem, to lead war unto Rome
To quit ourselves, hath taught now-desperate Rome
T'assail our Carthage; now the war is here.

MASINISSA   He is not blest not honest that can fear.

HANNO   Ay, but to cast the worst of our distress—   85

MASINISSA   To doubt of what shall be is wretchedness.
Desire, fear, and hope receive no bond,
By whom we in ourselves are never but beyond.°
On!

CARTHALON   Th'alarum beats necessity of fight.   90
Th'unsober evening draws out reeling forces,°
Soldiers, half men, who to their colours troop

With fury, not with valour; whilst our ships
Unrigged, unused, fitter for fire than water,
We save in our barred haven from surprise.   95
By this our army marcheth toward the shore,
Undisciplined young men, most bold to do,
If they knew how or what; when we descry
A mighty dust beat up with horses' hooves;
Straight Roman ensigns glitter; Scipio—   100
HASDRUBAL Scipio!
CARTHALON Scipio, advancèd like the god of blood,
   Leads up grim war, that father of foul wounds,
   Whose sinewy feet are steeped in gore, whose hideous voice
   Makes turrets tremble and whole cities shake;   105
   Before whose brows Flight and Disorder hurry;
   With whom march Burnings, Murder, Wrong, Waste, Rapes;
   Behind whom a sad train is seen, Woe, Fears,
   Tortures, lean Need, Famine and helpless Tears.
   Now make we equal stand in mutual view.
   We judged the Romans eighteen thousand foot,   110
   Five thousand horse; we almost doubled them
   In number, not in virtue; yet in heat
   Of youth and wine, jolly and full of blood,
   We gave the sign of battle; shouts are raised   115
   That shook the heavens; pell-mell our armies join;
   Horse, targets, pikes, all against each opposed,
   They give fierce shock, arms thundered as they closed.
   Men cover earth, which straight are coverèd
   With men and earth; yet doubtful stood the fight,   120
   More fair to Carthage, when lo, as oft you see
   In mines of gold, when labouring slaves delve out
   The richest ore, being in sudden hope
   With some unlooked-for vein to fill their buckets
   And send huge treasure up, a sudden damp   125
   Stifles them all, their hands yet stuffed with gold;
   So fell our fortunes, for look as we stood proud
   As hopeful victors, thinking to return
   With spoils worth triumph, wrathful Syphax lands
   With full ten thousand strong Numidian horse   130
   And joins to Scipio. Then lo, we all were damped;°
   We fall in clusters, and our wearied troops
   Quit all. Slaughter ran through us straight; we fly,

Romans pursue, but Scipio sounds retreat,
As fearing trains and night. We make amain   135
For Carthage most, and some for Utica,
All for our lives.—New force, fresh arms with speed!
You have sad truth of all. No more; I bleed.

BYTHEAS O wretched fortune! [*Tears his hair*]

MASINISSA   Old lord, spare thy hairs.
What, dost thou think baldness will cure thy grief?   140
What decree the senate?

Enter Gelosso with commissions in his hand, sealed

GELOSSO Ask old Gelosso, who returns from them,
Informed with fullest charge. Strong Hasdrubal,
Great Masinissa, Carthage' general,
So speaks the senate: counsel for this war   145
In Hanno Magnus, Bytheas, Carthalon,
And us, Gelosso, rests. Embrace this charge,
You never-yet-dishonoured Hasdrubal,
High Masinissa; by your vows to Carthage,
By god of great men, glory, fight for Carthage.   150
Ten thousand strong Massylians, ready trooped,
Expect their king; double that number waits
The leading of loved Hasdrubal. Beat loud
Our Afric drums, and whilst our o'er-toiled foe
Snores on his unlaced casque, all faint, though proud   155
Through his successful fight, strike fresh alarms.
Gods are not, if they grace not bold, just arms.

MASINISSA Carthage, thou straight shalt know
Thy favours have been done unto a king.

Exit [Masinissa] with Hasdrubal and the Page

SOPHONISBA My lords, 'tis most unusual such sad haps   160
Of sudden horror should intrude 'mong beds
Of soft and private loves; but strange events
Excuse strange forms. O you that know our blood,
Revenge if I do feign. I here protest,
Though my lord leave his wife a very maid,   165
Even this night, instead of my soft arms
Clasping his well-strong limbs with glossful steel,
What's safe to Carthage shall be sweet to me.
I must not, nor I am once ignorant
My choice of love hath given this sudden danger   170
To yet strong Carthage; 'twas I lost the fight;

My choice vexed Syphax, enragèd Syphax struck
Arms' fate; yet Sophonisba not repents;°
O we were gods if that we knew events.°
But let my lord leave Carthage, quit his virtue,   175
I will not love him, yet must honour him,
As still good subjects must bad princes. Lords,
From the most ill-graced hymeneal bed
That ever Juno frowned at, I entreat
That you'll collect from our loose-formed speech   180
This firm resolve: that no low appetite
Of my sex' weakness can or shall o'ercome
Due grateful service unto you or virtue.—
Witness, ye gods, I never until now
Repined at my creation; now I wish   185
I were no woman, that my arms might speak
My heart to Carthage. But in vain, my tongue
Swears I am woman still: I talk too long.

   Cornets, a march. Enter two Pages with targets and javelins,
   two Pages with torches; Masinissa armed cap-à-pie;° Hasdrubal
   armed

MASINISSA Ye Carthage lords, know Masinissa knows
Not only terms of honour, but his actions;°   190
Nor must I now enlarge how much my cause
Hath dangered Carthage, but how I may show
Myself most prest to satisfaction.°
The loathsome stain of kings, ingratitude,
From me O much be far! And since this torrent,   195
War's rage, admits no anchor, since the billow
Is risen so high we may not hull, but yield
This ample state to stroke of speedy swords,
What you with sober haste have well decreed
We'll put to sudden arms; no, not this night,   200
These dainties, this first-fruits of nuptials
That well might give excuse for feeble ling'rings,
Shall hinder Masinissa. Appetite,
Kisses, love's dalliance, and what softer joys
The Venus of the pleasing'st ease can minister,   205
I quit you all. Virtue perforce is vice;
But he that may, yet holds, is manly wise.°
Lo then, ye lords of Carthage, to your trust
I leave all Masinissa's treasure. By the oath

Of right good men stand to my fortune just.° 210
Most hard it is for great hearts to mistrust.

CARTHALON We vow by all high powers.

MASINISSA   No, do not swear;
I was not born so small to doubt or fear.

SOPHONISBA Worthy my lord—

MASINISSA   Peace, my ears are steel;
I must not hear thy much-enticing voice.   215

SOPHONISBA By Masinissa, Sophonisba speaks
Worthy his wife; go with as high a hand
As worth can rear; I will not stay my lord.
Fight for our country; vent thy youthful heat
In fields, not beds; the fruit of honour, fame,   220
Be rather gotten than the oft disgrace
Of hapless parents, children. Go, best man,
And make me proud to be a soldier's wife
That values his renown above faint pleasures.
Think every honour that doth grace thy sword   225
Trebles my love. By thee I have no lust
But of thy glory. Best lights of heaven with thee!
Like wonder, stand or fall, so though thou die,
My fortunes may be wretched, but not I.

MASINISSA Wondrous creature, even fit for gods, not men, 230
Nature made all the rest of thy fair sex
As weak essays, to make thee a pattern
Of what can be in woman! Long farewell.
He's sure unconquered in whom thou dost dwell,
Carthage' Palladium. See that glorious lamp,°   235
Whose lifeful presence giveth sudden flight
To fancies, fogs, fears, sleep and slothful night,
Spreads day upon the world; march swift amain;
Fame got with loss of breath is god-like gain!

> *The ladies draw the curtains about Sophonisba; the rest*
> *accompany Masinissa forth, the cornets and organs playing loud*
> *full music for the act°*

2.1

[*Dumbshow.*]° *Whilst the music for the first act sounds, Hanno,*
Carthalon, Bytheas, Gelosso enter; they place themselves to
counsel, Gisco, the empoisoner, waiting on them; Hanno,
Carthalon, and Bytheas setting their hands to a writing, which
being offered to Gelosso, he denies his hand, and, as much
offended, impatiently starts up and speaks

GELOSSO My hand, my hand? Rot first; wither in aged shame!

HANNO Will you be so unseasonably wood?

BYTHEAS Hold such preposterous zeal as stand against
The full decree of senate? All think fit.

CARTHALON Nay, most unevitable necessary   5
For Carthage' safety, and the now sole good
Of present state, that we must break all faith
With Masinissa. Whilst he fights abroad,
Let's gain back Syphax, making him our own
By giving Sophonisba to his bed.   10

HANNO Syphax is Masinissa's greater, and his force
Shall give more side to Carthage. As for 's queen°
And her wise father, they love Carthage' fate;
Profit and honesty are one in state.°

GELOSSO And what decrees our very virtuous senate   15
Of worthy Masinissa, that now fights
And, leaving wife and bed, bleeds in good arms
For right old Carthage?

CARTHALON   Thus 'tis thought fit:
Her father, Hasdrubal, on sudden shall take in
Revolted Syphax; so with doubled strength,   20
Before that Masinissa shall suspect,
Slaughter both Masinissa and his troops,
And likewise strike with his deep stratagem
A sudden weakness into Scipio's arms,°
By drawing such a limb from the main body   25
Of his yet powerful army; which being done,
Dead Masinissa's kingdom we decree
To Sophonisba and great Hasdrubal
For their consent; so this swift plot shall bring°
Two crowns to her, make Hasdrubal a king.   30

GELOSSO So, first faith's breach, adultery, murder, theft!
CARTHALON What else?
GELOSSO   Nay, all is done, no mischief left.
CARTHALON Pish! Prosperous success gives blackest actions glory;
    The means are unremembered in most story.
GELOSSO Let me not say gods are not.
CARTHALON   This is fit: 35
    Conquest by blood is not so sweet as wit;°
    For howsoe'er nice virtue censures of it,
    He hath the grace of war that hath war's profit.
    But Carthage, well advised that states comes on
    With slow advice, quick execution,   40
    Have here an engineer, long bred for plots,
    Called an empoisoner, who knows this sound excuse:
    The only dew that makes men sprout in courts is use.°
    Be 't well or ill, his thrift is to be mute;
    Such slaves must act commands and not dispute,   45
    Knowing foul deeds with danger do begin
    But with rewards do end; sin is no sin
    But in respects.°
GELOSSO Politic lord, speak low; though heaven bears
    A face far from us, gods have most long ears;   50
    Jove has a hundred hundred marble hands.
CARTHALON O ay, in poetry or tragic scene!°
GELOSSO I fear gods only know what poets mean.
CARTHALON Yet hear me, I will speak close truth and cease:
    Nothing in nature is unserviceable,   55
    No, not even inutility itself;
    Is then for nought dishonesty in being?
    And if it be sometimes of forcèd use,
    Wherein more urgent than in saving nations?
    State shapes are soldered up with base, nay faulty,   60
    Yet necessary functions; some must lie,
    Some must betray, some murder, and some all;
    Each hath strong use, as poison in all purges;°
    Yet when some violent chance shall force a state
    To break given faith, or plot some stratagems,   65
    Princes ascribe that vile necessity
    Unto heaven's wrath; and sure though 't be no vice,
    Yet 'tis bad chance: states must not stick too nice.°
    For Masinissa's death, sense bids forgive:°

Beware to offend great men and let them live;   70
For 'tis of empire's body the main arm:
He that will do no good shall do no harm.°
You have my mind.°

GELOSSO Although a stage-like passion and weak heat
Full of an empty wording might suit age,   75
Know I'll speak strongly truth. Lords, ne'er mistrust
That he who'll not betray a private man
For his country, will ne'er betray his country
For private men; then give Gelosso faith.
If treachery in state be serviceable,   80
Let hangmen do it. I am bound to lose
My life, but not my honour, for my country.
Our vow, our faith, our oath, why, they're ourselves,
And he that's faithless to his proper self
May be excused if he break faith with princes.   85
The gods assist just hearts, and states that trust
Plots before providence are tossed like dust.
For Masinissa—O let me slack a little
Austere discourse and feel humanity!—
Methinks I hear him cry, 'O fight for Carthage!   90
Charge home! Wounds smart not for that so just, so great,
So good a city'. Methinks I see him yet
Leave his fair bride even on his nuptial night
To buckle on his arms for Carthage. Hark!
Yet, yet I hear him cry, 'Ingratitude,   95
Vile stain of man, O ever be most far
From Masinissa's breast! Up, march amain!
Fame got with loss of breath is godlike gain'.
And see, by this he bleeds in doubtful fight,
And cries, 'For Carthage!' whilst Carthage—Memory,   100
Forsake Gelosso! Would I could not think,
Nor hear, nor be, when Carthage is
So infinitely vile! See, see, look here!
        Cornets. Enter two Ushers, Sophonisba, Zanthia, Arcathia.
        Hanno, Bytheas, and Carthalon present Sophonisba with a
        paper, which she having perused, after a short silence [Gelosso]
        speaks°

GELOSSO Who speaks? What, mute? Fair plot! What? Blush to break
    it?
How lewd to act when so shamed but to speak it!   105

SOPHONISBA Is this the senate's firm decree?
CARTHALON   It is.
SOPHONISBA Hath Syphax entertained the stratagem?
CARTHALON No doubt he hath, or will.
SOPHONISBA   My answer's thus:
  What's safe to Carthage shall be sweet to me.
CARTHALON Right worthy!
HANNO   Royalest!
GELOSSO   O very woman!°   110
SOPHONISBA But 'tis not safe for Carthage to destroy.
  Be most unjust, cunningly politic,
  Your head's still under heaven. O trust to fate;
  Gods prosper more a just than crafty state.
  'Tis less disgrace to have a pitied loss,   115
  Than shameful victory.
GELOSSO   O very angel!°
SOPHONISBA We all have sworn good Masinissa faith;
  Speech makes us men, and there's no other bond
  'Twixt man and man but words. O equal gods,
  Make us once know the consequence of vows—   120
GELOSSO And we shall hate faith-breakers worse than man-eaters.
SOPHONISBA Ha, good Gelosso, is thy breath not here?
     [Indicating the paper]
GELOSSO You do me wrong. As long as I can die,
  Doubt you that old Gelosso can be vile?
  States may afflict, tax, torture, but our minds   125
  Are only sworn to Jove. I grieve, and yet am proud
  That I alone am honest.—High powers, you know
  Virtue is seldom seen with troops to go.
SOPHONISBA Excellent man, Carthage and Rome shall fall
  Before thy fame.—Our lords, know I the worst?   130
CARTHALON The gods foresaw, 'tis fate we thus are forced.
SOPHONISBA Gods nought foresee but see, for to their eyes
  Nought is to come or past; nor are you vile
  Because the gods foresee, for gods and we
  See as things are; things are not for we see.°   135
  But since affected wisdom in us women
  Is our sex' highest folly, I am silent;
  I cannot speak less well, unless I were
  More void of goodness.—Lords of Carthage, thus:
  The air and earth of Carthage owes my body,   140

It is their servant; what decree they of it?

CARTHALON   That you remove to Cirta, to the palace
Of well-formed Syphax, who with longing eyes
Meets you. He that gives way to fate is wise.

SOPHONISBA   I go. What power can make me wretched? What evil   145
Is there in life to him that knows life's loss
To be no evil? Show, show thy ugliest brow,
O most black chance; make me a wretched story;
Without misfortune, virtue hath no glory.
Opposèd trees makes tempests show their power,   150
And waves forced back by rocks makes Neptune tower.
Tearless, O see a miracle of life:
A maid, a widow, yet a hapless wife.

   Cornets. Sophonisba accompanied with the Senators depart;
   only Gelosso stays

GELOSSO   A prodigy! Let nature run cross-legged,
Ops go upon thy head, let Neptune burn,   155
Cold Saturn crack with heat, for now the world°
Hath seen a woman!
Leap nimble lightning from Jove's ample shield,
And make at length an end! The proud hot breath
Of thee-contemning greatness, the huge drought°   160
Of sole self-loving vast ambition,
Th'unnatural scorching heat of all those lamps°
Thou rear'dst to yield a temperate fruitful heat,
Relentless rage, whose heart hath not one drop
Of human pity—all, all loudly cry,   165
'Thy brand, O Jove, for know the world is dry!'°
O let a general end save Carthage' fame;
When worlds do burn, unseen's a city's flame.
Phoebus in me is great; Carthage must fall;°
Jove hates all vice, but vows' breach worst of all.   170

   Exit

2.2

Cornets sound a charge. Enter Masinissa in his gorget and
shirt, shield, sword; his arm transfixed with a dart. Jugurth
follows with [Masinissa's] cuirass and casque

MASINISSA Mount us again; give us another horse.
JUGURTH Uncle, your blood flows fast; pray ye withdraw.
MASINISSA O Jugurth, I cannot bleed too fast, too much,
    For that so great, so just, so royal Carthage.
    My wound smarts not, blood's loss makes me not faint,   5
    For that loved city. O nephew, let me tell thee
    How good that Carthage is. It nourished me,
    And when full time gave me fit strength for love,
    The most adorèd creature of the city
    To us before great Syphax did they yield,   10
    Fair, noble, modest and, 'bove all, my own,
    My Sophonisba. O Jugurth, my strength doubles;
    I know not how to turn a coward, drop
    In feeble baseness I cannot. Give me horse;
    Know I am Carthage' very creature, and I am graced   15
    That I may bleed for them. Give me fresh horse.
JUGURTH He that doth public good for multitude
    Finds few are truly grateful.
MASINISSA O Jugurth, fie! You must not say so, Jugurth.
    Some commonwealths may let a noble heart,   20
    Too forward, bleed abroad and bleed bemoaned
    But not revenged at home; but Carthage, fie,
    It cannot be ungrate, faithless through fear,
    It cannot, Jugurth; Sophonisba's there.
    Beat a fresh charge.   25
        Enter Hasdrubal, his sword drawn, reading a letter; Gisco
        follows him
HASDRUBAL Sound the retreat; respect your health, brave prince;
    The waste of blood throws paleness on your face.
MASINISSA By light, my heart's not pale! O my loved father,
    We bleed for Carthage; balsam to my wounds,
    We bleed for Carthage. Shall's restore the fight?   30
    My squadron of Massylians yet stands firm.
HASDRUBAL The day looks off from Carthage; cease alarms;°
    A modest temperance is the life of arms.
    Take our best surgeon Gisco; he is sent
    From Carthage to attend your chance of war.   35
GISCO We promise sudden ease.
MASINISSA   Thy comfort's good.
HASDRUBAL [*aside*] That nothing can secure us but thy blood!
    [*To Gisco*] Infuse it in his wound, 'twill work amain.

GISCO O Jove—

HASDRUBAL   What Jove? Thy god must be thy gain;
   And as for me—Apollo Pythian!°
   Thou know'st a statist must not be a man.   40

        Exit Hasdrubal. Enter Gelosso disguised like an old soldier,
        delivering to Masinissa (as he [is] preparing to be dressed by
        Gisco) a letter, which Masinissa reading, starts, and speaks to
        Gisco

MASINISSA Forbear! How art thou called?

GISCO   Gisco, my lord.

MASINISSA Um, Gisco! Ha! touch not mine arm.—*(To Gelosso)*
   Most only man!°
   [*To Gisco*] Sirrah, sirrah, art poor?

GISCO   Not poor.°

        Masinissa begins to draw [his sword]

MASINISSA [*To Jugurth*]   Nephew, command
   Our troops of horse make indisgraced retreat;°   45
   Trot easy off.—Not poor!—Jugurth, give charge
   My soldiers stand in square battalia,
   Entirely of themselves.—°

        Exit Jugurth

                        Gisco, thou'rt old;
   'Tis time to leave off murder; thy faint breath
   Scarce heaves thy ribs, thy gummy blood-shot eyes   50
   Are sunk a great way in thee, thy lank skin
   Slides from thy fleshless veins; be good to men.—
   Judge him ye gods; I had not life to kill
   So base a creature.—Hold, Gisco, live;
   The god-like part of kings is to forgive.   55

        [*Sheathes his sword*]°

GISCO Command astonished Gisco.

MASINISSA   No return.°
   Haste unto Carthage; quit thy abject fears;
   Masinissa knows no use of murderers.

        [*Exit Gisco.*] *Enter Jugurth, amazed, his sword drawn*

   Speak, speak; let terror strike slaves mute;
   Much danger makes great hearts most resolute.   60

JUGURTH Uncle, I fear foul arms. Myself beheld
   Syphax on high speed run his well-breathed horse
   Direct to Cirta, that most beauteous city
   Of all his kingdom; whilst his troops of horse

With careless trot pace gently toward our camp,   65
As friends to Carthage. Stand on guard, dear uncle,
For Hasdrubal, with yet his well-ranked army,
Bends a deep threat'ning brow to us as if
He waited but to join with Syphax' horse
And hew us all to pieces. O my king,   70
My uncle, father, captain over all,
Stand like thyself, or like thyself now fall.
Thy troops yet hold good ground. Unworthy wounds,
Betray not Masinissa!

MASINISSA   Jugurth, pluck,
Pluck.
          [*Jugurth pulls out the dart from Masinissa's arm*]
          So, good coz.

JUGURTH   O god! do you not feel?   75

MASINISSA No, Jugurth, no; now all my flesh is steel.

GELOSSO Off, base disguise! High lights, scorn not to view°
A true old man.—Up, Masinissa, throw
The lot of battle upon Syphax' troops
Before he join with Carthage; then amain   80
Make through to Scipio; he yields safe abodes.
Spare treachery, and strike the very gods.°

MASINISSA Why wast thou born at Carthage? O my fate!
Divinest Sophonisba! I am full
Of much complaint and many passions,   85
The least of which expressed would sad the gods
And strike compassion in most ruthless hell.
Up, unmaimed heart, spend all thy grief and rage
Upon thy foe; the field's a soldier's stage
On which his action shows. If you are just   90
And hate those that contemn you, O you gods,
Revenge worthy your anger, your anger! O,°
Down man, up heart! Stoop, Jove, and bend thy chin°
To thy large breast; give sign thou'rt pleased and just;°
Swear good men's foreheads must not print the dust.°   95
          Exeunt

2.3

Enter Hasdrubal, Hanno, Bytheas

HASDRUBAL What Carthage has decreed, Hanno, is done.
  Advanced and born was Hasdrubal for state;
  Only with it his faith, his love, his hate
  Are of one piece. Were it my daughter's life°
  That fate hath sought or Carthage' safety brings,° 5
  What deed so red but hath been done by kings?
  Iphigenia! He that's a man for men,°
  Ambitious as a god, must like a god
  Live clear from passions; his full aimed-at end,
  Immense to others, sole self to comprehend, 10
  Round in's own globe; not to be clasped, but holds°
  Within him all; his heart being of more folds
  Than shield of Telamon, not to be pierced though struck.°
  The god of wise men is themselves, not luck.
    Enter Gisco
  See him by whom now Masinissa is not. 15
  —Gisco, is't done?

GISCO   Your pardon, worthy lord,
  It is not done; my heart sunk in my breast,
  His virtue mazed me, faintness seized me all.
  Some god's in kings that will not let them fall.

HASDRUBAL His virtue mazed thee? Um, why, now I see 20
  Thou'rt that just man that hath true touch of blood,
  Of pity and soft piety. Forgive?
  Yes, honour thee; we did it but to try
  What sense thou hadst of blood.—Go, Bytheas,
  Take him to our private treasury— 25
  [*Aside*] And cut his throat; the slave hath all betrayed.

BYTHEAS [*aside*] Are you assured?

HASDRUBAL [*aside*]   Assured, for this I know:°
  Who thinketh to buy villainy with gold
  Shall ever find such faith so bought, so sold.
  [*Aloud*] Reward him thoroughly.
    A shout [within], the cornets giving a flourish

HANNO   What means this shout? 30

HASDRUBAL Hanno, 'tis done; Syphax' revolt by this
  Hath secured Carthage; and now his force come in

And joined with us give Masinissa charge
And assured slaughter.—O ye powers, forgive!
Through rotten'st dung best plants both sprout and live;   35
By blood vines grow.

HANNO   But yet think, Hasdrubal,
'Tis fit at least you bear grief's outward show;
It is your kinsman bleeds. What need men know
Your hand is in his wounds? 'Tis well in state
To do close ill, but 'void a public hate.°   40

HASDRUBAL   Tush, Hanno, let me prosper, let routs prate;
My power shall force their silence, or my hate
Shall scorn their idle malice. Men of weight
Know, he that fears envy let him cease to reign;
The people's hate to some hath been their gain.   45
For howsoe'er a monarch feigns his parts,
Steal anything from kings but subjects' hearts.

Enter Carthalon leading in bound Gelosso

CARTHALON   Guard, guard the camp! Make to the trench!—Stand
    firm.

HASDRUBAL   The gods of boldness with us! How runs chance?

CARTHALON   Think, think how wretched thou canst be, thou art;   50
    Short words shall speak long woes.

GELOSSO   Mark, Hasdrubal.°

CARTHALON   Our bloody plot to Masinissa's ear
    Untimely by this lord was all betrayed.

GELOSSO   By me it was, by me, vile Hasdrubal;
    I joy to speak't.

HASDRUBAL   Down, slave!

GELOSSO   I cannot fall.   55

CARTHALON   Our trains disclosed, straight to his well-used arms
He took himself, rose up with all his force
On Syphax' careless troops, Syphax being hurried
Before to Cirta, fearless of success,
Impatient Sophonisba to enjoy.   60
Gelosso rides to head of all our squadrons,
Commands make stand in thy name, Hasdrubal,
In mine, in his, in all. Dull rest our men,
Whilst Masinissa, now with more than fury,
Chargeth the loose and much-amazèd ranks   65
Of absent Syphax, who with broken shout,
In vain expecting Carthage secondings,

Give faint repulse. A second charge is given;
Then look as when a falcon towers aloft
Whole shoals of fowl and flocks of lesser birds   70
Crouch fearfully and dive, some among sedge,
Some creep in brakes; so Masinissa's sword,
Brandished aloft, tossed 'bout his shining casque,
Made stoop whole squadrons; quick as thought he strikes,°
Here hurls he darts, and there his rage-strong arm   75
Fights foot to foot; here cries he, 'Strike, they sink!'
And then grim slaughter follows, for by this,
As men betrayed, they curse us, die, or fly, or both.
Of ten, six thousand fell. Now was I come
And straight perceived all bled by his vile plot.   80
GELOSSO Vile? Good plot, my good plot, Hasdrubal!
CARTHALON I forced our army beat a running march,
But Masinissa struck his spurs apace
Upon his speedy horse, leaves slaughtering;
All fly to Scipio who with open ranks   85
In view receives them. All I could effect
Was but to gain him.
HASDRUBAL   Die!
GELOSSO   Do what thou can,°
Thou canst but kill a weak old honest man.
    Gelosso departs guarded
CARTHALON Scipio and Masinissa by this strike
Their claspèd palms, then vow an endless love;°   90
Straight a joint shout they raise, then turn they breasts
Direct on us, march strongly toward our camp
As if they dared us fight. O Hasdrubal,
I fear they'll force our camp.
HASDRUBAL   Break up and fly.
—This was your plot.
HANNO   But 'twas thy shame to choose it.   95
CARTHALON He that forbids not offence, he does it.
HASDRUBAL The curse of women's words go with you.—Fly!—
You are no villains!—Gods and men, which way?—
Advise vile things!
HANNO   Vile?
HASDRUBAL   Ay.
CARTHALON   Not!
BYTHEAS   You did all.

HASDRUBAL Did you not plot?
CARTHALON   Yielded not Hasdrubal?   100
HASDRUBAL But you enticed me.
HANNO   How?
HASDRUBAL   With hope of place.
CARTHALON He that for wealth leaves faith is abject.
HANNO   Base.
HASDRUBAL Do not provoke my sword; I live.
CARTHALON   More shame,
    T'outlive thy virtue and thy once-great name.
HASDRUBAL Upbraid ye me?
HANNO   Hold!
CARTHALON   Know that only thou   105
    Art treacherous; thou shouldst have had a crown.
HANNO Thou didst all, all; he for whom mischief's done,
    He does it.
HASDRUBAL   Brook open scorn!—Faint powers,°
    Make good the camp.—No, fly!—Yes.—What? Wild rage!   110
    To be a prosperous villain yet some heat should hold,°
    But to burn temples and yet freeze, O cold!
    Give me some health!—Now your blood sinks! Thus deeds
    Ill-nourished rot; without Jove nought succeeds.
      Exeunt

Organ mixed with recorders for this act°

3.1

[*A bed is set out.*] *Syphax, his dagger twone about her hair, drags in Sophonisba in her nightgown petticoat; and Zanthia and Vangue following*

SYPHAX Must we entreat? Sue to such squeamish ears?
 Know, Syphax has no knees, his eyes no tears;°
 Enragèd love is senseless of remorse.
 Thou shalt, thou must; kings' glory is their force.
 Thou art in Cirta, in my palace, fool;   5
 Dost think he pitieth tears that knows to rule?
 For all thy scornful eyes, thy proud disdain,
 And late contempt of us, now we'll revenge;
 Break stubborn silence. Look, I'll tack thy head
 To the low earth, whilst strength of two black knaves°   10
 Thy limbs all wide shall strain. Prayer fitteth slaves;
 Our courtship be our force. Rest calm as sleep,
 Else at this quake; hark, hark, we cannot weep.

SOPHONISBA Can Sophonisba be enforced?

SYPHAX   Can? See.

SOPHONISBA Thou may'st enforce my body but not me.   15

SYPHAX Not?

SOPHONISBA No.

SYPHAX   No?

SOPHONISBA   No. Off with thy loathèd arms,
 That lie more heavy on me than the chains
 That wear deep wrinkles in the captive's limbs.
 I do beseech thee—

SYPHAX   What?

SOPHONISBA   Be but a beast,
 Be but a beast.

SYPHAX   Do not offend a power   20
 Can make thee more than wretched; yield to him
 To whom fate yields. Know, Masinissa's dead.

SOPHONISBA Dead?

SYPHAX   Dead.

SOPHONISBA   To gods' of good men shame.

265

SYPHAX Help, Vangue, my strong blood boils.
SOPHONISBA   O save thine own yet fame.°
SYPHAX All appetite is deaf; I will, I must;   25
    Achilles' armour could not bear our lust.°
SOPHONISBA Hold thy strong arm and hear, my Syphax: know
    I am thy servant now; I needs must love thee,
    For—O, my sex, forgive!—I must confess,
    We not affect protesting feebleness,   30
    Entreats, faint blushings, timorous modesty;
    We think our lover is but little man
    Who is so full of woman. Know, fair prince,
    Love's strongest arm's not rude; for we still prove°
    Without some fury there's no ardent love.   35
    We love our love's impatience of delay;
    Our noble sex was only born t'obey
    To him that dares command.
SYPHAX   Why, this is well.
    Th'excuse is good. Wipe thy fair eyes, our queen,
    Make proud thy head. Now feel more friendly strength   40
    Of thy lord's arm; come, touch my rougher skin
    With thy soft lip.—Zanthia, dress our bed.
    —Forget old loves and clip him that through blood
    And hell acquires his wish. Think not, but kiss;
    The flourish 'fore love's fight is Venus' bliss.   45
SOPHONISBA Great dreadful lord, by thy affection
    Grant me one boon. Know I have made a vow—
SYPHAX Vow? What vow? Speak.
SOPHONISBA   Nay, if you take offence,
    Let my soul suffer first, and yet—
SYPHAX   Offence?
    Not, Sophonisba; hold, thy vow is free   50
    As—come, thy lips!
SOPHONISBA   Alas, cross misery!
    As I do wish to live, I long to enjoy
    Your warm embrace, but, O my vow, 'tis thus:
    If ever my lord died, I vowed to him
    A most, most private sacrifice before   55
    I touched a second spouse. All I implore
    Is but this liberty.
SYPHAX   This, go obtain.
    What time?
SOPHONISBA One hour.

266

SYPHAX   Sweet, good speed, adieu!—
    [*Aside*] Yet, Syphax, trust no more than thou may'st view.—
    [*Aloud*] Vangue shall stay.
SOPHONISBA   He stays.
        Enter a Page delivering a letter to Sophonisba which she
        privately reads
SYPHAX [*aside to Zanthia*]   Zanthia, Zanthia,   60
    Thou art not foul, go to; some lords are oft
    So much in love with their known ladies' bodies
    That they oft love their vails. Hold, hold; [*giving her money*]
        thou'st find°
    To faithful care kings' bounty hath no shore.
ZANTHIA You may do much.
SYPHAX   But let my gold do more.   65
ZANTHIA I am your creature.
SYPHAX   Be, get, 'tis no stain;
    The good of service is however gain.°
        Exit [*Syphax*]
SOPHONISBA Zanthia, where are we now? Speak worth my service;°
    Ha' we done well?
ZANTHIA   Nay, in height of best.   70
    I feared a superstitious virtue would spoil all,
    But now I find you above women rare;
    She that can time her goodness hath true care°
    Of her best good. Nature at home begins;
    She whose integrity herself hurts, sins.
    For Masinissa, he was good, and so;   75
    But he is dead or, worse, distressed, or more
    Than dead, or much distressed. O sad, poor,
    Who ever held such friends! No, let him go;
    Such faith is praised, then laughed at, for still know,
    Those are the living women that reduce   80
    All that they touch unto their ease and use,
    Knowing that wedlock, virtue, or good names
    Are courses and varieties of reason,°
    To use or leave as they advantage them,
    And absolute within themselves reposed,
    Only to greatness ope, to all else closed.   85
    Weak sanguine fools are to their own good nice;
    Before I held you virtuous, but now wise.
SOPHONISBA Zanthia, victorious Masinissa lives,

My Masinissa lives! O steady powers,   90
Keep him as safe as heaven keeps the earth,
Which looks upon it with a thousand eyes.
That honest, valiant man! And Zanthia,
Do but record the justice of his love,
And my for-ever vows, for-ever vows.   95

ZANTHIA   Ay, true, madam; nay, think of his great mind,
His most just heart, his all of excellence,
And such a virtue as the gods might envy.
Against this, Syphax is but—and you know,°
Fame lost, what can be got that's good for—

SOPHONISBA   Hence!   100
Take, nay, with one hand.

ZANTHIA   My service.°

SOPHONISBA   Prepare
Our sacrifice.

ZANTHIA   But yield you, ay or no?

SOPHONISBA   When thou dost know—

ZANTHIA   What then?

SOPHONISBA   Then thou wilt know.

          Exit Zanthia

Let him that would have counsel 'void th'advice
Of friends made his with weighty benefits,   105
Whose much dependence only strives to fit
Humour, not reason, and so still devise°
In any thought to make their friend seem wise.
But above all, O fear a servant's tongue,
Like such as only for their gain to serve.   110
Within the vast capacity of place
I know no vileness so most truly base.
Their lord's their gain; and he that most will give,
With him they will not die but they will live.
Traitors and these are one; such slaves once trust   115
Whet swords to make thine own blood lick the dust.°

          *Cornets and organs playing full° music, [there] enters the
          solemnity° of a sacrifice; which being entered, whilst the
          Attendants [including Zanthia and Vangue] furnish the altar,°
          Sophonisba [sings a] song; which done, she speaks*

SOPHONISBA   Withdraw, withdraw.—

          All but Zanthia and Vangue depart

I not invoke thy arm, thou god of sound,°
Nor thine, nor thine, although in all abound

High powers immense. But jovial Mercury, 120
And thou, O brightest female of the sky,
Thrice-modest Phoebe, you that jointly fit°
A worthy chastity and a most chaste wit,
To you corruptless honey and pure dew
Upbreathes our holy fire.
　　　　[*She throws incense on the altar fire*]
　　　　　　　　　　　　Words just and few 125
O deign to hear. If in poor wretches' cries
You glory not; if drops of withered eyes
Be not your sport, be just; all that I crave
Is but chaste life or an untainted grave.
I can no more; yet hath my constant tongue 130
Let fall no weakness, though my heart were wrung
With pangs worth hell. Whilst great thoughts stop our tears,
Sorrow unseen, unpitied, inward wears.°
You see now where I rest, come is my end.
Cannot heaven virtue against weak chance defend? 135
When weakness hath outborne what weakness can—
What should I say?—'tis Jove's, not sin of man.
Some stratagem now, let wit's god be shown;
Celestial powers by miracles are known.
I have't; 'tis done!—Zanthia, prepare our bed.— 140
Vangue!
VANGUE　Your servant.
SOPHONISBA　　　　　　Vangue, we have performed
Due rites unto the dead.
　　　Sophonisba presents a carouse to Vangue [*which she has*
　　　drugged]
　　　　　　　　　　Now to thy lord,
Great Syphax, healthful cups; which done, the king
Is right much welcome.
VANGUE　　　　　　Were it as deep as thought,
Off it should thus.
　　　He drinks
SOPHONISBA [*aside*]　My safety with that draught. 145
VANGUE　Close the vault's mouth lest we do slip in drink.
SOPHONISBA　To what use, gentle negro, serves this cave°
Whose mouth thus opens so familiarly
Even in the king's bedchamber?
VANGUE　　　　　　　　　　O my queen,

This vault with hideous darkness and much length   150
Stretcheth beneath the earth into a grove
One league from Cirta.—I am very sleepy.—
Through this, when Cirta hath been strong begirt
With hostile siege, the king hath safely 'scaped
To . . . to . . .
   [Vangue falls down]

SOPHONISBA The wine is strong.

VANGUE   Strong?

SOPHONISBA   Zanthia!   155

ZANTHIA What means my princess?

SOPHONISBA   Zanthia, rest firm
And silent. Help us. Nay, do not dare refuse.

ZANTHIA The negro's dead!

SOPHONISBA   No, drunk.

ZANTHIA   Alas!

SOPHONISBA   Too late,
Her hand is fearful whose mind's desperate.°
It is but sleepy opium he hath drunk.   160
Help, Zanthia!
   *They lay Vangue in Syphax' bed, [remove some of his clothing]
   and draw the curtains*°
There lie, Syphax' bride; a naked man°
Is soon undressed; there bide, dishonoured passion.
   [There is a] knock within
Forthwith Syphax comes!

SYPHAX *[offstage] Way for the king!*

SOPHONISBA   Straight for the king!—I fly   165
Where misery shall see nought but itself.
Dear Zanthia, close the vault when I am sunk,
And whilst he slips to bed, escape; be true.
I can no more; come to me.—Hark, gods, my breath°
Scorns to crave life; grant but a well-famed death.   170
   *She descends [into the vault]. Enter Syphax ready for bed [with
   Attendants]*

SYPHAX Each man withdraw, let not a creature stay
Within large distance!
   [Exeunt Attendants]

ZANTHIA   Sir!

SYPHAX   Hence, Zanthia!
Not thou shalt hear; all stand without ear-reach

Of the soft cries nice shrinking brides do yield,
When—
ZANTHIA   But sir—
SYPHAX   Hence!—[*Aside*] Stay, take thy delight by steps,   175
Think of thy joys, and make long thy pleasures.
O silence, thou dost swallow pleasure right;
Words take away some sense from our delight.—
Music!—°
Be proud, my Venus; Mercury, thy tongue;   180
Cupid, thy flame; 'bove all, O Hercules,
Let not thy back be wanting; for now I leap°
To catch the fruit none but the gods should reap.
      Offering to leap into bed, he discovers Vangue
Ha! Can any woman turn to such a devil?°
Or—or—Vangue! Vangue!
VANGUE   Yes, yes.
SYPHAX   Speak, slave;   185
How cam'st thou here?
VANGUE   Here?
SYPHAX   Zanthia, Zanthia,
Where's Sophonisba? Speak at full, at full;
Give me particular faith, or know thou art not.
ZANTHIA Your pardon, just-moved prince, and private ear.°
SYPHAX Ill actions have some grace, that they can fear.   190
      [*Zanthia whispers to Syphax*]
VANGUE [*aside*] How came I laid? Which way was I made drunk?
Where am I? Think. Or is my state advanced?
O Jove, how pleasant is it but to sleep
In a king's bed!
SYPHAX   Sleep there thy lasting sleep,
Improvident, base, o'er-thirsty slave!   195
      Syphax kills Vangue
Die pleased a king's couch is thy too-proud grave.—
Through this vault, say'st thou?
ZANTHIA   As you give me grace
To live, 'tis true.
SYPHAX   We will be good to Zanthia;
Go cheer thy lady, and be private to us.°
ZANTHIA As to my life.
      She descends after Sophonisba
SYPHAX   I'll use this Zanthia,   200

And trust her as our dogs drink dangerous Nile,
Only for thirst, then fly the crocodile.°
Wise Sophonisba knows love's tricks of art;
Without much hindrance, pleasure hath no heart.
Despite all virtue or weak plots I must;   205
Seven-walled Babel cannot bear our lust.°

    Descends through the vault

3.2

    Cornets sound marches. Enter Scipio and Laelius with the
    complements of a Roman General° before them [at one door]. At
    the other door, Masinissa and Jugurth

MASINISSA Let not the virtue of the world suspect
  Sad Masinissa's faith, nor once condemn
  Our just revolt. Carthage first gave me life.
  Her ground gave food, her air first lent me breath.
  The earth was made for men, not men for earth.°   5
  Scipio, I do not thank the gods for life,
  Much less vile men or earth. Know, best of lords,
  It is a happy being breathes well-famed,
  For which Jove seiseth us.—Men, be not fooled°
  With piety to place, tradition's fear;   10
  A just man's country Jove makes everywhere.
SCIPIO Well urgeth Masinissa, but to leave
  A city so ingrate, so faithless, so more vile
  Than civil speech may name, fear not; such vice
  To scourge is heaven's most grateful sacrifice.   15
  Thus all confess, first they have broke a faith
  To thee most due, so just to be observed
  That barbarousness itself may well blush at them.
  Where is thy passion? They have shared thy crown,
  Thy proper right of birth; contrived thy death.—   20
  Where is thy passion?—Given thy beauteous spouse
  To thy most hated rival.—Statue, not man!—
  And last, thy friend Gelosso, man worth gods,
  With tortures have they rent to death.
MASINISSA [*weeping*]   O Gelosso,
  For thee full eyes.

SCIPIO   No passion for the rest?°   25
MASINISSA O Scipio, my grief for him may be expressed by tears,
      But for the rest, silence and secret anguish
      Shall waste, shall waste! Scipio, he that can weep
      Grieves not, like me, private deep inward drops
      Of blood. My heart! For god's rights, give me leave°   30
      To be a short time man.
SCIPIO   Stay, prince.
MASINISSA   I cease;°
      Forgive if I forget thy presence. Scipio,
      Thy face makes Masinissa more than man,
      And here before your steady power a vow
      As firm as fate I make: when I desist   35
      To be commanded by thy virtue, Scipio,
      Or fall from friend of Rome's, revenging gods
      Afflict me with your torture. I have given
      Of passion and of faith my heart.
SCIPIO   To counsel then;
      Grief fits weak hearts, revenging virtue men.   40
      Thus, I think fit, before that Syphax know
      How deeply Carthage sinks, let's beat swift march
      Up even to Cirta, and whilst Syphax snores
      With his, late thine—
MASINISSA   With mine? No, Scipio;
      Libya hath poison, asps, knives, and too much earth   45
      To make one grave. With mine? Not; she can die.
      Scipio, with mine? Jove say it, thou dost lie.
SCIPIO Temperance be Scipio's honour.
LAELIUS   Cease your strife;°
      She is a woman.
MASINISSA   But she is my wife.
LAELIUS And yet she is no god.
MASINISSA   And yet she's more;   50
      I do not praise gods' goodness but adore;
      Gods cannot fall, and for their constant goodness,
      Which is necessited, they have a crown
      Of never-ending pleasures; but faint man,
      Framed to have his weakness made the heavens' glory,   55
      If he with steady virtue holds all siege
      That power, that speech, that pleasure, that full sweets,
      A world of greatness can assail him with,

Having no pay but self-wept misery,
And beggars' treasure heaped,—that man I'll praise   60
Above the gods.

SCIPIO   The Libyan speaks bold sense.

MASINISSA By that by which all is, proportion,°
I speak with thought.

SCIPIO   No more.

MASINISSA   Forgive my admiration;
You touched a string to which my sense was quick.
Can you but think? Do, do! My grief, my grief   65
Would make a saint blaspheme. Give some relief;
As thou art Scipio, forgive that I forget
I am a soldier; such woes Jove's ribs would burst;
Few speak less ill that feel so much of worst.°
My ear attends.

SCIPIO   Before, then, Syphax join   70
With new-strengthed Carthage, or can once unwind
His tangled sense from out so wild amaze,
Fall we like sudden lightning 'fore his eyes;
Boldness and speed are all of victories.

MASINISSA Scipio, let Masinissa clip thy knees!   75
May once these eyes view Syphax? Shall this arm
Once make him feel his sinew? O ye gods,
My cause, my cause! Justice is so huge odds,°
That he who with it fears, heaven must renounce
In his creation.

SCIPIO   Beat then a close quick march.   80
Before the morn shall shake cold dews through skies,
Syphax shall tremble at Rome's thick alarms.

MASINISSA Ye powers, I challenge conquest to just arms.°

With a full flourish of cornets, they depart

Organs, viols and voices play for this act

4.1

Enter Sophonisba and Zanthia, as out of a cave's mouth°

SOPHONISBA Where are we, Zanthia?

ZANTHIA   Vangue said the cave
Opened in Belos' forest.

SOPHONISBA   Lord, how sweet
I scent the air! The huge long vault's close vein,
What damps it breathed! In Belos' forest, say'st?
Be valiant, Zanthia; how far's Utica
From these most heavy shades?   5

ZANTHIA   Ten easy leagues.

SOPHONISBA There's Masinissa, my true Zanthia.
Shall's venture nobly to escape, and touch
My lord's just arms? Love's wings so nimbly heave°
The body up, that as our toes shall trip   10
Over the tender and obedient grass,
Scarce any drop of dew is dashed to ground.
And see, the willing shade of friendly night
Makes safe our instant haste. Boldness and speed
Make actions most impossible succeed.   15

ZANTHIA But madam, know the forest hath no way
But one to pass, the which holds strictest guard.

SOPHONISBA Do not betray me, Zanthia.

ZANTHIA   I, madam?

SOPHONISBA   No,
I not mistrust thee, yet, but—

ZANTHIA   Here you may
Delay your time.

SOPHONISBA   Ay, Zanthia, delay,   20
By which we may yet hope—yet hope—alas,
How all benumbed's my sense! Chance hath so often struck,
I scarce can feel. I should now curse the gods,
Call on the Furies, stamp the patient earth,
Cleave my stretched cheeks with sound, speak from all sense, 25
But loud, and full of players' eloquence.—
No, no! What shall we eat?

ZANTHIA   Madam, I'll search
For some ripe nuts which Autumn hath shook down
From the unleaved hazel; then some cooler air
Shall lead me to a spring. Or I will try   30
The courteous pale of some poor foresters
For milk.
SOPHONISBA Do, Zanthia.—
        Exit Zanthia
                                    O happiness
Of those that know not pride or lust of city;
There's no man blessed but those that most men pity.
O fortunate poor maids, that are not forced   35
To wed for state nor are for state divorced!
Whom policy of kingdoms doth not marry,
But pure affection makes to love or vary;
You feel no love which you dare not to show,
Nor show a love which doth not truly grow.   40
O, you are surely blessèd of the sky;
You live, that know not death before you die.
        Through the vault's mouth, in his nightgown, torch in his
        hand, Syphax enters just behind Sophonisba
You are—
SYPHAX   In Syphax' arms, thing of false lip.
What god shall now release thee?
SOPHONISBA   Art a man?
SYPHAX Thy limbs shall feel. Despite thy virtue, know   45
I'll thread thy richest pearl. This forest's deaf,
As is my lust. Night and the god of silence
Swells my full pleasures; no more shalt thou delude
My easy credence. Virgin of fair brow,
Well-featured creature, and our utmost wonder,   50
Queen of our youthful bed, be proud.
        Syphax setteth away his light, and prepareth to embrace
        Sophonisba
                                    I'll use thee—
        Sophonisba snatcheth out her knife
SOPHONISBA Look thee, view this; show but one strain of force,
Bow but to seize this arm, and by myself,
Or more by Masinissa, this good steel
Shall set my soul on wing.—Thus, formed gods, see,   55
And men with gods' worth, envy nought but me!

SYPHAX Do, strike thy breast; know, being dead I'll use
    With highest lust of sense thy senseless flesh,
    And even then thy vexèd soul shall see,
    Without resistance, thy trunk prostitute   60
    Unto our appetite.
SOPHONISBA   I shame to make thee know
    How vile thou speakest; corruption then as much
    As thou shalt do; but frame unto thy lusts
    Imagination's utmost sin. Syphax,
    I speak all frightless; know, I live or die   65
    To Masinissa, nor the force of fate
    Shall make me leave his love, or slake thy hate.°
    I will speak no more
SYPHAX Thou hast amazed us. Woman's forcèd use,
    Like unripe fruit 's no sooner got but waste;°   70
    They have proportion, colour, but no taste.
    [*Aside*] Think, Syphax.—Sophonisba, rest thine own.—
    Our guard!
        Enter a Guard [*and Zanthia*]°
    —Creature of most astonishing virtue,
    If with fair usage, love and passionate courtings,   75
    We may obtain the heaven of thy bed,
    We cease no suit; from other force be free.
    We dote not on thy body, but love thee.
SOPHONISBA Wilt thou keep faith?
SYPHAX   By thee, and by that power
    By which thou art thus glorious, trust my vow.   80
    —Our guard, convey the royal'st excellence
    That ever was called woman to our palace;
    Observe her with strict care.
SOPHONISBA   Dread Syphax, speak,
    As thou art worthy, is not Zanthia false?
SYPHAX To thee she is.
SOPHONISBA   As thou art then thyself,   85
    Let her not be.
SYPHAX   She is not.
        The Guard seizeth Zanthia
ZANTHIA   Thus most speed;
    When two foes are grown friends, partakers bleed.
SYPHAX When plants must flourish, their manure must rot.
SOPHONISBA Syphax, be recompensed; I hate thee not.

Exit Sophonisba [with Zanthia and Guard]

SYPHAX   A wasting flame feeds on my amorous blood,   90
  Which we must cool or die! What way all power,
  All speech, full opportunity can make,
  We have made fruitless trial.—Infernal Jove,
  You resolute angels that delight in flames,
  To you all wonder-working spirits, I fly.   95
  Since heaven helps not, deepest hell we'll try.
  Here in this desert the great soul of charms,
  Dreadful Erichtho lives, whose dismal brow
  Contemns all roofs or civil coverture.
  Forsaken graves and tombs, the ghosts forced out,   100
  She joys to inhabit.
    Infernal music plays softly whilst Erichtho enters, and when
    she speaks ceaseth°
  A loathsome yellow leanness spreads her face,
  A heavy hell-like paleness loads her cheeks
  Unknown to a clear heaven; but if dark winds
  Or thick black clouds drive back the blinded stars   105
  When her deep magic makes forced heaven quake
  And thunder spite of Jove, Erichtho then
  From naked graves stalks out, heaves proud her head,
  With long unkempt hair loaden, and strives to snatch
  The night's quick sulphur. Then she bursts up tombs;°   110
  From half-rot cerecloths then she scrapes dry gums
  For her black rites; but when she finds a corpse
  New-graved, whose entrails yet not turn
  To slimy filth, with greedy havoc then
  She makes fierce spoil, and swells with wicked triumph   115
  To bury her lean knuckles in his eyes;
  Then doth she gnaw the pale and o'ergrown nails
  From his dry hand; but if she find some life
  Yet lurking close, she bites his gelid lips,°
  And sticking her black tongue in his dry throat,   120
  She breathes dire murmurs which enforce him bear
  Her baneful secrets to the spirits of horror.
  To her first sound the gods yield any harm,
  As trembling once to hear a second charm.
  She is—   125

ERICHTHO   Here, Syphax, here; quake not, for know
  I know thy thoughts. Thou wouldst entreat our power

Nice Sophonisba's passion to enforce
To thy affection, be all full of love.
'Tis done, 'tis done; to us heav'n, earth, sea, air   130
And fate itself obeys; the beasts of death,
And all the terrors angry gods invented
T'afflict the ignorance of patient man,
Tremble at us: the rolled-up snake uncurls
His twisted knots at our affrighting voice.   135
Are we incensed? The king of flames grows pale°
Lest he be choked with black and earthy fumes
Which our charms raise. Be joyed, make proud thy lust.
I do not pray you, gods; my breath's 'You must'.°

SYPHAX Deep-knowing spirit, mother of all high   140
Mysterious science, what may Syphax yield
Worthy thy art, by which my soul's thus eased?
The gods first made me live, but thou, live pleased.°

ERICHTHO Know then, our love, hard by the reverend ruins
Of a once-glorious temple reared to Jove,   145
Whose very rubbish, like the pitied fall
Of virtue much unfortunate, yet bears
A deathless majesty, though now quite rased,
Hurled down by wrath and lust of impious kings,
So that, where holy flamens wont to sing   150
Sweet hymns to heaven, there the daw and crow,
The ill-voiced raven and still-chattering pie
Send out ungrateful sound and loathsome filth;
Where statues and Jove's acts were vively limned,
Boys with black coals draw the veiled parts of nature   155
And lecherous actions of imagined lust;
Where tombs and beauteous urns of well-dead men°
Stood in assurèd rest, the shepherd now
Unloads his belly, corruption most abhorred
Mingling itself with their renownèd ashes;   160
Ourself quakes at it.
There once a charnel-house, now a vast cave,
Over whose brow a pale and untrod grove
Throws out her heavy shade, the mouth thick arms
Of darksome yew, sun-proof, for ever choke;   165
Within rests barren darkness; fruitless drought
Pines in eternal night; the steam of hell
Yields not so lazy air; there, that's my cell.

From thence a charm, which Jove dare not hear twice,
Shall force her to thy bed. But, Syphax, know,   170
Love is the highest rebel to our art.
Therefore I charge thee, by the fear of all
Which thou knowest dreadful, or more, by ourself,
As with swift haste she passeth to thy bed,
And easy to thy wishes yields, speak not one word,   175
Nor dare, as thou dost fear thy loss of joys,
T'admit one light, one light.

SYPHAX   As to my fate,
I yield my guidance.

ERICHTHO   Then when I shall force
The air to music and the shades of night
To form sweet sounds, make proud thy raised delight.   180
Meantime, behold, I go a charm to rear,
Whose potent sound will force ourself to fear.
    [*Exit Erichtho*]

SYPHAX Whither is Syphax heaved? At length shall's joy°
Hopes more desired than heaven? Sweet labouring earth,
Let heaven be unformed with mighty charms;   185
Let Sophonisba only fill these arms.
Jove, we'll not envy thee; blood's appetite
Is Syphax's god; my wisdom is my sense;
Without a man I hold no excellence.°
Give me long breath, young beds, and sickless ease;   190
For we hold firm, that's lawful which doth please.
            Infernal music, softly
                    Hark, hark, now rise infernal tones,
                        The deep-fetched groans
                    Of labouring spirits that attend
                    Erichtho.

ERICHTHO (*within*) Erichtho!   195

SYPHAX   Now crack the trembling earth and send
                        Shrieks that portend
                    Affrightment to the gods which hear
                    Erichtho.

ERICHTHO (*within*) Erichtho!   200
    A treble viol and a bass lute play softly within the canopy°
Hark, hark, now softer melody strikes mute
Disquiet nature. O thou power of sound,°
How thou dost melt me! Hark, now even heaven

Gives up his soul amongst us. Now's the time   205
When greedy expectation strains mine eyes
For their loved object; now Erichtho willed
Prepare my appetite for love's strict grips.°
O you dear founts of pleasure, blood and beauty,
Raise active Venus worth fruition   210
Of such provoking sweetness. Hark, she comes!°
    A short song to soft music above
Now nuptial hymns enforcèd spirits sing.
Hark, Syphax, hark!
    They sing [above]
            Now hell and heaven rings°
With music spite of Phoebus. Peace, she comes.
    *Enter Erichtho in the shape of Sophonisba, her face veiled, and
    hasteth in the bed, [set in the discovery space,]° of Syphax*
Fury of blood's impatient!—Erichtho,   215
'Bove thunder sit; to thee, egregious soul,
Let all flesh bend.—Sophonisba, thy flame
But equal mine, and we'll joy such delight,
That gods shall not admire, but even spite.
    *Syphax hasteneth within the canopy as to Sophonisba's bed,
    [and the curtains are closed]*

A bass lute and a treble viol play for the act°

5.1

Syphax draweth the curtains and discovers Erichtho lying with him°

ERICHTHO Ha, ha, ha!

SYPHAX Light, light!

ERICHTHO Ha, ha!

SYPHAX Thou rotten scum of hell!—
O my abhorrèd heat! O loathed delusion!

They leap out of the bed. Syphax takes him to his sword

ERICHTHO Why, fool of kings, could thy weak soul imagine°
That 'tis within the grasp of heaven or hell   5
To enforce love? Why, know, love dotes the Fates,
Jove groans beneath his weight. Mere ignorant thing,°
Know we, Erichtho, with a thirsty womb
Have coveted full threescore suns for blood of kings.
We that can make enragèd Neptune toss   10
His huge curled locks without one breath of wind;
We that can make heaven slide from Atlas' shoulder;
We in the pride and height of covetous lust
Have wished with woman's greediness to fill
Our longing arms with Syphax' well-strong limbs;   15
And dost thou think, if philtres or hell's charms
Could have enforced thy use, we would have deigned°
Brain-sleights? No, no! Now are we full
Of our dear wishes; thy proud heat, well wasted,
Hath made our limbs grow young. Our love, farewell!°   20
Know he that would force love, thus seeks his hell.

Erichtho slips into the ground as Syphax [attempts to strike her with] his sword

SYPHAX Can we yet breathe? Is any plagued like me?
Are we? Let's think. O now contempt, my hate
To thee, thy thunder, sulphur, and scorned name!
He whose life's loathed, and he who breathes to curse   25
His very being, let him thus with me
Fall 'fore an altar sacred to black powers,
And thus dare heavens:

Syphax kneels at the altar°
          —O thou whose blasting flames°
Hurl barren droughts upon the patient earth,
And thou, gay god of riddles and strange tales,°   30
Hot-brainèd Phoebus, all add if you can
Something unto my misery; if aught
Of plagues lurk in your deep-trenched brows
Which yet I know not, let them fall like bolts
Which wrathful Jove drives strong into my bosom!   35
If any chance of war or news ill-voiced,
Mischief unthought-of lurk, come, gift us all,
Heap curse on curse, we can no lower fall.
    Out of the altar the ghost of Hasdrubal ariseth°
ASDRUBAL Lower, lower.
SYPHAX   What damned air is formed
Into that shape? Speak, speak; we cannot quake;   40
Our flesh knows not ignoble tremblings. Speak,
We dare thy terror. Methinks hell and fate
Should dread a soul with woes made desperate.
ASDRUBAL Know me the spirit of great Hasdrubal,
Father to Sophonisba, whose bad heart   45
Made justly most unfortunate; for know,°
I turned unfaithful, after which the field
Chanced to our loss, when of thy men there fell
Six thousand souls, next fight of Libyans ten.°
After which loss we unto Carthage flying,   50
Th'enragèd people cried their army fell
Through my base treason. Straight my revengeful fury°
Makes them pursue me; I with resolute haste
Made to the grave of all our ancestors,
Where poisoned, hoped my bones should have long rest; 55
But see, the violent multitude arrives,
Tear down our monument, and me, now dead,
Deny a grave; hurl us among the rocks
To staunch beasts' hunger; therefore thus ungraved
I seek slow rest. Now dost thou know more woes,   60
And more must feel.—Mortals, O fear to slight
Your gods and vows. Jove's arm is of dread might.
SYPHAX Yet speak: shall I o'ercome approaching foes?
ASDRUBAL Spirits of wrath know nothing but their woes.
    Exit [Hasdrubal]. Enter a Messenger

MESSENGER My liege, my liege,
　　The scouts of Cirta bring intelligence
　　Of sudden danger; full ten thousand horse,
　　Fresh and well-rid, strong Masinissa leads,
　　As wings to Roman legions that march swift,
　　Led by that man of conquest, Scipio.
SYPHAX　　　　　　　　　　　　Scipio!　　　　　　　　7
MESSENGER Direct to Cirta.
　　　　　　A march far off is heard
　　　　　　　　　　　　Hark, their march is heard
　　Even to the city.
SYPHAX　　　　　　Help, our guard, my arms!
　　Bid all our leaders march; beat thick alarms!
　　I have seen things which thou wouldst quake to hear.
　　Boldness and strength! The shame of slaves be fear.　　7
　　Up, heart, hold sword! Though waves roll thee on shelf,°
　　Though fortune leave thee, leave not thou thyself.
　　　　　　Exit [Syphax,] arming [with the Messenger]

5.2

　　　　　Enter two Pages with targets and javelins; Laelius and Jugurth,
　　　　　with halberds; Scipio and Masinissa armed; cornets sounding a
　　　　　march
SCIPIO Stand!
MASINISSA　　　Give the word 'Stand!'
SCIPIO　　　　　　　　　　　　Part the file.
MASINISSA　　　　　　　　　　　　　　Give way.—°
　　Scipio, by thy great name but greater virtue,
　　By our eternal love, give me the chance
　　Of this day's battle. Let not thy envied fame
　　Vouchsafe t'oppose the Roman legions
　　Against one weakened prince of Libya.
　　This quarrel's mine; mine be the stroke of fight.
　　Let us and Syphax hurl our well-forced darts
　　Each unto other's breast. O—what should I say?—
　　Thou beyond epithet, thou whom proud lords of fortune　　1
　　May even envy—alas, my joy's so vast
　　Makes me seem lost—let us thunder and lightning°

Strike from our brave arms! Look, look, seize that hill!
Hark, he comes near. From thence discern us strike
Fire worth Jove; mount up, and not repute   15
Me very proud though wondrous resolute.
My cause, my cause is my bold heart'ning odds,°
That sevenfold shield; just arms should fright the gods.

SCIPIO Thy words are full of honour; take thy fate.

MASINISSA Which we do scorn to fear. To Scipio state   20
Worthy his heart! Now let the forcèd brass°
Sound on!
          Cornets sound a march. Scipio leads his train up to the mount °
               Jugurth, clasp sure our casque,
Arm us with care; and, Jugurth, if I fall
Through this day's malice or our father's sins,
If it in thy sword lie, break up my breast   25
And save my heart that never fell nor sued°
To aught but Jove and Sophonisba.—Sound,
Stern heart'ners unto wounds and blood, sound loud,
For we have namèd Sophonisba.
          Cornets, a flourish
                              So!
          Cornets, a march far off
Hark, hark, he comes. Stand blood! Now multiply   30
Force more than fury. Sound high, sound high! we strike
For Sophonisba!
          Enter Syphax armed, his Pages with shields and darts before;
          cornets sounding marches

SYPHAX   For Sophonisba!

MASINISSA Syphax!

SYPHAX   Masinissa!

MASINISSA   Betwixt us two,
Let single fight try all.

SYPHAX   Well urged.

MASINISSA   Well granted.—
Of you, my stars, as I am worthy you   35
I implore aid; and O, if angels wait
Upon good hearts, my genius be as strong
As I am just.

SYPHAX   Kings' glory is their wrong.°
He that may only do just act's a slave.
My god's my arm, my life my heaven, my grave   40

To me all end.

MASINISSA   Give day, gods, life, not death,°
To him that only fears blaspheming breath.
For Sophonisba!

SYPHAX   For Sophonisba!
      Cornets sound a charge; Masinissa and Syphax combat;
      Syphax falls; Masinissa unclasps Syphax' casque and, as
      [Masinissa is] ready to kill him, speaks Syphax

SYPHAX Unto thy fortune, not to thee, we yield.

MASINISSA Lives Sophonisba yet unstained—speak just—   45
Yet ours unforced?

SYPHAX   Let my heart fall more low
Than is my body, if only to thy glory
She lives not yet all thine.

MASINISSA   Rise, rise; cease strife.
Hear a most deep revenge: from us take life.°
      Cornets sound a march; Scipio and Laelius enter. Scipio
      passeth to his throne. Masinissa presents Syphax to Scipio's
      feet, cornets sounding a flourish
To you, all power of strength.—And next to thee,   50
Thou spirit of triumph, born for victory,
I heave these hands. March we to Cirta straight,
My Sophonisba with swift haste to win;
In honour and in love all mean is sin.
      Exeunt Masinissa and Jugurth

SCIPIO [*to Syphax*] As we are Rome's great general, thus we press   55
Thy captive neck, but as still Scipio,
And sensible of just humanity,
We weep thy bondage. Speak, thou ill-chanced man,
What spirit took thee when thou wert our friend,
Thy right hand given both to gods and us   60
With such most passionate vows and solemn faith,
Thou fled'st with such most foul disloyalty
To now-weak Carthage, strength'ning their bad arms,
Who lately scorned thee with all loathed abuse,
Who never entertain for love but use?   65

SYPHAX Scipio, my fortune is captived, not I,
Therefore I'll speak bold truth; nor once mistrust
What I shall say, for now, being wholly yours,
I must not feign. Sophonisba 'twas she,
'Twas Sophonisba that solicited   70

My forced revolt; 'twas her resistless suit,
Her love to her dear Carthage, 'ticed me break
All faith with men; 'twas she made Syphax false,
She that loves Carthage with such violence
And hath such moving graces to allure   75
That she will turn a man that once hath sworn
Himself on's father's bones her Carthage' foe,
To be that city's champion and high friend.
Her hymeneal torch burned down my house;°
Then was I captived when her wanton arms   80
Threw moving clasps about my neck. O charms
Able to turn even fate! But this in my true grief
Is some just joy, that my love-sotted foe
Shall seize that plague, that Masinissa's breast
Her hands shall arm, and that ere long you'll try   85
She can force him your foe as well as I.
SCIPIO Laelius, Laelius, take a choice troop of horse
And spur to Cirta. To Masinissa thus:
Syphax' palace, crown, spoil, city's sack
Be free to him; but if our new-leagued friend   90
Possess that woman of so moving art,
Charge him with no less weight than his dear vow,
Our love, all faith, that he resign her thee;
As he shall answer Rome, will him give up
A Roman prisoner to the Senate's doom;   95
She is a Carthaginian, now our law's.°
Wise men prevent not actions, but ever cause.°
SYPHAX [aside] Good malice, so, as liberty so dear,
Prove my revenge. What I cannot possess
Another shall not; that's some happiness.   100
      Exeunt, the cornets flourishing

5.3

      The cornets afar off sounding a charge; a Soldier, wounded, at
      one door [enters]; enters at the other Sophonisba, two Pages
      before her with lights, two Women bearing up her train
SOLDIER Princess, O fly! Syphax hath lost the day
   And captived lies; the Roman legions

Have seized the town and with inveterate hate
Make slaves or murder all. Fire and steel,
Fury and night, hold all. Fair queen, O fly!   5
We bleed for Carthage, all of Carthage die.

> *Exit [Soldier.] The cornets sounding a march; enter Pages with
> javelins and targets, Masinissa and Jugurth, Masinissa's beaver
> shut*

MASINISSA March to the palace.

SOPHONISBA   Whate'er man thou art,
Of Libya thy fair arms speak; give heart
To amazed weakness; hear her that for long time
Hath seen no wishèd light. Sophonisba,   10
A name for misery much known, 'tis she
Entreats of thy graced sword this only boon:
Let me not kneel to Rome, for though no cause
Of mine deserves their hate, though Masinissa
Be ours to heart, yet Roman generals°   15
Make proud their triumphs with whatever captives.
O 'tis a nation which from soul I fear,
As one well knowing the much-grounded hate
They bear to Hasdrubal and Carthage' blood;
Therefore with tears that wash thy feet, with hands   20
Unused to beg, I clasp thy manly knees.
O save me from their fetters and contempt,
Their proud insults and more than insolence.
Or, if it rest not in thy grace of breath
To grant such freedom, give me long-wished death;   25
For 'tis not much-loathed life that now we crave,
Only an unshamed death and silent grave
We will now deign to bend for.

MASINISSA   Rarity!
> *Masinissa disarms his head°*
By thee and this right hand thou shalt live free.

SOPHONISBA We cannot now be wretched.

MASINISSA   Stay the sword!   30
Let slaughter cease! Sounds soft as Leda's breast°
Slide through all ears.
> *Soft music [within]*
                        This night be love's high feast.

SOPHONISBA O'erwhelm me not with sweets; let me not drink
Till my breast burst, O Jove, thy nectar; think—

288

She sinks into Masinissa's arms

MASINISSA She is o'ercome with joy.

SOPHONISBA   Help, help to bear   35
  Some happiness, ye powers! I have joy to spare
  Enough to make a god.—O Masinissa!

MASINISSA   Peace!
  A silent thinking makes full joys increase.

        Enter Laelius

LAELIUS Masinissa!

MASINISSA   Laelius!

LAELIUS   Thine ear.

MASINISSA   Stand off.
    [*Sophonisba and her Women retire upstage*]

LAELIUS From Scipio thus: by thy late vow of faith   40
  And mutual league of endless amity,
  As thou respects his virtue or Rome's force,
  Deliver Sophonisba to our hand.

MASINISSA Sophonisba?

LAELIUS   Sophonisba.

SOPHONISBA [*to her women*]   My lord
  Looks pale, and from his half-burst eyes a flame   45
  Of deep disquiet breaks. The gods turn false
  My sad presage!

MASINISSA [*to Laelius*] Sophonisba?

LAELIUS   Even she.

MASINISSA She killed not Scipio's father, nor his uncle,
  Great Gnaeus.

LAELIUS   Carthage did.

MASINISSA   To her what's Carthage?

LAELIUS Know 'twas her father, Hasdrubal, struck off   50
  His father's head. Give place to faith and fate.

MASINISSA 'Tis cross to honour.

LAELIUS   But 'tis just to state;°
  So speaketh Scipio. Do not thou detain
  A Roman prisoner due to this great triumph;
  As thou shalt answer Rome and him.

MASINISSA   Laelius,   55
  We are now in Rome's power. Laelius,
  View Masinissa do a loathèd act,
  Most sinking from that state his heart did keep.°
  Look, Laelius, look, see Masinissa weep.

Know I have made a vow, more dear to me   60
Than my soul's endless being, she shall rest
Free from Rome's bondage.
LAELIUS   But dost thou forget
Thy vow, yet fresh, thus breathed: 'When I desist
To be commanded by thy virtue, Scipio,
Or fall from friend of Rome, revenging gods,   65
Afflict me with your torture'?
MASINISSA   Laelius, enough.
Salute the Roman; tell him we will act
What shall amaze him.
LAELIUS   Wilt thou yield her, then?
MASINISSA She shall arrive there straight.
LAELIUS   Best fate of men
To thee.
MASINISSA And Scipio.
        [Exit Laelius]
                    —Have I lived, O heavens,°   70
To be enforcedly perfidious?
SOPHONISBA [coming forward] What unjust grief afflicts my worthy
    lord?
MASINISSA Thank me, ye gods, with much beholdingness,
For mark, I do not curse you.
SOPHONISBA   Tell me, sweet,
The cause of thy much anguish.
MASINISSA   Ha, the cause?   75
Let's see; wreathe back thine arms, bend down thy neck,°
Practise base prayers, make fit thyself for bondage.
SOPHONISBA Bondage?
MASINISSA   Bondage, Roman bondage.
SOPHONISBA   No, no.
MASINISSA How then have I vowed well to Scipio?
SOPHONISBA How then to Sophonisba?
MASINISSA   Right which way?   80
Run mad!—impossible!—distraction!
SOPHONISBA Dear lord, thy patience; let it maze all power
And list to her in whose sole heart it rests
To keep thy faith upright.
MASINISSA   Wilt thou be slaved?
SOPHONISBA No, free.
MASINISSA   How then keep I my faith?

SOPHONISBA   My death   85
    Gives help to all: from Rome so rest we free;
    So brought to Scipio, faith is kept in thee.
MASINISSA Thou dar'st not die.—Some wine!—Thou dar'st not die.
    Enter a Page with a bowl of wine
SOPHONISBA How near was I unto the curse of man, joy!
    How like was I yet once to have been glad!   90
    He that ne'er laughed may with a constant face
    Contemn Jove's frown. Happiness makes us base.
    She takes [the] bowl into which Masinissa puts poison
    Behold me, Masinissa, like thyself,
    A king and soldier; and I prithee keep
    My last command.
MASINISSA   Speak, sweet.
SOPHONISBA   Dear, do not weep.   95
    And now with undismayed resolve behold,
    To save you—you (for honour and just faith
    Are most true gods, which we should much adore),
    With even disdainful vigour I give up
    An abhorred life.
    She drinks
                        —You have been good to me,   100
    And I do thank thee, heaven. O my stars,
    I bless your goodness, that with breast unstained,
    Faith pure, a virgin wife, tried to my glory,
    I die, of female faith the long-lived story,
    Secure from bondage and all servile harms,   105
    But more, most happy in my husband's arms.
    She sinks [into Masinissa's arms]
JUGURTH Masinissa, Masinissa!
MASINISSA   Covetous,
    Fame-greedy lady, could no scope of glory,
    No reasonable proportion of goodness
    Fill thy great breast, but thou must prove immense,   110
    Incomprehense in virtue? What, wouldst thou
    Not only be admired but even adored?
    O glory ripe for heaven!—Sirs, help, help, help!
    Let us to Scipio with what speed you can;
    For piety make haste, whilst yet we are man.°   115
    Exeunt, bearing Sophonisba in a chair

5.4

*Cornets, a march. Enter Scipio in full state, triumphal
ornaments carried before him and Syphax bound;°* [enter] *at the
other door Laelius*

SCIPIO What answers Masinissa? Will he send
  That Sophonisba of so moving tongue?
LAELIUS Full of dismayed unsteadiness he stood,
  His right hand locked in hers, which hand he gave
  As pledge from Rome she ever should live free.   5
  But when I entered and well urged his vows
  And thy command, his great heart sunk with shame,
  His eyes lost spirit, and his heat of life
  Sank from his face, as one that stood benumbed,
  All mazed t'effect impossibilities;°   10
  For either unto her or Scipio
  He must break vow. Long time he tossed his thoughts,
  And as you see a snowball being rolled,
  At first a handful, yet, long bowled about,
  Insensibly acquires a mighty globe,   15
  So his cold grief through agitation grows,
  And more he thinks, the more of grief he knows.
  At last he seemed to yield her.
SYPHAX   Mark, Scipio!
  Trust him that breaks a vow?
SCIPIO   How then trust thee?
SYPHAX O, misdoubt him not when he's thy slave like me. 20
  Enter Masinissa, all in black
MASINISSA Scipio!
SCIPIO   Masinissa!
MASINISSA   General!
SCIPIO   King!
MASINISSA Lives there no mercy for one soul of Carthage,
  But must see baseness?
SCIPIO   Wouldst thou joy thy peace,°
  Deliver Sophonisba straight and cease;
  Do not grasp that which is too hot to hold.   25
  We grace thy grief and hold it with soft sense;
  Enjoy good courage, but 'void insolence.
  I tell thee, Rome and Scipio deign to bear

SOPHONISBA   5.4

So low a breast as for her say, 'We fear'.

MASINISSA Do not, do not! Let not the fright of nations°   30
Know so vile terms. She rests at thy dispose.

SYPHAX To my soul joy! Shall Sophonisba then
With me go bound, and wait on Scipio's wheel?°
When th' whole world's giddy, one man cannot reel.

MASINISSA Starve thy lean hopes!—And, Romans, now behold   35
A sight would sad the gods, make Phoebus cold!
   Organs and recorders play to a single voice.° Enter in the
   meantime the mournful solemnity of Masinissa's presenting
   Sophonisba's body°
Look, Scipio, see what hard shift we make
To keep our vows. Here, take; I yield her thee.
—And, Sophonisba, I keep vow, thou art still free.

SYPHAX Burst, my vexed heart! The torture that most racks   40
An enemy is his foe's royal acts.°

SCIPIO The glory of thy virtue live for ever;
Brave hearts may be obscured, but extinct never.
   Scipio adorns Masinissa°
Take from the general of Rome this crown,
This robe of triumph, and this conquest's wreath,
This sceptre, and this hand; for ever breathe   45
Rome's very minion. Live worth thy fame,°
As far from faintings as from now base name.

MASINISSA [*to Sophonisba's corpse*] Thou whom, like sparkling steel,
   the strokes of chance
Made hard and firm, and, like wild-fire turned,°   50
The more cold fate, more bright thy virtue burned,
And in whole seas of miseries didst flame;
On thee, loved creature of a deathless fame,
Rest all my honour.
   Masinissa adorns Sophonisba°
                    O thou for whom I drink
So deep of grief, that he must only think,
Not dare to speak, that would express my woe—   55
Small rivers murmur, deep gulfs silent flow—°
My grief is here, not here [*indicating his heart, then mouth*].—[*To
   Attendants*] Heave gently, then,
Women's right wonder, and just shame of men.
   Cornets, a short flourish. Exeunt, [bearing Sophonisba's body];
   Masinissa remains [to speak the Epilogue]

EPILOGUE And now,   60
   With lighter passion, though with most just fear,
   I change my person, and do hither bear
   Another's voice, who with a phrase as weak°
   As his deserts, now willed me (thus formed) speak:
   If words well sensed, best suiting subject grave,°   65
   Noble true story, may once boldly crave
   Acceptance gracious; if he whose fires
   Envy not others nor himself admires;
   If scenes exempt from ribaldry or rage,
   Of taxings indiscreet, may please the stage;°   70
   If such may hope applause, he not commands,
   Yet craves as due the justice of your hands.
   But freely he protests, howe'er it is,
   Or well or ill, or much, not much amiss,
   With constant modesty he doth submit   75
   To all, save those that have more tongue than wit.
       [Exit]

APPENDIX

Felice's Ballad in *Antonio and Mellida*, 3.2

Edited by Martin Wiggins

The ballad sung by Felice at the end of Act 3 of *Antonio and Mellida*, identified only by its first line in the Quarto, is extant, under the title *The Pangs of Love and Lovers' Fits*, in a single copy printed by Richard Lant on 22 March 1559. This copy, now held by the Huntington Library, California, is the basis for the modernized text printed here. It was previously edited by J. P. Collier in 1840.[1]

The author is given as 'W.E.', which is generally taken to refer to the prolific early Elizabethan ballad writer William Elderton. Elderton was also an Attorney in the Sheriff's Court at the Guildhall, and in the 1570s he ran a company of players. Later in his life, he fell foul of the egregious Cambridge don, Gabriel Harvey (*c*.1550–1630), who represented him, after his death, as a notorious drunkard. He died in or before 1592.[2] The ballad is among his earliest extant works.

> And was not good King Solomon°
> Ravished in sundry wise
> With every lively paragon°
> That glisterèd before his eyes?°
> If this be true as true it was,   5
>   Lady, lady,
> Why should not I serve you, alas,
>   My dear lady?
>
> When Paris was enamourèd
> With Helena, Dame Beauty's peer,   10
> Whom Venus first him promisèd
> To venture on and not to fear,°
> What sturdy storms endurèd he,°
>   Lady, lady,
> To win her love ere it would be,   15
>   My dear lady?

[1] J. Payne Collier (ed.), *Old Ballads from Early Printed Copies of the Utmost Rarity* (London, 1840), 25–8.

[2] For a fuller account of Elderton, see Hyder E. Rollins, 'William Elderton: Elizabethan Actor and Ballad Writer', *Studies in Philology*, 17 (1920), 199–245.

Know ye not how Troilus°
Languished and lost his joy
With fits and fevers marvellous
For Cressida that dwelt in Troy,   20
Till pity planted in her breast,
  Lady, lady,
To sleep with him and grant him rest,
  My dear lady?

I read sometime how venturous   25
Leander was his love to please,°
Who swum the waters perilous
Of Abydon, those surging seas,
To come to her where as she lay,
  Lady, lady,   30
Till he was drownèd by the way,
  My dear lady.

What say ye then to Pyramus°
That promisèd his love to meet
And found by fortune marvellous   35
A bloody cloth before his feet?
For Thisbe's sake himself he slew,
  Lady, lady
To prove that he was a lover true,
  My dear lady.   40

When Hercules for Eronie°
Murdered a monster fell,
He put himself in jeopardy
Perilous as the stories tell,
Rescuing her upon the shore,   45
  Lady, lady,
Which else by lot had died therefore,
  My dear lady.

Anaxaretis beautiful°
When Iphis did behold and see   50
With sighs and sobbings pitiful
That paragon long wooèd he,
And when he could not win her so,
  Lady, lady,
He went and hung himself for woe,   55
  My dear lady.

Besides these matters marvellous,
Good lady yet I can tell thee more;
The gods have been full amorous,
As Jupiter by learnèd lore   60
Who changed his shape as fame hath spread,
    Lady, lady,
To come to Alcumena's bed,°
    My dear lady.

And if beauty breed such blissfulness,   65
Enamouring both god and man,
Good lady, let no wilfulness
Exsuperate your beauty then°
To slay the hearts that yield and crave,
    Lady, lady,
The grant of your good will to have,   70
    My dear lady.

EXPLANATORY NOTES

(Short references in brackets in the following are to the editors and editions listed on pp. xxvii–xxviii of the Note on the Texts.)

Antonio and Mellida

DEDICATION

Marston wrote the following dedication for the 1602 edition of the play:

To the only rewarder, and most just poiser of virtuous merits, the most honourably renowned Nobody,° bounteous Maecenas° of Poetry and Lord Protector of oppressed innocence, *Do, dedicoque.*°

Since it hath flowed with the current of my humorous blood   5
to affect, a little too much, to be seriously fantastical, here take, most respected patron, the worthless present of my slighter idleness. If you vouchsafe not his protection,° O thou sweetest perfection, female beauty, shield me from the stopping of vinegar bottles.° Which most wished favour if it fail me, then *Si nequeo*   10
flectere superos, Acheronta movebo.° But yet, honour's redeemer, virtue's advancer, religion's shelter and piety's fosterer, yet I faint not in despair of thy gracious affection and protection; to which I only shall ever rest most servingman-like, obsequiously making legs and standing, after our free-born English garb, bare-   15
headed.°

> Thy only affied slave and admirer,
> J.M.

2 *Nobody*: ironic joke. The same dedicatee is nominated in John Day's play, *Humour out of Breath* (1607).

Maecenas: famous art patron of classical Rome.

3–4 *Do, dedicoque*: 'I give, and dedicate [this work]'.

8 *his protection*: i.e. the protection of it (the work).

9 *stopping . . . bottles*: meaning unclear. Might refer to the release of bitter satire ('stopping' = 'unstopping'), or to the banning ('stopping' = 'preventing') of such work; or, most plausibly, simply to the recycling of the quarto's paper (suitably so because of the satire printed on it) as stopper linings for vinegar bottles.

298

10–11 *Si...movebo*: 'If I cannot bend the gods above to my will, I will move the powers below'. Tag modified from Virgil, *Aeneid*, vii. 312.

15 *bareheaded*: without a hat (where the doffing of the hat signals deference).

THE PERSONS OF THE PLAY

There is no character list in Q. This is based on Bullen. Several names refer to moral or other qualities.

Sforza: Milanese ruling family. Perhaps also with reference to *sforzare* (It.) = 'force', 'ravish'.
Felice: 'happy man' (It.).
Mazzagente: 'a killer of people' (It.).
Balurdo: 'balordo' = 'stupid' (It.).
Castilio Balthazar: reference to Baldassare Castiglione, author of *Il cortegiano*, a favourite Renaissance courtesy book.
Forobosco: 'a woodpecker'; also 'a sneaking fellow' (It.).
Cazzo: vulgar word for 'penis' (It.).
Dildo: 'artificial penis' (It.).

INDUCTION

Speech prefixes in the Induction are shown in single inverted commas to indicate that it is the actor of the part, not the character, who is to be imagined speaking.

S.D. *parts*: refers to the narrow strips of paper issued to each actor and bearing only his lines, plus short cues. The fictional situation here is not a rehearsal but a 'Greenroom' discussion prior to a performance. Hence, 'The music will sound straight for entrance' (ll. 1–2), which is the cue for the beginning of the performance itself. In fact, the play seems hardly rehearsed, as some actors are ignorant of what parts are played by other actors.

1 *'GALEAZZO'*: omitted in Q. So assigned in 1633 edn. However, the speaker perhaps should be 'Alberto' who leads the opening exchange.

2 *Are...perfect?*: 'are you fully prepared'. 'Piero's' reply shows that the primary implication is to do with line-learning, though he himself is more concerned with character-portrayal. 'Perfect' = 'word-perfect'.

4 *actors*: here the meaning would seem to be 'roles', in the sense of the playing of the characters. But there is no *OED* warrant for such a sense and perhaps the word should be 'actions'.

14 *stroke...strut?*: the conventional gestures and physical language of the tragic actor. See next note.

15–19 *Truth... state*: an apparent satire on the clichés of tragic acting as developed on the popular stage. Cf. Hamlet's strictures on acting and nature in *Hamlet*, 3.2.

21 *The... parts*: it was a regular practice in the Elizabethan theatre for an actor to play two or more roles in the same play.

31 *mountebanking*: the actor of Balurdo characterizes the role he plays as being (inadvertently) akin to that of a street entertainer ('mountebank') or clown.

Bergamasco's: a native of Bergamo and hence (to subtle Venetians) a simpleton.

34 *strenuous*: a Marston coinage, derided by Jonson.

35 *forerunning*: which runs before (like a fox in front of the hounds).

43 *wolf*: (1) ravening predator; (2) malignant ulcer.

44 *falling sickness*: literally 'epilepsy', but used of moral (especially sexual) failings.

52 *tailor's legs*: traditionally, tailors sat cross-legged at their work.

54 *the*: this edition. The line is left as unfinished in other editions.

57 *bella graziosa madonna*: [my] lovely gracious lady.

58 *nick*: point aimed at; but, with 'tickle' and 'titillation', also an obscene pun.

68 *Amazon*: one of a race of female warriors in Greek legend, popular in Elizabethan literature.

69 *I... it*: evidently the actor's voice is too manly, even though he presumably belongs to a boys' company. See Intro., p. xi.

72 *bear... hood*: be two-faced.

72–3 *idiot... by*: allusion to Thomas Kyd's *Spanish Tragedy* (printed 1594), 3.12.31.

75 *point*: (1) musical note; (2) lace on stays; (3) place (as obscene reference).

76 *truss my hose*: lace up my breeches (see previous note).

79 *resplendent fulgor*: shining brightness. 'Mazzagente' gives a sample of his character's bombast. See next note.

86 *Bragadoch*: braggart. From Braggadocchio in Spenser's *The Faerie Queene*.

88–9 *spruce... Spanish*: accent neat and refined as Spanish mixed with Italian. 'Attic' = 'pure', derived from the 'Attic style' in rhetoric, with its ideal of simple elegance.

90–1 *Milan... Italian*: 'Milan was under the German (High Dutch) Spanish rule bequeathed by Charles V' (Hunter). 'Italian' is 'Italians' in Q.

92–3 *vainglorious... Italian*: considered to be the characteristic national vice.

104 *Felicity*: personification of happiness.

105-6 *not . . . fortune*: did not [also] hang in the front of his [Felice's] own fortune. (And there may be a reference to the image of Opportunity in the emblem books, pictured with a forelock that could be grasped only by the quick and alert, as she, Opportunity, rushed by).

110-12 *'Tis . . . utterance*: roundabout for 'it cannot be expressed clearly in words'.

116 *a common arm*: the embrace of a (mere) commoner.

121 *yeasty . . . ale-knight*: 'beery breath of a boozer' (Hunter).

125 *Proteus*: Greek god, expert at shape-changing.

blind Gew: evidently a blind performing baboon. There are several contemporary references.

129-30 *should . . . part*: reference to *Antonio's Revenge*. However, Felice does not appear there and Galeazzo receives no development. Clearly, the Induction was written before the sequel was anything more than a good idea.

PROLOGUE

2 *gentle front*: genteel and welcoming brows. Marston refers to the select audience of the Paul's playhouse (and the other private theatres).

6 *least . . . hope*: the gentlest weight of unaccustomed hope.

8 *worthless . . . idleness*: Marston refers slightingly (and perhaps not ingenuously) to his own play, in the manner typical of the amateur dramatist.

10 *abstruse . . . faculties*: difficult and muscular qualities of style. (These Marston cultivated in the *Antonio* plays and in *The Malcontent*.)

20 *veil . . . wants*: conceal (or play down) our failings.

21 *sleek*: with reference to the sleekstone (polishing-stone).

1.1.30 *triumphs*: public celebrations accorded to conquering princes.

S.D. *sennet*: fanfare (to announce a ceremonial entrance).

petronels: large pistols.

divided files: two ranks.

48 *stomach*: (1) appetite; (2) pride.

58 *Rome . . . tried*: Rome itself has experienced this.

59 *train*: (1) fuse of gunpowder; (2) train of events.

Babel pride: i.e. towering ambition leading to confusion (with the obvious reference to the biblical Tower of Babel).

60 *Dimitto . . . attigi*: Seneca, *Thyestes*, 888: 'I renounce the powers above; I have attained all that prayers can achieve.'

71 *pistolets*: Gold coins of the (considerable) value then of six to eight shillings. A 'double pistolet' was presumably worth twice that.

78 *O...excelsissimum*: Seneca, *Thyestes*, 911: 'I am the highest of the gods.'

82 *carpet-boy*: milksop (where 'carpet' in a term of abuse implies 'to do with the boudoir').

93 *Milan*: customarily stressed on the first syllable.

95 *We'll...love*: we will embrace them with an amplitude of love (with wordplay on 'waste'/'waist').

99 S.D. *above...below*: on the upper stage, on the main stage. The general effect of the formal receptions here and after l. 116, overviewed by Mellida and her companions on the upper level as though on a balcony overlooking the royal presence, is clear enough, though the exact disposition of Piero's attendants on stage after l. 34 is not. Whether 'the rest stand still' includes them or whether they exit at that point is not evident, and Marston himself may not have worked out the precise detail. Apparent here, though, is the ironic contrast between public display and private opinion, so dear to Marston's world-view and to his dramaturgy. In effect, the ladies above play chorus to the dumb-shows below.

104 *flankers*: side-forts. Rosaline develops a metaphor drawn from the siege of a town, and this is animated here by the convention of using the upper level of playhouse stage areas to represent the tops of town walls and gates.

105 *Mary Ambree!*: a military heroine of the English ballads, referred to in a number of contemporary plays.

106 *Thy...clear*: either 'explain your choice', or, 'you are a woman of sharp discrimination'. In the first case, 'clear' is an imperative (and therefore also 'Good' = 'make good' of the previous line); in the second case, it is an adjective. (Q reads 'electious'.)

109 *glibbery*: slippery. One of Marston's coinages (from the verb 'glibber') derided by Jonson.

112 *paradiso...contente*: 'paradise of contented ladies'.

116 *Saint...Whiff*: satirical title for the braggart soldier, Mazzagente. 'Tir-lery' = 'trumpery'; 'Whiff' = 'puff of breath'. 'Saint Tristram' might be a misprint for 'Sir Tristram' (cf. *The Malcontent*, 1.1.89–90, where Prepasso is slightingly referred to as 'Sir Tristram Trimtram').

118 *For...passion*: 'for the sake of love's passion'.

119 *varnished*: Mazzagente is heavily made up with cosmetics.

134 *monkey'sh*: perhaps with wordplay on 'monkish' (Q's spelling).

151 *affection's adamants*: the magnets [i.e. wit and beauty] that draw men on to love.

154 *illustrate*: (1) describe; (2) add lustre to.

161 *double... man*: be twice the man.

164 *Hebe's cup*: Hebe is the cup-bearer to the classical gods.

165 *close-fight*: 'small ledges of wood laid cross one another... betwixt the mainmast and the foremast' (Smith, *Seaman's Grammar*, 1627), and used as a protection against boarders when ships fought at close quarters.

181 *by imposition of*: at the behest of.

193 *glory... sex*: i.e. Queen Elizabeth. 'Brittainy' (l. 191) is 'Britain'.

208 *little humours*: a trifling indisposition. Rosaline might be thought to be helping Mellida here to conceal her agitation at the disguised Antonio's fiction about himself, but at l. 247 she seems not at all to understand the significance of what is happening. We must therefore assume candour rather than intrigue.

217–18 *struck... mainmast*: threw down our mainmast.

222 *which... again*: indebted to Seneca, *Agamemnon*, 465 ff.

225 *Th'unequalled mirror*: the matchless image. (Q reads 'Th'unequall...').

252 *our... curious*: it is not our custom [as Amazons] to be over-demanding.

259 *Dirt... froth*: away with the affectations of courtly behaviour. Either Rosaline is excusing her own over-intimacy in claiming Florizell as her bed-mate; or Antonio, forgetting his disguise, has made room for Rosaline to exit first, and hence the following stage-direction.

2.1.3 *belly... ears*: proverbial.

4 *pug*: term of endearment, but here perhaps also with reference to Cazzo's diminutive stature.

13 *stomach*: Dildo means that he is angry; Cazzo misinterprets as hungry (see note to 1.1.48).

27 *Dutch*: used in a derogatory sense.

28 *rounce... hobble*: enacting the roar of the cannon.

29–30 *pluck... mark*: hide their plumes denoting their officer rank so that they would not be shot at.

31–2 *Don... Knighthood*: Rosicleer, corrupted here by Dildo, Balurdo, or the compositor, is the hero of a Spanish romance, translated, 1578, as *The Mirror of Princely Deeds and Knighthood*. There are other scornful references to this in Marston's plays (see *The Malcontent*, 5.1.75 and note).

33 *more... cable*: coiled cables and featherbeds (palliasses) were used as defences against gunshot in ship battles. Balurdo seeks to construct a bullet-proof jacket.

34 *cable hatband*: a twisted band worn round the hat.

42 *Whoa!*: this edition. Q has 'Who', modern editions 'Who?'.

45 *brief... semiquaver*: the long and the short of it (punning on 'breve'/ 'brief').

descant: a musical composition comprising variations on a theme. What may be intended here is a part song alluding to the bawdy meanings of the names of the two pages. 'Come off' of 1. 47 would then pick up the innuendo, and possibly also 'knock it' (its first meaning being 'strike up', i.e. the music).

49 S.D. *running... pace*: practising the steps of the coranto. The coranto was a lively dance, and Rosaline is presumably rehearsing for later court festivities. Felice's part in the complex entrance as observer signals Marston's intent of staging a demonstration of court affectation and inanity.

59 *Savourly*: pun on (1) 'wisely'; (2) 'stinkingly'.

62 *Pallas... brainpan!*: in classical myth, Pallas Minerva, goddess of wisdom, was born directly from Jupiter's head.

63 *vouchsafe... service*: allow me to be your acknowledged suitor.

80 S.D. *She spits*: such an act would not be considered as indecorous as it might today. Nevertheless, new codes of politeness were being urged, a matter at issue in this scene.

104 *applausive elocuty*: eloquence worthy of applause.

106–7 *how... flattery*: trout tickling was (and is) a skilful form of fishing.

110 *real*: i.e. regal. Marston uses 'real' to make Forobosco sound pretentious.

117 *thou... spurs*: spurs were commonly given as the prize for a sporting success.

119 *Egyptian louse*: refers to the plague of lice in Egypt in Exodus 8: 16–17.

139 *cry... candlelight*: i.e. cry out, as the bellman does, for light to illuminate your path at night (and, by application, referring to finding things out, especially villainy, that hide in darkness).

149 *tickle the measures*: leap high in dancing.

161 *run... ground*: 'make counterpoint variations on the ground-bass theme of love' (Jackson).

162 *erect... symmetry*: Mazzagente's affected way of inviting Mellida to stand up (to dance).

163–4 *Shine... night*: may your eye, as doleful as the depths of night, shine in the arena of sweet love-making.

168 *lay... lips*: (1) kiss you; (2) strike you on the mouth.

180 *that ... amorist*: inappropriate as a description of the supposedly dead Antonio, Mazzagente's phrase evidently refers to Galeazzo. As self-styled warrior rather than 'amorist', Mazzagente wishes he could invoke the power of his blade rather than the eloquence of courtship, a skill which Galeazzo more successfully possesses. NB 'Mazzagente' = 'killer of people'. See next line.

193 *the channel ... dirt*: the open sewer of this mortal world.

190–4 *O music ... woe*: a classic (and Platonic) statement of Marston's pre-occupation with the moral and therapeutic values of music (and dance). See Intro., pp. xii–xiii.

199 *Ohimè ... fato!*: 'alas, unfortunate wretch; O lamentable fate'.

200 *What ... ground?*: apart from this and the next line, there is no response to Antonio's extravagant behaviour in the scene. It would be possible on stage to indicate to the audience that Rosaline is trying to create a distraction with the witty dialogue that ensues (though we have been offered no motivation for such behaviour). Antonio evidently recovers, but curiously no one speaks to him/her again before the mass exit after l. 251.

212 *constant to afflict*: constant in afflicting.

216 *as ... head*: as the whim takes me.

233 *commonplaces*: Elizabethans recorded memorable sayings in common-place books, but Flavia refers also to the cheapening effect (becoming 'commonplace') of being one of Felice's many mistresses.

237 *What ... Balurdo?*: attributed to Rosaline in this edition, a continuation of Flavia's speech in all other editions. The emendation motivates Balurdo's borrowing of Felice's repartee as a reply, as Marston orchestrates a series of courtship duels: Mazzagente vs. Mellida, Galeazzo vs. Mellida, Alberto vs. Rosaline, Balurdo vs. Rosaline, and Felice vs. Flavia.

244 *by art*: through your face-painting.

245 *BALURDO ... change*: this edition. In Q, the line runs on from Felice's previous speech and ends 'chance'. However, when attributed to Balurdo, it expresses the latter's admiration for the wit duellists ('spark spirits' = 'sparkling wits') with their 'hard change' = 'harsh exchange of words'. The next line in Q is an enigmatic 'Laty dine', taken by editors to be a scrap of nonsense song sung by Felice, but it is assumed here to be the 'missing' speech prefix, some form of 'Balurdo', which the compositor failed to decipher.

254 *What ... see?*: Q gives these three lines to Antonio but the description in fact fits Antonio himself in his distraction (he fell down after l. 199 above). In contrast, Mellida has fulfilled her role in the dance with stoic self-control. Antonio's staying of Mellida (stage-direction after l. 251)

reveals his excitement, not hers. Dilke attributed ll. 252–3 to Mellida, but (NB) ll. 252–4 employ the second-person plural (Mellida's continued reserve), while ll. 255–69 the second-person singular (Antonio's excited familiarity), as throughout the whole exchange.

268 *doubles*: folded pieces of cloth. Marston (as Jackson notes) develops the metaphor from 'rolled up'.

297 S.D. *[They kiss]*: this might be the occasion for the accidental dropping of the note.

3.1.31 *like … Dutchman*: Dutch (and German) painters were held in high esteem in England in the period.

33 *sot*: blockhead.

54 *rests*: remains.

65–6 *Your … take*: Lucio maintains that the heraldry on Andrugio's armour will betray him but he is interrupted in his urging his master to take the '*shepherd gown*' (opening stage-direction) which he has brought as a disguise. (The passage is part of the play's concern with identity.)

84 *A … man*: i.e. Lucio himself.

98 *chequer-roll*: list of servants on the exchequer pay-roll.

my blood: i.e. Andrugio's family, in the sense of the Italian royal house.

104 S.D. *They sing*: Q reads '*cantant*' (i.e. plural). Perhaps the Page sings and is accompanied by Andrugio and/or Lucio.

117 *struck … height*: 'produced the most exalted kind of music' (Hunter).

115 *No … fall*: echoes Seneca, *Thyestes*, 925. Compare *The Malcontent*, 2.1.26.

3.2 S.D. *unbraced*: with doublet unfastened. Conventionally symbolizing going to or rising from bed.

9 *traverse light*: i.e. the light that passes through the traverse or partition, and hence the satirist or discloser of secret vice.

22 *Is … blessedness*: 'does any blest condition exist' (Jackson).

24 *Nectar … ambrosian*: nectar and ambrosia are the drink and food, respectively, of the Olympian gods.

27 *ambergris*: whale secretion, used in the manufacture of perfume.

31 *minikin*: literally, a high lute string; hence, squeaky voice. (Cf. 5.2.10.)

43 *Pegasus*: winged horse of Greek mythology, associated with the Muses and poetry.

52 *feared fears*: feared himself, fears others.

73 *red beard*: taken to be a self-reference by Marston.

98 *straight*: 'narrow, single width, as opposed to broadcloth' (Jackson).

99 *ell*: forty-five inches. Castilio is presumably buying a cheap cloth.

104 *crossed*: receipted (as having been paid).

107 *she . . .* : either an obscene expression has been censored in the publication, or Marston left room for a colourful gesture by the actor.

116 *potato pie*: potatoes were thought to be an aphrodisiac.

3.2 S.D. *Enter . . . faces*: Marston creates in dumbshow a striking 'School of Vanities'. See Intro., p. xiii.
setting of faces: trying out different expressions.

121 *look*: Q has 'loof' which has been ingeniously but improbably explained; and also emended to 'loaf'. The problem of emendation is compounded by the fact that we cannot guess confidently to what 'them' and 'they' refer.

146–50 *ay . . . red*: this edition. Q and all other editions give all the lines to Flavia. But there are spaces in Q after 'lip' (l. 146) and 'little' (l. 148) that suggest comic byplay in the original which, it is assumed here, Q's compositor could not accurately decipher.

157 *beauty!*: Flavia refers to Rosaline's gift, which she then kisses. But perhaps the word should be 'bounty' (i.e. the gift of the 'bounteous lady' of l. 156).

152–7 *prethily . . . sweethly . . . kith*: Flavia suddenly acquires a lisp as a courtly affectation.

160 *Take . . . paper*: this is the note given to Mellida by Antonio at 2.1.295. Presumably, and despite a change of location in 3.1, it has lain on stage ever since.

164 *whinny*: this edition. Q has 'wighy'.

173 *gondolets*: small gondolas.

178–9 *O . . . morte*: 'O wretched traitress, condemned, base fortune, by denying me revenge, you cause me savage death'. Source unidentified.

181–2 *Alma . . . Mellida*: 'Kind and gracious fortune, be favourable to me; and may the vows of my dear Mellida prove fortunate'.

184 *A . . . stairs*: 'Mellida hears people climbing the stairs to her chamber' (Hunter).

222 *Viva . . . fato*: 'May hope live'. Source unidentified.

244 S.D. *Enter . . . attire*: Jackson points out the symmetrical balancing of Antonio's and Mellida's transvestism in the play. When Mellida was dressed as a woman, so was Antonio. Now both are dressed as men.

262 *And . . . [etc.]*: a popular, contemporary ballad, nine stanzas long in its extant form (of which only the first line is given by Q). For the entire ballad, see Appendix below. Felice presumably sings

alongside Piero's next speech and the bustle and excitement of the clearing of the stage that leaves himself and Castilio alone. The actor would have sung as much of the ballad as seemed appropriate in terms of timing.

263–5 *Fly . . . about*: a burlesque of *The Spanish Tragedy*, 3.2.22–3. Piero's collapse into inarticulacy at ll. 176–7 was perhaps inspired by the same passage.

266–7 *Maledetta . . . mal?*: 'Accursed fortune, that with hard luck . . . What shall I do, what shall I say, to escape so great an evil?'.

273–5 *I . . . anger*: from Ephesians 4: 26.

4.1 S.D. *sea gown*: i.e. the disguise offered by Felice at 3.2.212–15.

24–6 *O . . . Mellida*: The passage appears in Q thus: 'O, this is naught, but speckling melancholie. | I have beene | That Morpheus tenderskinp [ ] Cosen germane | Beare with me good | *Mellida*.' It is usually rendered in later editions as a breakdown in rationality on the part of the character. The present edition borrows 'morphews' (='infects with scurvy') and a reordering of several phrases from Jackson; and emends Q's 'tender skinp' to 'the tender-skinned'. If we then assume that Antonio (ll. 24–6) claims to have been suffering the (temporary) relationship of cousin–german–ship with Melancholy, the passage works as the rational discourse that the character, after his flights of mental wandering, claims to be striving to achieve.

30 *they . . . up*: now newly cut up [by Lucio], they had already sprouted.

32 *thou . . . world*: you follow the example of the rest of the world.

36–7 *They . . . plate*: from Seneca, *Thyestes*, 453.

47 *Tyrian purple*: denoting royal or imperial rank, dye originally from Tyre.

45–65 *Why . . . soul*: imitated from Seneca, *Thyestes*, 342 ff., a classic statement of Stoic morality.

69 *wade upon*: emendation from Jackson. Q reads 'made open'.

75 *ground*: (1) cause; (2) shore.

80 *devilish art*: this edition. Q reads 'diuelslast', for which many emendations have been proposed.

87 *O . . . lares!*: Seneca, *Hercules Oetaeus*, 756: 'O household gods, wretched household gods!'

121 *a-raising . . . house*: (1) rebuilding the fortunes of our house; (2) constructing a poor hovel.

147 S.D. *runs a note*: gives a note to start on (?).

breaks it: interrupts it (?).

149 S.D. *They sing*: Q has 'Cantant' (i.e. plural). Perhaps Antonio accompanies the page.

181-98 *Spavento... morir*: 'Terror of my heart, sweet Mellida, true medicine against sad death, sweet Mellida, heavenly saviour, Mellida, sovereign of my hope, true trophy, Mellida.

> MELLIDA My own beloved and delightful soul, Antonio, delightful in beauty, courteous Antonio, my lord and chaste love, beautiful Antonio, food for my senses, dear Antonio.
>
> ANTONIO O my heart swoons in a sweet kiss.
>
> MELLIDA The senses die in longed-for desire.
>
> ANTONIO Can there be a purer beauty in heaven?
>
> ANTONIO Give me a kiss from that blessed mouth. Let me gather the perfumed air that hovers there on those sweet lips.
>
> MELLIDA Give me the empire of your pleasing love which blesses me with eternal honour, for thus is it fitting for me to die.'

'This reads like an adaptation of a dialogue from pastoral drama' (Wood). See Intro., p. xv.

201 *sit*: this edition. Some editors replace the following 'and' with 'then' to emend what is more probably a printing omission.

204 *kissing commas*: perhaps formed by analogy with 'kissing-comfits'. Some editions excise one of the line's 'kissings' to produce the acceptable reading: 'amorous kissing commas'.

206 *Dull... clips*: I am a dull clod and no man unless I am prepared to embrace such sweet favour.

215-16 *yet... censure*: but some personal consideration [that Marston was half Italian?] may soften the edge of the harsher censure [of the audience]. Modern editions then give the Page an exit, but he remains to witness what happens next and reports it to Antonio (ll. 278 f.).

223 *tweered*: peeped. *OED* spelling is 'twired', but the original is retained here to to preserve the rhyme with 'peered' of the same line.

227-8 *dun... kettle*: 'probably a reference to an inn-sign depicting Guy of Warwick's "Dun Cow" and his kettle' (Wood).

231 *give... reverence*: a commoner would customarily remove his hat in the presence of nobility.

237 *peevish elf*: obstinate child.

240-1 *is... England*: reminds commentators of *Hamlet* (or of an *ur-Hamlet*).

269 *leave distress*: cease distressing us.

294-5 *When... rise*: it is hard enough for you to escape detection when unarmed, so why now appear in your armour?

297-8 *Fortune... it*: based on Seneca, *Medea*, 159-60. Lucio's compressed reply means: 'Valour then is praised only in those whose position gives them the capacity to display it.'

299 *Numquam... esse*: Seneca, *Medea*, 161: 'There can never fail to be –.' 'A place for honour' is left unsaid.

303 *blood-true-honoured*: honoured truly by the noble shedding of blood.

5.1 S.D. *Painter*: there is a scene with a Painter in the 1602 (revised) version of *The Spanish Tragedy*, to which this is evidently an allusion.

S.D. *two pictures*: the two pictures are possibly miniatures, in that 'limn' of l. 5 (and following) is a technical term in miniature painting.

9 *Aetatis suae 24*: in the twenty-fourth year of his age. Lines 7–9 are often used to date the play.

12 *Is... a—*: the Painter perhaps completes the question with a disparaging gesture, unless an obscene term has been censored in the printing.

16–17 *a device, an impresa*: an allegorical picture, usually with a motto ('mott'), carried on a knight's shield at a tournament.

17 *by synecdoche*: with the part standing for the whole.

21 *keel... mouth*: 'to keel' is literally 'to prevent liquid from boiling over' (by cooling it). Dildo evidently drools at the itemizing of the food.

22–4 *I... much*: there are bawdy references in 'ewe mutton' (= 'prostitute'), 'stewed plums', 'Hold pottage', and 'kitchen-stuff'.

35–6 *And... wood*: lines from two popular songs, the first: 'How should I your true love know?'; the second, 'Hey jolly Robin'.

37 *painted things*: i.e. court ladies wearing cosmetics.

38 *I... conceit*: I have thought of something that will be pleasing as a device.

54 *verse... rope*: make verses about you that will drive you to hang yourself.

56–8 *Munera... munera*: 'Gifts alone subdue, gifts alone confer beauty; court Wisdom with a gift and she will become Love. Gifts, gifts'.

65–6 *Farewell... comedy*: the character announces his exit from the play, although the original actor continued as Andrugio.

74–5 *grace... countenance*: favour and patronage.

5.2.1 *prize*: i.e. the gilt harp brought on at the beginning of the scene.

20 *knock... head*: do not succeed in singing the melody.

23 *above line?*: successful. (Expression derived from tennis.)

25–7 *Do... Balurdo*: parody of a popular song, 'Monsieur Mingo'. See *2 Henry IV*, 5.3.74–6.

30–1 *Lady... Fiddlestick*: bawdy reference (to penis).

32 S.D. *Enter... Balurdo*: modern editions indicate that the Page is brought on to receive the harp from Balurdo, which seems unnecessarily heavy-

handed. This edition assumes that the Page's entrance is to motivate Balurdo's exit (see l. 40) to dress for the masque.

33 *It . . . it*: Jackson suggests that Balurdo tries to blow the harp.

52–3 *Prince of Milan*: i.e. Mazzagente; but evidently Marston is confused, because the reference should be to the Prince of Florence, Galeazzo.

60 *makes . . . faces*: rehearses six different facial expressions.

62 *paints*: (1) uses cosmetics; (2) embroiders the truth. Cf. 'colour' (same line) = (1) 'complexion'; (2) 'plausibility'.

72 *Boys . . . close*: evidently Piero sends the Pages up (or even off-) stage to make room for the ensuing activities.

76 *Splendente Phoebo*: 'While the sun shines'. The burning-glass (a lens or concave mirror to concentrate the sun's rays) was a stock emblematic device.

95–6 *coxcomb . . . bauble*: respectively, the head-dress and sceptre of the professional fool, but the bauble was also used to suggest the penis, as here.

99 *take you down*: (1) humble you; (2) have sex with you.

102 *Splendescit . . . tenebris*: 'It shines only in the dark'.

106 *ignis fatuus*: will o' the wisp.

108 *ride*: with bawdy reference (= 'have sex with you').

111–12 *The . . . presence*: weapons were not allowed into the presence chamber.

113 *above E la*: higher than the top note of the scale.

115 *pricked*: written down (plus bawdy reference: 'prick' = 'penis').

120 *red lattice*: common inn-sign of a tavern or bawdy house.

125 *lapis*: 'stone'.

127 *avis*: 'bird'.

130 *thing*: bawdy reference (= 'penis').

132 *truss . . . point*: tie up my codpiece lace (i.e. retire from the love combat).

134–6 *flyboats . . . him*: small, fast vessels floating round the large galley so that he cannot be boarded (= approached).

179–80 *I . . . adore*: I take joy in my situation; namely, that him whom I loathed previously I now honour, love, indeed adore.

180 S.D. *still flutes*: recorders (?).

209 *poor John*: dried hake.

232 *Sic . . . umbras*: Virgil, *Aeneid*, iv. 660: 'Thus, thus it pleases me to descend into the shades.'

248 *anything*: also 'any thing', to yield a bawdy reference (see note to l. 130 above).

264 *checkroll*: variant of 'chequer-roll'. See note to 3.1.98.

267–8 *pricking... parts... stiff*: a series of bawdy references begun by Rosaline in l. 264.

270 *Lydian wires*: Lydian music in ancient Greece was soft and gentle.

EPILOGUE

1–21 *armed Epilogue*: Jonson provides his *Poetaster* (1601) with an armed Prologue and, presumably, deliberately echoes Marston.

Antonio's Revenge

THE PERSONS OF THE PLAY

There is no list in Q. For names other than those below, see notes to 'Persons in the Play' of *Antonio and Mellida*, p. 2.

Strozzo: from *strozzare* (It.), to strangle.

Nutrice: 'a nurse', 'foster-mother' (It.).

PROLOGUE

1 *clumsy*: benumbed. Mocked by a character in Jonson's *The Poetaster*, as is 'ramps', next note.

ramps: obsolete verb meaning either or both of 'climb up', and 'tear'.

9 *our weak... devoir*: our duty which we will perform, however weakly.

11–12 *sweat... issue*: Hercules was reputed to have impregnated fifty women in a single night. Further references in *The Malcontent*, 2.4.8 and 4.2.87–91.

14 *Uncapable of*: either 'unable to feel' or 'unable to endure'.

30 *weigh... scale*: be judged weighty by a judicious audience.

1.1.14–15 *this... breast*: my cunning has stopped his heart.

18 *scouts*: advance guard (perhaps referring to the constellations).

20–1 *raised... ground*: incited to murder Andrugio for this reason.

44 *Huge plunge*: great difficulty. (Piero is vexed at having to placate Strozzo, his inferior.)

46 *claw*: flatter.

54 *His... prowess*: Piero refers to Andrugio's courageous confrontation of him in *Antonio and Mellida*, 5.2.

57–8 *Could . . . love?*: could I avoid appearing to approve Antonio's marriage? (See *Antonio and Mellida*, 5.2.)

60 *Judas kiss*: Piero embraces Antonio in *Antonio and Mellida*, 5.2.

80 *lagged censure*: tardiness in granting approval.

90 *Stygian*: black as the river Styx (of the classical underworld).

97 *reconciliation*: i.e. that between her husband, Andrugio, and Piero at the end of *Antonio and Mellida*.

1.2.10 *courts your presence*: invites you to appear at court.

26 *Bacchus*: wine (from the Roman god of wine).

35 *spur-royals*: English gold coins, worth fifteen shillings then.

36 *Saint Ursula*: British saint, famous for her dream of impending martyrdom.

51–2 *Virtue . . . vanity*: virtue does not decay with each small whim of fragile vanity. 'Flam' (='whim' or 'caprice') is this edition's emendation of Q's 'flame'.

63–4 *to . . . encounter*: to prevent (or outstay) your encounter with joy.

64 S.D. *[They withdraw]*: Maria, Lucio, and Nutrice withdraw to a part of the stage remote from those entering.

67 *Aurora's horse . . . rings*: Aurora is the classical goddess of dawn. To 'tread the ring' was an equestrian feat.

69 S.D. *[starts in dismay]*: it is not clear in what manner Antonio behaves at this point. Already anxious and depressed, perhaps he hears something ominous (such as a cry from Mellida), but the ensuing action gives no support to that.

71 *pass . . . stock*: strike at him with a fatal thrust (i.e. with a sword).

72–3 *horned . . . eyes*: the reference is to cuckoldry.

82 *touch*: the test for gold (together with the touchstone of l. 81); and, metaphorically, for the truth. A coin proved counterfeit was called a 'slip' (l. 84). Meanwhile, Balurdo implies that Mazzagente's nose is a false one (as worn by a syphilis victim).

85 S.D. *writing tables*: notebook for jotting down noteworthy sayings, etc.

91 *my device*: Balurdo also plans a 'device' or heraldic design in *Antonio and Mellida*, 5.1.

98 *'Wehee Purt'*: assumed to be onomatopoeic for a horse's whinny and snort.

106 *Two . . . meagre ghosts*: the first clear reference to the *Hamlet* story. See Intro., p. xvii.

110–14 *at . . . stand*: borrowed from Virgil, *Aeneid*, iii. 175–6 and vi. 699–700.

114 *forced . . . stand*: with effort, pulled myself together.

119 *blazing comet*: comets were considered to be evil omens.

123 *Deus imperat astris*: 'God rules the stars'.

124 *my nose straight bled*: another evil omen.

125 *doubled I my word*: repeated the Latin tag (i.e. for protection).

131 *bewrayed*: (1) betrayed [what should be hidden], my fear; (2) beshitted myself.

136 *gelid*: icy and congealed. (A Marston coinage formed on 'gelid' (='cold as ice') and 'gealed' (='jellied'). Used also at 2.1.74 and *Sophonisba*, 4.1.119.

148 *Signor Renaldo*: 'perhaps the Paduan Giulio Renaldi (fl. 1596) is intended' (Hunter).

192 S.D. *The curtain is drawn*: evidently a curtain is drawn over a practical window at the upper stage level. See Intro., p. xiii.

198 S.D. *as at first*: i.e. appearing still as on his first entrance at the opening of the play ('unbraced', etc.).

206 *Behold my stomach*: Q reads 'stomach's', followed by most editions, which assume that Piero then fails to complete his sentence. But the stage picture is of the character's offering his unprotected breast to the avenger's blade (though Piero of course calculates that he will remain safe). Cf. a similar moment in the dumbshow at the beginning of 3.1.

216 *luxurious twines*: lustful embraces.

223 *Erebus*: hell.

239 *Give seeming passion*: Q and subsequent editions print this as a stage-direction, sometimes emending to the literary 'gives', sometimes moving it to after 'feign'. Including it in Piero's aside points up his pleasure in his deception and restores two pentameter lines.

251 *Slow . . . sin*: bringing slow comfort to those suffering greatly is a speedy wrongdoing.

261 *attaint*: (1) convicted (of the crime of lust); (2) tainted (by lust).

280 *wreathe our arms*: either 'fold our arms' (in the traditional body-language of melancholy); or 'entwine our arms together' (in fellow feeling). Probably the former.

300 *whilst . . . coz*: as here, Q seems to indicate that Pandulfo breaks off mid-sentence. However, this works against the character's stoic pose and his careful orchestration of the moment. Perhaps this should read, 'whilst we say on, fair coz'; i.e. 'make our speech as Chorus'.

S.D. *Music sounds softly*: the music, played offstage, presumably above, gently underscores and defines the elegiac mood of the remainder of the scene.

331 *soul's fair liege*: i.e. the reason must be sovereign to the soul, a corner-stone of the Stoic philosophy that Pandulfo adumbrates here.

337 *bidd'st a fig*: value at nothing.

339 *act*: a complicated pun in which (1) Pandulfo refers both to the event that has just taken place and the 'act' of the theatrical display which he is concerned to construct; and (2) Marston refers to the act end and act interval of his own play which the 'sad tone' of the playhouse band will underscore.

2.1 S.D. *The... kneeling*: the first of three elaborate dumbshows in the play (see Intro., p. xiii). The 'hearse' is the decorative feature constructed around the place where the coffin lies. The occasion is a kind of lying in state for Andrugio in Piero's court. The 'streamers' are pennons or ensigns denoting high rank.

1–5 *Rot... live*: Piero precisely reverses the invocation of eternal fame for Andrugio that the occasion demands.

8 *snaky vengeance*: probably a reference to the three avenging deities, or Furies, of the classical world who tortured the guilty and were repre-sented as serpent-headed.

20 S.D. *Enter... on*: commentators refer to a similar event in *The Spanish Tragedy*, 4.3. See also Intro., p. xiv.

25 *half... conger*: Q reads 'half fish, and half fish' which, although Balurdo frequently talks nonsense, seems unlikely because dull. This edition assumes a compositorial error and that the 'correct' reading is supplied by l. 29.

26–71 *council... counsel*: Balurdo appears to pick his way through a laboured pun on 'council' = 'political body' and 'counsel = 'private advisory capacity'. See also ll. 50 and 59.

73 *humming murmur*: a murdered body's wounds were thought to begin to bleed again in the presence of the murderer and so identify him. The immediacy of Felice's body to Pandulfo's senses (he can smell, hear, and see it) implies that it is still on stage and therefore 'hung up' in Mellida's window (from 1.2), though the staging of the dumbshow at the beginning of the scene makes this difficult, though not impossible, to imagine.

74 *gelid*: see note to 1.2.136.

81–2 *A... take*: 'a wise man may be subject to injustice, but can never suffer injury from it' (Jackson).

89 *he... shrug*: the shrug here is rather a shudder of unease than a gesture of disdain. Even so obdurate a villain as Piero is temporarily affected by Pandulfo's dignified grief and eloquent moralizing.

114 *strike on both sides*: agree with two opposing points of view (i.e. speak hypocritically).

115-29 *'Tis... king*: a battery of quotations and half quotations from Seneca underlie this passage. The climax of the most quoted play, *Thyestes*, points forward to the banquet of flesh with which Marston's own play will end.

135 *rifted chawn!*: yawning abyss.

142 *old Fortunatus*: a character in a popular sixteenth-century tale of German origin. On it Dekker based a successful play of the same name shortly before *Antonio's Revenge*.

148-51 *The... heaven*: Pandulfo develops an elaborate military/nautical metaphor expressing the idea that if imprisoned he can always escape to heaven by way of suicide. 'Sheathèd' means 'enclosed in the body'; the 'precious shot' is the soul.

149 *corbèd*: the sense is obvious from the context, but the word, in Q 'corb'd', is obscure. Commentators relate it to 'corbeil', recorded later, which is a little bucket filled with earth and set on breastworks to provide 'portholes' for firing at the enemy. Perhaps it should be 'corded' = 'fastened with a cord'.

152-62 *Slave... wise*: based on Robert Whittinton's translation, 1547, of Seneca's *De Remediis Fortuitorum*, a classic source of Stoic concepts. (For further use by Marston, see note to 4.2.34-8.)

159 *menace of mortality*: threat of death.

168 *Pandulfo's slave*: i.e. his body, which is a slave to his soul.

2.2 S.D. *Antonio... black*: Hamlet dresses in black (in mourning for his dead father) and enters with a book (2.2.166); while Hieronimo's book in *The Spanish Tragedy* (3.13) is, like Antonio's, a volume of Seneca.

6 *covert*: hiding-place.

19 *defame*: 'repudiate and so dishonour' (Hunter).

26 *cant*: evidently a pun: = (1) niche, shrine; (2) hypocritical language.

28 *endeared intimate*: beloved as a close friend.

37 *self-own*: this edition, and meaning 'owned-up-to' or 'acknowledged' [by itself]'. Q has 'self-one', retained in modern editions (and listed in *OED* as the only example of this formation). Antonio contrasts the self-admitted guilty, who may not be trusted thereafter, with the completely blameless.

43 S.D. *[Shows book]*: i.e. the book of the opening stage-direction. The quotation (somewhat abbreviated from the original) tells an educated Paul's audience that the writer is Seneca (see next note).

47–9 *Ferte...habet*: based on Seneca, *De Providentia*, vi. 6: 'Endure with fortitude; in this you may surpass God; for he is beyond suffering of ills, you are above it. Despise grief; either it is relieved, or it relieves you. Despise fortune; it has no weapon with which to strike your soul.'

55 *But...brain*: only the idle speculation of a cold, unfeeling mind.

64 s.D. *[beneath the stage]*: this edition. Mellida has been consigned to the 'castle vault' (2.1.41) and goes 'from the grate' (s.D. after l. 123 of this scene.). In 5.2, Balurdo, sent to the 'palace dungeon' (at 4.1.269) speaks from 'under the stage' and then climbs on to stage by way of a stage trap. For the present scene, the trap is evidently equipped with a grating.

69 *close*: it means both 'complete' and 'bring to a close musically', thus underlining the operatic effect of the synchronized laments from different parts of the stage and from offstage. Cf. 'bears his part' (l. 73), meaning 'sings his part in the harmony'.

77 *Phoebe*: poetical term for the moon.

83 *Can...thought*: can encompass through the greatest power of inspiration.

116–17 *force...sickness*: adopt an expression to conceal my suffering. (This might be an aside, so that Antonio contemplates convincing Mellida that he is able to put grief behind him. If not, he expresses the intention to deceive the court about his true feelings. In either case, the depth of his suffering is made evident to Mellida at ll. 122–3.)

130 *Some...despair*: Piero's call for doleful music to feed Antonio's despair is Marston's excuse to construct an elaborate stage ritual crossed by irony. The 'prostrate' Antonio, adopting Mellida's grating as his tomb, pronounces his own epitaph, while Piero's ditty is softly played offstage and Piero himself watches gloatingly. It is the perfect expression of narcissistic self-absorption in Antonio. See next note.

133 *Ne plus ultra*: 'nothing beyond'. This is the motto purportedly set on the pillars of Hercules (mountains) at the entrance to the Mediterranean, the limits of the (classical) known world. See also 'Herculean woe' (l. 134) with its reference to heroic passion (and perhaps to Hercules' own agonizing death).

142 *wreathe my tender arms*: a conventional expression of melancholy. See 1.2.280 and note.

153 *Heu...mea?*: Seneca, *Octavia*, 632: 'Alas, to what purpose are my effort and prayers?'

161 *Here's...leg*: Antonio removes his hat and bows in pretended deference, but in talking about it he half reveals the deceit.

172–3 *She's... her*: this edition. Q has a redundant 'most' before 'false', a colon before 'because', a comma after the second 'fair', and mislineation. The reading here allows Piero a conventionally cynical association in women of beauty and vice and a typical recognition and repetition of the decision 'I'll marry her' of l. 173 with ''Tis firm, I'll marry her'. And the reading restores two efficient, pentameter lines.

186 *Rush me in*: 'me' = 'for me'; it is Strozzo who will rush in.

217 *Tragoedia Cothurnata*: tragedy in buskins (the lifts of the tragic actor); i.e. stately or formal tragedy. There may be a reference to *The Spanish Tragedy*, 4.1.160.

221 *Capienda... est*: based (inaccurately) on Seneca, *Agamemnon*, 154: 'In the midst of ills, we must take the headlong path.'

3.1 S.D. *A... state*. The second of the three act-opening dumbshows, this puts together hints from *Richard III* and the *Hamlet* story to create a piece of stylized theatre that moves the plot sharply along, for only here do we get evidence that Piero's wooing of Maria is apt to succeed.

3.2.31 *Non... mori*: 'to die is not miserable, but to die miserably'.

S.D. *[Enter... tomb.]*: there is a similar piece of action in *The Second Maiden's Tragedy*, 4.4. We must infer from references at ll. 6, 13, and 21 that the tomb is set on stage. Evidently, a finely melodramatic entrance is intended.

43 *banks of rest*: restless spirits in the classical underworld were ferried across the Styx by Charon to reach the haven of rest on the other side.

47 *Nemesis*: goddess of vengeance.

51 *Scelera... vincis*: Seneca, *Thyestes*, 195–6: 'You do not avenge crimes unless you surpass them.'

S.D. *her... ears*: conventionally a sign of distraction or madness, here Maria makes her state of undress a kind of virtue by contrast with the cosmetic decorum of daytime behaviour. Cf. her sentiments at 1.2.46–51.

60 *Bacchanal or Jason's wife*: a bacchanal is one of the frenzied Bacchae of classical mythology. Jason's wife, Medea, killed her children in a murderous frenzy.

66–73 *O... Ulciscar*: Seneca, *Thyestes*, 13–15, 75–81, with the additions 'Antonio' and 'Ulciscar', and other minor changes: 'O whoever you are, harsh judge of shades, who allot fresh punishments for them [the dead], or you, lying trembling beneath a hollow rock and fearful of the imminent collapse of the mountain, or you, who shudder at the fierce gaping of greedy lions and the clutches of dread ranks of furies, hear the words of Antonio now hastening towards you: "I shall be revenged"'.

74–5 *appease... affections*: calm your mutinying spirits (i.e. the emotions which are betraying your reason).

81 *'tis idle*: this edition. Q reads 'thy idle', and later editions assume that Maria fails to complete her sentence; but the phrase as emended reappears at l. 95 in virtually the same verbal formula, if slightly rearranged.

84 *Forget not duty*: Maria urges her son's duty towards his parents (i.e. herself) whereas Antonio contemplates his duty towards his father.

103 *Lucio*: as Q. Modern editions change to 'Julio', but the audience has never heard the name and will be unable to identify him. Lucio is one of those on stage, and he has appeared to join Antonio's enemies in the dumbshow at the head of the scene.

104–6 *laid... bed... couch... sleep*: referring punningly (and ominously) to both rest and death.

110 *Pythagorean axioms*: reference to the belief attributed to Pythagoras that the souls of men might transmigrate to animals after death.

124 S.D. *[Pandulfo]... beneath*: cf. *Hamlet*, 1.5.151 and later. See also next note.

130 *GHOSTS... wounds*: this edition. In Q and subsequent editions the second 'Piero's wounds' is given to Antonio, which makes a weak repetition; whereas a second echo (the first is 'murder!' at l. 125) is theatrically compelling. Cf. *Hamlet*, 1.5.157 and later in the same scene.

141–2 *close... strain*: the closing cadence in the melody of revenge.

151–2 *Venit... quidem*: based on Seneca, *Thyestes*, 494–5: 'At last vengeance has come into my hands, and come in full.'

158 *How... together*: how closely you harmonize with each other.

174 S.D. *[under the stage]*: modern editions invent an entrance for the Ghost, but the assumption here is that Antonio wards off a reappearance. Cf. *Hamlet*, 1.5.157 and the stage-direction after l. 195.

206 S.D. *but... blood*: a burlesque of the ritual of the Requiem Mass.

215 *Blood... blood*: proverbial.

3.3.10 *Aristotle's 'Problems'*: the *Problemata* was first published in Latin in 1583 and in English, in chapbook form, in 1595. It discusses 'scientific' topics such as those that Nutrice mentions.

28–31 *My... rosin*: in Q and most editions, the line is printed as part of Balurdo's song, but a case can be made for its having a literal meaning outside the song. (NB Though the line metrically fits the song, it fails to rhyme.)

39 *tobacco*: i.e. to take as snuff.

44–5 *I... voice*: refers to the mock knighting in *Antonio and Mellida*, 5.2.

58 S.D. *Maria ... bed*: the whole episode inevitably recalls *Hamlet*, 3.5, but with the important difference that Gertrude, unlike Maria, does not see the ghost.

64 *plighted ... breast?*: faith which you plighted to this breast.

72 S.D. *Enter ... poniard*: this is clearly intended to recall Piero's entrances in 1.1 and 1.2.

83 *Pardon ignorance*: forgive your mother because she did not know (i.e. that Piero had murdered her husband).

85 *feignèd habit*: Antonio will adopt a fool's costume in 4.1.

89 S.D. *Lo ... curtains*: the Ghost takes on a stage-managerial role which is ambiguous for Maria, both kindly and threatening, as she is ushered towards a symbolic death.

92 *eat your dead again*: spirits return to their graves at first light.

4.1.3 *put ... cavalier*: dress like an impoverished courtier.

13–15 *he ... thought*: he has a licence to speak unpunished (confirmed by custom and guaranteed by self-interested statesmen) as unlimited as free thought itself.

19–22 *canonical ... apocrypha*: the metaphor rests on a contrast between the 'canonical' books of the Bible proper and the 'apocryphal' or inauthentic books.

25 *that ... fool*: Machiavelli's *Discourses*, 3.2, recommends that it is a good idea at times to pretend to be a fool.

35 *too slight a thought*: i.e. the notion of disguising himself, humiliatingly, as a fool.

47 *first innating cause*: the first cause, in scholastic parlance, or God.

49 *zany*: imitate grotesquely.

54 *dead ... defame*: totally insensitive to see infamy.

64 *no motion of him*: there has been no thought of him.

70 S.D. *bare[headed]*: Jackson takes 'bare' to mean unarmed, but Lucio is so characterized elsewhere, including 5.3 where arms would be plainly inappropriate. He is bare-headed because he is in attendance on the duke.

76–7 *Just ... just!*: honourable, correct. Antonio puns, and it is unnecessary that he should be heard by Piero. In fact, the ironic comedy is the greater if he is not, and hence the added 'asides' in this edition.

100–6 *Puff ... Puff*: in every case of its occurrence here, 'puff' might indicate Antonio's action in blowing bubbles rather than be a spoken word. Either way, it represents a pungent comment on a world of insubstantial folly and is integral to a striking piece of 'theatre of the absurd', staged by both Antonio and Marston.

107 *unvulgar*: Balurdo learned the word in 3.2 and uses it now inappositely.

108 S.D. *(affectedly)*: translation of Q's 'ficte', evidently intended to indicate that Piero speaks as though to a small child.

118 *Too . . . wits*: too probing in the vulnerable minds of those whose composure is not secure.

125 *Dud-a, dud-a*: baby-talk. See note to l. 107.

126 *monopoly*: exclusive privilege of selling some commodity, conferred by the monarch as a favour.

  S.D. *still* flutes: recorders.

151 *unnooked*: glossed by editors as 'without deception' and derived from 'nook' = 'to hide in a corner'. But perhaps it should read 'uncooked' (cf. 'unsalted', l. 115, and 'decocting', l. 163).

161 *Supreme Efficient*: i.e. the first cause, God. See l. 47 and note.

166–7 *In . . . ista*: adapted from Virgil, *Aeneid*, ix. 427–8: 'Turn your sword on me, O noblemen; he has done nothing, nor she.'

171 *threefold guard*: reference either to Cerberus, three-headed watchdog of the classical underworld, or to the Styx, over which the dead had to cross to face the final judgement.

186 *that . . . quaff*: so that his keen hopes [to be duke] might satisfy their boundless craving in a totally unlimited way.

  me: for me.

193 *death's entreats*: entreaties to be killed.

222 *dearly I*: I loved him dearly too.

243 *where you must be*: i.e. before the Judgement Seat of God.

252 *I . . . coals*: I would not submit to this humiliation.

254 *Marry-muff*: common expression of contempt.

276–81 *Why . . . goodnight*: recalls Bottom's passion in *A Midsummer Night's Dream*, 5.1.271–301; but Gair suggests it is cobbled together out of a number of ballads.

290 *May . . . thoughts*: provided it [the telling] does not depress you.

298 *guiltless blots?*: disgraces of which he is innocent.

303 *changed earth*: changed to earth (i.e. she died).

317 *Lethe*: river of the classical underworld whose waters, when drunk, induced forgetfulness.

4.2.1 *thou may'st*: i.e. permit such things as Mellida's death.

  9 *high-lone*: meaning 'completely alone', but with the connotations (typical of seventeenth-century usage) of the unassisted toddling of a baby.

23 *Golgotha*: the site of the Crucifixion in Matthew 27: 33; 'the place of a skull'.

27 *with supporting him*: by allowing you to support him.

29 *The ... earth*: i.e. the Stoic sage, the man who controls his passions. But Bullen plausibly transposes ll. 29 and 30 and assumes 'the domineering monarch' to be fortune.

33 *Non ... assentio*: Seneca, *De Providentia*, v. 6 (slightly misquoted): 'I am not God's slave, but I assent to his doings.'

34–8 *I ... cunning*: paraphrased from Robert Whittinton's translation, 1547, of Seneca's *De Remediis Fortuitorum*. Borrowings continue to l. 55.

41–2 *age ... defaced*: experience knows that young loves that seem so blessed are often spoiled by the rude buffets of older age.

44–5 *that ... good*: Pandulfo contrasts the hope that Antonio speaks of, which is only a 'may be' until death cancels it, with the 'good' which was actual (and which must not therefore be grieved over).

53 *spokeshaves of the church?*: those who pare away the wealth of the church for their own use (a spokeshave being a carpenter's tool for planing curves).

54 *maw to restitution?*: 'inclining to restore what you have swallowed up' (Hunter).

63 *Oft ... unsound*: often the love of gold makes more justly-based friendships unstable.

87 S.D. *They ... openeth*: the stage trap is opened from beneath (perhaps the same that provided Mellida's grating in 2.2 and will provide Balurdo's prison in 5.2). Striking the stage with daggers appears to be an echo of *The Spanish Tragedy*, 3.12.

88 *boy*: presumably the Page who entered after l. 23. Marston here notably rings the changes with his use of music to underscore mournful and ritualized events. It has been suggested that Alberto mistakes Antonio's 'boy' to refer to the dead Felice, which provides a resonant meaning for l. 90. In performance, such an interpretation would be easily conveyed to the audience.

98–106 *Death ... just*: other dirges spoken and not sung occur in *The Spanish Tragedy*, 2.5 and in *Cymbeline*, 4.2.

102 *none shall save*: none shall be saved.

104 *Virtue ... assume*: i.e. the virtuous live after death.

111 *Gordian knot*: too intricate to be untied, it was cut by Alexander the Great.

113 *triple Hecate*: Hecate, goddess of the underworld, is represented iconographically as having three faces.

116 *Etna ... Pelorus*: Typhon, a monster in Greek mythology, was thrown under Etna by Jupiter; and the Giants heaped Pelion on Mount Ossa in their war against the gods. Marston's image appears to combine the two legends. Pelorus is a separate place-name.

117 *cast ... chance*: throw dice for high stakes (aiming at the Duke).

5.1 S.D. *Enter ... triumph*: the last of the dumbshows, this one designed, in complex sequence, to sketch out the beginning of the downfall of Piero. Andrugio's presence (and his histrionic gesture) determine the inevitability of what follows.

1-2 *Venit ... sceleribus*: adapted from Pseudo-Seneca, *Octavia*, 629-30: 'The day comes, the hour, in which, for his crimes, he will pay back his foul soul.'

4 *Vindicta*: a Latinized and feminized equivalent of the Greek god of revenge, Nemesis.

8 *Wheel to a head*: swell up (like a boil) to form a circular head.

5.2 S.D. *Balurdo ... stage*: see note to 4.2.87 S.D.

2 *hunger ... walls*: proverbial.

6 *Sir ... ghost*: Balurdo had contemplated being a ghost in *Antonio and Mellida*, 2.1.

7 *put on the rope*: i.e. he risks being hanged for escaping from prison.

12-13 *Sing ... death*: Balurdo confuses the legendary qualities of the swan (which sings before it dies) and the unicorn (which can purify water poisoned by snakes by dipping its magical horn into it).

30 *labouring ... firm*: endeavouring to raise public support.

78-9 *opportunity ... foretop*: see note to *Antonio and Mellida*, Induction, 105-6.

5.3.19 *Io ... Hymen*: i.e. praise to the god of wedding.

20 *Bacchus ... Lyaeus*: alternative names for the god of wine, hence wine itself.

24 *Let quaff carouse*: let the healths go round.

30 *I ... full*: I would like to make my favours to the dead as full as possible. (It is ironically meant.)

49 S.D. *While ... houses*: the Ghost of Andrugio is placed on the upper level at the rear of the stage, probably in the same place as Felice was hung up in 1.2.

51 S.D. *[A ... space]*: this interpretation of the stage action depends on the assumption that the dead body will be concealed in the same place. See stage-direction after l. 152.

54 *Here ... revenge*: the character expresses his own function in the event and recalls Kyd's use of the Ghost of Andrea in *The Spanish Tragedy*.

323

64 S.D. *pluck . . . tongue*: Hieronimo bites out his own tongue in *The Spanish Tragedy* and Lavinia has hers cut out in *Titus Andronicus*. But closest in content and tone, in the drama of the period, to the torture and death here of Piero are the final moments of the Duke in *The Revenger's Tragedy*. And a general influence is Seneca's *Thyestes*.

69 *black blood*: the murderous 'humour' of melancholy.

80 *thy father's gorge*: i.e. Piero's gorge in his role as father.

105 *Sa, sa*: fencer's cry when delivering a thrust (from French *ça, ça*).

114 S.D. *The . . . Andrugio*: i.e., presumably, the Ghost disappears from view by means of the closing of the curtains on the upper level and the actor then withdraws backstage.

128-9 *Thou . . . state*: Hercules' sixth labour was to cleanse the Augean stables.

137 *Having . . . blood*: Antonio, challenging the role of poor orphan, asserts that he has exacted more blood from Piero's family than Piero's crimes extorted from Antonio's kin.

141 *to either part*: to either side in a dispute.

145-6 *and . . . know*: if we knew nothing beyond [this world], we could not bear to carry on living.

146-8 *constraint . . . corruption*: Christian prohibition [against suicide] forces us to remain in this mortal body.

151 S.D. *The . . . departeth* i.e. the actor of Piero withdraws from the stage area after the body of Piero has been concealed by the closing of the discovery-space curtains.

169-84 *Sound . . . tears*: Antonio's final speech modulates from funeral elegy into epilogue in a mannerist fashion typical of Marston. The 'gentle presence' (l. 182) is both invoked at some future time and is already there. In place of a formal epilogue, and true to the ritual framing of the play, there is a song.

The Malcontent

THE PERSONS OF THE PLAY

Altofronto: 'lofty brow' (It.); disguised as Malevole = 'ill-wisher' (It.).
Mendoza: from *mendoso* (It.) = 'faulty'.
Celso: 'high', 'eminent', 'noble' (It.).
Bilioso: 'choleric (It.). (Not particularly appropriate for the character as developed in the play.)
Prepasso: 'usher' (It.). Literally, 'before the door'.
Ferneze: Farnese was an aristocratic family of Parma.
Ferrard: from *ferrare* (It.) = 'to tie laces'. Also, 'to shoe a horse'.

Equato: suggests 'equable'.
Guerrino: 'prisoner of war' (It.). Also, 'child of war'.
Bianca: 'fair' (It.).
Maquerelle: from *macarello* (It.) = 'bawd' (French form).

DEDICATION (FOR THE 1604 EDITIONS)

BENIAMINO IONSONIO
POETAE
ELEGANTISSIMO
GRAVISSIMO

AMICO
SVO CANDIDO ET CORDATO
IOHANNES MARSTON
MVSARVM ALVMNVS

ASPERAM HANC SVAM THALIAM
D.D.°

Dedication: 'John Marston, disciple of the Muses, gives and dedicates
this, his harsh comedy, to his frank and heartfelt friend, Benjamin
Jonson, the weightiest and most finely discerning of poets'.
D.D.: *dat, dedicatque* (i.e. 'gives and dedicates').

TO THE READER (FOR THE 1604 EDITIONS)

I am an ill orator, and in truth use to indite° more honestly than
eloquently, for 'tis my custom to speak as I think and write as I
speak.

In plainness, therefore, understand that in some things I have
willingly erred, as in supposing a Duke of Genoa,° and in taking   5
names different from that city's families, for which some may
wittily° accuse me, but my defence shall be as honest as many
reproofs unto me have been most malicious, since, I heartily protest, 'twas my care to write so far from reasonable offence that even
strangers in whose state I laid my scene should not from thence   10
draw any disgrace to any, dead or living. Yet, in despite of my
endeavours, I understand some have been most unadvisedly over-
cunning in misinterpreting me, and with subtlety as deep as hell
have maliciously spread ill rumours,° which, springing from themselves, might to themselves have heavily returned. Surely I desire to   15
satisfy every firm spirit, who in all his actions proposeth to himself
no more ends than God and virtue do, whose intentions are always

simple; to such I protest that, with my free understanding,° I have
not glanced at disgrace of any but of those whose unquiet studies
labour innovation, contempt of holy policy, reverend comely super-   20
iority, and established unity. For the rest of my supposed tartness, I
fear not but unto every worthy mind it will be approved so general°
and honest as may modestly pass with the freedom of a satire. I
would fain leave the paper;° only one thing afflicts me, to think that
scenes invented merely to be spoken should be enforcively pub-   25
lished to be read, and that the least hurt I can receive is to do
myself the wrong.° But, since others otherwise would do me more,°
the least inconvenience is to be accepted. I have myself, therefore,
set forth this comedy, but so that my enforced absence must much
rely upon the printer's discretion; but I shall entreat slight errors in   30
orthography may be as slightly o'erpassed, and that the unhand-
some shape which this trifle in reading presents may be pardoned
for the pleasure it once afforded you when it was presented with the
soul of lively action.

Sine aliqua dementia nullus Phoebus.°   35

J.M.

1 *indite*: compose.

5 *Duke of Genoa* Genoa had no dukedom. Marston had invented one
  already in *Antonio and Mellida*.

7 *wittily*: wisely.

14 *ill rumours*: i.e. covert accusations of satirical references to contemporary
  persons and events. This is Marston's customary (probably disingenuous) plea of innocence in this matter.

18 *free understanding*: clear (of malice) cast of thought.

22 *approved so general*: found acceptable because not aimed at the particular.

24 *leave the paper*: give up writing.

26–7 *to ... wrong*: i.e. by publishing the play himself.

27 *others ... more*: other people would publish the play in even worse state.

35 *Sine ... Phoebus*: 'No poetic inspiration without some measure of madness'. A common classical idea, replacing, in QB, QA's *Me mea sequenter
  fata*: 'Let my destiny pursue me'.

PROLOGUE

Evidently not used at the Globe, it appears only in QC, placed at the end
of the text. It is headed: 'An imperfect Ode, being but one staff [=
'stanza'], spoken by the Prologue'. Marston presumably, but not certainly, wrote it for the reader, and hence its position here.

To wrest each hurtless thought to private sense   5
   Is the foul use of ill-bred impudence:
     Immodest censure now grows wild,
        All over-running.
   Let innocence be ne'er so chaste,
        Yet at the last   10
        She is defiled
   With too nice-brained cunning.
     O you of fairer soul,
        Control
     With an Herculean arm   15
        The harm;
  And once teach all old freedom of a pen,°
Which still must write of fools whiles't writes of men.

17 *old . . . pen*: the traditional licence for satire.

THE PLAY

In the quartos, there is an epigraph squeezed into the top corner of the page on which the play text begins: *Vexat censura columbas* = 'censorship disturbs the doves' (from Juvenal, *Satires*, ii. 63).

1.1 S.D. *vilest . . . music* a symbolic representation, organized by Malevole, of the moral state of the court. See note to 'breathes' (l. 10) below.

3 *Babylon*: in the Elizabethan/Jacobean period, Babel and Babylon were identified as the same by, amongst others, biblical commentators.

4 *Here's a noise*: a reference to Malevole's music and its inappropriateness to the ducal presence.

9 S.D. *Enter . . . Guerrino*: making a grand entrance, Duke Pietro is ushered in by Ferrard, Equato, and Celso, who actually appear first, and is then closely attended by Guerrino.

10 *breathes*: the music is evidently vocal. Malevole requires the musicians to 'Howl again' at l. 23.

13 S.D. *Malevole . . . chamber*: Malevole might be intended to call from offstage, but his recognition of Ferrard makes this improbable. That the 'chamber' is above is indicated by Pietro's command to 'Come down' at l. 18.

15 *Ganymede*: Jupiter's cup-bearer and from that, the generic name for a minion. 'Catamite' of l. 17, a male prostitute, is a corruption of it.

18–19 *cur . . . snarl . . . dogged*: references to Diogenes, the cynic philosopher ('cynic' derives from the Greek for 'dog'). See also 'duke's hounds' (= 'flatterers') of l. 53 and 'dogg'st of l. 55.

21 *goatish-blooded*: lecherous.

22 *gum . . . fret*: taffeta was stiffened with gum which caused it to fray. 'Fret' also suggests 'annoy' and 'eat'.

23 *Howl again!*: see note to 'breathes' at l. 10. Some editors take this to be a stage-direction.

25 *prodigious affections*: people with outrageously passionate temperaments.

33 *The . . . him*: see notes to *The Dutch Courtesan*, 1.2.77, and *Sophonisba*, 1.1.42–3.

51 *policy*: crafty strategem.

66–7 *Phew . . . strangely*: a reference to the belief that diabolic possession brought with it the gift of tongues.

74 *duke's ox*: the suggestion is that Bilioso is being horned (i.e. cuckolded) by Pietro.

77 *Sir Patrick Penlolians*: unidentified. It may be a nonce coinage analogous to 'Sir Tristram Trimtram' of ll. 89–90.

87–8 *Paris . . . Helen; Guinevere . . . Sir Lancelot*: two pairs of legendary adulterers, one from ancient Greece, the other from Arthurian Britain.

89–90 *Sir . . . whim-wham*: 'the cry of the ape-ward when the ape was to climb the pole and display his feats of agility' (Bullen). A 'Jackanapes' is an ape trained to imitate human behaviour, here a 'fool' or 'coxcomb'. A 'whim-wham' is a 'trifle' or 'silly idea'.

91–3 *Catito . . . trap, ride . . . ring*: 'cat' (or 'tipcat') and 'trapball', which were children's games, and 'riding . . . ring' all had sexual connotations (involving objects being placed in rings or hollows). Riding at the ring was an equestrian sport in which the rider thrusts his spear through a suspended ring. ('Catito' might be a corruption of 'cat in the hole' which existed later in Scotland as a game.)

93 *the . . . welkin*: either the eyelids or the rims of the eyes take on a dark blue colour ('welkin' = 'sky') as a sign of debauchery.

94 *Pompey the Huge*: cf. Shakespeare's *Love's Labour's Lost*, 5.2.674.

95 *You run—*: presumably Pietro is interrupted in his attempt to tax Malevole on his volubility.

96 *Guerrino*: quartos have 'Guerchino', which might be Malevole's deliberate corruption (= 'squint-eyed').

96–7 *that . . . flatterer!*: Marston evidently has an idea here about Guerrino which he fails to develop through the play.

107 *becco, a cornuto*: both words come in Elizabethan English to mean 'cuckold'. Literally, a *becco cornuto* (It.) is 'horned billygoat' (= 'cuckold').

118 *Maquerelle*: 'Maquerelle' here has four syllables to rhyme (on the last two) with 'tell me'.

121 *Blurt o'rhyme*: to hell with rhyming. (Malevole pronounces judgement on his inability to sustain his jingle about Maquerelle.)

122 *honest villain*: Malevole is honest in being candid in his malevolence, whereas Aurelia's villainy is kept 'close' = 'secret'.

130 *fillips his brows*: flicks at his forehead (i.e. puts cuckold's horns on him). The image is enclosed in a reference to playing the children's game of 'blind–man's–buff'.

141 *In . . . soul*: with regard both to the harmony of her body and the harmony of her soul.

156–7 *the thaw . . . apprehension*: the thawing of her iciness into pleasure proceeds from the heat of her lewd imagining.

166 *his son*: i.e. the son of Mendoza and Aurelia, who then marries his half-sister (by Mendoza and his legal wife).

171 *simony*: the practice of buying or selling ecclesiastical benefits.

172 *cope of salvation*: i.e. heaven.

178 *Show shrewd*: this edition. QC has 'shue, should', emended by editors to 'should show' and 'should have'. Malevole is intent on inciting Pietro to violent reaction. 'Shrewd' here = 'sharp' or 'grievous' and assumes a misreading. 'Adultery', as here, is followed by an exclamation mark in QC.

180 *damn*: editions sometimes follow Q's 'dam' and gloss 'choke', an attractive reading even if unsupported by *OED*.

195 *this affected strain*: this assumed style (i.e. of a malcontent).

200 *struck again*: struck in response.

209 *Ops*: goddess of plenty. (Celso, in his incorruptibility, can be entrusted with her soul.)

213 *time it*: temporize, i.e. conform to the time. (This is the Machiavellian compromise with idealism that Altofronto has had to learn. Cf. ll. 225–7.)

215 *bore with*: the sense required here is 'favoured' though *OED* provides no example.

238 *Impure*: this is Q's reading, and a little flat. Perhaps it should be 'impudent', meaning 'shameless', a word and idea that gathers round Mendoza during the play. See 1.2.20 and 34; 2.4.94; and 5.2.162.

242 *the . . . burst*: 'the faction is split by internal quarrels' (Hunter).

246 S.D. *shifteth his speech*: i.e. Malevole readopts the discourse of the Malcontent. Whether this involves a change in the manner of speaking as well as in register is not clear, but the two probably go together.

247 *father of maypoles!*: i.e. a tall, skinny person. Commentators see here a reference to Sinklo the actor, who appears in the Induction and who evidently acted in the play when it transferred to the Globe.

252 *high forehead*: another reference to cuckoldry (because Bilioso's cuckold's horns push up his nightcap), but also, ironically, reminding the spectator of 'Altofronto'.

263 *a chain*: the reward for Malevole promised at ll. 178-9.

264 *impart*: i.e. tell him why Malevole is in favour. Perhaps an aggressive response from Malevole forces Bilioso to change tack.

272 *my young wife*: i.e. Bianca, one of Aurelia's waiting ladies, though Marston is slow to identify what appears later as a classic January/May relationship.

276 *in state of grace*: i.e. in favour with the Duke.

279 *them are*: those who are.

289 *Castilio*: satiric reference to Baldassare Castiglione, author of a favourite courtesy book, translated into English (1561) as *The Courtier*. Cf. 'Castilio Balthazar' in the *Antonio* plays. Bilioso is the obverse of Castiglione's model courtier.

290 *privy key*: the key, held by a court officer, to the privy chamber. There are references at 1.2.116-17 and 2.1.20-1 to Mendoza's ability to penetrate secret places, and there may be also a sexual reference here to his adultery with Aurelia.

292-3 *Leave...me*: an emblematic episode demonstrating Mendoza's growing influence.

298-304 *Aegisthus, Orestes!*: Aegisthus, from Greek legend, was the lover of Clytemnestra who cuckolded Agamemnon and was killed in revenge by his (and her) son, Orestes.

317 *training*: following in the train of.

the cloth: i.e. the canopy of state carried in procession above great personages.

319-20 *lampreys...sides*: according to popular belief, lampreys had a row of eyes on each side (actually gills) and were thus the type of the ever-vigilant courtier.

331-3 *those...Phaeton!*: Phaeton lost control of the chariot of the sun and Jupiter had to intervene to save the earth from conflagration.

333-6 *In...unutterable!*: an allusion to *Hamlet*, 2.2.304 ff. ('What a piece of work is a man...').

337 *only*: i.e. for himself alone.

338 *Phoebus*: i.e. Apollo, god of poetry.

1.2.4 S.D. *Ferneze...speech*: in a comic pantomime, Maquerelle receives jewels from Ferneze without Aurelia's noticing the fact.

37 *heaven's dog*: the dog-star. (It made its appearance at the hottest time of the year. Ferneze mistakenly assumes a cause/effect relationship.)

36–8 *Was...eyes*: an inaccurate quotation, by Marston or Ferneze, from Guarini's *Il Pastor Fido*, 2.1. There are similar borrowings at ll. 40–1 and 47–8.

58, 61 *Nay...swear; Look...comes*: more *Hamlet* quotations (1.5.148 ff.; and 2.2.169).

73 *election*: Aurelia claims predestination as the reason for her doting on Mendoza, not her free and rational choice.

81 *smock-grace?*: intimate (sexual) favour.

89–90 *given hopes*: the hopes they give to others.

103 *sir*: this edition. Q and all other editions have 'sit'. Mendoza challenges Pietro's anger and his drawn sword by baring his chest ('bare heart').

104 *this centre*: the earth (as the centre of the Ptolemaic universe).

108 *loose thee*: 'release you from your misery' (Hunter). But some editions read 'lose' = 'destroy'.

118 *closer passages*: more secret goings-on.

119 *of revelation*: to reveal all.

125 *so loathed reject*: a rejection as of something loathsome.

131 *cold phlegm*: apathetic, dull person (phlegm being the humour that produces such qualities in humans).

135 *arras pictures*: tapestries (presumably depicting erotic activities).

136 *oiled hinges*: i.e. to prevent doors' creaking, for secret passage.

140 *deserve me*: be worthy of my generosity.

154 *advancèd birth*: noble family (i.e. the Medicis).

172 *As...young*: she-bears were popularly thought to lick their cubs literally into (bear-like) shape. (More lines borrowed from Guarini.)

2.1 S.D. *whilst...playing*: see Intro., p. xii.

4 *centaurs*: Ixion, intent on embracing Juno, encountered only a cloud in her shape and begot centaurs.

9 *clock-lines*: i.e. the strings on which the weights ('plummets') are suspended. The image is of the cease of (lust's) activity when the strings are fully paid out.

11 *salt sallow*: salacious and unhealthy.

26 *Unde...refert*: misquotation from Seneca, *Thyestes*, 925–6: 'Whence ye fall, not whither, is what matters.'

2.2.1 *Dipsas*: a character in Lyly's *Endimion*, an old enchantress, and also a bawd in Ovid's *Amores*; but originally a fabulous snake, the bite of which afflicted victims with unquenchable thirst. All three references seem appropriate.

9 *Janivere*: January, an old husband married to a young wife, May, as in Chaucer's *Merchant's Tale*. The reference is to Bilioso. See note to 1.1.267.

17 *close stock!*: secret thrust (fencing term, with sexual allusion).

18 *restoratives...Jasons?*: Jason's wife, Medea, restored his father, Aeson, to youth with magic potions. QA reads 'Jason' which, if correct, means that the whole speech is directed to Bianca; but the association of Medea and Maquerelle is attractive.

21 *fox-stones?*: fox's testicles (reputed to be aphrodisiac, as were the other items in Malevole's list and the 'fried frogs' of l. 30).

24 *country fashion*: bawdy pun, and perhaps an allusion to *Hamlet*, 3.2.111.

28-9 *posset...drink*: posset curdled three times, and with no whey remaining. (This speech is reassigned to Bianca in QC. And this version alone of the quartos has ll. 30-1.)

40-1 *'When...began'—Agamemnon, Menelaus!*: first line of a popular ballad (also sung by Falstaff in *2 Henry IV*, 2.4.32-3) about Sir Lancelot, famous cuckolder of King Arthur. Agamemnon and Menelaus are also legendary, cuckolded kings.

48 *Slaves...rise?*: textually a much disputed line which reads in QB: 'Slaves I favour, I marry shall he, rise'. The meaning intended in this edition is: 'Are slaves now in favour [at court]? Yes. And shall Mendoza rise?'

51-3 *Mounts...fall*: the allusion is to Aesop's fable of the tortoise and the eagle, used here to comment on court rising and falling. Malevole refers to Mendoza's privileged but precarious position in Pietro's court. 'Shell-fish' of l. 52 is 'tortoise'.

55-60 *'I...leagued'*: Malevole recalls Bilioso's lines of 1.1.277-9.

64 *seise*: 'take possession of (legal spelling from QC).

69 *It...so*: evidently Pietro's considered commitment to Mendoza's plan of 1.2.148-64. But perhaps Pietro and Mendoza rediscuss the idea *sotto voce* during ll. 45-68, which would make those lines an aside. Lines 54-68 were added in QC to the text of QA,B. They would only serve to extend further such a private discussion.

70-2 *where...dogged*: a somewhat obscure passage, possibly corrupt. Jackson (whose version is adopted here) paraphrases: 'where a prince seeks revenge it is necessary that those parties whom his own pious demeanour and sense of his high office forbid him to confront directly, be spied on by someone else'.

loft: lofty.

74 *run in self-faction*: 'run alongside the prince, in the same course of conduct' (Hunter). 'Self' = 'the same'. Mendoza urges a stratagem of spying and is, l. 81, instantly rewarded with the job.

83 *BILIOSO*: the line is attributed to Mendoza in the quartos. The emendation has the effect of producing a trio of time-serving responses, followed by Celso's ironic criticism.

85 *(aside)*: QBC read *tacite*, literally 'silently', i.e. said to no one. Equato, like Ferrard, is now merely another flatterer.

2.3.1–3 *three . . . drink*: i.e. the recipe proposed earlier at 2.2.27–9, with a development of the idea of the three curds remaining in separate layers, unmixed and 'distinct'.

7–8 *'Tis . . . me?*: Maquerelle repeats her trick of 1.2.5 ff. of soliciting rewards for information. 'How does't with me?' = 'how does it suit me', 'it' being the pearl she has already won.

12 *eryngoes*: candied, sea-holly root (regarded as an aphrodisiac).

13–14 *amber of Cathaia*: 'amber' = 'ambergris', a delicacy and restorative; here from 'Cathaia' = 'Cathay'.

14 *lamb-stones*: lamb's testicles, a delicacy, here from Russia ('Muscovia').

20 *fortifieth the back*: a strong back was considered a prerequisite of sexual vigour.

23 *art to seem honest?*: the knack of appearing chaste (despite engaging in sexual encounters).

27 *forging of veins*: painting of false veins on top of cosmetic material (to look life-like).

32–3 *keep . . . pale*: a metaphor from horse-keeping: too-good feeding makes the horse (= husband) jump over the fence (= pursue other women).

41–6 *Men . . . woman*: from *Il Pastor Fido*, 3.5.

46–7 *from . . . beauties!*: parody of the Litany in the Book of Common Prayer.

47 S.D. *[Music within]*: the music is played from offstage and anticipates the romantic/erotic accompaniment to Ferneze and Aurelia's love-making, i.e. the song with which the next scene begins. The music modulates neatly between the scenes and the episodes.

51 *sentinel*: Maquerelle is intended to be the guardian of the Duchess' bedchamber (in 4.1.18–19 we learn she lies in 'the outward chamber'). She will now exit through the upstage door through which Ferneze will enter in the next scene. Meanwhile, as the song is sung, Mendoza will enter through the other door and remain, lying in wait.

2.4.2 S.D. *is . . . sword*: i.e. Ferneze runs on to Mendoza's sword (held ready for that event).

6 *prince's*: this might perhaps read 'princess'' (singular, possessive) and thus refer to the Duchess. In any case, 'prince' in early modern usage could apply to women as well as men.

7–8 *Argus'...Hercules*: in Greek mythology, Argus had a hundred eyes and Hercules great sexual powers.

23 *He...him*: anyone who loves Pietro should rail at him (to convince him he does wrong).

29 *loves*: who loves.

62 *pent*: hemmed in, trapped. QC reads 'spent', which yields the (less effective?) sense of 'exhausted'.

64 *Too full of phlegm*: over-phlegmatic (i.e. having too much of the bodily humour phlegm, which in excess makes a person cold and unpassionate).

66 *stand in honour*: defend the honour.

73 *Instantly!*: QB has 'Instantly?'; QC 'Instantly.'.

78 *of Medicis*: see 1.2.154.

87 *the...night*: i.e. in the middle of the night when lechery thrives.

88 *The...dew*: i.e. the moon.

102 *God arrest thee!*: punning on 'rest'/'arrest'.

110 *Huguenot*: French Protestant (evidently used here to connote 'hypocrite').

115 *Rochelle*: La Rochelle was a centre of French Protestantism.

118–20 *deny...parish*: Elizabethan Anglicanism accepted the monarch's authority in 'things indifferent', i.e. in all matters which did not involve central tenets of doctrine. In denying this, Malevole would ally himself with the radical puritans who sought to vest supreme ecclesiastical authority in elders; and such elders would accordingly be 'popes' in their own parishes.

123 *Et...fuit*: adapted from Ovid, *Heroides*, i. 53: 'And now there are cornfields where Sion once was.'

126 *sacredest place*: i.e. the sanctuary.

128 *Hic finis Priami*: 'such was Priam's end' (adapted from Virgil, *Aeneid*, ii. 554).

134 *cross-points*: literally, steps in a variety of court dances, but here with the metaphorical sense of deceit, crafty footwork.

135 *true Frenchman's legs*: the pox, or 'French' disease, sometimes forced sufferers to adopt a straddle stance.

139–40 *What...limbo?*: i.e. as though Ferneze has returned from the underworld, and intended as a joke by Malevole; but also part of a moral plan by Altofronto.

157 *Now . . . skull*: Malevole, in a theatrically self-referential moment typical of Marston's dramaturgy, identifies himself as the writer of a play moving towards its climax.

3.1.1 *youth of day*: early morning (as Malevole's entry at l. 35 confirms).

8-9 *As . . . fast*: this edition. Normally regarded by editors as an uncompleted sentence because the quartos end with 'so'. However, the latter is QA's misreading of a (presumably shortened) speech-prefix for Bilioso which it consequently fails to supply (thus assigning l. 10 to Pietro). QB then provides *Mend(oza)* as a speech-prefix, failing to notice that the character has exited. In any case, there is no theatrical justification for Pietro's 'good old simile' not to be completed, as indeed it in fact has been (and certainly we would not expect Bilioso to commit the solecism of interrupting his Duke).

11-14 *I . . . thirst*: From *Il Pastor Fido*, 3.6.

22 *Physic . . . Sincerity*: neither work is extant, but the first is evidently of the neo-Stoic school (consolation literature) and the second a type of puritan pamphlet. Perhaps Marston invented both of them.

24-7 *Seneca . . . coward*: Roman philosopher and playwright (and favourite reading of Marston) who preached stoic attitudes on austerity, self-restraint, and fortitude in the face of suffering, and yet who famously lived in luxury and committed suicide.

32 *due compliments advance*: use ceremonies appropriate to his position.

33 S.D. *patent*: i.e. his commission as ambassador (the 'letters' of l. 29).

49 *Elder of Israel*: referring to Bilioso as an elderly example of the 'Children of Israel and/or as one of the 'elders' of the Puritan church (cf. 2.4.118-20 and note).

58-9 *Hymen . . . robe*: Hymen, god of marriage, was traditionally represented as robed in saffron.

62 *there*: i.e. in the bordello.

66 *When*: whereas. Malevole is constructing an ambitious contrast between the comparative safety of a woman left alone in a brothel and the dangerous vulnerability of a woman abandoned in an Italian court. (An extra irony lies in the fact that Bianca is the woman in question.)

70 *bound . . . sweets*: 'garlanded and perfumed with a profusion of flowers' (Hunter).

71 *heating delicates*: 'refined foods that inflame the blood' (Hunter).

72-83 *Soft . . . out?*: prose in the quartos, and admittedly 'rough' verse here (following Jackson); but Jacobean writers were not absolutists in these matters.

82–3 *Ulysses . . . out*: when Ulysses failed to return home to Ithaca at the end of the Trojan war, his wife, Penelope, was beset by suitors but remained chaste.

96 *near*: this edition, for quartos' 'neere' and other editions' 'ne'er'. The multitude, Celso reports, is changing its allegiance ('faint reformation') back towards Altofronto because of the 'envy and malice' of their new leader ('envy' = 'ill-will'; 'they' is understood before 'Produce').

99–100 *For . . . draw*: the image is of two people with a double-handed saw cutting through wood together although pulling in opposite directions.

105 *suit*: means either 'petition' or 'apparel'. Malevole says either: 'I will change what I now ask of fortune'; or, 'I will change my disguise required by my misfortune'.

106 *whose only force*: whose power alone.

110 *for conveniency*: for a convenient opportunity.

111 *Upon . . . myself*: to re-establish myself in power at the moment their alliance breaks up.

115 *snibs*: (1) reproves; (2) snuffs (candles; i.e. by cutting off the wick).

124 *second cause*: ulterior motive.

127 *Illo . . . ho!*: falconer's cry to lure the hawk. Also, possibly, a reference to *Hamlet*, 1.5.118, and see next note.

old truepenny?: possibly a reference to *Hamlet*, 1.5.152.

131 *futuens gratis*: 'copulating for free'.

134 *sergeant*: court officer who arrested offenders.

138 *bum-cracks*: farts.

142 *gives . . . am*: suggests to me that I am.

146–7 *Neminem . . . oriundum*: adapted from Seneca, *Epistles*, xliv. 4: 'There is no slave not descended from kings, no king not descended from slaves.'

166 *So, so!*: possibly an Anglicized version of *ça, ça* (cf. *Antonio's Revenge*, 5.3.106), i.e. accompanying a thrust with an imaginary weapon.

168 *As Lent and fishmongers*: i.e. very well, because the restrictions on eating meat in Lent brought fishmongers great profit.

cap-à-pie?: from head to foot. (Sometimes taken to refer to the Duke, but Malevole excitedly queries how he himself should be armed.)

175 *state's life*: a political future.

176 *No reason, marry*: no question, certainly.

179 *Lacedaemonian*: a whore, probably from the slang 'laced mutton' = 'whore'.

202 *Our excellency*: Mendoza refers to himself as already the new duke.

203 *Why . . . emperor?*: Why were you not born an emperor?

208 *remember greatness!*: remember the greatness I have promised you.

3.2.1 *a fault*: a break in the line of scent. The hunt is to be imagined as happening just offstage (evoked by the cornets). Those entering detach from it for a moment.

27 *sirenical*: like the sirens (whose singing cast a spell on the hearer).

30 *crotchets*: (1) quarter-notes (in music); (2) whimsical fancies.

   closes: (1) cadences (in music); (2) embraces.

32–3 *one . . . one?*: Pietro means 'all in one song', with a secondary reference to 'all these moods in one woman'. The Page wordplays bawdily, as Pietro's response shows.

54–5 *to . . . horns!*: reference to the pastime of baiting the bull at the stake.

58 *tip-tap*: i.e. light blows given alternately, and referring to an elegant but ineffectual fencing bout (contrasted with the no-nonsense of Malevole's 'home-thrusting tongue').

4.1.1 *Medam*: an affected pronunciation.

  8 *Cunnycourt*: women's quarters in the palace (with a pun on 'cunny' = 'women's genitalia', plus, possibly, a further pun on 'coney court' = 'rabbit warren').

17 *tongue-tied hatch*: door made to open silently (its tongue having been tied).

30–1 *'most . . . ladies'*: quotation from Philip Sidney's dedication of *Arcadia*, but with 'dear' here meaning 'expensive', as well as being a term of endearment.

40 *'quit*: acquit.

47–9 *'Twas . . . often*: said in fact by a character in *Il Pastor Fido*, 1.3.

53 EMILIA: this edition. All other editions follow Q in ascribing the line to Bianca; but Emilia claims Ferrard as her servant at l. 45. Alternatively, ll. 45–6 belong to Bianca.

54 *Ulysses' bow*: Penelope insisted that suitors must string and draw Ulysses' bow in order to claim her hand (see note to 3.1.82–3).

62–3 *Les . . . brawl?*: all evidently the names of dances, although only the first and last are otherwise known. The brawl, introduced to the English court from France, is punned on at l. 65. 'Quanto' might be a linguistic variation of 'coranto', referred to at l. 68.

69–70 *two . . . honour*: a series of dance steps, though the galliard and coranto were dances in their own right.

71 *Daedalus, thy maze!*: in Greek legend, Daedalus constructed the famous maze for Minos of Crete.

72–3 *the . . . honour!*: a bawdy construing of Guerrino's 'fall back, and then honour' (='stepping back and curtsey') of l. 70.

125 *I . . . Ethiop*: i.e. he attempted to redeem a sinner by marrying her. (To wash an Ethiop white was a proverbial impossibility.)

149 *thy*: this edition. All others read 'the'.

155 *Address . . . council*: 'prepare for a public meeting of the council of state (to ratify the change in government)' (Hunter).

157 *Our . . . sudden*: we will be instantly there.

169-70 *praemium . . . scelus*: 'the prize he seeks is uncertain, the crime certain'. Adapted from Seneca, *Phoenissae*, 632-3.

174 *Omit . . . person*: omit no detail to make me attractive.

175-6 *due adieu*: 'consider me as having made a suitably ceremonious farewell' (Hunter). Some editions read 'dieu, adieu'.

180, 182 *selected, deformed*: ironic transformations of 'elected' and 'reformed', Calvinist terms.

184 *ordained*: the disguised Pietro returns Mendoza's religious language.

188 *go . . . him*: walk, thanks to him.

197 *ring*: i.e. the one given to Malevole at l. 171.

198 *Westphalian . . . zaza*: pig-faced hussar. Westphalia was famous for pigs: and the corruption of 'hussar' to 'zaza' is a conjecture (Harris) as the word is otherwise unrecorded. But another possibility is the corruption of 'Saracen', used as a generalized term of abuse.

199 *Castle of Comfort*: the Genoese citadel is ironically caught up in a Court of Love allegory.

200 *Command . . . letter*: require a warrant in our name to be issued immediately.

206 *Thou'st*: thou must.

211 *Shoots . . . belly*: as Harris. Not in QA, and QBC place the words in brackets in the right-hand margin. Most editions print them as though they were a stage-direction. If so, 'his' would have to refer to the actor of Mendoza or Malevole, whereas clearly it refers to the horse of Mendoza's metaphor.

4.2.13 *Cross-capers, tricks!*: each is a feat of dance-like, physical dexterity and each implies deceit.

14 *eldern guns*: popguns made of elder wood.

85-8 *Agamemnon, Prince Arthur, Hercules*: all three were legendary cuckolds. Arthur was reported as having defeated the Saxon kings in twelve battles. Hercules' 'wenches' were the daughters of Thespius, and there were, as Pietro points out, fifty of them. Hercules' back supported the heavens when he replaced Atlas. See 2.4.8.

94 *a dangerous sore*: a too compassionate surgeon does not make a good job of cleaning out a wound.

99–100 *born . . . coal- basket*: i.e. born only to carry out the most menial of tasks.

103 *so*: this edition. All other editions read 'son', which makes little sense as Pietro is set on reformation, not finding a new heir to replace Mendoza. ('Soon' would also be possible.)

108 *great duke*: customary English way of referring to the Grand Duke of Tuscany.

110 *for . . . dishonour*: it was in fact Mendoza who banished Aurelia, and after Bilioso had left for Florence (4.1.147). Marston may be in error here, or we may replace 'banishing' with 'brandishing' and thus create a different (and quite compelling) sense. 2.4.75 would suggest another possible emendation in 'blazing'.

117 *turn straight again?*: return straightway.

118 *turn straight again*: change my allegiance.

124, 128 *Alcmena, Amphitryo*: husband and wife in Greek mythology. Alcmena was tricked into a sexual union by Jupiter and bore Hercules, and so the passage is all about cuckoldry, especially Bilioso's. Hence, 'a cloth for your old worship's brows', to wipe away the sweat (ll. 129–30) that breaks out on Bilioso at the thought of his being cuckolded.

137 *Golgotha*: boneyard.

142 *all of one piece*: made of the same material (and this leads to the tailoring metaphor that follows).

158 S.D. *Enter . . . Celso*: quartos follow this with 'Altofront, Ferneze, Celso, Pietro' in italics, which some editors incorporate into Malevole's speech that follows.

162 *Give leave*: give me leave.

166 *A . . . all!*: may all have hearty faith (in providence).

171 *close can temporise?*: can wait secretly for the time to be ripe.

173 *lest . . . suspect*: in case ignorance (of Malevole's plans) excites suspicion.

5.1 S.D. *at . . . opposite*: the two characters enter from the two upstage doors opposite each other. They can be imagined to come together while singing their 'duet'.

4 *pox*: omitted in all editions, originally, presumably, as an act of press censorship. But it is also possible that Marston cut the word and expected the actor to supply the omission with an obscene gesture.

12 *the . . . other*: sexual innuendo complicates the proverbial notion of one man's rise at the fall of another.

14 *officers*: i.e. of the law.

15–16 *some must be citizens*: this part of the sequence ironically dispenses with the idea of evident contrasts because it was commonly assumed that citizens were indeed readily cuckolded by the gentry. Perhaps such irony infects the other contrasts.

27 *sign*: i.e. of the zodiac. Maquerelle proceeds to wring jokes out of the zodiacal names that follow by their (not always obvious to us) appropriateness. Cancer refers to the 'crabbed' nature of the 'precisian'; Libra (the scales) is associated with lawyers (and the Michaelmas Law Term began during the ascendancy of Libra—see l. 37 below and note); and Scorpio refers to venereal disease.

30–1 *Chaldean*: Babylonian (an astrologer).

37 *be at the term*: is away at the law-courts.

38 *stones?*: (1) jewels; (2) testicles (i.e. sexual favours).

46 *buff-jerkin!*: a soldier's leather jacket (cf. 'buff-captain' of 4.1.197).

48 *this duchess' easiness?*: i.e. readiness to be persuaded to unchastity.

54 *fine*: fee.

66–8 *sect... dead*: Maquerelle refers to the Family of Love, a radical Protestant sect, to whom this belief was attributed.

73 *Mully*: a term of endearment.

76 *Rosicleer or Donzel del Phoebo*: heroes of the Spanish romance, *The Mirror of Knighthood*. (Cf. Addition B, ll. 28–9.)

89 *Cleopatra, Portia*: heroic female suicides from classical history, together with their choices of death.

95 *cockatrice*: slang for whore; but perhaps 'cicatrice' may be intended.

96 *feather*: the foolish gallant wore a feather in his hat for fashion's sake. See Addition A, ll. 33–47 and note.

100 *Stultorum... omnia*: Cicero, *Epist.Fam.*, ix. 22: 'the whole world is full of fools.'

105–6 *put her to 't*: exert pressure on her.

106 *Women... moment*: women are easily inflamed.

112 *thou... see*: a comma after 'pand'ress' and a full-stop after 'see' would give a different and possible reading for the line.

125 *'Hence... go!'*: he is quoting Bilioso at 2.2.61 and thus making it appear that the two characters have not met since Bilioso's return from Florence, which ignores 4.2.104–30. However, it is possible that Marston intended to cut the 4.2 meeting when he added ll. 121–50 here.

129 *Si... homines*: Ovid, *Tristia*, ii. 33: 'If as often as men sin...' Bilioso then adapts what follows: 'Jupiter sent down his thunderbolts, soon he would run out of them.'

133 *Nemo...sapit*: from Pliny, *Nat. Hist.*, VII. xl. 131. Bilioso translates.

165 *Per...iter*: Malevole translates Mendoza's last line back into its original Seneca, *Agamemnon*, 115.

172 *conduits*: i.e. the mouth and nostrils through which the brain, according to contemporary theory, purged itself by means of spittle and snot.

178 *Cazzo!*: perhaps this should read 'Celso!' and thus anticipate the summons of l. 178. (Cf. *Antonio's Revenge*, 2.1.17, 20.)

201 *led in by Mercury*: Mercury was often the 'presenter' of Jacobean masques, appropriate in his role as guide to the dead spirits (see 5.2.93–6).

203 *Some...ladies*: proverbial expression. 'Far-fet' = 'exotic', 'fetched from afar'.

205 *your*: this edition. Quartos read 'our'. Mendoza gives Celso licence in the devising.

215 *deservèd ranks*: those who support him because of his desert.

220 *antique*: former; plus, possibly, 'antic' = 'fantastic', 'grotesque'.

228 *That...him*: who admits no authority he must obey but God's.

5.2.3 *drop your torch*: allow your torch to drop pitch.

9 *Revelling-scaffolds!*: banks of seating (for the court spectators and not actually represented here on stage; perhaps the actor of Bilioso gestures towards the playhouse auditorium).

9–10 *oaths enough*: i.e. to deter gate-crashers. Overcrowding at court masques was a frequent and serious problem.

14 *all...feather*: clothed in felt (with bawdy secondary meaning), and a hat with a feather. For satire on feathers as fashionable accoutrements, see 5.1.96 and note, and Addition A, ll. 33–47 and note.

16 *falling-bands*: turned-down collars (and provoking a bawdy joke in 'the falling fashion').

20 *poting-stick*: thin iron rod used to crimp pleats in a ruff (here rumpled by an afternoon nap; and part of a bawdy joke).

22 *Signor St. Andrew Jaques*: possibly, satire on Scottish lords and on King James himself. This is made the more likely by the fact that 'Jaques' is omitted in QBC.

25 *Marshal Make-room*: his name denotes his function as usher (see note to ll. 9–10 above).

32 *red...legs*: generally taken to be a reference to Marston himself, as these were among his physical attributes.

33–4 *Quidlibet-in-Quodlibet*: Whichever-you-will-in-Whatever-you-will. (Justice Quodlibet is referred to in *The Dutch Courtesan*, 4.5.51.)

41 *o'erpoise slight rites*: outweigh trivial formalities (like marriage).

62 *You'st*: you must.

84-5 *'Life...vanity'*: from an epigram in Thomas Bastard's *Chrestoleros* (1598), 4.32. Bastard was a member of the literary circle at the Middle Temple to which Marston also belonged and had become an Anglican clergyman, as Marston was later to do.

93 *Cyllenian...ghosts*: Mercury was born on Mount Cyllene; and see note to 5.1.196 above.

102 *Mercury...lawyer*: Mercury was the god of eloquence and so the ideal advocate.

103-4 *Nay...lawyer*: lawyers were often held to be thieves.

111 *birth*: this edition. All others read 'breath' but the repetition is clumsy and 'birth' restores a needed rhyme in a sequence of couplets, as well as (paradoxical) good sense.

124 *agree*: (1) agree to dance; (2) find spiritual harmony in the dance. The symbolic import of the restored relationship is thus subtly stressed.

S.D. *change*: evidently a unit of dancing involving a change of partners. However, while Ferneze changes from Maquerelle to Bianca, the other principals keep their original partners. See also note to 147 S.D. above.

137-8 *jealousy to a citizen*: see note to 5.1.15-16.

139-40 *empty...damnation*: the handbasket was evidently a kind of badge for cheap prostitutes (= 'sixpenny damnations').

147 *AURELIA*: this edition. Quartos read 'Maria'. Some modern editions change the previous speech-prefix to 'Malevole' to solve an evident problem but thus confuse the careful patterning discussed below in the note to ll. 106-47 S.D..

will: presumably a noun rather than a verb.

S.D. *Celso...unmask*: By a happy mistake and confused by the masks, Mendoza calls on Altofronto to woo Maria on his behalf. In the complex sequence that follows, and framed by the choreography of the dance, three separate dialogues take place: Altofronto/Maria; Pietro/Aurelia; and Ferneze/Bianca plus Maquerelle. (Unless we assume a clumsy attempt at seduction on Ferneze's part, it would seem that Marston has forgotten that Bianca is married. Perhaps Emilia was intended here. Irrespective of that, it would make some sense to substitute Celso for Ferneze in that exchange (i.e. 125-32). Altofronto's and Pietro's revealing of themselves to their respective wives takes place during the dance (that is, the first 'measure').

149 *No*: in effect there are two unmaskings for Altofronto. Mendoza first sees 'Malevole', and then Altofronto reveals his true self (as Mendoza

acknowledges in his roll-call of the ghosts from the past now circling round him, l. 150).

182 *still conceit*: always keep in mind.

187 *thrust . . . apricots*: i.e. pushed around. (Apricots were commonly grown against a sun-lit wall.)

192–3 *put it up*: put up with it.

196 *vows*: assumed to indicate retirement to a life of contemplation and religious retreat; alternatively, to a renewal of marriage vows.
suburbs: areas of ill-repute where the brothels were situated.

200 *idle actors*: (1) minor participants in the story; (2) actors now out of work because the play is over.

EPILOGUE

8 *reformèd Muse*: assumed to refer to the reforming effect of Jonson and *The Poetaster*.

11 *Though . . . labour*: though some men labour at it.

14 *Thalia*: Muse of Comedy. (There may be a reference to Jonson's next comedy here, and to Jonson in 'another's' of l. 13.)

15 *desertful lamps*: well-deserving powers of illumination.

Webster's additions to QC of The Malcontent

THE PERSONS OF THE PASSAGES

PASSARELLO° fool to Bilioso

[*In the Induction*]
DICK BURBAGE°
HENRY CONDELL° } Originally played by themselves
JOHN LOWIN°
A THEATRE PATRON Originally played by Will Sly°
DOOMSDAY JR. Originally played by John Sinklo°
A TIREMAN°

Passarello: from *passarella* (It.) = 'little plaice' or 'flounder'.
Richard Burbage: major actor with the Chamberlain's/King's Men, 1590–1627. He played Altofronto in the Globe production as the Induction shows.
Henry Condell: actor with the Chamberlain's/King's Men, 1590–?1619.

ADDITION A

John Lowin: actor with Worcester's Men, then King's Men, 1603 to closure.
Will Sly: actor with the Chamberlain's/King's Men, 1594–1608.
John Sinklo: actor with the Chamberlain's/King's Men, ?1594–1604.
A Tireman: property and wardrobe keeper.

ADDITION A The Induction

   Enter a Theatre Patron, a Tireman° following him with a stool
TIREMAN Sir, the gentlemen will be angry if you sit here.°
PATRON° Why? We may sit upon the stage at the private house.
  Thou dost not take me for a country gentleman, dost? Dost
  think I fear hissing? I'll hold my life, thou took'st me for one
  of the players!   5
TIREMAN No, sir.
PATRON By God's slid, if you had, I would have given you but
  sixpence for your stool.° Let them that have stale suits sit in
  the galleries. Hiss at me! He that will be laughed out of a
  tavern or an ordinary shall seldom feed well or be drunk in 10
  good company. Where's Harry Condell, Dick Burbage and
  Will Sly? Let me speak with some of them.
TIREMAN An't please you to go in,° sir, you may.
PATRON I tell you no. I am one that hath seen this play often and
  can give them intelligence for their action.° I have most of 15
  the jests here in my table-book.
   Enter Doomsday
DOOMSDAY° Save you, coz!
PATRON O cousin, come, you shall sit between my legs here.
DOOMSDAY No indeed, cousin; the audience will then take me
  for a viol da gamba and think that you play upon me. 20
PATRON Nay, rather that I work upon you, coz.
DOOMSDAY We stayed for you at supper last night at my cousin
  Honeymoon's, the woollen-draper. After supper we drew
  cuts° for a score of apricots, the longest cut still to draw an
  apricot. By this light, 'twas Mistress Frank Honeymoon's 25
  fortune still to have the longest cut. I did measure for the
  women.
   Enter Dick Burbage, Harry Condell, John Lowin
What be these, coz?
PATRON The players.—God save you!
BURBAGE You are very welcome.   30
PATRON I pray you know this gentleman, my cousin; 'tis Master
  Doomsday's son, the usurer.
CONDELL [*to the patron who has doffed his hat*] I beseech you, sir,
  be covered.°

344

PATRON No, in good faith, for mine ease. Look you, my hat's the 35
handle to this fan.° God's so, what a beast was I, I did not
leave my feather at home. Well, but I'll take an order with
you.°

Puts his feather in his pocket [and replaces his hat on his head]

BURBAGE Why do you conceal your feather, sir?

PATRON Why, do you think I'll have jests broken upon me in the 40
play, to be laughed at? This play hath beaten all your gallants
out of the feathers. Blackfriars hath almost spoiled Blackfriars for feathers.°

DOOMSDAY God' so, I thought 'twas for somewhat our gentlewomen at home counselled me to wear my feather to the 45
play. Yet I am loath to spoil it.

PATRON Why, coz?

DOOMSDAY Because I got it in the tilt-yard. There was a herald
broke my pate for taking it up.° But I have worn it up and
down the Strand° and met him forty times since, and yet he 50
dares not challenge it.

PATRON Do you hear, sir, this play is a bitter play?

CONDELL Why, sir, 'tis neither satire nor moral,° but the mean
passage of a history.° Yet there are a sort of discontented
creatures that bear a stingless envy to great ones, and these 55
will wrest the doings of any man to their base, malicious
applyment. But should their interpretation come to the test,
like your marmoset they presently turn their teeth to their
tail and eat it.°

PATRON I will not go so far with you, but I say, any man that 60
hath wit may censure, if he sit in the twelvepenny room.°
And I say again, the play is bitter.

BURBAGE Sir, you are like a patron that, presenting a poor
scholar to a benefice, enjoins him not to rail against anything
that stands within compass of his patron's folly. Why 65
should not we enjoy the ancient freedom of poesy? Shall
we protest to the ladies that their painting makes them
angels, or to my young gallant that his expense in the brothel
shall gain him reputation? No sir, such vices as stand not
accountable to law should be cured as men heal tetters, 70
by casting ink upon them. Would you be satisfied in anything else, sir?

PATRON Ay, marry would I. I would know how you came by this
play.

CONDELL Faith, sir, the book° was lost, and because 'twas pity 75
so good a play should be lost, we found it and play it.

PATRON I wonder you would play it, another company having
interest in it!

CONDELL Why not Malevole in folio with us, as Hieronimo° in
    decimo-sexto° with them? They taught us a name for our play;   80
    we call it *One for Another*.

PATRON What are your additions?

BURBAGE Sooth, not greatly needful, only as your salad to your
    great feast, to entertain a little more time, and to abridge the
    not-received custom of music in our theatre.° I must leave   85
    you, sir.
    Exit Burbage

DOOMSDAY Doth he play the Malcontent?

CONDELL Yes, sir.

DOOMSDAY I durst lay four of mine ears, the play is not so well
    acted as it hath been.   90

CONDELL O no, sir, nothing *ad Parmenonis suem*.°

LOWIN Have you lost your ears, sir, that you are so prodigal of
    laying them?

DOOMSDAY Why did you ask that, friend?

LOWIN Marry, sir, because I have heard of a fellow would offer   95
    to lay a hundred-pound wager that was not worth five
    bawbees;° and in this kind you might venture four of your
    elbows.° Yet God defend your coat should have so many!

DOOMSDAY Nay, truly, I am no great censurer, and yet I might
    have been one of the College of Critics° once. My cousin   100
    here hath an excellent memory indeed, sir.

PATRON Who, I? I'll tell you a strange thing of myself; and I can tell
    you, for one that never studied the art of memory, 'tis very
    strange too.

CONDELL What's that, sir?   105

PATRON Why, I'll lay a hundred pound I'll walk but once down
    by the Goldsmiths' Row in Cheap,° take notice of the signs,
    and tell you them with a breath° instantly.

LOWIN 'Tis very strange.

PATRON They begin as the world did, with Adam and Eve.   110
    There's in all just five and fifty. I do use to meditate much
    when I come to plays, too. What do you think might come
    into a man's head now, seeing all this company?

CONDELL I know not, sir.

PATRON I have an excellent thought:° if some fifty of the Gre-   115
    cians that were crammed in the horse-belly had eaten garlic,
    do you not think the Trojans might have smelt out their
    knavery?

CONDELL Very likely.

PATRON By God, I would they had, for I love Hector° horribly.   120

DOOMSDAY O, but coz, coz:

'Great Alexander, when he came to the tomb of Achilles,
Spake with a big loud voice, "O thou thrice blessèd and
happy!"'°

PATRON Alexander was an ass to speak so well of a filthy cullion.   125

LOWIN Good sir, will you leave the stage? I'll help you to a
private room.

PATRON Come, coz, let's take some tobacco.—Have you never a
Prologue?

LOWIN Not any, sir.   130

PATRON Let me see, I will make one extempore. Come to them
and, fencing of a congee with arms and legs,° be round with
them.— Gentlemen, I could wish for the women's sakes you
had all soft cushions.—And gentlewomen, I could wish that
for the men's sakes you had all more easy standings.—°   135
What would they wish more but the play now? and that they
shall have instantly.

    [*Exeunt*]

S.D. *Patron*: like *Doomsday* (l.17 below), this edition. The two characters
are identified in speech-prefixes and stage-directions in QC by the
names of the actors who originally played them, namely Sly and Sinklo.

S.D. *Tireman*: we do not know if this role was played by an actual 'tireman'
or by a small-part actor. Perhaps such a distinction did not always apply.

1 *Sir...here*: Patron wrongly assumes that, because spectators regularly
sat on the stage of the Blackfriars Playhouse (where the play was
originally performed), he can do the same at the Globe, for which the
Induction was written. However, there was no such practice there
(probably because sightlines forbade it).

8 *sixpence...stool*: evidently the price of the hire of the stool at
the Blackfriars, but Patron implies that he might have given more.

13 *go in*: go backstage. The tireman is anxious to get Patron offstage so that
the play might begin.

15 *intelligence...action*: advice on how to play their roles.

23–4 *drew cuts*: i.e. as in a lottery. The whole passage of ll. 22–7 is given
added point by *doubles entendres* ('cuts' = 'cunts'), and the original
spelling of 'apricot' as 'apricock' enhances the effect. Evidently, Sly and
Sinklo, as Patron and Doomsday, play a comic double-act throughout
the scene.

34 *be covered*: put your hat back on. Patron has doffed his hat out of respect
and introduces a passage reminiscent of banter between Osric and
Hamlet (*Hamlet*, 5.2), including an expression common to each, 'for
mine ease'. (Burbage, onstage here as himself, played Hamlet.)

35–6 *my...fan*: Patron uses his hat as a handle to fan himself with the
hat's enormous feather.

37–8 *I'll... you*: I'll make an arrangement with you.

41–2 *This... feathers*: at 5.1.96 we hear 'no fool but has his feather'. Black-friars, the area where the play was first produced, was the centre of the feather trade, so that satirical references to feathers, the passage implies, would be bad for the trade.

48–9 *Because... up*: the feather came from the helmet of a combatant at the 'tiltyard' where chivalric contests were staged. These were overseen by heralds.

50 *the Strand*: a newly fashionable area.

53 *neither... moral*: i.e. not as bitter as a satirical play, but neither is it a morality play.

53–4 *but... history*: either 'an insignificant piece of story-telling'; or 'a play that lies somewhere between ("mean") the other two kinds'. Probably the former.

58–9 *like... it*: it was held that monkeys when introduced to meat-eating would devour their own tails. Presumably, Condell is saying that malicious interpreters of the play are forced to eat their own words.

61 *twelvepenny room*: a box adjacent to the stage costing one shilling.

75 *the book*: Presumably the playhouse copy of the play text. For an account of the losing, refinding, and playing of the play, see Intro., pp. xviii–xx.

79 *Hieronimo*: hero of Thomas Kyd's *The Spanish Tragedy* (1587) which had evidently been performed, perhaps illicitly, by one of the boy companies.

79–80 *folio... decimo-sexto*: these page sizes in books (large and small in format) represent the adult actors at the Globe and the child actors at the Blackfriars.

84–5 *to... theatre*: see Intro., pp. xi–xii.

91 *ad Parmenonis suem*: 'compared with the pig of Parmeno'. Parmeno, an accomplished mimic, was adjudged the best maker of pig noises; his rival turned out to be a real pig. Plutarch tells the story in his *Table Talk*.

97 *bawbees*: Scottish halfpennies. (Possibly a reference to the poor retainers who accompanied James I to the English court.)

97–8 *four... elbows*: fools' coats were often equipped, for comic effect, with four elbows.

100 *College of Critics*: i.e. a fictitious group of self-appointed theatre critics.

107 *Cheap*: Cheapside (with its goldsmiths' shops).

108 *with a breath*: taking only one breath.

115 *excellent thought*: Patron thinks of the stink of garlic when he looks at the audience in the public playhouse.

120 *Hector*: hero of the Trojan war. Perhaps in Patron's head is the common notion that the British were descended from the Trojans.

122–3 *Great...happy*: Doomsday misquotes John Harvey's translation of Petrarch's Sonnet 187. The lines support Hector's adversary (and vanquisher), Achilles.

131 *fencing...legs*: i.e. make an extravagant bow with arms and legs (as though in a posture to sword-fight).

132–4 *Gentlemen...standings—*: Patron parodies the Epilogue of *As You Like It*. 'Standings' contains a sexual pun (= 'erections').

ADDITION B After Act 1, Scene 2

Enter Malevole and Passarello

MALEVOLE Fool, most happily encountered! Canst sing, fool?

PASSARELLO Yes, I can sing fool if you'll bear the burden,° and I can play upon instruments, scurvily, as gentlemen do. O that I had been gelded! I should then have been a fat fool for a chamber, a squeaking fool for a tavern, and a private fool 5 for all the ladies.

MALEVOLE You are in good case° since you came to court, fool. What, guarded,° guarded?

PASSARELLO Yes, faith, even as footmen and bawds wear velvet,° not for an ornament of honour but for a badge of 10 drudgery; for now the duke is discontented, I am fain to fool him asleep every night.

MALEVOLE What are his griefs?

PASSARELLO He hath sore eyes.

MALEVOLE I never observed so much. 15

PASSARELLO Horrible sore eyes, and so hath every cuckold, for the roots of the horns spring in the eyeballs, and that's the reason the horn of a cuckold is as tender as his eye, or as that growing in the woman's forehead twelve years since, that could not endure to be touched.° The duke hangs down his 20 head like a columbine.°

MALEVOLE Passarello, why do great men beg fools?°

PASSARELLO As the Welshman stole rushes when there was nothing else to filch, only to keep begging in fashion.

MALEVOLE Pooh! Thou givest no good reason; thou speakest like 25 a fool.

PASSARELLO Faith, I utter small fragments as your knight courts your city widow with jingling of his gilt spurs, advancing his bush-coloured° beard, and taking tobacco. This is all the mirror of their knightly compliments.° Nay, I shall talk when 30

my tongue is a-going once! 'Tis like a citizen on horseback,°
evermore in a false gallop.

MALEVOLE And how doth Maquerelle fare nowadays?

PASSARELLO Faith, I was wont to salute her as our English-
women are at their first landing in Flushing:° I would call   35
her whore. But now that antiquity leaves her as an old piece
of plastic° t' work by, I only ask her how her rotten teeth fare
every morning, and so leave her. She was the first that ever
invented perfumed smocks for the gentlewomen, and
woollen shoes, for fear of creaking, for the visitant. She were   40
an excellent lady, but that her face peeleth like Muscovy
glass.°

MALEVOLE And how doth thy old lord,° that hath wit enough to
be a flatterer and conscience enough to be a knave?

PASSARELLO O excellent! He keeps, beside me, fifteen jesters to   45
instruct him in the art of fooling, and utters their jests in
private to the duke and duchess. He'll lie like to your
Switzer° or lawyer: he'll be of any side for most money.

MALEVOLE I am in haste; be brief.

PASSARELLO As your fiddler when he is paid. He'll thrive, I'll   50
warrant you, while your young courtier stands like Good
Friday in Lent: men long to see it because more fatting days
come after it; else he's the leanest and pitifull'st actor in the
whole pageant. Adieu, Malevole.

MALEVOLE O world most vile, when thy loose vanities,   55
Taught by this fool, do make the fool seem wise!

PASSARELLO You'll know me again, Malevole.

MALEVOLE O ay, by that velvet.

PASSARELLO Ay, as a pettifogger by his buckram bag.° I am as
common in the court as an hostess's lips in the country;   60
knights and clowns and knaves and all share me;° the court
cannot possibly be without me. Adieu, Malevole.

   [*Exeunt*]

2 *bear the burden*: (1) sing the refrain; (2) support my folly.

7 *case*: covering (i.e. his clothes).

8 *guarded*: trimmed with braid.

9–10 *even . . . velvet*: under Elizabethan sumptuary laws, ordinary citizens
were forbidden to wear velvet and other expensive materials. The laws
were often defied, and they were repealed in 1604, at the time that
Webster probably wrote the additions.

19–20 *that . . . touched*: commentators refer to one Margaret Griffith of
Montgomeryshire, who was described in a pamphlet of 1588 as having
a horn growing from her forehead.

21 *columbine*: A flower drooping in form but also with horn-like parts suggesting cuckoldry.

22 *beg fools?*: the crown could grant the custody of idiots (and their property) to petitioners.

29 *bush-coloured*: assumed to be a reference to the reddish tail ('bush') of the fox.

29–30 *the . . . compliments*: a reference to the chivalric romance, *The Mirror of Knighthood*.

31 *citizen on horseback*: citizens were not regarded as expert equestrians.

35 *Flushing*: the garrison town and landing-place for soldiers in the Dutch War. The women expected there would be prostitutes.

37 *plastic*: pliable, susceptible of being moulded.

41–2 *Muscovy glass*: mica.

43 *thy old lord*: i.e. Bilioso.

48 *Switzer*: Swiss mercenary soldier.

59 *pettifogger . . . bag*: a pettifogger was an inferior type of lawyer. Lawyers were noted for carrying buckram bags

59–61 *Ay . . . without me*: 'Passarello speaks as the incarnation of Folly' (Jackson).

ADDITION C After Act 3, Scene 1, S.D. *Exit Pietro* (after l. 33)

Enter Bianca [to Bilioso, already on stage]

BILIOSO Madam, I am going ambassador for Florence. 'Twill be great charges to me.

BIANCA No matter, my lord, you have the lease of two manors come out next Christmas; you may lay your tenants on the greater rack for it;° and when you come home again, I'll   5
teach you how you shall get two hundred pounds a year by your teeth.

BILIOSO How, madam?

BIANCA Cut off so much from housekeeping; that which is saved by the teeth, you know, is got by the teeth.   10

BILIOSO 'Fore God, and so I may! I am in wondrous credit, lady.

BIANCA See the use of flattery. I did ever counsel you to flatter greatness and you have profited well. Any man that will do so shall be sure to be like your Scotch barnacle,° now a block, instantly a worm, and presently a great goose. This it is to   15
rot and putrefy in the bosom of greatness.

BILIOSO Thou art ever my politician. O, how happy is that old lord that hath a politician to his young lady! I'll have fifty

351

gentlemen shall attend upon me; marry, the most of
them shall be farmers' sons, because they shall bear their   20
own charges;° and they shall go apparelled thus: in sea-
water green suits, ash-colour cloaks, watchet stockings,
and popinjay-green° feathers. Will not the colours do excellent?

BIANCA Out upon't! They'll look like citizens riding to their   25
friends at Whitsuntide, their apparel just so many several
parishes.°

BILIOSO I'll have it so. And Passarello my fool shall go along
with me; marry, he shall be in velvet.

BIANCA A fool in velvet?°   30

BILIOSO Ay, 'tis common for your fool to wear satin; I'll have
mine in velvet.

BIANCA What will you wear then, my lord?

BILIOSO Velvet too. Marry, it shall be embroidered, because I'll
differ from the fool somewhat. I am horribly troubled with   35
the gout. Nothing grieves me but that my doctor hath forbidden me wine, and you know your ambassador must drink.
Didst thou ask thy doctor what was good for the gout?

BIANCA Yes; he said ease, wine and women were good for it.°

BILIOSO Nay, thou hast such a wit! What was good to cure it,   40
said he?

BIANCA Why, the rack: all your empirics could never do the like
cure upon the gout the rack did in England; or your Scotch
boot.° The French harlequin° will instruct you.

BILIOSO Surely, I do wonder that thou, having for the most part   45
of thy lifetime been a country body, shouldst have so good a
wit.

BIANCA Who, I? Why, I have been a courtier thrice two months.

BILIOSO So have I this twenty year, and yet there was a gentleman usher called me coxcomb t'other day, and to my face,   50
too. Was't not a back-biting rascal? I would I were better
travelled, that I might have been better acquainted with the
fashions of several countrymen;° but my secretary, I think he
hath sufficiently instructed me.

BIANCA How, my lord?   55

BILIOSO 'Marry, my good lord', quoth he, 'your lordship shall
ever find amongst a hundred Frenchmen forty hot-shots;
amongst a hundred Spaniards, threescore braggarts; amongst
a hundred Dutchmen, fourscore drunkards; amongst a hundred Englishmen, fourscore and ten madmen; and amongst a   60
hundred Welshmen—'

BIANCA What, my lord?

BILIOSO 'Fourscore and nineteen gentlemen.'°

BIANCA But since you go about a sad embassy, I would have you go in black, my lord.   65

BILIOSO Why? Dost think I cannot mourn unless I wear my hat in cypress like an alderman's heir? That's vile, very old, in faith.

BIANCA I'll learn of you shortly. O, we should have a fine gallant of you, should not I instruct you! How will you bear yourself   70
when you come into the Duke of Florence' court?

BILIOSO Proud enough, and 'twill do well enough. As I walk up and down the chamber, I'll spit frowns about me, have a strong perfume in my jerkin, let my beard grow to make me look terrible, salute no man beneath the fourth button;° and   75
'twill do excellent.

BIANCA But there is a very beautiful lady there. How will you entertain her?

Enter Passarello

BILIOSO I'll tell you that when the lady hath entertained me! But to satisfy thee, here comes the fool.—Fool, thou shalt stand   80
for the fair lady.

PASSARELLO Your fool will stand for your lady most willingly and most uprightly.°

BILIOSO I'll salute her in Latin.

PASSARELLO O, your fool can understand no Latin.   85

BILIOSO Ay, but your lady can.

PASSARELLO Why then, if your lady take down your fool, your fool will stand no longer for your lady.

BILIOSO A pestilent fool! 'Fore God, I think the world be turned upside down too.   90

PASSARELLO O no, sir; for then your lady and all the ladies in the palace should go with their heels upward, and that were a strange sight, you know.

BILIOSO There be many will repine at my preferment.

PASSARELLO O ay, like the envy of an elder sister that hath her   95
younger made a lady° before her.

BILIOSO The duke is wondrous discontented.

PASSARELLO Ay, and more melancholic than a usurer having all his money out° at the death of a prince.

BILIOSO Didst thou see madam Floria today?   100

PASSARELLO Yes, I found her repairing her face today. The red upon the white showed as if her cheeks should have been served in for two dishes of barberries° in stewed broth, and the flesh to them a woodcock.

BILIOSO A bitter fool!°—Come, madam, this night thou shalt enjoy   105
me freely, and tomorrow for Florence.

Exeunt [Bilioso and Bianca]

PASSARELLO What a natural fool is he that would be a pair of
bodice to a woman's petticoat, to be trussed and pointed to
them!° Well, I'll dog my lord; and the word° is proper, for
when I fawn upon him he feeds me, when I snap him by the   110
fingers he spits in my mouth.° If a dog's death° were not
strangling, I had rather be one than a servingman; for the
corruption of coin is either the generation of a usurer or a
lousy beggar.°

[*Exit*]

4–5 *you . . . it*: you may extort more from your tenants in rent (i.e. in new leases).

14 *Scotch barnacle*: it was commonly believed that the metamorphic life-cycle of the barnacle goose proceeded from a shell growing on a tree-trunk ('block'), to (according to this passage) a worm, and finally to the mature goose. 'Block', 'worm', and 'great goose' all have insulting connotations.

20–1 *bear . . . charges*: pay for themselves. (Farmers' sons, the satirists complained, wasted their landed wealth in fashionable pursuits.)

23 *popinjay-green*: parrot green.

26–7 *just . . . parishes*: i.e. made up of different colours like the parishes on a map.

30 *A . . . velvet?*: see note to Addition B, ll. 9–10 above.

39 *he . . . it*: i.e. these things are effective in causing it.

43–4 *Scotch boot*: instrument of torture, designed to crush the leg.

44 *French harlequin*: a *commedia dell'arte* character. The precise meaning is unclear; but there may also be a reference to Old French 'Herlekin', the name of a mythical devil.

53 *several countrymen*: men of different countries.

56–63 *your . . . gentlemen*: conventional characteristics attributed to the different nationalities, the Welsh one being a pretention to gentility.

75 *salute . . . button*: i.e. never make a low bow.

82–3 *stand . . . uprightly*: with sexual pun (on the male erection).

96 *made a lady*: i.e. by marrying a gentleman.

99 *out*: i.e. out on loan.

103 *barberries*: fruit of the berberis. The elaborate simile appears to suggest that Madam Floria's cheeks stand out bright red against her otherwise white flesh like the red berries served with the woodcock.

105 *fool!*: QC's 'fowle' also allows a punning reference to Passarello and back to the woodcock in its sauce (previous speech).

107–9 *a pair...them!*: the bodice was tied with laces ('points') to the petti-coat, but Passarello also puns, in 'trussed', on 'fool'/'fowl'.

109 *the word*: i.e. 'dog'.

111 *spits...mouth*: apparently as a sign of affection.

dog's death: dogs that caused a nuisance were frequently hanged in the period.

112–14 *for...beggar*: for the vitiating effect of money [received as wages] leads only to the practice of usury or beggardom. (The metaphor turns on the idea of the spontaneous generation of vermin out of decaying matter = 'corruption'.)

ADDITION D After Act 4, Scene 2 (i.e. a new beginning for Act 5)

Enter Bilioso and Passarello

BILIOSO Fool, how dost thou like my calf in a long stocking?

PASSARELLO An excellent calf, my lord.

BILIOSO This calf hath been a reveller this twenty year. When Monsieur Gundi° lay here ambassador, I could have carried a lady up and down at arm's end in a platter; and I can tell you, there were those at that time who, to try the strength of a man's back and his arm, would be coistered.° I have measured calves with most of the palace, and they come nothing near me. Besides, I think there be not many armours in the arsenal will fit me, especially for the head-piece. I'll tell thee—

PASSARELLO What, my lord?

BILIOSO I can eat stewed broth as it comes seething off the fire, or a custard as it comes reeking° out of the oven: and I think there are not many lords can do it. [*Sniffs at his pomander*] A good pomander, a little decayed in the scent, but six grains of musk ground with rosewater and tempered with a little civet° shall fetch her again presently.

PASSARELLO O ay, as a bawd with aqua-vitae!

BILIOSO And what, dost thou rail upon the ladies as thou wert wont?

PASSARELLO I were better roast a live cat, and might do it with more safety. I am as secret as thieves to their° painting. There's Maquerelle, oldest bawd and a perpetual beggar. Did you never hear of her trick to be known in the city?

BILIOSO Never.

PASSARELLO Why, she gets all the picture-makers to draw her picture; when they have done, she most courtly finds fault with them one after another and never fetcheth them. They, in revenge of this, execute her in pictures as they do in Germany,

5

10

15

20

25

and hang her in their shops. By this means she is better known   30
to the stinkards than if she had been five times carted.°

BILIOSO 'Fore God, an excellent policy!

PASSARELLO Are there any revels tonight, my lord?

BILIOSO Yes.

PASSARELLO Good my lord, give me leave to break a fellow's   35
pate that hath abused me.

BILIOSO Whose pate?

PASSARELLO Young Ferrard, my lord.

BILIOSO Take heed, he's very valiant. I have known him fight
eight quarrels in five days, believe it.   40

PASSARELLO O, is he so great a quarreller? Why then, he's an
arrant coward.

BILIOSO How prove you that?

PASSARELLO Why thus: he that quarrels seeks to fight; and he
that seeks to fight seeks to die; and he that seeks to die seeks   45
never to fight more; and he that will quarrel and seeks means
never to answer a man° more, I think he's a coward.

BILIOSO Thou canst prove anything.

PASSARELLO Anything but a rich knave, for I can flatter no man.

BILIOSO Well, be not drunk, good fool; I shall see you anon in   50
the presence.
                          Exeunt

4 *Monsieur Gundi*: probably a reference to Jerome Gondi who was a
French diplomat in England in the spring of 1578.

7 *coistered*: word recorded only here. Old French *coustille*, a two-edged
dagger, from which 'coistrel' is ultimately derived, suggests 'castrated'.
('Castrate' is first recorded by *OED* in 1613.)

13 *reeking*: steaming.

16 *civet*: perfume derived from the civet cat, used here to 'fetch', or revive
the scent of, the pomander.

22 *their*: i.e. the ladies'.

31 *carted*: carried in a cart (i.e. through the streets of London as part of the
punishment of a bawd).

46 *answer a man*: accept a person's challenge to duel.

ADDITION E After Act 5, Scene 1, line 9—'. . . a beast'

> *Enter Passarello [carrying a bowl of wine. Malevole and Maquerelle
> are already onstage]*

MAQUERELLE O fool, will ye be ready anon to go with me to the revels? The hall will be so pestered anon.

PASSARELLO Ay, as the country is with attorneys.

MALEVOLE What hast thou there, fool?

PASSARELLO Wine. I have learned to drink since I went with my lord ambassador. I'll drink to the health of Madam Maquerelle.

MALEVOLE Why, thou wast wont to rail upon her.

PASSARELLO Ay, but since I borrowed money of her. I'll drink to her health now as gentlemen visit brokers, or as knights send venison to the city: either to take up more money or to procure longer forbearance.

MALEVOLE Give me the bowl. I drink a health to Altofront, our deposed duke. [*Drinks*]

PASSARELLO I'll take it. [*Takes bowl and drinks*]° So! Now I'll begin a health to Madam Maquerelle. [*Drinks*]

MALEVOLE Pooh! I will not pledge her.

PASSERELLO Why, I pledged your lord.

MALEVOLE I care not.

PASSARELLO Not pledge Madam Maquerelle? Why, then will I spew up your lord again with this fool's finger.

MALEVOLE Hold! I'll take it. [*Takes bowl and drinks*]

MAQUERELLE Now thou hast drunk my health.—Fool, I am friends with thee.

PASSARELLO Art? Art?
    'When Griffon saw the reconcilèd quean
        Offering about his neck her arms to cast,
    He threw off sword and heart's malignant stream,
        And lovely her below the loins embraced.'°
    Adieu, Madam Maquerelle.
    Exit Passarello

6–15 *I'll ... drinks*]: Passarello pledges Malevole's toast before beginning his own.

25–8 *'When ... embraced'*: parody of a translation by Richard Haydocke of a passage of Ariosto's *Orlando Furioso*. Passarello substitutes 'quean' (= 'whore') for the original's 'King'.

ADDITION F after Act 5, Scene 1, line 163 (evidently intended as a substitution and lengthening for 5.1.155-163–)

[*Malevole and Mendoza are onstage, alone*]

MENDOZA Hast been with Maria?

MALEVOLE As your scrivener to your usurer, I have dealt about taking of this commodity; but she's cold, frosty. Well, I will go rail

> upon some great man, that I may purchase the bastinado, or
> else go marry some rich Genoan lady and instantly go travel. 5
> MENDOZA Travel when thou art married?
> MALEVOLE Ay, 'tis your young lord's fashion to do so, though
>   he was so lazy, being a bachelor, that he would never travel
>   so far as the university; yet, when he married her, tails off,
>   and *cazzo* for England! 10
> MENDOZA And why for England?
> MALEVOLE Because there is no brothel-houses there.
> MENDOZA Nor courtesans?
> MALEVOLE Neither; your whore went down with the stews, and
>   your punk came up with your Puritan.° 15

14–15 *your... Puritan*: i.e. the brothels ('stews') were closed by puritanism
but re-emerged differently styled. Malevole suggests that the prostitutes
sought legitimacy by changing their name to 'punk' and that puritanism
enhanced 'punkdom' by its (notorious) sexual hypocrisy.

The Dutch Courtesan

FABULAE ARGUMENTUM

(Provided by Marston for the 1605 quarto and placed after the Prologue)
    The difference betwixt the love of a courtesan and a wife is the full
scope of the play, which, intermixed with the deceits of a witty city
jester, fills up the comedy.

THE PERSONS OF THE PLAY

Franceschina: name of the serving maid in the *commedia dell'arte*.
Mary Faugh: 'marry, faugh!' was a popular expression of disgust.
Freevill: 'free will'.
Beatrice: 'blessed' (It.).
Crispinella: diminutive of Lat. *crispus* = 'curled' or 'quivering'.
Putifer: either from It. *putiferio* = 'stench'; or from *putifarre*, derived
    from the biblical Potiphar, misapplied to mean 'loose woman'.
Tysefew: from Fr. *tisonner* + *feu* = 'poke-fire', or *tison* = 'firebrand'.
Caqueteur: 'chatterer', 'prattler' (Fr.).
Malheureux: 'unhappy', 'unfortunate' (Fr.).
Cocledemoy: derivation not clear: 'cuckold' + *moi*; or, possibly, from
    'cockle-demois' = 'shells of some sort', representing money.

Mulligrub: 'mulligrubs' = 'stomach ache', 'attack of depression'.

Reinscure: 'reins' = 'kidneys' (the seat of the affections).

EPIGRAPH

In the right hand margin of the opening page of dialogue in Q is the epigraph, *Turpe est difficiles habere nugas* = 'It is shameful to accomplish difficult trifles' (from Martial, *Epigrams*, II. lxxxvi. 9) .

PROLOGUE

8 *We...delight*: disingenuous denial of the Horatian ideal (famously expressed by Jonson) of mixing instruction and delight.

16 *passionate man*: usually taken to mean Malheureux, but possibly Marston himself and 'his slight play'.

1.1 S.D. *with lights*: the lights denote a night-time scene. They are torches and will accompany the departing gentlemen through the streets.

2 *sorrowful nose*: Malheureux implies that Mulligrub is weeping for the loss of the goblets.

5-6 *nest of goblets?*: set of goblets of graduated sizes, each fitting inside another.

6 *hammered out*: i.e. beaten out so as to be unrecognizable.

11 *In...thus*: in fact, anything but, as Freevill engages in a flight of mock-epic narration.

13-14 *The...street*: Freevill explains that because the tavern was full, Cocledemoy had to have a downstairs room next to the street, not the 'parlour' where he pretended he wanted to be.

18 *blind harper*: seemingly a Homeric figure, but blind harpers were proverbial.

19 *uncaseth*: takes his instrument out of its case. (The Elizabethan harp was a small, portable instrument.)

24 *last day*: i.e. the day of Judgement.

25 *have day*: postpone payment (i.e. his punishment).

31 *preposterously*: literally, 'backside first'.

32-3 *bids...them*: 'The unpaid harper wastes his irony on an empty room' (Jackson).

36 *Which...heavens*: i.e. because the goblets have not been recovered.

39 *Hic finis...Priami!*: Virgil's *Aeneid*, ii. 554: 'Such was the fate of Priam' (but misquoted).

41 *sins of the cellar*: i.e. Mulligrub's cheating over the drinks he serves (with pun on 'seller'). See 3.2.37–8.

65–4 *Englishmen . . . Countries*: Queen Elizabeth supported the Dutch against the Spanish in order to postpone the attack by Spain on the English mainland. (There may also be a bawdy reference in 'Low Countries'.)

67–8 *hole . . . in*: find shelter (even if he has to put his head in the hole in the pillory as a punishment for fornication); plus a sexual pun on 'hole' (vagina).

69 *club of Hercules*: a symbol of forceful restraint here, though elsewhere often of sexual potency.

73 *middle*: i.e. in the genital area.

82 *publican*: pun on 'public one' (with reference to the gospel formula of 'publicans and sinners').

102 *civil*: (1) civilian; (2) courteous.

103 *take say*: (1) carry say (which is a serge-like material); (2) make trial (i.e. of her lady's lovers, and so 'miscarry' = 'become pregnant').

106 *case?*: (1) situation; (2) receptacle (i.e. pudenda).

109 *give to lose*: Q reads 'loose' which would give the meaning 'give money to live loosely'. The present reading means 'give money to lose everything'.

118 *French crown*: (1) coin; (2) syphilis (symptoms of which included baldness, and hence the pun on crown).

the French—: i.e. syphilis. Not clear whether the printed text is censored or Marston left room for the actor to supply comic byplay.

118–19 *justus . . . justum!*: nominative form in the three genders of Latin for 'just'.

127 *Give . . . fee!*: i.e. his lawyer's fee for delivering a mock defence of the institution of prostitution.

134–4 *Bonum . . . melius*: 'a good thing is better for being shared'.

139–40 *Family of Love?*: Dutch religious sect rumoured to practise free love, and, ironically here, the name for Franceschina's brothel. Evidently, the Mulligrubs are members of the sect (see 3.3.51).

141 *Tannakin*: a Dutch or German diminutive of 'Anna'.

1.2.1 *Mary, Mary*: as Q. Perhaps the first 'Mary' should read 'Marry'.

8 *restitution is Catholic*: the restoration of stolen goods was a precondition of atonement according to the Catholics, whereas Cocledemoy claims to believe in Protestant reliance on God's grace. Commentators see a reference to Mary Faugh's membership of the Family of Love with its communistic ideas. See note to 1.1.139–40.

11 *tempus praeteritum*: 'the time has passed' (and pagan miracles have therefore ceased after the coming of Christ).

12-13 *fire... temple?*: Diana is the classical goddess of chastity.

19 *wicked... Fridays*: Anglicans (as well as Catholics) were required to abstain from the eating of meat on Fridays, though Puritans did not observe the practice.

20 *Hang toasts!*: Cocledemoy's favourite oath, in effect his catch-phrase. 'Toasts' probably derives from the expression 'toasts-and-butter', meaning 'cowards', and is therefore part of Cocledemoy's self-presentation as an aggressive, martial figure.

23 *barber-surgeons*: barbers often combined their primary job with that of surgery. Mary Faugh makes work for them by spreading diseases in her office of a bawd.

24 *diet-drink?*: literally, 'medicinal potion'; here, medicine for venereal disease.

30 *twelve companies*: the twelve major Livery Guilds of London.

38 *Wahahowe!*: usually taken to be the cry of the falconer to lure the falcon; but also an expression of a sense of sexual excitement or appreciation.

48-9 *death's head*: ring with a figure of a skull, often worn by bawds and prostitutes.

51 *Clerkenwell... Bridewell*: the first a district of London frequented by prostitutes, the second a prison.

52 *Dixi*: 'I have spoken' (a Latin term marking the formal end of a legal argument).

56 *lies for*: lies in wait for.

59 *Tully's 'Offices'*: Cicero's *De Officiis*, a popular moral textbook in the period.

61-2 *I... him*: a 'stoup' is a tankard, and Cocledemoy sees Mulligrub as one of his own barrels which he, Cocledemoy, will empty. There may be a second strand of reference to do with falconry, in which 'draw' means 'entice', 'stoop' is the falcon's swoop onto the quarry or lure, and 'to tilt' is 'to thrust at'.

71-2 *syringe... lotium*: sexual allusions (= 'penis', 'semen').

77 *proportion*: probably, a disproportion in the balance of the four humours that determine a person's temperament. Malheureux's phlegmatic composure is instantly undermined by seeing Franceschina.

78 *aderliver*: one of Franceschina's Dutch terms; actually 'alderliefest' = 'dearest'.

86-7 *Curtian gulfs*: a reference to the fate of Marcus Curtius, Roman hero who in 362 BC leapt, in full armour and on horseback, into a chasm (=

'gulf') that had opened up in the forum. His self-sacrifice caused the chasm to close.

96 *cockatrice*: literally, a fabled basilisk that could kill with a look, but here and elsewhere, a prostitute.

96–7 *that ... suppository*: Freevill refers to Ariosto, author of the comedy, *I Suppositi* (*The Substituted Ones*), and avails himself of an unsubtle pun on 'suppository' (cf. 'clyster-pipe' of l. 12 above).

99 *he ... livery*: i.e. he is a member of one of the Livery Companies of London (see l. 30 above) and is thus legitimized.

109–16 *The ... nightingale*: the setting for the song survives (see *Renaissance News*, 13 (1960), 222–32). In Renaissance iconography the nightingale's sleeping with its breast against a thorn represented the sufferings of love.

122 S.D. *seems to overhear*: i.e. is seen to overhear (by the audience).

2.1 S.D. *with music*: i.e. with musical instruments (for the serenade).

8 S.D. *[at the window]*: there was a practical window on the upper acting level at Blackfriars. (See Intro; p. XIII).

18 *your protested due*: what, I have declared, belongs to you by right.

50 *Nothing ... extreme*: this edition. Q reads 'But not to be extreme | Nothing in love's extreme'. Freevill observes that in love not being extreme is itself a kind of extremeness; whereas his love admits no moderation ('receives no mean').

52 *I give you faith*: I believe you.

65 S.D. *The nightingales sing*: evidently a sound-effect from offstage, perhaps made on a portable organ.

79 *O ... habent*: a phrase from Maximianus, a minor Latin author quoted in Montaigne's *Essays*. Florio, Montaigne's 1603 translator, renders it: 'O miserable they, whose joys in fault we lay'.

80 *cross doth fall*: runs contrary.

89 *Diaboli ... est!*: another quotation in Montaigne (see note to l. 79 above), here from St Jerome. Florio translates: 'The devil's master-point lies in our loins.'

104–40 *he ... putes*: Freevill's lines comprise a tissue of quotations from Montaigne.

125 *This ... floor!*: this argument is more than you can bear.

126 *the world's eye*: the common gaze (with reference to the heaven's eye = 'the sun').

139–40 *Absentem ... putes*: a Martial epigram quoted in Montaigne (and inaccurately by Marston). Florio translates: 'Of marble you would think she were, | Or that she were not present there'.

145 *ut vales, domine!*: 'welcome, sir'.

146 *Ago tibi gratias*: 'I give you thanks'.

151 *bulchin*: gallant (literally, bull-calf).

152 *Frank Frailty*: a comic appelation for Franceschina.

155 *prattling*: a translation of Caqueteur's name.

163 *Quamquam te Marce fili*: the opening of Cicero's *De Officiis*: 'Although, Marcus, my son ...'

164 *barber-surgeon*: see 1.2.23 and note.

173 *pray ye be covered*: please put your hat back on.

174–6 *And ... have?*: probably quoting from a ballad.

194 *catastrophonical*: a Cocledemoy coinage from 'catastrophe' (comic term for 'buttocks') and 'phonos' (Greek for 'sound'), i.e. 'farting'.

197 *trim*: (1) barber; (2) cheat.

209 *Northern barber*: taken by Jackson to be anti-Scottish satire; hence the adopted name, 'Andrew Shark', and, presumably, an adopted Scottish accent.

211–12 *All ... breasts*: as playing cards have white backs, so knaves would appear innocent.

2.2 S.D. *with her hair loose*: characteristic display of the distracted mind.

24 *kept counsel for thee*: kept your secrets.

28 *two-shilling ... men*: Inns of Court men were students and lawyers of the four London Law Societies. Two shillings was a substantial payment and the joke Marston makes here is unclear. He had been himself a law student and many of the Blackfriars audience were from that world. Perhaps the point being made is that the Inns of Court men were gullible enough to pay well over the odds for services rendered.

29 *flat-caps*: citizens and traders, so-called from the woollen caps typical of the apprentice. There would be few in the Blackfriars audience (see previous note).

38–9 *Mine ... twopence*: literally, 'I must become an infidel and sell myself for any price I can get'.

43–4 *Neapolitan pock*: i.e. syphilis.

49–50 *Give ... friend*: welcome my friend properly (i.e. with a kiss).

53–9 *Mine ... go*: the song is a version of No. 19 in Robert Jones's *First Book of Songs and Airs*, 1600. Lines 54 and 56 are extra to the song, presumedly addressed to the reluctant Malheureux. Perhaps Franceschina attempts to match her actions to the words of the song.

66 *house-surgeon*: i.e. the physician who attends the brothel to deal with problems related to venereal disease.

89 *unproved sluttery*: untested slut, virgin. Q reads 'Vnproude', which might also modernize as 'unproud'.

95 *Video meliora proboque*: from Ovid, *Metamorphoses*, vii. 20: 'I see and approve the better way.' But Medea, whose line it is, continues: 'but follow the worst', which lies behind Malheureux's next line. Medea also has a ruinous passion—for Jason—which she cannot repress.

108 *Or*: this edition. Q reads 'Of'.

164 *your sudden enjoying*: the immediate enjoyment of you.

206 *that ... man*: i.e. the soul.

2.3.3 *as many irons*: i.e. Cocledemoy will be put in irons to the same weight ('charge' = 'weigh').

4 *Cheapside*: London district where the goldsmiths' shops were situated.

5 *the loss*: i.e. the goblets stolen by Cocledemoy before the play begins.

8 *our wines are: Protestants* 'Protestant' here means 'Anglican', as opposed to the Puritan sect to which the Mulligrubs belong. At 5.3.102–8, Cocledemoy stigmatizes Mulligrub's wine as 'Popish'.

9 *fry ... butter*: 'presumably to stimulate violent thirst in their customers' (Jackson).

14 *Andrew Shark*: 'Andrew' = 'a Scotsman'; 'Shark' = 'a cheat'. See note to 2.1.209 above.

16 *Master Quicquid*: Master Whoever (a nonsense name).

19 *this two year*: taken by some commentators to provide an internal dating for the play, i.e. two years after James I's accession to the English throne and his subsequent descent on England, accompanied by a large contingent of Scottish courtiers.

22 *polled*: (1) clipped; (2) plundered.

29–30 *What's ... court*: barbers were thought of as regular purveyors of (often false) news.

31 *poll*: (1) clip the hair; (2) have intercourse with (from 'pole' = 'penis').

50 *Paris Garden*: the bear-baiting arena on Bankside in Southwark.

50–1 *green onions*: ?leeks (cf. the Welsh reference in 'toasted cheese').

58 *privy searchers*: (1) spies; (2) sanitary inspectors; (3) probers of private parts.

65 *ball*: i.e. a ball of soap (part of the shaving process).

76 *free*: i.e. not apprenticed, or contracted as a worker. Mulligrub is evidently about to offer him work as he himself gains promotion.

76–7 *one ... Council*: i.e. he will reach the first rung of metropolitan government.

78 S.D. *He sings*: what he sings is unknown. Jackson suggests 'Andrew, dost leave me?'.

103 *rosa solis!*: cordial made of spirits and spices, to act as a restorative. Literally, 'rose of the sun', or the plant sundew.

105–6 *'tis...term*: i.e. one week's cheating in the term-time, the period when the courts were in session and so London was crowded with visitors; plus a play on 'cutting' = 'fleshmongering' (an alternative source of income for Mrs Mulligrub).

109 *Master Creak's noise*: the band will play both for Mulligrub (to cheer him up) and, with theatrical economy, for the audience as entr'acte entertainment.

3.1 S.D. *Enter... Putifer*: at some point in the scene they sit down, as we can presume from l. 100. It probably happens here at the beginning, and so chairs or stools are available.

3 *Sh'a 't*: Q has 'sha'te' = 'thou shalt have it'.

15 *John-a-Stile*: a fictitious name for an unnamed party in a legal action; 'Joe Bloggs'.

16 *ployden's*: lawyer's (derived from the name of the Tudor lawyer, Edmund Plowden, also spelt 'Ployden').

21 *with a curs'y*: with a bow, i.e. 'politely' (including 'curtsy' and 'courtesy', and allowing wordplay with 'curse').

25–46 *Let's... quality*: Crispinella, like Freevill, here deploys a good deal of unacknowledged Montaigne.

40 *fashion of the time*: Q has 'fashion of time'.

44 *called in*: banned.

60 *broke my skull*: racked my brains.

66–7 *blanks... prize*: sexual punning, continued in the following lines. 'Blanks' and 'prize' refer to male fertility. 'Coral' (l. 68 ff.) is developed as an extended and witty metaphor for male sexual vigour and potency ('coral' = 'penis', erect or not).

103–4 *pieced above*: i.e. with a false hair-piece ('pieced' = 'added to').

105 *in the—*: obviously 'middle' completes the bawdy reference. Whether censorship operates here, or Crispinella butts in, or Tysefew completes the line with an obscene gesture, or he teasingly leaves the line unfinished is not clear.

107 *Lord Mayor's pageant*: reference to the annual Lord Mayor's Show and its procession through the London streets on 29 October. The giants mentioned may be Corineus and Gogmagog.

121 *a motion*: Beatrice means 'a proposal', but Crispinella playfully misinterprets it to mean 'a puppet show' and proceeds to name some popular ones.

133–4 *fill up a room*: make up the numbers.

136 *in your visitation*: in visiting you. See 1.1.45–52.

168–9 *I...hip*: I have him at a disadvantage (term from wrestling).

169 *I'll...ring*: I'll take the ring as a forfeit.

192–4 *singles...back*: dance steps, with a sexual reference in 'falling back'.

195 *the provision...ours*: we have a responsibility for the night's arrangements.

206 *Babylon?*: i.e. the biblical city of sin. The implication is that Franceschina is the Whore of Babylon.

208 *The...nature*: i.e. Adam, the first to encounter sin and the Fallen World.

210 *In...formas*: the opening line of Ovid's *Metamorphoses*: 'My spirit prompts me to tell of bodies changed into new forms.'

215 *Lindabrides?*: a character in the Spanish romance, *The Mirror of Princely Deeds and Knighthood* (translated into English in 1578).

3.2 S.D. *[at...door]*: the upstage façade at the Blackfriars through which the actors made their entrance was equipped with two doors.

3 *good*: of sound credit; or, as Shylock defines the word in a passage that may lie behind ll. 3–6 here, 'sufficient'. (See *The Merchant of Venice*, 1.3.)

[Reads]: this edition, on the assumption that Burnish is checking over the details of the bond (though the actual wording may be imagined to be ampler).

10–11 *without...psalm*: i.e. without Cocledemoy's singing a psalm before he is hanged (as the condemned man customarily did), i.e. because he will believe himself to be damned.

11 *that...neck!*: and so can only die once.

17 *Secure yourself*: rest assured.

19 *greater things*: sexual boasting, about his genitalia.

24–5 *ball...shaved?*: Cocledemoy is claiming to sell various soaps. See 2.3.65 and note.

29 *The...cursed!*: proverbial. Cocledemoy is the fox.

30 *My...rheum*: my mouth waters.

31 *bowl*: i.e. the standing cup.

34–6 *a penurious...fortnight*: 'Because of lack of learning this parson has been relegated to a very poor parish where he does not eat well (hence, infrequency of "stools"). In even a poor parish the parson can usually depend on a tithing pig; this is a *very* poor one where the tithe consists of only pigs' tails' (Wine).

36–7 *works of supererogation!*: good deeds performed beyond the needs of ensuring personal salvation in the Roman Catholic faith and so available to other sinners. (Cocledemoy claims to be beyond them.)

37–8 *spigot-frigging...elements*: Cocledemoy accuses Mulligrub of tampering with the spigots of his barrels and mixing water with his wine.

42–4 *Only...carts!*: Cocledemoy progresses by degrees from the rungs of the ladder the criminal climbs (at his execution), to the knots of the halter at the top, to the cart for carrying his corpse away.

3.3.5 *Knew me*: unconscious sexual innuendo, of a kind that occurs frequently in the next few lines.

8 *Cheap*: i.e. Cheapside. See note to 2.3.4.

19 *go upon my score*: (1) keep an account with me; (2) have a sexual success with me.

21–2 *piece...serves*: (1) game in season; (2) have sex with me at the right moment.

23 *'s cap's...wool*: see note to 2.2.29.

29 *score it up*: note down the expression for later use.

55 *Sir Aminadab Ruth*: names to suggest a Puritan.

103 *cozened on't*: cheated out of it.

115 *Roger!*: conventional name for a servant.

126 *out of my skin*: scared out of my wits.

133 *take my sleeves*: the sleeves were often separate from the main part of the garment.

134 *I'll...for 't*: the meaning is not clear. 'Gossip' = 'take part', 'chatter idly', and 'give a name to' (in the religious sense). All three yield a reasonable sense.

151 *I'll...you*: i.e. 'I'll make a cuckold out of you' (give you horns).

155 *music*: this again is music to harmonize with Mulligrub's mood and entr'acte music for the audience. See 2.3.109 and note.

4.1.5 *Rank handsomely*: arrange yourselves elegantly (for the dance).

S.D. *Enter...Freevill*: in the original stage-direction, it is not made clear if the entering masquers perform their own dance first (which is promised at 3.1.203–4) and then take out partners (e.g. Freevill with Beatrice) from those present, or take partners immediately. In the light of l. 5 above (and see note), probably the latter, and hence the amplification of the stage-direction as here. Marston may have left latitude for the production to decide. Perhaps Malheureux was intended also to be a masquer (see 3.1.240–1), but the present stage-direction does not allow that.

7 *even*: fairly.

14 *soft*: peaceful.

23 *mettle*: (1) spirit; (2) metal.

24 *copper*: red. But also 'worthless', because copper was an alloy.

25 *Quicksilver!*: Tysefew continues the punning. Crispinella is 'mercurial' = 'quick-witted'.

27 *wisp*: figure of straw for a scold to rail at (meaning herself).

33 *babble*: (1) idle talk; (2) fool's sceptre (bauble).

34-5 *unwholesome reversions*: 'venereal disease inherited after the husband's death' (Jackson).

47-8 *Euphues... Lies!*: three romances: *Euphues and his England*, by John Lyly, 1580; *Palmerin de Oliva*, translated by Anthony Munday, 1588; and *Legend of Lies*, a title evidently invented by Marston. Tysefew says that Crispinella has got her wit out of books.

55 *swallowed flap-dragons*: reference to a game in which raisins are set a-flame in brandy and picked out and swallowed while still burning.

56 *stabbed arms*: the gesture of dripping blood into a glass and drinking it.

61 *By—*: not clear why the oath is not completed. Either it was censored in the printing or the actor was intended to complete it with a gesture.

65 *taken drink*: sworn [upon it] with a drink.

71 *mantle*: i.e. to cover the non-existent hump previously referred to.

83 *Hymen*: i.e. marriage. Hymen is the Greek god of marriage.

4.2.3-4 *hath... life*: has been accepted as the real thing.

4 *they... possessed*: they (those just addressed offstage from Sir Hubert's household) are firmly convinced.

5 *Of... quarrel*: this edition. Q reads 'Of force most, most all quarrel', which for some editors yields some sense if 'they' of l. 4 = 'men in the abstract (who...)'. 'Still' here means 'now as previously' (i.e. the dispute has not been resolved amicably).

39 *whore and knave*: the whore is obviously Franceschina, but the knave has been identified as both Freevill (anticipating his disguise as Don Dubon) and Cocledemoy. Neither convinces and perhaps Malheureux is intended.

45-6 *Nor... blood*: 'nor do strict virtues which are always unalloyed have any sensible proportion to a temperament weakened by passion'.

47 *with side wind*: by indirect means.

4.3.1 *cacafuego*: Spanish for 'spitfire'.

4 *mentula*: Latin for 'penis'.

6 *wagtail*: contemptuous term for a prostitute. ('Tail' = 'female genitalia'; cf. 'gosling', l. 13, and 'up-tail', l. 17.)

10–12 *Hadamoy . . . oteeston*: Cocledemoy's 'Greek' is actually mere gibberish, intended to impress.

14 *bush*: i.e. 'buss' (= 'kiss'). Also at 5.1.97.

25, 26 *bate, seets*: bath, sheets.

26 *begar, tartar*: by God, torture.

33 *cock-stones*: either, the testicles of a male chicken; or, kidney beans (in either case, employed as an aphrodisiac).

37 *stale*: variously glossed as 'an old hand', 'slippery', 'experienced', 'inured'. Bullen conjectures it should read 'tall'.

4.4.13 *Crispinella*: in both lines, Q has a short form, 'Crisp' and 'Cris', which some editions retain as a spoken diminutive.

17 *by the—*: another unfinished oath. Sir Lionel is interrupted, or censorship took place in the printing.

21–2 *cough . . . everlastings*: either 'everlasting cough', or 'terminal cough'.

33 *men of nightcaps*: 'elders' (i.e. those seeking the comfort of nightcaps); or, possibly, 'men of law'.

36, 39 *Matre, Mestre*: master.

38 *No point*: not at all.

59 *Unlace, good nurse*: i.e. Putifer is to unlace Beatrice's bodice.

72 *common woman*: i.e. a whore.

80 *dove-like . . . gall*: the dove was thought to possess no gall, the source of bitterness in other creatures.

90–1 *Were . . . saved*: the meaning is unclear. If we emend 'Two' to 'It' (= 'the world') we get a typical satirist's jibe at the scarcity of virtuous women.

4.5.6 *presantment*: presently (= 'immediately').

7 S.D. *[except the Constables]*: this edition. No re-entry is marked for them.

8 *Wahahowe!*: again, Cocledemoy's hunting cry. See 1.2.88 and 4.3.1.

9 *cupping-glasses*: normally 'glasses used in cupping blood'. Perhaps Mulligrub means 'drinking companions' here.

15 *Bonus nochues*: Spanish *buenos noches* = 'goodnight'.

16 *ubiquitari*: 'people who are everywhere at once' (Latin).

20 *if . . . mercy!*: i.e. if God may be so merciful to me.

29–31 *watch . . . tailors*: the watch were not full-time law-enforcers but tradesmen elected to serve by local residents. Cf. a similar group in *Much Ado About Nothing* on whom these are partly modelled.

369

50 *grub*: root out (and playing on 'Mulligrub').

51 *Quodlibet*: 'what you please' (Latin); term for a scholastic debate.

56–7 *matter in us scabs*: (1) reason in us rascals; (2) pus in us sores.

62 *Illo, ho, ho!*: a variant of Cocledemoy's hunting cry.

65 *stock*: (1) tradesman's supply; (2) the stocks (that Mulligrub is put in).

72–3 *fiddle...fist*: beat him till he farts. The next word, 'Fough', is his response to the imaginary smell.

75 *light——*: the missing word is evidently 'tails'. Censorship seems feeble as the word has been paraded earlier in its sexual sense. Again, perhaps the actor supplies the sense with a gesture.

85 *one...Council!*: cf. Mulligrub's earlier boast (2.3.76–7) which, strictly speaking, Cocledemoy did not hear.

93 *saved*: i.e. by knocking on an unsecured door, as bellman, to warn the household to lock up (as well as his own savings in 'knowing' Mistress Mulligrub).

110–11 *receipt for cutpurses*: a receiving place where pickpockets exchange stolen items for cash, i.e. Cocledemoy alleges that Mulligrub is a fence.

111 *black book*: a register in which the names of criminals were recorded.

114 *mittimus*: a Justice of the Peace's warrant for committal to prison.

Newgate: a London prison.

117 *end of your worship*: the end your worship is coming to. The constable uses 'worship', a title for the gentry, with irony and is repaid by 'good-man' (l. 118), a term for those below the rank of gentry.

129–30 *God...music*: Cocledemoy exercises his privileged position in the play by addressing the audience and cueing the music for the entr'acte.

5.1.6 *pred-a*: prayed.

10 S.D. *the curtain*: part of the regular furnishings of the stage, hanging on the upstage façade and concealing the discovery-space.

14 *puisson*: poison.

20 *trat*: troth.

58–9 *Farewell...hell!*: this edition. Q reads 'Strumpets are fit, fit for som-thing. *Farewell.* | *All save Frevile departs.* | *Fre.* I, for Hell!' The rearrangement 'restores' a likely looking couplet and creates a more dramatically satisfying exit.

100 *as thee!*: is as thee.

5.2.6–7 *the...wormwood*: standard practice to encourage weaning.

23 *Honorificabilitudinitatibus*: famous as the longest known word (see *Love's Labour's Lost*, 5.1.41): 'the state of being loaded with honours' (medieval Latin).

43 s.d. *discovers himself*: removes his disguise. Cf. 5.3.32.

68 *mean*: moderation (as in the classical notion of the 'golden mean').

75 *Oysters...oysters!*: Crispinella mocks Tysefew with a street-cry to match his (l. 74).

93 *ill-fortuned*: translation of Malheureux's name.

114 *wronged in wine*. Presumably 'drunk'; but a possible alternative meaning is that the judge had been the victim of low-quality wine sold by Mulligrub.

116 *justice' nose*: i.e. inflamed by wine.

124 *motion*: (1) proposal; (2) movement.

125 *For...wheels*: criminals were normally carried on carts to execution (though, for theatrical convenience, not in 5.3). But also, 'to go upon wheels' = 'to hurry'; and 'the world goes upon wheels' was proverbial (as well as the title of a play).

134 *turn...ill*: do not follow the fashion of the time and decry everything.

5.3 s.d. *Enter...sergeant*: in fact, it appears that Cocledemoy dons the disguise as he talks to the audience (ll. 1-6). 'So now will I fit myself' (l. 2) = 'now I will furnish myself (with these clothes)'; and 'Fit...everybody' (ll. 3-4) expresses his pleasure at the result.

3-4 *Fit...tail*: i.e. as accommodating as the prostitute's 'tail' (= 'pudendum') which provides an exact fit for each of her customers' genitals.

47 *tired*: (1) exhausted; (2) pulled in at the end of a line, i.e. like a fish.

49 *merely it blood!*: made up entirely of sexual passion.

74 *somebody it is*: in fact neither Pliny nor Cicero, but Ecclesiastes 4: 12.

92 *piece of mutton*: i.e. (sexually) a piece of flesh (and 'mutton' was a cant word for 'prostitute').

102 *vessels*: (1) wine casks; (2) women's bodies.

103 *juice...Babylon*: i.e. Italian wines (from the identification of the Whore of Babylon with the Pope and hence 'Popish' = 'Italian').

105 *Trojan*: by tradition, it was held that Britain was founded by Brutus, great-grandson of Aeneas, as a new Troy.

106-7 *tam...Mercurio*: 'as much for Mars (= war) as for Mercury (= trade)'.

107 *muscadine and malmsey*: foreign, sweet wines, for the importing of which Mulligrub is being criticized. Muscadine came from Malaga; Malmsey from Monemvasia in (modern-day) Greece.

115 *upright*: with bawdy reference to an erection.

134 *euphoniae gratia*: 'for the sake of euphony'. Cocledemoy's alternative (and erroneous) translation of *euphoniae* is probably based on the subtitle of John Lyly's romance, *Euphues: The Anatomy of Wit*, 1579.

140 *seven liberal sciences*: i.e. the seven subjects of the medieval university curriculum.

nine cardinal virtues: Cocledemoy has added two to the traditional seven in scholastic philosophy.

155 *Heliconian*: Mount Helicon was the classical home of the Muses.

156 *middle region*: evidently a part of the theatre auditorium, possibly the middle gallery of three; as well as the inevitable, sexual joke.

Sophonisba

THE PERSONS OF THE PLAY

Masinissa, Syphax, Hasdrubal, Hanno, Scipio, Laelius, and Sophonisba were historical figures involved in the Second Punic War, 218-202 BC.

Gelosso: name adapted by Marston from the historical Masinissa's son (Gulussa).

Jugurth: name adapted by Marston from the historical Masinissa's grandson (Jugurtha).

Gisco: name borrowed by Marston from Hasdrubal's father.

Messenger: borrowed by Marston as part of the formal machinery of classical tragedy.

Erichtho: Thessalian witch, imported by Marston from Lucan's *Civil Wars*, vi.

DEDICATION (from the 1606 quarto)

TO THE GENERAL READER

Know that I have not laboured in this poem to tie myself to relate anything as an historian but to enlarge everything as a poet; to transcribe authors, quote authorities and translate Latin prose orations into English blank verse hath in this subject been the least aim of my studies.° Then, equal reader, peruse me with no pre-   5
pared dislike; and if aught shall displease thee, thank thyself; if aught shall please thee, thank not me; for I confess in this it was not my only end.°

Jo[hn] Marston.

1-5 *Know . . . studies*: Marston evidently refers implicitly and slightingly to Jonson's *Sejanus' Fall*, printed in 1605 with notes citing historical authorities. He had himself contributed verses to that volume.

7-8 *in . . . end*: i.e. in writing a tragic poem, as opposed to a comedy where, he would claim, the primary purpose is to please (see *The Dutch Courtesan*, Prologue, l. 8 and note).

ARGUMENTUM (from the 1606 quarto)

A grateful heart's just hate, ingratitude;°
And vow's base breach with worthy shame;
A woman's constant love, as firm as fate;
A blameless counsellor, well born for state;
The folly to enforce free love: these, know,°   5
This subject with full light doth amply show.

1 *hate*: this edition, though Kemp, retaining Q's 'haight' glosses it
'height'. Other editions emend to 'height'. Though Q's spelling elsewhere of 'hate' is 'hate', the structure and punctuation of the Argumentum, as well as the sense, favour the present reading.

5 *The . . . love*: the folly of trying to enforce love that must be freely given.

(Appended to the end of the text of the 1606 quarto)

After all, let me entreat my reader not to tax me for the fashion of the
entrances and music of this tragedy, for know it is printed only as it was
presented by youths, and after the fashion of the private stage. Nor let
some easily amended errors in the printing afflict thee since thy own
discourse will easily set upright any such unevenness.

EPIGRAPH (printed in the 1606 quarto in the right-hand margin after the
opening speech by the Prologue and assumed here to be not a continuation of that speech but an addition for the printed text by the author)

Nec se quaesiverit extra.

= 'Nor will he have looked outside himself'. Adapted from Persius,
Satires, i. 7.

1.1 S.D. *[A dumbshow.]*: the formal style of the play is established by this
unusual dumbshow in which the Prologue is introduced, flanked by the
two main parties. He is presumably accompanied by 'two Pages with
torches', and each party also has 'two Pages with lights'. See next note.

lights, lights: these are evidently a source of illumination different from
the 'torches' of the same stage-direction. Presumably candles or tapers.

2 *the . . . Rome*: the only nation able to awe Rome.

14 *black*: i.e. in a melancholy mood, which will lead to angry reprisals. See
note to ll. 42–3.

16 *Apollo . . . Hymen*: god of music and poetry, god of marriage. (The torch
is a typical attribute of Hymen.)

17 *louring Juno*: Juno was the goddess of married love and opposed to
Venus (see next note).

18 *Sits . . . Venus*: Venus was the goddess of beauty and erotic love. The line
implies that this marriage, as a love match, is one that honours Venus
rather than Juno.

23-4 *oil... holy dew*: both traditionally associated with divine blessing.

25-6 *what... hopes*: the author has only limited hopes with regard to what you will understand of this.

42-3 *Not... vexations*: in Renaissance physiology, man contains within him a mixture of the four humours (blood, phlegm, choler, and melancholy), the proportions of which determine his psychological state. For Syphax, 'black' melancholy is predominant and his composure is therefore disturbed.

56 *Hannibal*: famous Carthaginian general who inflicted a number of defeats on the Romans but was then recalled to Africa and defeated by Scipio (202 BC).

63 *two-necked eagles*: anachronistic reference to the double-headed eagle of the Holy Roman Empire. Syphax refers to the Roman eagle of the legion's standard and hopes that Scipio will overrun Carthage.

68-9 *thy... blood*: Marston errs (though not later at 5.3.48-9). Gnaeus Cornelius Scipio was Scipio's uncle and Publius Cornelius Scipio his father. Both were killed in Spain in 211 BC fighting Hasdrubal.

82 *Prove... Syphax*: deny your blessings to Syphax.

88 *wing a vessel*: i.e. set rapid sail.

91 *palms*: i.e. the generals' palms of victory, but with a secondary reference to the shaking of hands on a new alliance. Cf. 2.3.89-90.

91-3 *make... arms*: i.e. while we are driven by our discontent, add together his forces and ours (which are 'unsuspected').

98 *their wrong*: the wrong they have done to me.

104 *bear... right*: carry with it no rational justification as right action.

1.2.4 *I undo*: this edition. All others repeat Q's 'under', which conceals Zanthia's action and wordplay. See next note.

5 *You... undone*: 'punning elaborately on four sense of "undone": (1) ruined; (2) unbuttoned, unlaced; (3) deflowered; (4) un-done = not copulated with' (Jackson).

8 *ceremony*: i.e. the ritual activities around the bedding of the newly wed wife, which we shall now see. Barring the door to the bridegroom is a custom in a number of cultures. Marston prepares for the subsequent 'bed' scenes elsewhere in the play (in 3.1 and 4.1).

11-12 *figures in locution... about-phrases*: elaborate, circuitous expressions (rather than the discourse of candid behaviour).

16-17 *form... vice*: ceremonial gloss can neither make actions better nor eliminate immorality.

22 *imperfect mixtures*: the four humours (see note to 1.1.42-3), says Zanthia, are mixed imperfectly, thus creating female instability which requires

ceremony to give it discipline. Through Sophonisba, on the other hand, the play presents an ideal of womanhood to which Zanthia herself will provide an exemplary opposite.

31 *You . . . high*: not only 'you walk on built-up soles', but also 'you are very proud'. Marston effectively develops an undercurrent of antagonism (on Zanthia's part) during the exchange.

32 S.D. *the curtains*: i.e. the curtains of the bed. This is evidently a free-standing structure that either sits in the discovery-space (see Intro., p. 0) or, more likely, has been set on stage at the beginning of the scene.

[seeks to] enter: Q seems to have Masinissa enter here, but his real entrance is the ceremonial one after l. 35 ('admit').

35 S.D. *Enter . . . quivers*: the boys are costumed appropriately as Cupids. 'Anticly' means as masque figures, to perform the anti-masque. Hence, their 'fantastic measure' = 'grotesque dance'.

39 *Smooth-chinned*: Apollo was traditionally represented as beardless, un-usual in a mature man in the Jacobean period.

40 S.D. *white ribbon*: the maiden girdle worn by unmarried women, sym-bolically loosed on the wedding-night by the bridegroom.

42 *Io*: Greek and Latin expression of joy.

43 S.D. *[Chorus . . . voices]*: a musical consort of cornets, portable organ, and choir provides an epithalamium as part of the wedding-night cere-mony. The choir is perhaps the four boy masquers. The consort is either offstage or might be located 'above'.

45–7 *her . . . her*: her who only professes virtue but does not practise it.

54 *bands*: i.e. the bonds of matrimony.

57 *Atlas*: the Titan whose punishment for revolt was to be condemned to support the heavens.

44–57 *A . . . shame*: Sophonisba's reply takes the form of a sonnet, spoken, presumably, but perhaps with musical accompaniment.

80 *our . . . back*: our intended security has failed. (A ship's anchor 'comes back' when it fails to catch on the seabed. Here, the anchor is Hanni-bal's strategy of attacking Rome.)

86–8 *To . . . beyond*: i.e. concern about the future makes us miserable; desire, fear, and hope are unresolvable emotions which continually draw us, anxious, towards the unknowable. (Lines 87–8 are adapted from Montaigne, 1.3.25.)

91 *unsober evening*: 'unsober' because the troops had been drinking (in celebration of the marriage) and were consequently 'reeling'.

131 *damped*: i.e. discouraged.

172–3 *struck . . . fate*: determined the fate of the battle.

174 *events*: outcome.

188 S.D. *cap-à-pie*: Marston makes a theatrical contrast to the earlier Masinissa 'in his nightgown'.

190 *his actions*: the actions appropriate to it (honour), i.e. not just the language.

193 *prest to satisfaction*: ready to offer satisfaction.

206-7 *Virtue ... wise*: enforced virtue is in effect a vice, whereas the man who has the opportunity to err and does not is truly wise.

210 *stand ... just*: justly take care of my interests.

235 *Carthage' Palladium*: the Palladium was a statue of Pallas Athene (or Roman Minerva) supposed to confer safety on the city of Rome, and thus deployed with irony here. Sophonisba is seen as the Carthaginian equivalent and her safe-keeping is of vital concern for Masinissa and for Carthage.

239 S.D. *the cornets ... act*: see Intro., p. xii.

2.1 S.D. *[Dumbshow.]*: the dumbshow, an exordium to the act, formally makes a graphic statement about the temporizing versus the honest politician, which is a strong, if minor theme of the play, related to the play's concern with Stoic notions of integrity.

12 *more ... Carthage*: a greater increase to the Carthaginian side.

14 *Profit and honesty*: the advantageous action and the just action.

24 *Scipio's arms*: i.e. both Scipio's personal valour and his forces.

29 *For their consent*: as a reward for their agreement.

36 *as wit*: as conquest by cleverness.

43 *is use*: is being put to use.

48 *in respects*: according to the context (i.e. not absolutely).

52 *O ... scene!*: a self-referential irony, suggesting that divine justice operates only in poetry and tragedy, not in real life.

55-73 *Nothing ... mind*: Carthalon carefully constructs a Machiavellian justification of state violence towards moral codes. Marston creates the passage out of Machiavelli himself and Montaigne.

63 *as ... purges*: as there is poison in all purges (i.e. evil to create a beneficial effect).

68 *stick too nice*: be over-scrupulous (i.e. like those princes who ascribe their politic actions to 'heaven's wrath' or 'bad chance'. Such 'nicety' is not required).

69 *For ... forgive*: common sense dictates that the killing of Masinissa is justifiable.

72 *He ... harm*: he who is inclined to do you no good should not be allowed to do you harm.

103 S.D. *[Gelosso] speaks*: this edition. The next two lines of dialogue (104–5) have no speech-prefix in Q and later editors ascribe them to Sophonisba, thus making her revulsion at the plan immediately evident. But this is to miss the point of the whole episode, in which all the others (including Gelosso—see note to l. 110 below) misinterpret l. 109, and are able to do so because Sophonisba's responses until then have been non-committal. So Gelosso's ll. 104–5 show him as a moral commentator, drawing out the implications of the others' treachery and their lack of courage in speaking to Sophonisba. The 'short silence' is theirs as well as Sophonisba's.

110 *very woman!*: Gelosso sees frailty and (typically female) inconstancy in Sophonisba's ambiguous response, ironically counterpointing Carthalon's and Hanno's enthusiasm for her (for the very vice that Gelosso assumes).

116 *very angel!*: deliberate contradiction of 'very woman'. (See previous note.)

135 *for . . . see*: because the gods and we see things as they are; things are not as they are because we see.

155–6 *Ops . . . Neptune . . . Saturn*: Ops is the Roman goddess of plenty, here standing for the earth; Neptune, god of the sea, standing for the sea; Saturn, god of melancholy, a cold, moist humour. Gelosso offers a catalogue of impossibilities.

160 *thee-contemning greatness*: tyrannic power that despises you (i.e. Jove, to whom ll. 58–65 are in part addressed).

162 *those lamps*: the heavenly bodies (referring to ambitious leaders).

165–6 *cry . . . dry!*: i.e. the tyrants call down Jove's thunderbolt—'brand'—on themselves.

169 *Phoebus . . . great*: Phoebus = Apollo, god of prophecy, here inspiring Gelosso in his oracular 'Carthage must fall'.

2.2.32 *looks . . . Carthage*: ceases to look with favour on Carthage.

40 *Apollo Pythian!*: i.e. Apollo as the deity of the oracle at Delphi.

43 *Most only man!*: peerless man. (Masinissa's praise of Gelosso is occasioned by the warning in the letter that Gisco is a poisoner.)

44 *Sirrah . . . poor*: Masinissa tries to comprehend why anyone should take on such a base role as poisoner.

45 *make indisgraced retreat*: beat an orderly retreat.

48 *Entirely of themselves:*—composed only and continuously of themselves (in order to avoid infiltration).

55 S.D. *[Sheathes his sword]*: supplied by Jackson in place of empty brackets in Q. Kemp reads 'Gisco attempts to drink his own poison'; but that is

to place the focus on Gisco, whereas it is Masinissa's moral choice not to punish (with death) that should concern us.

56 *No return*: i.e. Masinissa requires no return for his magnanimity in the way of service.

77 *High lights*: illustrious ones.

82 *Spare . . . gods*: if you spare treachery, you strike at the very gods.

92 *Revenge . . . anger*: take revenge worthy your anger on those who have provoked your anger.

93 *Down . . . heart!*: down with my weak humanity and up with my courage.

93-4 *Stoop . . . breast*: i.e. nod (with approval).

95 *print the dust*: be laid low.

2.3.3-4 *Only . . . piece*: only in exercising his political (or statesman-like) craft are his various emotions harmonized.

4-5 *Were . . . brings*: this edition. Q has 'song to' for 'sought or'. Modern editions variously emend 'song' to 'sung' or 'said', with only a small improvement in Q's mangled sense. Ironically, and throughout his speech, Hasdrubal develops a quasi-Stoic justification for his ruthless treatment of individuals, in contrast to the more complex responses of the true Stoics in the play, Masinissa, Sophonisba, and Gelosso. Their personal integrity and sense of moral responsibility translate in Hasdrubal into selfish ambition and a steely determination untutored by humanitarian considerations. By extirpating his passions, he becomes, he thinks, like the true Stoic, god-like. See next note.

7 *Iphigenia!*: with devastating laconicism, Hasdrubal refers to the death of Agamemnon's daughter, sacrificed by her father to secure from the gods favourable winds for the sea-journey by the Greeks to Troy.

10-11 *sole . . . globe*: only to understand himself, contained within his head.

13 *Telamon*: father of Ajax. The son carried the father's mighty shield.

27 *Assured*: This edition. Q and all subsequent editions read 'Afeared'. Hasdrubal is decisive and not timid here, as he then reports.

40 *'void*: avoid.

51 *Short . . . woes*: a version of the Senecan tag, popular with Marston: 'Light woes speak, heavy ones strike dumb' (*Hippolytus*, 607).

74 *Made stoop*: caused to submit. But 'stoop' is also a falconry term for the action of swooping on the prey and so refers back to 'falcon towers aloft' of l. 69.

87 *gain him*: i.e. capture Gelosso.

89-90 *strike . . . palms*: clasp hands (in military alliance).

108 *Brook...powers*: 1633 reading. Q has 'Brode skorne oppen faind powers'. The whole speech, ll. 108–13, enacts Hasdrubal's (non-Stoical) incoherence but was further garbled by the compositor. See next note.

110 *To...hold*: this edition, to give the meaning: 'being a successful villain should afford some emotional warmth'. Hasdrubal then contrasts that with his own deadly situation where a sacrilegious act has produced a freezing effect. (Q reads 'To be a prosperous villain yet some heat some hold').

3.1 S.D. *Organ...act*: see Intro., p. xii.

2 *has no knees*: never kneels in supplication.

10 *two black knaves*: i.e. Zanthia and Vangue, both negroes.

24 *save...fame*: save your reputation while you still have it.

26 *Achilles' armour*: made by Hephaestus (god of fire). Contrary to the impression given by this allusion, however, Achilles' near total invulnerability in battle did not derive from his armour.

34 *Love's...rude*: 'not even the most violent expressions of love are barbaric' (Jackson).

63 *vails*: commentators suggest a complex pun: (1) servants (metaphorically); (2) gratuities (anticipating what happens next); (3) veils (i.e. literal protectors of the 'ladies' bodies'). But there may be textual corruption here. (Deighton would emend to 'maids' which yields a straightforward meaning.)

67 *good*: this edition, to yield the sense: 'the good of being in service is to gain in whatever way is possible'. For 'good' Q reads 'god'. Syphax's philosophy is directly refuted below. See l. 101 and note.

68 *Speak...service*: speak what is worthy of my service.

72 *time her goodness*: fit her morals to the needs of the moment: temporize.

83 *courses...reason*: activities and abstract ideas dependent on rational interpretation.

99 *is but—*: either Zanthia interrupts herself or, more likely, fills the sense out with a contemptuous gesture.

101 *Take...hand*: i.e. take payments only from one direction. Sophonisba develops the idea of the baseness of reward-seeking servants in ll. 109–16. Perhaps she has witnessed the bribery in ll. 60–3.

106–7 *Whose...reason*: whose great dependence on him causes them only to flatter his mood and not advise what is just and reasonable.

116 *such...dust*: either 'trust such slaves, and you whet swords...' or 'such slaves, once in your trust, will whet swords...'

S.D. *full*: swelling.

116 S.D. *solemnity*: ceremonial procession (probably involving the setting up of the altar; see next note).

S.D. *altar*: this is presumably carried on but not placed centre-stage as the bed will need to be accommodated later in the scene. Indeed, the bed is probably already onstage and visible. (See note below to S.D. after l. 161.) Jackson suggests that the altar is adorned with images of the classical gods referred to in ll. 118-25.

118 *god of sound*: i.e. Apollo, god of music.

120-2 *Mercury...Phoebe*: Mercury was the most cunning of the classical gods. Phoebe was the surname of Diana in her aspect of moon goddess; she was also the goddess of chastity.

132-3 *Whilst...wears*: a re-use of the Senecan tag. See 2.3.51 and note.

146-7 *vault's mouth...cave*: this is evidently represented onstage by the stage trap. At what point it is opened is not certain, but probably at the end of the 'solemnity' which it might otherwise impede.

159 *fearful*: as Q and all editions. One might expect 'fearless', but perhaps 'fearful' here means 'able to cause fear' = 'dreadful'.

161 S.D. *They...curtains*: the bed is evidently onstage from the beginning of the scene, or at least visible in the discovery-space. Cf. the use of the bed and its curtains in 1.2.

162 *naked*: defenceless (because of the drug).

169 *I...more*: I can say no more.

179 *Music!—*: presumably offstage music is supplied here, which will add to the effect of grotesque travesty.

181-2 *Hercules...wanting*: see *The Malcontent*, 4.2.87-8 and note.

184 *Can...devil?*: the devil was popularly conceived as literally black in hue.

189 *just-moved*: justly aroused to strong emotion.

private ear: i.e. a word with you in private.

199 *be...us*: keep our secret.

201-2 *as...crocodile*: 'Dogs on the banks of the Nile were supposed to drink by snatches, running from fear of the crocodiles' (Bullen).

206 *bear our*: this edition. Q reads 'bear out'.

3.2 S.D. *with...General*: either 'accompanied by the insignia proper to a general'; or, 'with a general's company of men', i.e. his personal guard.

5 *The...earth*: 'the world was made for men to enjoy, men were not made to serve their native earth (punning on "earth" = "grave")' (Jackson).

9 *seiseth us*: this edition. Q reads 'sees these thus' and O reads 'fees these thus', for both of which ingenious explanations have been offered. The

assumption here is that Q's compositor failed to read a favourite (legal) expression of Marston's and O tried to clear things up. 'To seise' is 'to put someone in legal possession of place or property'. The idea is more or less repeated at l. 11; and see also *Antonio and Mellida*, 5.2.217.

25 *full eyes*: i.e. eyes full of tears.

28–30 *he...blood*: the Senecan idea again, noted at 2.3.51 and 3.1.124–5. It is especially apposite here in this extended test of Masinissa's stoic capacity to endure. See next note.

30–1 *give...man*: allow me to grieve for a short time as a man should. (Cf. Macduff's 'I must also feel it as a man', *Macbeth*, 4.3.223.)

48 *Temperance...honour*: may Scipio's sense of personal honour express itself as temperance (as opposed to anger in the face of Masinissa's insult in telling him he lies).

62 *proportion*: i.e. the harmony in nature which in Stoic doctrine guarantees that the world is organized rationally.

69 *Few...worst*: few can manage to speak less passionately who feel as much pain as I do.

78 *Justice...odds*: having justice on one's side gives such an advantage.

83 *I...arms*: I demand victory for the just side.

4.1 s.d. *Organs...act*. See Intro., p. xii.

s.d. *a cave's mouth*: this entrance might be expected to be made from the stage trap, but its previous use as the opening of the vaulted passage from Syphax's palace makes that unlikely though not impossible.

9 *nimbly*: this is a reading from a proof-correction in Q of 'justly'. While having no certain authority, it provides an 'improvement' in vividness.

67 *slake thy hate*: slake my hatred of you.

70 *fruit 's*: this edition. Q reads 'fruites'.

73 s.d. *Enter...Zanthia]*: logically, the guard should enter *via* the stage trap, but such niceties may be superfluous here. Q gives no re-entry for Zanthia and this edition picks this as the likeliest moment. She has, narratively speaking, simply lurked nearby, knowing that Syphax would soon arrive.

101 s.d. *Infernal...ceaseth*: eerie music accompanies Erichtho's entrance and is probably played beneath the stage. Note the care with which Marston orchestrates the effect with '*when she speaks ceaseth*'. The music accompanies Syphax's description of Erichtho and creates a ghostly atmosphere for her entrance after l. 124. One might expect this entrance to be made from the stage trap, but its previous use as the opening of the vaulted passage from Syphax's palace makes that improbable Perhaps

Marston imagined an entrance from a tomb or suchlike (see ll. 100–1) but left the details to the production.

110 *quick sulphur*: i.e. lightning.

119 *gelid*: see note to *Antonio's Revenge*, 1.2.136.

136 *king of flames*: i.e. the sun.

139 *my ... must'*: my word is 'you must' (because I command, not entreat).

143 *but ... pleased*: but you make me live a life of pleasure.

157 *well-dead men*: men who have died well (and therefore are in 'assurèd rest', l. 156).

183 *shall 's joy*: shall we enjoy.

189 *Without a man*: i.e. outside man and his physical and sensual being. Lines 186–90 constitute a 'credo' at direct variance with that of Masinissa and Sophonisba.

201 S.D. *within the canopy*: the phrase is repeated in the stage-direction after l. 218 where it clearly refers to the discovery-space. The stage-direction after l. 210 might incline us to see the music here as also taking place 'above'. However, the discovery-space is intended, we see, from the same reference to the 'canopy' to represent the bed area, and in fact erotic melodies from there would be appropriate. In which case, during the whole episode, the audience is to register music played from three distinct, offstage areas. See note to l. 212 below.

203 *Disquiet*: unruly, disturbed.

208 *grips*: i.e. embraces, though the Elizabethan form of 'gripes' also carries the secondary meaning of 'pangs'.

210–11 *worth fruition Of*: worthy of the enjoyment of.

213 *hell and heaven*: Marston underlines the rich aural effect in which music, both instrumental and vocal, is created in different offstage areas to register the dangerous ambiguity of Syphax's consorting with demonic forces.

214 S.D. *in ... space]*: the setting of the bed here in the discovery-space is assumed from the reference to 'the canopy' of the last stage direction of the scene.

S.D. *A ... act*: see Intro., p. xii.

5.1 S.D. *Syphax ... him*: at this stage, it is clear that the audience can see the bed and its occupants. Either it is set in the discovery-space or it has been set on the main stage between the acts. As the scene also requires the use of the stage trap and an altar, and the latter must also have been set between the acts, the discovery-space is the likely place. Be that as it may, the audience is to imagine that sexual intercourse has taken place in the narrative time between the acts.

4 *fool of kings*: most foolish amongst kings.

7 *his*: its (i.e. love's).

8–20 *Know...young*: Erichtho has fulfilled her aim of rejuvenating herself by taking in the vigorous Syphax's semen.

17 *thy use*: my use of you.

28 S.D. *at the altar*. With the discovery-space occupied by the bed, the altar was evidently set up on the open stage between the acts, possibly with the actor of Hasdrubal already inside it. Marston had planned a similar effect in *Antonio's Revenge*, 3.1.

30 *thou*: i.e. the sun god.

god of riddles: as deity of the Delphic oracle, Phoebus Apollo's prophecies were delivered in a riddling form.

38 S.D. *Out...ariseth*: see note to the stage-direction in l. 28 above.

45–6 *whose...unfortunate*: i.e. Hasdrubal's evil heart made him, justly, very unfortunate.

49 *next...ten*: 'alongside a force of ten thousand Libyans' (Jackson).

52 *fury*: presumably this is a reference to an avenging goddess, but it is also possible that it is Hasdrubal's own revenging anger that earns the hatred and violence of the people.

76 *roll...shelf*: drive you onto the rocks.

5.2.1 *Part the file*: form up in two lines.

12 *lost*: i.e. for words.

17 *my odds*: the overwhelming odds which embolden my heart.

20–1 *state...heart*: I wish an outcome worthy of his magnanimity.

22 S.D. *Scipio...mount*: Scipio might have been intended to exit at this point and reappear on the upper level to watch the fight, but there is little to be gained theatrically by such a manœuvre. The stage-direction is possibly not a stage-direction at all but a literary note aimed at the reader.

26 *nor sued*: this edition. Q has 'nor's adue' and some modern editions emend to 'nor's due'.

38 *Kings'...wrong*: it is kings' freedom to commit evil actions that is their glory.

41 *not*: 1633 ed.'s emendation of Q's 'and'. If the latter stands, the death is Syphax's, to contrast with Masinissa's 'life'.

49 *from...life*: i.e. receive life at our hands.

79 *Her...torch*: the celebratory torch of Sophonisba's wedding to Masinissa, but metaphorically standing for the spiritual impact on Syphax and his household.

96 *now our law's*: now within the jurisdiction of Roman law (as a subject Carthaginian).

97 *Wise . . . cause*: wise men do not merely anticipate actions, they seek to cause them.

5.3.15 *Be . . . heart*: 'is bound to us in love' (Jackson).

28 S.D. *disarms his . . . head*: takes off his helmet (thus revealing himself to Sophonisba).

31 *Leda's breast*: Leda was raped by Zeus in the shape of a swan. The soft breast of the swan seems to be transferred to Leda here.

52 *'Tis . . . state*: it is contrary to the demands of personal honour. | But just according to the demands of state.

58 *Most . . . keep*: falling away entirely from the condition maintained by his customary courage.

70 *And Scipio*: and I return the same to Scipio.

76 *wreathe . . . arms*: bend your arms behind your back (in readiness to be tied thus as a prisoner).

115 *whilst . . . man*: before I break down in unmanly tears.

5.4 S.D. *Enter . . . bound*: Scipio, as the conquering leader, is accorded a Roman triumph, with martial music, ornaments registering his triumph (including perhaps the crown of l. 44) and 'in full state' (which perhaps refers to the triumphal robe and laurel wreath of l. 45).

10 *All . . . impossibilities*: quite confounded as to how to achieve impossible tasks.

23 *see baseness*: know himself reduced to baseness.

30 *the fright of nations*: he who is feared of nations.

33 *Scipio's wheel?*: i.e. his chariot wheel, the traditional place for prisoners conquered in battle.

36 S.D. *play . . . voice*: play in unison (without harmonizing).

the . . . body: Masinissa goes to one of the doors to meet and then accompany Sophonisba's body borne in funeral procession on a hearse or (as at the end of 5.3) in a chair.

40–1 *Burst . . . acts*: the historical Syphax reportedly died of grief in Rome, but Marston retains Syphax's obdurate villainy to the end.

43 S.D. *Scipio . . . Masinissa*: the following lines explain precisely how this happens.

47 *very minion*: true favorite.

50 *wild-fire*: inflammable liquid used as a weapon; ignited, it could not be extinguished.

54 S.D. *Masinissa . . . Sophonisba*: perhaps Masinissa 'adorns' Sophonisba's body with the crown, wreath, sceptre and robe he has himself just received, thus recognizing her heroic achievements as warrior of the heart.

57 *Small . . . flow*—: final instance of the Senecan idea that has become a major motif of the play. See 2.3.51; 3.1.132–3; and 3.2.28–30.

(EPILOGUE)

63 *Another's*: i.e. the playwright's.

65 *well sensed*: full of matter (not the trivia of the comic plays).

70 *taxings indiscreet*: scandalous satire.

Appendix : Felice's Ballad in *Antonio and Mellida*, 3.2

1 *And*: not in the 1559 text, but metrically necessary and supplied by Marston.

Solomon: biblical king of Israel, who 'loved many strange women', and had 700 wives and 300 concubines (1 Kings 11:1–3). He was induced by his wives to worship foreign gods, causing rebellions and, after his death, the division of the kingdom.

3 *paragon*: mate, consort in marriage.

4 *glisterèd*: sparkled, glittered.

9–12 *When . . . fear*: Paris abducted Helen, the most beautiful woman in the world, with the connivance of Venus, goddess of love; in doing so he caused the Trojan war.

13 *sturdy*: violent, rough.

17 *Troilus*: Trojan prince whose love for Cressida was recounted in Chaucer's *Troilus and Criseyde*; his name was trisyllabic in Elizabethan pronunciation. Cressida eventually betrayed him.

26 *Leander*: lover who nightly swam the Hellespont from Abydos to Sestos to meet Hero. The story was later the basis of Christopher Marlowe's poem, *Hero and Leander* (1593).

33 *Pyramus*: in Ovid's *Metamorphoses*, Book 4, Pyramus makes an assignation with Thisbe in the forest. Awaiting his arrival she is scared away by a lioness, leaving behind a cloak which the animal soils with blood. On finding this, Pyramus assumes she has been killed, and commits suicide. Shakespeare later used the story for the play-within-a-play of *A Midsummer Night's Dream* (1595). The name is misprinted as 'Priamus' in the 1559 copy of the ballad.

41 *Hercules*: mightiest of the Greek heroes.

Eronie: probably a misrendering of Hesione, a Trojan maiden whom Hercules saved from being sacrificed to a sea-monster. Her father then offered her to Hercules in marriage, but later went back on his word, causing the hero to attack Troy. The 1559 reading is retained here for metrical reasons.

49-50 *Anaxaretis . . . see*: in Ovid's *Metamorphoses*, Book 14, Anaxarete of Cyprus treats her lover Iphis with such disdain that he hangs himself at her door.

60-3 *As Jupiter . . . bed*: Jupiter, ruler of the classical gods, often changed his shape in order to visit and have sex with mortal woman. He visited Alcmena in the form of her husband Amphitryon, and fathered Hercules on her. Ovid told the story in Book 9 of his *Metamorphoses*.

68 *Exsuperate*: overcome.

GLOSSARY

abstract extract

accomplished complete

accordance harmony

addictions inclinations

admiration wonderment

affect affection (*AR*, 1.2.272; 4.1.73); disposition (*DC*, 2.2.172); *v.* love (*AM*, 2.1.243; *AR*, 2.1.112; *M*, 1.1.32; *S*, 3.1.30)

affied assured (*AM*, Ded. 16); betrothed (*AR*, 2.2.51)

all one united

alone exclusively (*AR*, 5.3.34)

ambergris perfume (from whale secretion)

amorist lover

and if even if (*AR*, 1.2.70)

antic carved with grotesque figures (*M*, 1.2.135)

anything at all (*M*, 1.1.182)

apish imitative

applyment application

apt well-fitted

art learning (*AR*, 4.1.20)

artificial feigned

assay tasting of food before sovereign eats (*AM*, 4.1.42)

assured engaged (*AR*, 1.2.27)

astoning stunning

at adventure however chance determines (*AR*, 3.2.168)

attached arrested (*AM*, 3.1.17)

aunt whore (*DC*, 1.2.8)

balsamum ointment

ban curse (*AM*, 3.2.201)

banquet repast of sweetmeats, fruit, and wine

barb mow (*M*, 3.1.42)

barmed fermented

bastinado beating

baubled carrying fool's baton

bead-roll catalogue

beat up rouse (*AR*, 1.1.108)

beaver visor

beeking warming

be garzon by God's son (oath)

bellman night watchman

belly-act copulation

bezzled drink-befuddled

billets pieces of wood, cut as fuel (*M*, 2.2.5)

blaze proclaim (*AR*, 3.2.39)

blood family (*AM*, 3.1.98); gallant (*AR*, 1.2.100)

blowze wench

blurred defiled (*AM*, 1.1.213; *AR*, 1.1.34)

boots matters

brack crack (*AR*, 2.2.213); flaw in cloth (*AM*, Ind. 54)

brackish salt, lascivious

bragget drink made of honey and ale

brain-caught captured by cunning

bravo bold ruffian (*DC*, 4.3.37)

breaks errors in versification (*M*, Ep. 8)

breath utterance (*S*, 4.1.139)

broad-horn cuckold

buff-captain officer in leather jerkin

bully sweetheart (*AM*, 5.1.70)

bur prickly flower-head

burly bombast (*AR*, 4.2.72)

busk corset stiffening

busk-points laces on stays

buss kiss

bustles up bestirs itself (*AR*, 2.1.9)

cack shit

canary wine from Canaries (*AM*, 2.1.12)

cap-à-pie from head to foot

capricious witty (*DC*, 1.2.64)

carcanet chain set with jewels

case pair (*AM*, 2.1.25)

casque helmet

cast cast off (*AM*, 2.1.111; *DC*, 1.2.157); pair (*M*, 2.2.1)

casting-bottle bottle for sprinkling scent

cast up reckon (up) (*DC*, 2.3.110; *S*, 1.2.85); vomit up (*AR*, 5.2.33); found guilty (*DC*, 5.2.117)

caudle warm drink of wine and gruel, often given to sick

cazzo (It.) 'penis' (used as expletive)

cerecloth winding-sheet

chafing-dish censer

chap-fallen with lower jaw hanging open

chaps jaws

charm spell

chawn split open

check rebuke (*AM*, Prol. 23)

check-roll list of servants

choke conceal (*AR*, 1.1.74)

chopines platform shoes

Christ-tide Christmas

chub-faced plump-cheeked

cittern guitar

clip embrace

close *v.* meet (*M*, 4.2.174); *adj.* stingy (*M*, 5.1.209); *adj.* secret (*S*, 2.3.40)

closed engaged in hand to hand combat (*S*, 1.2.118)

closely secretly (*M*, 3.2.52)

close to deal with (*M*, 3.1.201)

clyster-pipe enema syringe

coasts regions (*M*, 5.2.94)

cockall one that beats all

cog cheat

cog a die cheat at dice

coil uproar (*AM*, 2.1.32)

collect conclude (*S*, 1.2.180)

collogue speak deceitfully and flatteringly

comfits sweetmeats

common customs whoring

complot *n.* plot (*DC*, 5.2.99); *v.* conspire (*AR*, 3.2.41; 5.2.47)

conceit *v.* imagine (*AM*, Ind. 94, 96; 4.1.13); *v.* understand (*AM*, 5.2.77)

condition identity (*AM*, 1.1.168)

condole grieve for (*AR*, 5.3.81 S.D.)

confound destroy

conjure solemnly demand (*M*, 2.2.92)

consort combination of musical instruments (*AR*, Prol. 26); company (*AR*, 5.3.62)

consul-queller consul-killer

contemn despise

cony rabbit

conycatching cheating

cornets of horse troops of cavalry

cornute *v.* cuckold

corruptless incorruptible (*S*, 3.1.124)

courtship art of being a courtier (*M*, 2.4.134)

cousin-german first cousin

coverture shelter

coxcomb fool's cap

coz cousin (term of affection)

crackers firecrackers

cresset-light oil lamp on pole

crudities undigested pieces of food

crumped crooked

cuirass chest armour

cullion knave

culverin cannon

curious expert (*AR*, 5.3.44); intricate (*DC*, 1.1.132); obscure (*AM*, 5.2.77)

current make value judgement (*AM*, Ind. 26)

Curson Christian

cut fashion (*AM*, Ind. 98; 1.1.147; *M*, 5.2.13)

cypress black veiling

daintiness choiceness (*DC*, 1.1.132)

damnation damned person (*DC*, 1.2.24)

damps fog (*AR*, 1.2.145)

daw jackdaw

decoct concoct

defenced fortified (*M*, 5.2.165)

delicate charming (*DC*, 2.1.167); delicious (*DC*, 4.3.26)

depaint depict in words (*AM*, 5.2.226)

descry spy out

desperate despairing

despite contempt

device advice (*AM*, 5.1.40); heraldic design (*AR*, 1.2.96)

diaper patterned

diet feed (*DC*, 3.3.18)

digest think over (*AR*, 3.2.90)

ding beat (*AM*, Ind. 81); throw himself (*AR*, 4.1.208)

discourse consider (*AM*, 3.2.55)

disease disturb

disgorge vomit up

disport entertainment

distemperance unbalancing of the humours

distempered put off balance

divulsed torn asunder

doit coin (Dutch) of small value

dotes causes to dote (*S*, 5.1.6)

double bend (*AM*, 4.1.77)

doubt suspect

drab prostitute

drab-keeper pimp

draught earth-closet (*M*, 4.2.138); drinking capacity (*DC*, 2.1.156); extract (*AM*, Ind. 98)

draw infer (*M*, To the Reader, 11)

dressed treated medically for wounds (*S*, 2.2.41 S.D.)

dropsy unbounded thirst

dry-shaved cheated

dulness stupidity

dusky gloomy (*AM*, Ind. 61)

eager imperfectly tempered (*DC*, 4.2.44)

easy credulous (*DC*, 2.1.53); effortless (*DC*, Prol. 1)

ecliptic obscuring

ejaculatories short prayers (*DC*, 4.2.10)

elate elevated (*AM*, Ind. 8)

eld old age

elected, election chosen, choice

elixed distilled

embraid upbraid

empiric empirical physician (quack)

enchased ornamented

endear win the affection of (*AR*, 2.1.45)

enhanceress 'enhancer', one who raises the price

enlarge expatiate on

entertain welcome

essay attempt

exequies funeral ceremonies

exhale evaporate (*AR*, 1.2.145)

exordium introductory part

extractive essence

fact crime (*DC*, 5.2.110)

fame infamy (*M*, 2.4.144)

fearless of not doubting (*S*, 2.3.59)

fence shield (*AM*, 2.1.35)

feodars holders of land of an overlord on condition of homage and service

fetch trick

fico obscene gesture

firk strike

fist fart (*DC*, 2.1.154; 4.5.73, 126)

flamen priest

flaws squalls (*AM*, 1.1.217)

fleer sneer, jeer

fleet migrate (*AR*, 3.2.111)

flesh-fly blow-fly

flourish fanfare

flux discharge

foil contrast

foist rogue

footcloth horse's caparison

fore-horse lead horse in a team

foutra obscene oath

frau Dutchwoman

free to invested in (*S*, 5.2.90)

frieze coarse woollen cloth

front forehead

frothy worthless (*AR*, 2.1.146)

fub cheat

fulgor splendour

fume steam

furniture equipment

furze evergreen shrub (type of)

gaged pledged

gain capture (*S*, 2.3.87)

galliass large war galley

galls sores

gargalise gargle

girn grimace, pull face

glavering deceitful, to flatter

glibbed made smooth

glibbery slippery

glossed shining (*AR*, 1.2.8)

glossing putting a finish on (*M*, 4.2.144)

goatish-blooded lecherous

God's bores God's wounds (oath)

GLOSSARY

God's me   God save me (oath)
God's nigs   oath
goose   fool
gorge   capacity to devour (AR, 5.3.80)
gorget   throat armour
graced   accepted with applause (M, 5.1.207)
great (of)   pregnant (with) (AR, 1.2.138; 2.2.120)
great slop   loose breeches
grincome   syphilis
gripe   hand in position for grasping (AR, 4.2.30)
grogram   coarse fabric
grow off   separate (DC, 2.1.99)
gudgeon   type of small fish, gullible person

halberd   long-handled weapon with blade
hale   draw (AR, 1.1.78)
half-clammed   half stuck together
halter-worthy   deserving to be hanged
hangers   straps on swordbelt (AM, 2.1.149)
hard-bound   constipated
harquebus   early type of musket
hearty   heart-felt
heedy   heedful
high-fronted   high-browed, noble
high-nolled   high-peaked
holds   resists (S, 3.2.56); will take place (DC, 3.1.189)
honey   flatter (AR, 1.1.84)
horn-mad   enraged by being cuckolded
horselike   stupid
hospital   poor house
hot-reined   lecherous
hot-shots   reckless hotheads
huddle   old miser (M, 1.1.72)
hull   float (S, 1.2.197)
humorous   moody, capricious
humours   moods
hymeneal   pertaining to marriage

idle   foolish
ill   sinful (DC, 2.1.22)
illustrate   adj. illustrious

imbraids   upbraids
imparloured   closeted
impostumed   abscess-like
inamorate   lover
incestuous   lecherous (AR, 1.2.215)
incomprehence   beyond comprehension
incubus   demon that visits people in their sleep
inhumed   buried
innovation   civil disturbance (M, To the Reader, 20)
insensibly   imperceptibly (S, 5.4.15)
instant   ready (AR, 5.1.9); present (S, 4.1.14)
insufficient   incompetent (DC, 2.1.108)
intestine   innate (AM, 1.1.79); internal (AM, 1.1.216)
inward   intimate (M, 4.1.183; DC, 3.3.2)

jades   vicious, worthless horses
jealous   suspicious (AM, 2.1.278)
jowl   head and shoulder parts, cut of a fish (DC, 3.3.31)
jubilee   time of rejoicing
jumbler   adulterator (DC, 5.3.109)

kennel   gutter
knocked   copulated with (M, 3.1.145)
knurly   gnarled

lackey   dance attendance on (AR, Prol. 28)
languishings   lingering diseases
lapped   wrapped
lavishness   openness of speech (M, 5.2.57)
lavolta   lively dance
lazy   sluggish (S, 4.1.168)
lepered   diseased
level   position of taking aim (AM, 3.2.130)
lewd   poor (DC, 5.3.15); immoral (AM, 3.2.277; AR, 2.2.193; S, 2.1.105)
lewdly   ignorantly (DC, 4.4.88)
lickerish, lickerous   greedy, eagerly desirous
light   immoral (AR, 2.2.23, 31); merry (DC, 2.2.62); unstable (AR, 2.2.18)
lime-twig   snare

390

limn paint (often used of miniatures; not so at *S*, 4.1.154)

linstock stick to hold gunner's lighted match

lint tinder

lists tournament ground

lotium stale urine used as 'dye' for hair by barbers

lumpish dull

luxury lasciviousness

maim serious blemish

main mainland (*AM*, 1.1.190); ocean (*M*, 4.1.133)

make a leg(s) bow

make-please flatterer

make stand halt

malapert impudent

malign betray (*DC*, 3.1.238)

man escort (*DC*, 5.2.126); manhood (*AM*, 1.1.161)

mangonist one who patches up inferior goods for sale

masquery masquing attire

maugre in spite of

maws jaws

maze *n.* amazement (*M*, 4.2.169) *v.* confound (*S*, 5.3.82)

mazed confounded (*M*, 2.4.83)

mean moderation (*DC*, 5.2.68; *S*, 5.2.54); performer of middle part in musical harmony (*AM*, 5.2.18)

measure dance (*DC*, 2.3.61); moderation (*DC*, 2.2.103)

mechanical engaged in manual labour

merely only (*M*, To the Reader, 25); utterly (*M*, 2.1.3)

metheglin strong herb made of herbs and honey

metreza mistress

mineral medicinal drug

minikin high-pitched (voice)

minioning caressing

misgone in state of error (*DC*, 2.2.219)

mistrust suspect (*AM*, 5.2.69–70)

modestly moderately (*M*, To the Reader, 23)

mundifieth cleans

murr attack of catarrh

murrain plague

musk-cod scented fop

nap pile (of textile)

nappy with a nap, rich-piled

naunt aunt (affectionate)

next alongside (*DC*, 1.1.16)

nice coy (*DC*, 1.2.132; *S*, 3.1.174); fastidious (*AM*, 1.1.25; *S*, 2.1.37; 3.1.87); refined (*DC*, 2.1.13)

nice-brained ingenious

niceness coyness (*AM*, 1.1.173; *M*, 5.1.104)

nicer-stomached with delicate digestion

night-rails dressing-gowns

noise musical consort (*DC*, 2.3.62, 109)

no jot not at all

nolled *see* high-nolled

note example (*M*, 4.1.37)

obligation written contract (*DC*, 3.2 S.D.)

obloquy disgrace

observe obey (*M*, 5.1.189); treat with reverence (*M*, 1.1.310)

of proof impenetrable

old old-fashioned (*M*, Add. C, 67)

once at once (*AM*, 5.2.270); for once (*S*, 5.4.66); one day (*M*, 3.1.87)

ope come into the open (*M*, 2.1.29)

opinion idea based on sense impressions

opposite opponent (*M*, 4.1.216)

oppressed in decline (*M*, 1.1.98)

ordinary eating-house

ostent ostentation

owes owns (*S*, 2.1.140)

paints uses cosmetics (*DC*, 3.3.8)

pale *n.* enclosure (*S*, 4.1.31); *v.* weaken (*DC*, 4.1.37)

pantable slipper

passage issue (*AM*, 5.2.273)

passion compassion

pathetically passionately

paunched stabbed

peise weight (*AR*, Prol. 29)

perdy by God (oath)

peregal equal

periphrasis circumlocution
pest plague
pinion wing
pinked ornamented with perforations
pipe of breath windpipe
pistolets pistols
place preferment (*S*, 2.3.101);
   employment (*S*, 3.1.111)
point *v.* punctuate (*AM*, 4.1.203); *n.*
   musical phrase (*AM*, 4.1.136); *n.* stop
   (*AM*, 5.2.70)
points laces
poise, poiser weigh, weigher
polecat prostitute
politic scheming; social (*DC*, 2.1.70)
pomander perfume ball
pomatum pomade
port expensive style (*AM*, Ind. 24);
   place of refuge (*M*, 2.4.152)
position proposition (*M*, 1.1.30)
posset hot milk curdled with wine
posy motto engraved on inside
   of ring
prank it show oneself off
precise rigorous (*DC*, 4.2.45)
precisian puritan
presence royal presence-chamber
   (*AM*, 2.1.38; 3.2.110–11; *AR*, 3.2.58;
   M, 1.1.27; 5.2.96)
present(ly) immediate(ly)
priapism state of having a permanent
   erection
prick spur (*AM*, 4.1.257)
printing dyeing (*AM*, 2.1.238)
private room theatre box
proper own; respectable (*DC*,
   3.3.7, 8)
prostitution prostitute (*DC*,
   1.1.145–6)
provide prepare (*M*, 2.4.71)
puff to say 'pooh!' or the like (*AR*,
   1.1.51; 4.1.100 ff.)
pug term of endearment
punk whore
purfled with embroidered border
putry putrid

quaint ingenious
quelquechose trifle
quick living (*DC*, 5.2.78)

racked stretched, as in torture (*AR*,
   5.2.22)
ragg'd harsh (*AM*, 1.1.225)
ramping wild, violent
rank take up position (*M*, 2.4.44)
rased scratched (*AR*, 2.1.83)
rases cuts (*AR*, 3.2.168)
real royal (*AM*, 2.1.110)
rebato support for ruff
receipt recipe (*M*, 2.3.6); place of
   refuge, for thieves (*DC*, 4.5.110)
red bloody (*S*, 2.3.6)
regency, regenty government, rule
reparation repair (*AM*, 2.1.241)
resistless irresistible (*S*, 5.2.71)
respective respectful (*AR*, 3.3.21)
retain hold back (*AR*, 5.1.22)
returns replies (*M*, 5.1.160)
reversion succeeding to the possession
   of something when the
           present incumbent dies/retires
rheum cold
rivel(led) wrinkle(d)
routs gangs (*AR*, 4.1.114); rabble (*S*,
   2.3.41)
rowels spurs (*see* walking rowels)
ruffled boot boot with turned-over top
rustiest-jawed foulest-mouthed

sad grave, earnest
sans without
sarcenet fine silk
say saying (*AM*, 3.2.164)
scant cramped (*AM*, 5.2.72)
scattered distracted (*AM*, 2.1.252)
scene of up *levee*
sconce head (*DC*, 5.3.71); candlestick
   (*M*, 2.1 S.D.)
score add up bills
scout dismiss scornfully (*DC*, Prol. 10)
scud move sharply
scuffle fight at close quarters
sectary dissenter
secure unsuspecting (*DC*, 2.1.20)
security culpable self-confidence (*AM*,
   1.1.50; *DC*, 3.1.213)
seise take legal possession of (*AM*,
   5.2.217)
seisin legal possession (*AM*, 2.1.172)
sennet fanfare

sentences   moralizings (*DC*, 2.2.6)
sergeant   arresting officer
serpigo   ringworm
serrant   earlier
servant   courtly lover
shark   *n.* swindler; *v.* swindle
short-heels   wanton person
shotten herring   emaciated person
siddow   tender
silly   innocent
singled   left alone (*M*, 3.1.60)
slatted   bashed (*M*, 4.1.161)
sleights   wiles, ruses
sliftered   cloven
slightly   without attention (*M*, To the Reader, 31)
slip   counterfeit coin (*AM*, 5.2.21)
slop   *see* great slop
slough   cast snakeskin
slurred   smeared (*AR*, 3.2.55)
smugged   smartened up
sonnet   love poem or song
sometimes   former (*DC*, 1.2.92)
sore   to a painful degree (*AR*, 2.2.137)
souse   plunge deeply (*M*, 4.1.132)
spangs   spangles (*AM*, 3.2.17)
spitting   censoriousness (*AR*, 4.1.4)
spongy   flexible (*AM*, 4.1.56)
sprig   spray-shaped ornament (*AM*, 5.1.82)
spurned   kicked
spurt   brief period (*M*, 1.2.17)
staff   stanza (*M*, Prol. 2)
stale   made common (*DC*, 1.1.92); unfashionable (*M*, Add. A, 8; 5.2.13)
standing collar   high, fashionable collar
standing cup   cup with stem and base
St. Antony's fire   the skin disease, erysipelas
state   nobles (*AM*, 5.2.217; *AR*, 1.2.45; 5.2.26); rank (*S*, 3.1.192); royal demeanour (*AM*, Ind. 113); sovereign (*AM*, 3.1.6); state affairs (*S*, 4.1.36); statecraft (*M*, 3.2.65); throne (*AM*, 2.1.150 S.D.; 4.1.47; 5.2.139)
stateful   dignified
stick   hesitate (*AR*, 2.1.31)
still   always
stilled   distilled (*S*, Prol. 24)

still flutes   recorders (?)
stinkards   stinking fellows
stomach   appetite, anger (*AM*, 2.1.13; *AR*, 5.2.67)
stone-bows   crossbows for shooting stones
stoned   gelded
stone-horse   stallion
stoop   swoop (falconry)
strangury   disease of the urinary organs
strike   bushel (*AM*, 2.1.78)
strong   flagrant (*DC*, 4.5.109)
stub-bearded   short-bearded
studious   diligent (*DC*, 2.1.63)
stuff   of poor (woollen) material (*M*, 3.1.144; *DC*, 4.5.27)
suckets   sweetmeats
sugar-candy   sweet (*AM*, 3.2.120)
supple-chapped   glib-mouthed
surfling   painting
surquedries   arrogance (*AR*, 3.2.123); excesses (*AM*, 3.2.11)
swagger   carry on (*DC*, 2.2.1)
swart   black
sweets   embraces (*AR*, 1.1.26); flowers (*AM*, Prol. 1; *AR*, 4.1.311); *v.* sweetens (*AR*, 3.2.160)
'swill   God's will (oath)
synagogue   church (puritan term)

table-book   notebook for jotting down memorable sayings etc.
tack   addition (*DC*, 5.3.147)
tails off   turns tail (*M*, Add. F, 10)
taken up   reprimanded (*DC*, 3.1.99)
take up   borrow (*M*, 1.1.44)
taking   plight (*DC*, 4.5.89)
targets   shields
tax   oppress (*S*, 2.1.125)
taxings   satirical attacks (*S*, 5.4.70)
tell-clock   clock-watcher
tells   counts
tent   probe and clean (a wound) (*M*, 4.2.94)
tester   canopy
tetters   skin eruptions
thick   thick-set (*DC*, 2.3.101)
tilting-staff   spear used in tournaments
tipstaves   court ushers

393

tire accoutrements (*AM*, 3.2.18)
tiring-man backstage dresser
tiring-things head-dress
touch sound (*AR*, 1.2.300)
touch-hole vent in firearm for igniting charge
touse rumple
towards approaching (*M*, 3.2.10); in preparation (*DC*, 3.3.62)
toy trifle, whim
trains tricks (*S*, 1.2.135; 2.3.56)
traverse closet (*AM*, 3.2.9)
trencher platter
tripe-wife tripe-seller
troops assemblies (*S*, 2.1.128)
turn edge become blunt (*AR*, 2.2.176)
twone twined

unbraced with clothes unfastened
uncollected off guard (*DC*, 2.2.223)
unconscionable without conscience
under-offices menial occupations
underpoised undervalued
unexpressed inexpressible (*AM*, 5.2.220)
unhele uncover
unhonest dishonourable
unkind unnatural
unlace untie laces of stays
unnooked unweighed-down
unpeerable, unpeered peerless
unperegal peerless
unpranked unadorned
unrespective without respect (*AR*, 4.1.283)
unsalted natural
unshale expose
untruss unfasten
unused unprecedented (*AM*, 3.2.66); unusual (*AR*, Prol. 29)
unvulgar unrefined
usherless without announcement
usquebaugh whisky

velour kind of velvet

venery lechery
verge boundary of community (*AR*, 5.3.150)
via away
viced squeezed
viol da gamba stringed instrument, held between legs to play; early version of cello
virtual capable of producing effects (*M*, 3.1.207)
virtue courage (*S*, 1.2.113)
vively vividly
voids spits out (*AR*, 4.1.5)
vow-band sworn bond

wainscot fine quality (imported) oak
waiter attendant
walking rowels ornamental spurs
wanton-sick malingering
watchet pale blue
weak enfeebling (*DC*, 5.2.34)
welkin sky
welladay alack (expression of lamentation)
well-humoured equable
whist pent up (*AM*, 1.1.47)
wimble nimble, active
wink shut the eye
wit intelligence (*DC*, 2.2.207)
withers neck and shoulder joints of horse
wittol willing cuckold
wizard wise man
wood mad
woodcock fool
word motto (*AM*, 5.1.21; 5.2.76; *AR*, 5.2.54)
wreath garland, crown
wrought embroidered (*AM*, 5.1.82)

yet even though (*M*, 4.2.39)

zany imitate grotesquely
zounds by God's wounds (oath)

394

OXFORD

MORE OXFORD PAPERBACKS

This book is just one of nearly 1000 Oxford Paperbacks currently in print. If you would like details of other Oxford Paperbacks, including titles in the World's Classics, Oxford Reference, Oxford Books, OPUS, Past Masters, Oxford Authors, and Oxford Shakespeare series, please write to:

UK and Europe: Oxford Paperbacks Publicity Manager, Arts and Reference Publicity Department, Oxford University Press, Walton Street, Oxford OX2 6DP.

Customers in UK and Europe will find Oxford Paperbacks available in all good bookshops. But in case of difficulty please send orders to the Cash-with-Order Department, Oxford University Press Distribution Services, Saxon Way West, Corby, Northants NN18 9ES. Tel: 01536 741519; Fax: 01536 746337. Please send a cheque for the total cost of the books, plus £1.75 postage and packing for orders under £20; £2.75 for orders over £20. Customers outside the UK should add 10% of the cost of the books for postage and packing.

USA: Oxford Paperbacks Marketing Manager, Oxford University Press, Inc., 200 Madison Avenue, New York, N.Y. 10016.

Canada: Trade Department, Oxford University Press, 70 Wynford Drive, Don Mills, Ontario M3C 1J9.

Australia: Trade Marketing Manager, Oxford University Press, G.P.O. Box 2784Y, Melbourne 3001, Victoria.

South Africa: Oxford University Press, P.O. Box 1141, Cape Town 8000.

BEN JONSON
THE ALCHEMIST AND OTHER PLAYS
Edited with an Introduction by Gordon Campbell

Contains *Volpone*; *Epicene*;
The Alchemist; *Bartholomew Fair*.

THOMAS MIDDLETON
A MAD WORLD, MY MASTERS AND OTHER PLAYS
Edited with an Introduction by Michael Taylor

Contains *A Mad World, My Masters*; *Michaelmas Term*;
A Trick to Catch the Old One;
No Wit, No Help Like a Woman's.

(*Forthcoming January 1996*)

FOUR REVENGE TRAGEDIES
Edited with an Introduction by
Katharine Eisaman Maus

Contains *The Spanish Tragedy*; *The Revenger's Tragedy*;
The Revenge of Bussy D'Ambois;
The Atheist's Tragedy.

AN ANTHOLOGY OF SEVENTEENTH-CENTURY FICTION
Edited with an Introduction by Paul Salzman

Contains *Urania, Book One*; extracts from *The Princess
Cloria*; *The Blazing World*; *Don Tomazo*;
extracts from *Mr Badman*; *Incognita*;
The Unfortunate Happy Lady.

WORLD'S CLASSICS
Seventeenth-century texts

APHRA BEHN

OROONOKO AND OTHER WRITINGS

Edited with an Introduction by Paul Salzman

The Fair Jilt, *Memoirs of the Court of the King Bantam*,
The History of the Nun, *The Adventure of the Black Lady*,
and *The Unfortunate Bride* are complemented by a
generous selection of Behn's poetry, ranging from public
political verse to lyrics and witty conversation poems.

APHRA BEHN

THE ROVER AND OTHER PLAYS

Edited with an Introduction by Jane Spencer

Contains *The Rover*; *The Feigned Courtesans*; *The Lucky
Chance*; *The Emperor of the Moon*.

(Forthcoming November 1995)

JOHN BUNYAN

THE PILGRIM'S PROGRESS

Edited with an Introduction by N. H. Keeble

JOHN FORD

'TIS PITY SHE'S A WHORE
AND OTHER PLAYS

Edited with an Introduction by Marion Lomax

Contains *The Lover's Melancholy*; *The Broken Heart*;
'Tis Pity She's a Whore; *Perkin Warbeck*.

THE NEW OXFORD BOOK OF
SEVENTEENTH CENTURY VERSE
Alistair Fowler

'Fowler's volume is full of blessings, not all of them expected. It is erudite and scholarly.' Blair Worden, *Sunday Telegraph*.

Oxford Paperbacks